Writing and F

Theory, Practice, and Research

Edited by

Chris M. Anson
University of Minnesota

National Council of Teachers of English
1111 Kenyon Road, Urbana, Illinois 61801

NCTE Editorial Board: Donald R. Gallo, Richard Lloyd-Jones, Raymond Rodrigues, Dorothy Strickland, Brooke Workman, L. Jane Christensen, *ex officio*, John Lansingh Bennett, *ex officio*

Staff Editor: Michelle Sanden Johlas

Cover Design: Michael J. Getz

Interior Design: Tom Kovacs for TGK Design

NCTE Stock Number 58749

Library of Congress Cataloging-in-Publication Data

Writing and response: theory, practice, and research / edited by
   Chris M. Anson.
         p.   cm.
   Includes bibliographies.
   ISBN 0-8141-5874-9
   1. English language—Rhetoric—Study and teaching.   I. Anson,
Christopher M., 1954–
PE1404.W6934   1989
808'.042'07—dc19   88-38343

Contents

Introduction: Response to Writing and the Paradox of
Uncertainty   1
   Chris M. Anson

I   Toward a Theory of Response in the Classroom Community

1. Reconceiving Literacy: Language Use and Social Relations   15
   David Bleich

2. Images of Student Writing: The Deep Structure of Teacher
   Response   37
   Louise Wetherbee Phelps

3. Transactional Theory and Response to Student Writing   68
   Robert E. Probst

4. A Horse Named Hans, a Boy Named Shawn: The Herr
   von Osten Theory of Response to Writing   80
   Russell A. Hunt

II   New Perspectives for Responding to Writing

5. Learning to Praise   103
   Donald A. Daiker

6. The Use of Rogerian Reflection in Small-Group Writing
   Conferences   114
   Dene Thomas and Gordon Thomas

7. Showing Students How to Assess: Demonstrating
   Techniques for Response in the Writing Conference   127
   Richard Beach

8. Responding to Student Journals   149
   Toby Fulwiler

9. The Writer's Memo: Collaboration, Response, and
   Development   174
   Jeffrey Sommers

10. Response in the Electronic Medium   187
    Geoffrey Sirc

III Studies of Response in the Instructional Context

11. Response to Writing as a Context for Learning to Write   209
    Martin Nystrand and Deborah Brandt

12. The Student, the Teacher, and the Text: Negotiating
    Meanings through Response and Revision   231
    Cynthia Onore

13. The Semantics of Error: What Do Teachers Know?   261
    Susan V. Wall and Glynda A. Hull

14. A Theoretical Framework for Studying Peer Tutoring as
    Response   293
    Ann Matsuhashi, Alice Gillam, Rance Conley, and
    Beverly Moss

15. The First Five Minutes: Setting the Agenda in a Writing
    Conference   317
    Thomas Newkirk

16. Response Styles and Ways of Knowing   332
    Chris M. Anson

    Contributors   367

Introduction: Response to Writing and the Paradox of Uncertainty

Chris M. Anson
University of Minnesota

In Melville's "Bartleby, the Scrivener" (1856), a young, sedate copyist takes on employment in the office of the narrator, an aging and unambitious lawyer. At first Bartleby is the picture of efficiency, faithfully performing all his copy work with great precision and accuracy. But to the bewilderment of the office staff, he begins resisting any and every request or admonition, eventually tormenting the narrator with his complete indifference to the social and institutional system in which he is so mechanically working. Mysteriously turning his back on everyone around him, Bartleby becomes a human completely alone in the midst of humanity.

In trying to explain Bartleby's "perverse" resistance, the narrator is finally drawn to a rumor about the scrivener's previous manner of life. As a clerk in a Washington post office, Bartleby had been responsible for opening, reading, and preparing to burn hundreds of undeliverable letters — "errands of life" destined to die in the flames without ever reaching their intended audiences. Ironically, as a reader of letters for which there could be no true response — no "hope for those who died unhoping," no "good tidings for those who died stifled by unrelieved calamities" — Bartleby becomes a man who himself loses the will to respond. The process of response, as "Bartleby" reminds us, is so fundamental to human interaction that when it is short-circuited, whether by accident or design, the result can hardly be interpreted as anything but a loss of humanity.

. At a time when efforts are being made to understand the social and interpersonal nature of writing, we are beginning to recognize not only how important response is to the development of literacy, but also how little we know about it. In the scientific orientation of writing studies, the processes of composing and reading texts are often represented in a highly objective, rational manner, as if the whole business were relatively normative and stable. Consequently, response to writing is often seen procedurally, as something which, from an instructional perspective, can be regulated and institutionalized as a coherent part of any writing program.

From both the student's and the teacher's perspective, however, response to writing is often difficult and tense. For the teacher, it is the schizophrenia of roles — now the helpful facilitator, hovering next to the writer to lend guidance and support, and now the authority, passing critical judgment on the writer's work; at one moment the intellectual peer, giving "reader-based" feedback (Elbow 1981), and at the next the imposer of criteria, the gatekeeper of textual standards. For students, as for all writers, response can generate its own special anxieties: misguided expectations as their private creations struggle with the public nature of discourse; conflicts of ego as the instinct to present themselves at their best battles with the fundamental need to share their doubts and imperfections at the very moment when they are most vulnerable.

As teachers and as agents of the theories we generate in the field of writing studies, we have tried to circumvent these tensions and complexities with the certainties afforded by simple procedures and activities. Like farmers with new chemicals, we grasp at the slightest success of this or that treatment, forgetting for the moment that nothing in our human world, least of all writing, can be so simple.

Occasionally, the keys to unlocking the complexities of writing have, in fact, been elegantly simple, lying in plain view but for our lack of vision to see them. More often than not, however, the field of composition has erred when it has too hastily trusted and laid claim to certainty — when it has assumed, for example, that some new key will work with great accuracy and consistency; that it will always work, no matter what the writing, in the same way; that it will work at different stages of intellectual development and writing proficiency; that it will work across contexts, from the classroom to the newspaper office to the chemist's lab; and that it will work among diverse personalities, from the introspective, moody, or defensive to the out-going, self-consuming, or manic.

Instead of providing solutions, the urge for certainty has often created new problems by encouraging simpleminded, mechanical procedures for teaching or learning highly complex skills and processes. Guised in the cloak of reliability and efficiency, such procedures are instructionally very attractive, and teachers adopt them rapidly, often in spite of their deepest convictions about the complexities of the writing process. Easily promulgated and passed along, both the methods and their underlying philosophical origins begin to saturate the habits and assumptions of the profession. Over time, yesterday's new approaches become today's "current/traditional" paradigm that unconsciously drives our national ideology of learning and fuels many teachers' behaviors — and students' expectations — in the classroom.

This penchant for inheriting and passing on traditional teaching methods is nowhere better illustrated than in the area of response to student writing. The philosophical and pedagogical sources of conventional practice can be traced at least to the late nineteenth century, when the need for curricular and administrative changes in the schools created new attitudes toward learning and new methods of teaching. During this time, enrollments increased dramatically as more people found the incentive (and the means) to attend college. But where once small classes of socially advantaged "apprentice" students could receive personal and detailed response to their work by highly qualified master educators with time to devote to their teaching, now students found themselves in large classroom sections, taught by overburdened and underpaid assistants often hired by the term (Lunsford 1986). True response suffered. Discussion, negotiation, language in real use — these became ready-made evaluations churned out twenty or thirty at a time.

The influence of these circumstances on teacher responses to student writing is reflected in Harvard University's newly instituted composition program in the 1890s and early 1900s — a program that in many ways paved the way for the next half century of American writing instruction. Under the direction of Adams Sherman Hill, fifth Boylston Professor of Rhetoric and Oratory, students were fed through a kind of "grammar machine," a well-oiled mechanism designed to purge the new middle-class enrollee of his linguistic barbarisms. (Women had yet to achieve a status that entitled them to the same treatment.) One goal of the program is described in *Freshman English and Theme-Correcting in Harvard College* (Copeland and Rideout 1901):

> The first effort of the instructors . . . is not to make the daily themes interesting, but to make them correct. [The] daily exercises are the only material from which to teach punctuation, spelling, grammar, the right use of words, the principles of structure, and whatever else ill-prepared youths need to learn. The special kind of subject [descriptions of the writer's new surroundings] is prescribed merely that the students may have a fairer chance to make themselves interesting. If they succeed, so much the better; but first they must seek correctness, and live in the hope that the other things may be added unto them. (9)

> For this, the habitual use of correct and intelligent English, is what the instructors try to drill into the Freshmen. (2)

Thus, what began as an efficient way for 11 instructors to teach 630 freshmen soon invaded and captured the program developers' philosophy, until response to writing became totally mechanized. At the start of the school year, instructors and students were supplied with an "English Composition Card," written by Hill and published by Charles W. Sever. On it were printed special marks of correction: "Cst." for "faulty construction"; "K" for "awkward, stiff or harsh"; "P" for "fault in punctuation"; "S" for "sentence objectionable in form"; and so on. Aided by the card, instructors combed student essays for errors and marked them with the correction symbols. The spirit of this response method is reflected in a "specimen theme," written by a Harvard freshman in October 1899 (Copeland and Rideout 1901, 86).

As described by Copeland and Rideout, the justifications for the comments on this student's paper are fairly characteristic of the program as a whole:

> It will be seen at once that the instructor's marks — made very hastily, as must happen where so many pages have to be read in a short time — are directed at a few salient defects. Besides the uncertainty of punctuation, the too frequent use of present participles is pointed out to the writer as one of his particular weaknesses. The only comments on the substance deal with the vagueness of one passage, and a questionable attempt at being imaginative. (10)

That such an ideology of response has prevailed in American writing instruction since Hill's "English Composition Card" is not difficult to discern: it is hard to overlook the card's educational durability, laminated as it is to the inside front and back covers of most typical composition textbooks. Symbolically sandwiching in everything else rhetorical, the card is still, in many contexts, the first and last word on writing.

But we have, in fact, known better all along — if not about how and when to respond to student writing, at least that real, substantive response is in one form or another fundamental to language development. Some eighteen years before the specimen theme was written, Harvard began to require the "correction of bad English as part of the examination for admission" to the college. This move simply reinforced much of what was already happening in secondary schools, where students spent most of their "writing time" parsing sentences, working on penmanship, and memorizing dozens of numbered rules of grammar and usage. Some educators, however, were already pointing out the futility of divorcing these principles from actual use — from sustained

Use fewer present participles, and avoid nominative absolute constructions

K.

P. The day being clear, which by the way seems to be the exception and not the rule here, we set out for that Mecca of all visitors to Boston—Bunker Hill.

Vague. Our first experience in the subway was rather enjoyable because it was something entirely new.

P. Arriving at the monument we sat down for a few moments to rest, then, my friend who had been sick lately, not feeling able to attempt the climb to the top, I commenced the tedious journey. The winding stairway on which I counted two hundred and ninety-four steps, seemed interminable, but at last I reached the summit.

verb?

P. The sun being bright I obtained a few snap-shots of the city below, from one of the windows, with my camera which I had not, for a wonder, forgotten to bring along. On the way down, the hollow shaft in the center of the structure gave forth weird echoes which seemed like the voices of the brave sons of the Revolution for whom the pillar was erected. After signing the register I went forth to join the throng which greets new-comers to Boston with: "Have you been to Bunker Hill yet? Well you really ought to go."

P.

Choppy.

? ?

Figure 1. Specimen Theme

discourse, and from the response that follows. In a speech delivered
to the Massachussetts Association of Classical and High School Teachers
on April 4, 1890, L. B. R. Briggs, one of Hill's colleagues, bemoaned
the lack of attention teachers were giving to the substance and meaning
of student writing:

> I once saw a number of themes from a school that is at least the
> equal of any in the country. These themes had been read and
> marked. On the outside of each was a diagram drawn by the boy
> and containing the words *Penmanship, Spelling, Punctuation,* and —
> I think — *Composition,* with a blank opposite each word. Each
> category had its maximum figure; and the sum of the maxima
> was one hundred. The teacher filled the blanks with marks, added
> these marks together, and thus gave the boy a percentage. The
> themes may have been discussed in the class; but so far as written
> criticism is concerned, they might almost as well have been let
> alone. Whatever the teacher put on them, beyond the figures, was
> infinitely small, and — as geometry teaches — might be neglected.
>
> One theme was sent to me as a specimen of the best work in the
> school. The writer had taken a formidable subject and had wrestled
> with it manfully. Yet though his theme was remarkably long, a
> few commas in the text and two or three words in the margin
> were almost all the guidance that he got from the instructor. He
> lost three or four marks, — for punctuation, I believe; but the
> instructor added to his score a well-earned bonus for general
> excellence, and marked the theme *one hundred.*
>
> Having secured permission to criticise this theme, I spent an hour
> or two upon it, trying to point out both its faults and its merits.
> The boy had done so much that it was a shame to see his teacher
> doing so little. There were a hundred things to say about the
> composition; and the boy, by the strong intelligence of his work,
> showed himself able to apply them all. Yet it was nobody's
> business to examine his writing minutely. Nobody had time for
> him. (Briggs 1890, 311)

While we might wonder what Briggs had in mind for his hundred
comments, his observation, buried in the annals of pedagogical history,
still rings true. For it is time — or lack of it — that so often manages
to redeem us from the admission that we have corrected, circled,
checked, and assigned points to our students' writing but forgotten,
in the arduous and painful process, to listen to what they have been
saying.

But even with world enough and time, the sort of minute examination
of the theme which Briggs advocates might have done no more for
the student's development than his teacher's formulaic approval. In
addition to finding useful ways to ease the "paper load" through
alternative response methods, we would do well to study what we

are as teachers, what role we play in the development of students' writing abilities. That role, which for centuries vested us with the authority and wisdom to find fault in the quest for perfection, is now finally weakening under the scrutiny of its appropriateness in helping writers grow, and not wither, from its manifestation in our response. For if we agree with David Bleich in the opening essay of this collection, then we must admit that, as the best teachers we can be, we are finally not fundamentally different from anyone who takes the time to interact, in a truly intersubjective and meaningful way, with our students. And to the extent that we deny ourselves and our students the opportunity for such natural social interaction, then we are sterilizing language and weakening the chance for its fullest development in our students' lives.

Whether we are looking back over our own careers or over the span of the last century's educational changes, the new ideas and methods now taking hold in response to writing seem clear and theoretically sound compared with the misguided and provincial efforts of the past. And if we have not yet found them, the answers are still near, we think — just around the corner from our present state of mind. Collections of essays on topics of central importance to educational practice may well suggest that we are on the brink of certain and lasting reform. And, by showing something of how far we have come in our assumptions about student learning and how best it is fostered through response to writing, the essays here speak with the same vitality and promise that has become the hallmark of the emergent field of composition studies.

But the essays' vitality lies in their questions, and they promise with caution. They remind us that what is new is not always guaranteed to work — at least not immediately, not simply, not without considerable thought. They remind us that if and when the new fails us, the old rarely provides the best respite for recovery. They remind us, finally, that we are and always must be suspended in the paradox of uncertainty, caught between tradition and reform, evidence and belief, the enigmas of success and the mysteries of failure. Paradoxically, it is this uncertainty, this feeling at each thread of conviction, this tentative balance along the fragile line of our students' literacy, that creates the most meaningful changes in how we think about what we do and how we go about doing it.

The essays gathered here do not generally speak with certainty. Instead, the goal of the collection is to raise questions, to challenge our common assumptions about response to writing, many of which we have inherited blindly from the certainties of our educational ancestors. Some of the essays are reflective, standing back to consider the social and educational ethos in which we now respond to students and ask them to respond to their own and each other's writing. Others are sharply focused, examining the minutiae of such response — its benefits, its limitations, its way of reflecting attitudes toward and beliefs about writing. Together, these essays may suggest a finality, a certainty sanctioned by their publication. But like the process their authors invariably experienced in creating them, they are designed to invite response — and in so doing, they invite us to further revise the text of our profession.

Part I begins introspectively, as its four authors examine the past, present, and potential assumptions underlying our theories of response. In the opening essay, David Bleich takes issue with the dominant conception of literacy and its way of restricting social and pedagogical change. Drawing on the work of language philosophers, feminist epistemologists, linguistic ethnographers, and researchers of infant language acquisition, Bleich paints language development as a nec- essarily intersubjective, highly social phenomenon. Consequently, "re- sponse" to writing must be understood in terms of the "collective and communal character of any language situation," which necessitates a focus not on what individuals say but on what they say to one another.

Fundamental to large-scale changes in our conception of literacy is the need to understand the relationship between our individual prac- tices and the way these practices are informed by our membership in a discipline that exerts its own historical or temporal influences over us. In "Images of Student Writing: The Deep Structure of Teacher Response," Louise Wetherbee Phelps shows how different response practices are, in fact, manifestations of personal, historical, intellectual, empirical, and paradigmatic perspectives. Suggesting that the theories underlying teaching practices evolve toward greater depth, Phelps points out the dangers of impeding this natural movement by cutting off theory development because of the need to solve immediate pedagogical problems.

The next two essays demonstrate the sorts of transformations in our reading of student writing that occur as a consequence of new theory. In "Transactional Theory and Response to Student Writing," Robert Probst illustrates the effect of reader-response theory, particularly as espoused by Louise Rosenblatt, on new thinking about the language of response. Questioning teachers' established roles as diagnosticians and gatekeepers, Probst argues that we must abandon the illusion that we can read with precision and objectivity, instead developing an epistemology of response that values all that is idiosyncratic and subjective in the creation of meaning. Further describing this change in attitude and stance, Russell Hunt next urges us to recognize the importance of natural, meaningful response through "whole language" approaches to literacy. Using as a metaphor the famous story of Clever Hans, the nineteenth-century German horse who was thought to be able to add and subtract, Hunt reminds us of the power of language embedded in real, functional contexts in providing unconscious, intersubjective cues to encourage true language development.

Turning from theory to practice, Part II brings together new perspectives on the methodology of responding to student writing. As Donald Daiker aptly shows in the opening essay, teachers must remember from the start the importance of a simple but powerful concept in all response: praise. Drawing on research studies that show an alarming paucity of praise in teachers' commentary, Daiker argues for the benefits of positive response: decreased writing anxiety, an enhanced attitude toward oneself as a writer and one's writing process, and greater motivation to write and revise. Following from this belief in the importance of positive commentary, Daiker then shows how praise can be incorporated into various levels of a student text.

The growing emphasis on peer response informs the next two essays on small-group writing conferences. Using insights from Rogerian counseling theory, Dene Thomas and Gordon Thomas offer a new perspective on the kinds of active learning encouraged by small-group conferences. Drawing on their analysis of conference-group sessions, they make specific recommendations for the role, directedness, and language structure of the teacher-facilitator. Richard Beach then provides a scheme for helping students to acquire the skills of self-assessment. Each natural stage of self-assessment — describing, judging, and selecting or testing appropriate revisions — carries with it specific instructional techniques for guiding students toward the kind of critical response to one's own texts that is so central to the improvement of writing ability.

Three further chapters reflect the breadth and diversity of response methods. Almost entirely unexamined, for example, is the question of how one responds to the loose, expressive writing typically found in student journals. Turning response to student writing in a new direction, Toby Fulwiler's article shows how sensitive we must be to the perceived purpose and nature of the discourse we read. Next, Jeffrey Sommers describes a method that places the teacher in the role of collaborator. The "writer's memo," a vehicle for metacommentary, allows students to explore and express their own developing intentions and writing processes to the teacher, who comes to see the students' writing in new ways and can respond more openly and freely to it. Finally, Geoffrey Sirc offers a critique of computer programs that "respond" in one form or another to writing. Arguing that current programs are severely limited in what they can provide by way of response, Sirc offers an alternative perspective in which computer technology becomes an adjunct to, and not a replacement for, real human response.

Part III draws together six studies of response to writing, ranging from descriptive analyses of teacher interactions with students to more empirical research on the relationship between response and the improvement of writing ability. In "Response to Writing as a Context for Learning to Write," Martin Nystrand and Deborah Brandt report results from their studies that the social, collaborative context of peer conferences not only helps students to revise more copiously but enhances their attitudes toward writing through the natural, functional reciprocity of discussion and review. As Cynthia Onore shows in "The Student, the Teacher, and the Text: Negotiating Meanings through Response and Revision," a curriculum based on inquiry can do much to help the teacher assume a more productive role in the classroom, closer to the role of the peer. The traditional classroom, with its established structure of authority and expectations, is unsuited to a model of growth which privileges both gains and losses in the nonlinear movement toward literacy. Drawing from case studies of three under-graduate students reacting to teacher responses, Onore reveals the complexity and idiosyncratic effects response can have on writers as they explore their way toward a finished text. By reinterpreting data that failed to reveal an expected relationship, Onore cautions us against the potential myopia of taking too empirical a view of our research.

Keeping the focus on teachers, Glynda Hull and Susan Wall examine the implications of new theories of interpretation for responding to error. In a study of elementary, secondary, and college teachers' responses to an editing task, they suggest that the interpretation of error is often a function of the institutional and ideological contexts of the reader. To assume that hard-and-fast criteria exist even within the boundaries of easily identifiable features of texts is to ignore the functional, contextual, and interpersonal features of discourse.

Next, Ann Matsuhashi, Alice Gillam, Rance Conley, and Beverly Moss widen traditional conceptions of response by examining peer tutoring as a response event. Through a careful study of one beginning peer tutor's response process, the authors raise important questions about how students read texts in progress and how such readings reflect the development of writing ability.

Bringing together both teachers and students into a dynamic interchange of response, Thomas Newkirk then provides a descriptive study in which he analyzes several tape-recorded one-on-one tutorial sessions. By illustrating differences in the way each teacher sets the agenda in the conference, Newkirk depicts response as a dialectic encounter involving complex roles. And, for the teacher's part, that role may require more silence, more attentive listening, than what we are used to. The focus remains on the teacher in the last chapter, as I describe a study in which writing instructors responded to essays reflecting different ways of viewing the world. Drawing on the developmental scheme of William Perry, I show how teachers themselves either encourage or inhibit intellectual growth, in terms of their own attitudes toward writing as manifested in their responses.

Throughout this book is an underlying belief in the importance of response, in all its forms, to the development of writing abilities. Clearly, no single method, no set theory, no specific research findings, no matter how conclusive, will provide everything we should know about or act upon in this rich and complicated process. But in gathering together the opinions, speculations, methods, and findings of twenty-two scholars and teachers who find the issue of response a constant source of interest and challenge, it is my hope that this volume moves us a little further toward a more complete understanding of the relationship between response and students' development as writers.

References

Briggs, L. B. R. 1890. The Correction of Bad English as a Requirement for Admission to Harvard College. *The Academy* 5:302–12.

Copeland, C. T., and H. M. Rideout. 1901. *Freshman English and Theme-Correcting in Harvard College.* New York: Silver, Burdett.

Elbow, P. 1981. *Writing with Power.* New York: Oxford University Press.

Lunsford, A. A. 1986. The Past — and Future — of Writing Assessment. In *Writing Assessment: Issues and Strategies,* edited by K. L. Greenberg, H. S. Wiener, and R. A. Donovan, 1–12. New York: Longman.

I Toward a Theory of Response in the Classroom Community

1 Reconceiving Literacy: Language Use and Social Relations

David Bleich
University of Rochester

Most people studying literacy today believe that it is better to be literate than to be illiterate. The topic itself has become important because of difficulties arising in the usual techniques of bringing people into literacy within schools and universities. Those of us living in literate societies see literacy as an almost natural technical skill that must be acquired in order to maintain a minimum capability as a social being. Because of this, a certain degree of handwringing has set in as it becomes clear that many people don't move into literacy very easily, and that many who do show no inclination to cultivate it to ever higher levels of sophistication. Thus, some studies show how important literacy is to contemporary civilization and how thoroughly social life depends on it, while other studies seek to disclose the history of how and why nonliterate societies became literate. In either case, the aim is to provide reasons and backgrounds that will facilitate the large-scale cultivation of literacy today and tomorrow.

While I do not wish to dispute that literacy is basic to our techno-logical way of life, I do want to draw new boundaries around the concept, which will perhaps weaken the old divisions between the literate and the illiterate, and which will render the scholarly and pedagogical handling of the subject a more socially active project. In our local communities of "English" and "composition" teachers, use of the term "literacy" is often taken to be a pompous synonym for the menial and remedial tasks of "teaching writing" or "finally getting students to write a literate sentence." Most of us do not yet believe that the subject of literacy is likely to change our traditional notion of "English": a burden to the unprivileged and a luxury to the privileged. But literacy could transform "English" into the subject that stands the best chance of disclosing the means of social change and provides the best opportunity for all peoples to use and cultivate their natural social legacies. Literacy should be understood as comprising all varieties of language use. Bearing this principle in mind, I am proposing it as a context for this collection of studies on responding to student writing. I will try to show why literacy should be thus reconceived and how such a change might bring new responsibilities to those of us who earn our livelihood as custodians of the native language.

Language as a Social Entity

During the last two or three decades, in which Chomsky's concept of language was vigorously pursued, language use was not a real academic subject. Early in the development of his thought, Chomsky presented his well-known distinction between *competence* and *performance* to enable linguists to study competence as a relatively abstract and clearly circumscribed subject that was understood to be the mental essence of language. Performance, which pertains much more to what we now ordinarily think of as language use, was not a part of this subject; instead, it was offered as a "mystery" of language rather than a set of problems with potentially useful solutions. Moreover, both competence and performance were tacitly understood to refer to capabilities and behaviors of *individuals*; whatever each of these things were, they appeared as features of single human beings: if we could understand a single person's "competence," we would then understand the language competence of all people, while differences in individual performance were of no theoretical interest. Because it is essentially not located within an individual, but always exists in groups of two or more people, performance was decisively excluded as an object of study. This feature of performance seems to render it a social subject, one definitely not susceptible to the kind of "pure" scientific treatment that Chomsky wished for language.

When he proposed it, Chomsky's distinction appeared to be bold. Most studies of language performance, such as the painstaking efforts of the Sterns (1907) to observe how infants acquire language, seemed not to issue any really new understanding. They treated language as Chomsky did — as something rooted purely in individual development. If this individualist perspective was to be held, it seemed imaginative not to proceed in any empirical way but to attempt to abstract the process in the hope of reaching a biological, genetic basis for language: in principle, the right sort of abstraction would make it reasonable to look for a genetic foundation of language.

While Chomsky's strategy may or may not yield the results he wants, it has become increasingly held that even if a language-acquisition device were found, it would not be understood as an explanation of language. Put another way, the "whatness" of language now tends to be understood as something completely bound up in human social existence, regardless of what its biological components are. Even as a tactic of study and inquiry, it now seems inconclusive to understand language as something whose "essence" may be traced to genetic information. In the same way that Freud's understanding of individual psychology shows it to be embedded in family and social existence, it is likely that our understanding of language will have a similar array of psychological and political aspects that are at work even in the newborn's first efforts to negotiate its interpersonal environment.

While few dispute the fundamental role of grammar in the Chomskyan sense, many researchers have now accepted the necessity of understanding language as a social entity. This change is both epistemological and political, and represents in part the infusion of what has recently come under the heading of feminist epistemology, as well as related considerations offered in the 1930s by G. H. Mead and L. S. Vygotsky. As a background to the claims I will make about how literacy ought to be reconceived, it is useful to review several thoughts of both Mead and Vygotsky, of the feminist epistemologists, and of some more recent work, especially by women, on infantile language acquisition.

Development of Language as Social Response

In taking up the issue of whether mind and self should be thought of as prior to society, Mead ([1934] 1962) argues that mind and self are creatures of society and not the reverse. He writes,

> [I]f you regard the social process of experience as prior to the existence of mind and explain the origins of minds in terms of the interaction among individuals within that process, then . . . the origin of minds [and] the interaction among minds cease to seem mysterious or miraculous. (50)

Mead outlines how the individual mind has always been considered the primary datum in Western thought, and how in this century the mind has been understood to be "biological both in its nature and its origin." If this is so, he argues, the act of explanation is solipsistic. The mind explains both itself and other minds. The idea of sharing knowledge, or of an explanation being accepted by another, must be understood as either a mystery or the result of a power struggle in which one mind prevailed. The common phenomenon of mutual or intersubjective knowledge would always have to give way to its being a function of some one person rendering it so.

On the other hand, if you assume that intersubjectivity is the prior term, it is easy to see how the individual mind is *derived* from it, how a single person can define and feel that singleness on the basis of having responded to the situation of intersubjectivity. Mead makes a similar point with regard to the self:

> [S]elf-consciousness involves the individual's becoming an object to himself by taking the attitudes of other individuals toward himself within an organized setting of social relationships and unless the individual had thus become an object to himself he would not be self-conscious or have a self at all. Apart from his social interactions with other individuals, he would not relate the private or "subjective" contents of experience. (225–26)

For experience to acquire meaning, for it to be known as private experience to begin with, the individual must have first objectified him- or herself, and to have done this is to have internalized the attitudes of others toward oneself. Self-objectification is the key to understanding subjective experience as intersubjectively grounded. Even a feeling such as "I am in pain" cannot be understood as separate from its social meaning of "I need help from you." Furthermore, as I have discussed in Chapter 2 of *Subjective Criticism* (1978), self-objectification is achieved with, by, and through the infantile acquisition of language.

In his work on the "higher psychological functions," Vygotsky ([1930] 1978) presents a perspective similar to Mead's. First consider his description of how an infant's grasping behaviors turn into pointing. Subsequently, he presents a similar argument for the conversion of sensorimotor intelligence into linguistic intelligence:

> We call the internal reconstruction of an external operation *internalization*. A good example of this process may be found in the development of pointing. Initially this gesture is nothing more than an unsuccessful attempt to grasp something, a movement aimed at a certain object which designates forthcoming activity. . . . When the mother comes to the child's aid and realizes his movement indicates something, the situation changes fundamentally. Pointing becomes a gesture for others. The child's unsuccessful attempt engenders a reaction not from the object he seeks but *from another person*. Consequently, the primary meaning of that unsuccessful grasping is established by others. . . . At this juncture there occurs a change in that movement's function: from an object-oriented movement it becomes a movement aimed at

> another person, a means of establishing relations. *The grasping*
> *movement changes to the act of pointing.* . . . It becomes a true
> gesture only after it objectively manifests all the functions of
> pointing for others and is understood by others as such a gesture.
> Its meaning and functions are created first by an objective situation
> and then by people who surround the child. (56)

The keynote of Vygotsky's work on the development of language and
thought is the principle that social action on motor behavior creates
internal intelligence. This case is paradigmatic: the interpersonal response to physical movement converts it into *gestures*, which, in the
normal case, are understood to be purposely initiated by people. The
idea of intelligence, in other words, has no meaning as an independent
faculty, but only as an internalized form of the capacity for social
interaction.

In his essay on the relation between speech and tool use ([1930]
1978), Vygotsky further argues that adult human tool use is different
from ape or infantile tool use primarily because language is bound
up, attached, or fused with it. Although speech functions and other
(nonspeech) motor developments are in one sense separate from one
another, they are actually growing toward one another in a reciprocal
relationship: "The history of the process of the *internalization of social*
speech is also the history of the socialization of the children's practical
intellect" (27). Vygotsky also implies something described by Piaget:
when "practical activity" ("sensorimotor intelligence" in Piaget) and
speech converge, language has been acquired. The child sees, in one
act or mental stroke, the congruence of speech and behavior, or names
and things. To internalize speech is both to make language into a
specifically human tool, and to make human tool use into a specifically
social behavior. Language acquisition is both a process of internalization
of social speech and a process of socialization of individual practical
"sensorimotor" intelligence.

Many elements in the social epistemology of Mead and Vygotsky
are now found in several feminist critiques of traditional scientific
inquiry. While many such works are germane, Naomi Scheman's essay,
"Individualism and the Objects of Psychology" (1983) is especially
relevant here. In it, Scheman claims that the conventional idiom of
philosophy and science is "socially masculine," and that it assumes
the epistemological priority disputed by Mead. For Scheman, individualism and objectivity are linked, and thought put forth on those
grounds is actually governed by the ideal of a "world filled with self-
actualizing persons pulling their own strings, capable of guiltlessly
saying 'no' to anyone about anything, and freely choosing when to

begin and end all their relationships" (240). To include equally a feminine accent on scientific discourse would be

> to suggest . . . that the psychological individualists might be wrong, and we are responsible for the meaning of each other's inner lives, that our emotions, beliefs, motives and so on are what they are because of how they — and we — are related to the others in our world — not only those we share a language with, but those we more intimately share our lives with. (241)

As things are now, the "underpinnings of philosophical psychology, metaphysics, epistemology, ethics, and political theory [are] the essential distinctness of persons and their psychological states, the importance of autonomy, the value of universal principles in morality, and the demand that a social theory be founded in an independent theory of persons, their natures, needs, and desires" (241). Scheman argues, then, for an epistemology of relatedness that applies as a principle of explaining how people work together and how groups of people are made up of interlocking roles. Unlike Mead and Vygotsky, she does not speak of origins and priorities, but implies instead that if two entities, such as the individual and the group, the language and its interpersonal locus of action, are isolated as "things," they are always ultimately to be understood in the light of one another and cannot be indefinitely understood in their isolated sense.

Certain studies of infantile language acquisition, while not explicitly claiming these epistemological perspectives, have proposed formulations which seem to depend on them. Colwyn Trevarthen and Penelope Hubley (1978), in their study of infants in the first year, find evidence of what they see as an "innate intersubjectivity." They see it appearing in two stages, the first at two or three months, the second at about nine months. Of this latter stage, they say:

> [A]t 9 months there is attainment of functional control, of intrinsic origin, for the use of innate and practised communicative abilities so they can be related to physical objects that have been brought inside the field of shared experience and shared knowledge. (223)

By adducing the spontaneous appearance of a field of shared experience, they stipulate an "innateness" hypothesis for intersubjectivity, which then yields the view that "structures of intelligence" are "at a deeper level" structures of intersubjectivity — a view bearing strong resemblances to Vygotsky's, with the exception of the idea of innateness. What most researchers study as a purely cognitive development is here understood to be intersubjective development. Notice the different accent on the idea of innateness. In Chomsky's case, the formal description of the "steady state" of adult language is supposed to provide the formulae for genetic findings. But in the present case a *qualitative behavioral style* is taken as evidence of the innate predisposition to think intersubjectively, so to speak, and in consequence, to develop language as an inherently social phenomenon. Trevarthen and Hubley do not propose a search for a genetic correlative of innate intersubjectivity, but they show, in a way related to Mead's, that to *think* of mental development in terms of intersubjectivity promises better and more comprehensive explanations of infantile language acquisition.

From the presuppositions of intersubjectivity, two elements not usually found in purely cognitive approaches to language — affect and dialogue — become central. In the work of Maureen Shields (1978, 1984), these elements constitute the social world's priority in infantile language development. Like Trevarthen and Hubley, Shields aims to change and enlarge the idea of cognition:

> The impact of the personal and social world on the child is almost always described in terms of affective rather than cognitive consequences. . . . There are words about thinking, wanting, liking, being friends. There are claims for possession, assignments of roles, words for sharing play proposals, threats, protests, appeals of social rules. In so far as children can use this repertory, it appears reasonable that the terms of it refer to internal representations of behaviour as much as words like *mug* or *chair* refer to representations of experienced objects. (1978, 530–31)

Shields argues that just as there is no separating the cognitive from the affective in children's mental development, there is no way to separate the individual capability for, and use of, language from the enduring situation of dialogue: "The young baby appears to be genetically programmed to give preferential attention to the human voice and the human face, and to respond with pleasure to human exchanges" (1984, 30–31). Shields therefore proposes that "dialogue is the basic form of thought" and that language should be understood as "the internalisation of the voices of others . . . the subject-to-subject relationship will promote and develop our ability to act as our own subjects when we consciously examine our ideas and think things out" (1984, 30–31). Shields maintains that the affective character of interpersonal relations makes them the more potent influence on the growth of mental life. In addition, the preexistence of intersubjectivity makes possible *both* the dialectic of object cognition and the dialogue that governs object cognition. Intersubjectivity is the framework that will explain the intermingling of the cognitive and the affective, as well as the interdependence of individual and collective manifestations of language. Perhaps it is just as useful to see this outlook as a belief system, as an epistemology. As a belief system, we may more easily discern its ethical and political values; as an epistemology, we may see what sort of language instances ought to be studied. In any case, Shields's work is a departure from the abstract scientism of Chomsky and from the solemn pretenses of value-free knowledge taken on by those pursuing an objective cognitive science.

Writing as the Manifestation of Social Purpose

In the same way that for Shields the study of language use in intrasocial contexts *is* the study of language, the study of literacy for us is the study of language use in intrasocial situations. This meaning for literacy already suggests that to be literate is to have a socially governed strategy or set of customs and habits for *any* use of language, either oral or written. To study literacy is to study the social prompts and styles that call for the use of language. In this connection, it is worth taking a few moments to see how Derrida derived his concept of writing. His formulations make it easier to understand literacy in the more general sense I am now proposing.

In his study of Husserl, Derrida ([1967] 1973) asks whether the sign, or any piece of language, may be understood in the two senses Husserl claims for it — expression and indication — or whether, as Husserl also acknowledges, these two senses are so "interwoven" that they cannot be separated. Husserl believes that while the two senses cannot be separated in any actual use of language, in the "solitary mental life" or in "transcendental subjectivity" only expression exists, because indication — the referring of something to someone, or of someone to something — is not a feature of this private area of meaning. Derrida argues that a private area of meaning can have no relation to language — cannot be thought of as part of the sign — because to use the idea of "sign" is to presuppose its already having been established in its combined form of expression and indication. To imagine a separation between ordinary indicative meaning and inner expression is to stipulate a meaning somehow more fundamental, more "primordial," than the meaning which came about from the recursive *use* of language to begin with. To think of a meaning at all means to acknowledge the primordiality of the sign itself.

Derrida explains how the concept of "presence" makes it possible for Husserl to clear away indicative meanings from expressive ones.

Presence may be described as an irrefutable momentary consciousness of sense that is separable from consciousness tied to language. The mere fact of self-consciousness (or self-presence) provides an intuitive demonstration of its priority to language. In this way, Husserl stipulates the unchangeable palpability of subjectivity, an ineradicable self-possession on which all mental life is founded. Derrida argues that this momentary experience of certainty is illusory just because the moment cannot be held, because it is a feature of time, because the "now" is a series of *repetitions* of consciousness, because the "digital" character of self-presence is founded on the digital character of language, and in particular, of speech — the voice.

The human voice, Derrida argues, gives at once the illusion of the subjectivity of meaning and the demonstration of its permanent exteriority. On the one hand, one hears oneself speak; the speaking and the hearing coincide and give the sense of "absolute proximity" of meaning and subjectivity. There seems to be an incontrovertible bond between the "meaning-intention" and its expression in sound while it is at the same time heard. Because of this bond, the act of speech seems "alive." At the same time, however, the exteriority of the sound and its necessary movement in time forces all other exteriority to appear, creates the occasion for "the world" to appear as a noninterior phenomenon: "The voice *is* consciousness." It is this view that leads Derrida to reject any possibility of a split either between indication and expression, or between these two and some inner, silent subjective "sense" that precedes the word. Derrida sees Husserl as the last effort of Western metaphysics to preserve the ideality of that subjective sense, because of his extraordinary effort to utilize it as the cornerstone of a new edifice of utterly certain knowledge.

The final focus of Derrida's discussion is perhaps less the denial of the existence of an authoritative subjective sense than the declaration of its contingent relation to the materiality ("exteriority") of the word. It is this materiality that he calls *writing*. Any palpable rendition of language is necessarily written. In actual writing, this exteriority is obvious. But to understand speech also as writing is to unify all manifestations of language as having the same sort of palpability, the same inextricability of indication and expression, and the same unidentifiable relation to whatever may be "inside" subjective consciousness. While I may wish to dispute the claim that this relation is unidentifiable, we can in any case proceed with the present line of thought by understanding any and all use of language as *writing*. In so doing, we may begin to change the traditionally held view of literacy as something radically distinct from orality, as some special honored feature of civilization whose functions are different from the familiar forms of speech and symbolic expression.

In this connection, consider the comments given in Lévi-Strauss's essay, "A Writing Lesson" ([1955] 1973). He observes that when viewed from the usual perspective, "one might suppose that [writing's] emergence could not fail to bring about some profound changes in the conditions of human existence" (298ff). He argues, however, that "the only phenomenon with which writing has always been concomitant is the creation of cities and empires, that is the integration of large numbers of individuals into a political system, and their grading into castes or classes." In general, writing "seems to have favored the exploitation of human beings rather than their enlightenment," and in contemporary civilization, "the fight against illiteracy is . . . connected with an increase in governmental authority over citizens. Everyone must be able to read, so that the government can say: Ignorance of the law is no excuse." We should not, of course, construe these remarks to mean that literacy is not also the means of political emancipation, as Paulo Freire has shown (1970). The point is rather that writing in the traditional sense, like every other tool or device that has emerged in human civilization, is immediately a function of the then prevailing social interests, and it becomes one of a vast array of customary opportunities and capabilities. Thus, if the written word was ever thought to have magical power, it is because other things also had magical power, and as Lévi-Strauss describes, when an outsider brings writing into a nonliterate group, it is assimilated into the practices that already exist for social intercourse. Even though the transistor seemed to create a "revolution," American *values* that dictated the manufacture of new consumer goods have remained exactly the same after the transistor as before it.

Literacy, therefore, is the name for the way language and social purpose interact. Literacy covers speech, art, science, and all symbolic forms in the sense defined by Cassirer (1953), but the accent for us is not on the "pure" idea of writing, as it is for Derrida, or on the final limiting role of language, but on how the materiality or exteriority of language is integrated with social purposes, interests, and relations.

Literacy, Orality, and Language as Markers of Social Relations

One of the most promising techniques of studying language use with these considerations in mind has been the ethnographic investigation of whole communities. Although anthropologists have been using it for quite some time now, Shirley Brice Heath's (1983) exhaustive study of three communities in the Carolinas has pointed up, probably in the first consequential way, its special usefulness for understanding literacy. Her study took ten years to complete, and she was thus able to chart *development* and *change,* particularly how oral speech habits and customs were related to how literacy was acquired. In addition, Heath was what we should call an integrated or involved researcher — not merely an observer, but someone who had a real pedagogical function in the communities she was studying. This fact also represents an important departure from the usual "scientific" research procedures, and, as I will discuss shortly, it is an especially necessary one for understanding literacy. Here, then, are three general propositions she derived from the new turn she took in the study of literacy:

> First, patterns of language use in any community are in accord with and mutually reinforce other cultural patterns, such as space and time orderings, problem-solving techniques, group loyalties, and preferred patterns of recreation. In each of these communities, space and time usage and the role of the individual in the community condition the interactional rules for the occasions of language use . . .
>
> Second, factors involved in preparing children for school-oriented, mainstream success are deeper than differences in formal structure of language, amount of parent-child interaction, and the like. The language socialization process in all its complexity is more powerful than such single-factor explanations in accounting for academic success.
>
> Third, the patterns of interactions between oral and written uses of language are varied and complex, and the traditional oral-literate dichotomy does not capture the ways other cultural patterns in each community affect the uses of oral and written languages. (1983, 344)

Each of these formulations urges us to abandon the idea of literacy as a trainable skill and to establish the principle that attention to literacy in any of its aspects entails simultaneous attention to the community, the culture, and the process of language socialization. Heath observes, for example, that "Roadville parents [white community] bring up their children in the drama of life by carefully scripting and rehearsing them for the parts they must play" (346). This means that a great many instructions are given, say, to show how to behave in church, use the proper table manners, and use the proper forms of address. As the child enters school, these "scripts" actually become a model and a preparation for the formal writing activities typical in the schools. It is an ethical and cultural matter to train children in certain kinds of behavior and to do it in just this scripted way. These ways greatly resemble the social rules in school, as well as the technical rules of reading and writing. The underlying mental, social, and affective structures of school literacy are, in other words, already part of the children's culture throughout the first five or six years of growth.

"In the drama of Trackton life [black community] . . . children will experience numerous shifts of scene and cast, and players will take on different roles on different occasions. . . . As they become conversationalists, they draw from their viewing of others' performances on the plaza, they imitate motions, facial expressions, and extraneous sounds to set the background for their discourse" (346–47). This situation, of course, is not scripted in advance by the parents; children, in a sense, socialize themselves — not in an any less complex way — but in a way altogether different from the way of the American school. The family life and socialization style of the black families, even through — and perhaps because of — the generations of slavery, have retained their ancestral forms, without, that is, some purposeful attempt to retain what is "theirs" in the face of white domination. This spontaneous dramatic style is no less firm as a cultural habit than the "scripting" style, but it is abruptly halted in its natural inclination to grow. The black child's entrance into school is a radical cultural disjunction. The old style remains in a secondary, and perhaps subversive role, while the new habits are laboriously learned from scratch. One can see, in this light, that one cannot "teach" literacy as if it can be acquired on top of any community and family background a child happens to have. Put in the more abstract terms I used earlier, the materiality of language is, in a sense, uniform in a particular culture, while different cultures have different *kinds* of materiality, both oral and written.

This is the reason Heath reduces the importance of the oral-literate dichotomy that Walter Ong, in particular, has tried to document. Although Ong's study, *Orality and Literacy* (1982), is quite useful in alerting us to the history of oral forms and of writing, he seems eager to retain a strong dichotomy between orality and literacy and to make a case for the superiority of the latter. Ong tries to show that writing "restructures" consciousness:

> By separating the knower from the known, writing makes possible increasingly articulate introspectivity, opening the psyche as never before not only to the external objective world quite distinct from itself but also to the interior self against whom the objective world is set. Writing makes possible the great introspective religious traditions such as Buddhism, Judaism, Christianity, and Islam. All of these have sacred texts. (105)

Ong claims that because in writing the audience is not immediately present, the possibility for introspection is enhanced; the accumulating cultural habit of introspection that results is the enabling factor for great religions. But Ong goes further. Writing made it possible to use "Learned Latin," a language which, he says,

> effects even greater objectivity by establishing knowledge in a medium insulated from the emotion-charged depths of one's mother tongue, thus reducing interference from the human life-world and making possible the exquisitely abstract world of medieval scholasticism and of the new mathematical modern science which followed on the scholastic experience. Without Learned Latin, it appears that modern science would have got under way with greater difficulty, if it had got under way at all. (114)

In addition to being "insulated from the emotion-charged depths of one's mother tongue," Learned Latin is "devoid of baby-talk, insulated from the earliest life of childhood where language has its deepest psychic roots." Finally, Learned Latin was "written and spoken only by males," based on academia "which was totally male" and learned "outside the home in a tribal setting which was in effect a male puberty rite setting, complete with physical punishment and other kinds of deliberately imposed hardships" (113).

What, then, are the features of "consciousness as restructured by writing" — objectivity, religion, and science — in their *decisively masculine form*, complete with puberty rites and punishments? Ong actually provides good evidence for Naomi Scheman's (1983) claim, cited earlier, that the language of science is "socially masculine." Paying homage to values such as detachment, and particularly, the insularity of masculine thought, Ong seems actually to fear the consequences of proceeding with cultural work in the mother tongue, with its roots in baby-talk and other basics of human emotional life. In large part, the case for separating literacy from orality and for seeing literacy as superior is a case for prolonging purely masculine cultural forms, and exclusively masculine groups. If one takes Ong's claims seriously, one would in fact wish to *advocate* learning dead languages to be used by purely masculine groups. The circumstances he describes regarding the social milieu of Learned Latin resemble the milieu faced by the Trackton children as they enter the American school. An original, family-based language and its attached values and social forms is to be rendered secondary to a new "scripted" language mastered *exactly because* it does not retain the emotional and social history of the mother tongue.

Does anyone really advocate this meaning of literacy? Ong's support of a separate and better literacy must also be related to the fact that, as a Catholic priest, he is himself a member of an exclusively masculine group with demonstrated social, political, and intellectual interests in the growth of society. Ong's case for a separate and better literacy is a political one. The politics of Scheman's and Heath's epistemology are no less clear, but they seem to enhance the interests of groups which are less exclusive and less privileged. Like Lévi-Strauss, Heath sees for traditional literacy no special power. In her 1984 essay with Thomas, Heath writes:

> In spite of all the claims about consequences of literacy, recent research has shown that the changes which have come with literacy across societies and historical periods have been neither consistent nor predictable. We cannot make generalizations about literacy as a causal factor, nor indeed as a necessary accompaniment of specific features of a society. The prior conditions and cooc-curring contexts of literacy in each society determine its forms, values, and functions. (68)

In discussing Luria's (1976) study of illiterates, Ong is able to see that the thought processes of the purely oral person and those of the literate questioner are incommensurate: that is, the illiterate person seems to be speaking a different language altogether. What Ong does not see is something Heath's perspective makes it possible and valuable to see, namely, the affirmative value of the oral idiom — the social values that are presupposed and suffused in the nonliterate societies. Once identified, these values could just as soon be part of a literate society as an illiterate one. (It is hard to judge what Luria's own views of his materials are; what he says seems to be doctrinaire Marxism, and seems to assume the superiority of the literate mind.)

Ong takes up the following sequence from Luria's *Social Cognition*. The respondent is a twenty-two-year-old illiterate peasant.

Q: Try to explain to me what a tree is.
A: Why should I? Everyone knows what a tree is, they don't need me telling them.
Q: Still, try and explain it.
A: There are trees here everywhere; you won't find a place that doesn't have trees. So what's the point of my explaining?
Q: But some people have never seen trees, so you might have to explain.
A: Okay. You say there are no trees where these people come from. So I'll tell them how we plant beetroots by using seeds, how the root goes into the earth and the leaves come out on top. That's the way we plant a tree, the roots go down . . .

Q: How would you define a tree in two words?
A: In two words? Apple tree, elm, poplar. (Luria 1976, 86–87)

About the first question, Ong observes that this intelligent respondent reacts to the question "by trying to assess the total puzzling context (the oral mind totalizes)" (Ong 1982, 56). Why this answer is especially oral it is hard to tell. On every occasion that I had to take an intelligence test or any other test, even in elementary school, my response to the test question was that no one really wants to know the answer to this question; it has an ulterior political purpose which puts my dignity on the line. My response also "totalized" the context, and yet I was the epitome of the literate student.

As I read this passage, the peasant is not merely unable to play this game, but is *unwilling*. The researcher's interrogative behavior is intrusive, personally and culturally. For the respondent, explaining what a tree is may be necessary if he were really in a place where there were no trees and someone really wanted to know. When this hypothetical purpose is finally explained to the respondent, the description of tree *planting* is perhaps a more reasonable response, because the peasant includes information not only about what a tree *is* but what *his relation* to it is. The questioner, however, is looking for an abstract essentialist *definition* of a tree, some kind of description, often found in Latin in science books, in genus and species terms, i.e., a plant of such and such a variety and structure. It is inconceivable to Ong and the researcher that such a definition may be a useless burden to someone who works with trees and needs other kinds of knowledge.

Meanwhile, the passage shows something about the respondent's own sense of what language is, namely, an item that ought to bear some *correspondence to the social relation* of the speakers. The respondent is resisting the questioner's initiatives, because to him, such a question seems illegitimate. When the respondent asks, three times, "What's the point?" he receives no answer. The first two of the researcher's questions are actually in the imperative voice, while the peasant's answers are in the interrogative. On these grounds alone the whole inquiry is suspicious. But once we know that the researcher is coming to the peasant "from above," and that the peasant sees this, it is easy to conclude that the problem of this whole inquiry lies in the embeddedness of language in social relations, the assumption of this principle by the peasant, and the attempt to use language in its less social "literate" form by the researcher.

This is just the point raised by Margaret Donaldson (1978) in her critique of Piaget. Donaldson is concerned that by Piagetian measures and experimental techniques, children do not look very bright. She observes that children's answers to Piaget's questions were cued by the schedule of questions, and then, when the schedule was altered in a way that made the questions imply much less that the children's answers were wrong, their answers were "right" much more often. In other words, she argues, when the situation itself was less intimidating, either through the use of fewer questions or experimental materials that were already familiar items to the children, their "performance" seemed much better, and they seemed to know more at an earlier age than Piaget's measures suggested.

The social situations of Piaget's experimental children and Luria's experimental illiterates are analogous. Neither Piaget nor Luria come to their subjects with the purpose of *contributing* to their lives and situations. In their roles as pure observers, and perhaps as manipulating observers, they superimpose an intimidating authority on the social scene of the people being studied. Believing in the ideal of objectivity, the researchers overlook the meaning and role of this new research scene, and attribute the subsequently gained knowledge only to the subjects under study, without regard for their own behavior within the context of the research. In contrast, Heath announced herself from the outset to be an integral part of the research situation; she came as a researcher and teacher — that is, someone with something to contribute as well as someone with the hope of reaching new understanding. She became a member of the community of interest, and while she was also a member of the literate privileged majority, her work played a part in the actual lives of the communities. It is this social action on the part of the researcher that weakens and can eliminate the boundary between the oral and the literate and can establish the single but supple and politically respectful category of language use.

If only speculatively, Deborah Tannen has gone a step further. At the conclusion of her recent essay, "Oral and Literate Strategies in Spoken and Written Discourse" (1983), she observes that "oral strategies may underlie successful discourse production and comprehension in the written as well as the oral mode." Behind this thought is not that the oral is inherently better or that the literate is less than necessary, but that the oral mode has an accent on the dialogic and the interactive that is not easily seen when one accepts Ong's description of the solitariness and insularity of writing. Tannen's point is also important because social interest is a missing element in Derrida's reconceptualization of writing: Once Derrida makes the key synthesis, his concentration is entirely on language as the "play of traces"; his own writing strives to enact this play and it readily becomes just another species of individual, and perhaps narcissistic, linguistic performance rather than an advance in the social handling of language. As Ralph Cohen (1985) has argued, the kinds or genres of writing are the normal reflections of social interests, yet Derrida is not inclined to move outside the allegedly limiting function of textuality. If we combine Tannen's and Cohen's terms, both the oral and the written will be understood as "mixed genres," with elements of each always found in the other, and with both always tied to a real human community.

In her long study of "two and a half hours of naturally occurring conversation at Thanksgiving dinner among six participants [one of whom was Tannen] of various ethnic backgrounds," Tannen (1983) observed a language-use trope she calls "overlapped or simultaneous speech" among three of the participants, and her reflection on this feature bears on her sense of the relation between oral and literate discourse styles:

> The preference for overlapping talk in some settings has been reported among numerous ethnic groups — Armenian-American, Black-American, West Indian, Cape Verdian-American, to name just a few. This preference sacrifices the clear relay of information for the show of conversational involvement, and in that sense, it is typically interactive or oral as opposed to literate in style. The effect of overlapping or "chiming in" with speakers who share this style is to grease the conversational wheels. But when speakers use this device with others who do not expect or understand its use, the effect is quite the opposite. The other speaker, feeling interrupted, stops talking. A paradoxical aspect of this style clash is that the interruption is actually created by the one who stops talking when she or he was expected to continue. Yet this reaction is natural for anyone who assumes that in conversation only one person speaks at a time. Such a strategy is literate in style in the sense that it puts emphasis on content, on uttering a complete message, on a kind of elaborated code. (86)

The basic difference between oral and literate styles is that the former is context-dependent, and the latter content-dependent, or "lexicalized." What gives expository writing its independent cast is the extra vocabulary and extra explanation that comes, so to speak, with the "main thought." It looks as if it does not matter who the author is or who the reader is. On the other hand, the oral style always requires the participation of other speakers. The "extra language" of expository or literate discourse comes, in oral situations, from other participants. Preliminarily, then, we can stipulate a certain equivalence between the oral and literate styles.

But only preliminarily. What Tannen is describing are different styles of social conduct, which she observes in her study of discourse, but which appear in other forms of social behavior in each group. *The discourse is itself not the issue,* but is only a mark of underlying attitudes toward interpersonal comportment. Thus, if "chiming in" is important, if interruption is expected, if "cheerleading" (i.e., the response of a black congregation to a sermon) is appreciated, all of these add up to a certain mode of relatedness among people, where the speech is in a literal sense a speech *act,* or a palpable element in a relationship. This is a demonstration of the "exteriority" or "materiality" of language. Of course the meanings of the words count and are necessary, but meaning is not just in words but in the modes of exchange, in the choice of when to present the words, in the preestablished systems of mutual uptake, and in the way all speakers sense that the exchange of language is an exchange of responsibility, commitment, caring, and involvement.

In the literate style, even though Basil Bernstein (1964) calls it an "elaborated code," the discourse depends much more narrowly on the meaning of the words. To interrupt, when this style obtains, is to injure the presentation of "meaning." The language itself takes on a much fuller referential sense: what the discourse refers *to* — something beyond the speaking situation — is understood to be the point of the contribution. More words, perhaps involving holding the floor longer by oneself, enhance the contribution. Notice also, however, how much more prominent the individual speaker becomes, how much more set off he or she is from the group in this style of conversation. We are reminded of the Greek rhetorical style admired by Ong, which, not coincidentally, finds its way, through the universal use of the word "rhetoric" to describe writing textbooks, into the contemporary approach to writing instruction in colleges and universities. We are furthermore led to Ong's other values — abstraction, objectivity, and the desire for insularity when attending to how we say things. The literate style tends to mute the social presence of any group and implicitly depends on an elitist social organization recalling the time when literacy and privilege were intimately associated with one another.

The literate style is weighted in favor of an individual-priority sense of society, even as we move, historically, into contemporary times. Ong's point about how introspection is enhanced by writing is related to the idea that *thought* or meaning is "more basic" than words (consider the familiar freshman complaint that "I know what I want to say, but I just can't find the right words"), which, in turn, is related to the idea that an inviolably private human soul lies "deeper" than the palpable social and bodily presence of the individual among members. In religious cosmology, individual souls are "saved" because of their private acts of contrition, and their completely private pact with God, a pact to which other people can have no access and of which they can have no knowledge. The gradual separation of literacy from orality in the West developed from these values of the priority of the individual.

But in the light of Derrida's considerations, this was in no sense a necessary development. In fact, to take the word seriously as a human, social speech act shows the underlying kinship of literacy and orality, and what is required for that kinship to emerge is the adoption of values which set no priorities between the two entities, individual and community. Each of these two items simultaneously constitutes the other. This mutuality is reflected in the "overlapping" conversational style, in context-dependent talk, and a series of other verbal-interaction strategies that are not permitted to disturb the decorum of formal adult life in the West.

In her concluding speculation about the underlying oral elements in written discourse, Tannen argues that "imaginative literature has more in common with spontaneous conversation than with the typical written genre, expository prose" (89). Why should this claim come as a surprise? In the memory of almost all people living today, I would answer, "literature" is something that first appeared in the schoolbooks as something "taught." Even though British education gets to resemble American ways more and more, in Britain, literature is much more a part of everyday life: more often than here, schoolchildren have some other acquaintance with the indigenous national literature than through school, and the literature itself has more of an independent life outside of school.

But if our familiarity with literature comes mainly from the stiff, "literate" presentational forms of the school, Tannen's claim that "literary language builds on and perfects features of mundane conversation" (90) will seem surprising. It is because there is so little practice, in the schools, of "interpersonal involvement" that Tannen must conclude, after careful study, that "literary language, like ordinary conversation, is dependent for its effect on interpersonal involvement" (90). But where else could literary language have come from? Only because the spontaneous social connections between literacy and literature are systematically severed, only because written texts become "sacred," because interpreters become privileged clerics, that the "oral" character of literature is lost, and the social distinction between literature and expository prose is obscured.

Social Responsibility and Response to Literacy

The foregoing sense of what literacy is derives, as I have suggested, from many sources and developments in the recent study of language use. In my own thinking, the general idea of literacy has been a necessary explanatory concept for the understanding of literary response. As I have discussed at some length in Chapter 4 of *Subjective Criticism* (1978) and in some later work as well, the interest in literary response resulted from a need to socialize and humanize the English classroom. In this context, the idea of "response to literature" is not ultimately a literary project but one that concerns how language is taught in any classroom. The term "response" refers not only to what a person says or writes after reading a written text, but to a social system of answering the language initiatives of other people. In this way, we are shifting our attention from the individual focus of "what a person says" to the social focus of "what people say to one another." The idea of response has served to introduce into formal scrutiny the collective and communal character of any language situation and the necessity for collaborative efforts in the study of language use.

The essays in this volume all make use of this wider idea of response and work to integrate it toward the far-reaching aims of literacy studies. The term "response" now reminds us that teachers as well as students are respondents — correspondents, actually — in the disciplined exchange of thought about language. These essays will suggest that to consider response is at the same time to explore the *responsibility* of teachers to include their own social interests as part of the subject matter of language use, writing, reading, and literacy. The idea of response suggests that teachers are in the *same community* as students and that classroom responsibilities, in regard to the study of literacy, are mutual and shared. Just what these responsibilities are, is, of course, not yet determined, and part of the purpose of this volume is to begin discussion of a new allocation of responsibility, a new program of social initiative, as well as of new ideas about the nature of literacy.

In reconceiving literacy in this comprehensive way, we are also helping to create a more permeable boundary between teaching and research. All subjects, including the so-called "hard" sciences, are finally a matter of language — though, of course, not of language alone. We hear a great deal about "computer" or "media" literacy;

this usually means a person is competent or knowledgeable about computers or television. But with a more comprehensive sense of literacy, computer literacy will also refer to the person's alertness to the social roles and actions of "computer language," to the changes in values promoted by any generic development in language. The one social institution in which all of these languages appear is the classroom. The relations among the classroom's membership, its constituents, the customs and conventions of dialogue, the distribution and diffusion of authority — all these bear on the particular mode of literacy being used and explored. The teaching of literacy always includes research; research always includes teaching. This is a new subject for the academy, and one that will make the academy more available to all its subjects.

References

Bernstein, B. B. 1964. Elaborated and Restricted Codes: Their Social Origins and Some Consequences. *American Anthropologist* 66 (6): 55–69.

Bleich, D. 1978. *Subjective Criticism.* Baltimore: Johns Hopkins University Press.

Cassirer, E. 1953. *The Philosophy of Symbolic Forms,* vol. 1. New Haven: Yale University Press.

Cohen, R. 1985. The Attack on Genre; The Regeneration of Genre. Paper presented for The Patten Lectures, Indiana University, Bloomington.

Derrida, J. [1967] 1973. *Speech and Phenomena.* Translated by D. B. Allison. Evanston, Ill.: Northwestern University Press.

Donaldson, M. 1978. *Children's Minds.* New York: Norton.

Freire, P. 1970. *Pedagogy of the Oppressed.* New York: Herder and Herder.

Heath, S. B. 1983. *Ways with Words.* New York: Cambridge University Press.

Heath, S. B., and S. Thomas. 1984. The Achievement of Preschool Literacy for Mother and Child. In *Awakening to Literacy,* edited by H. Goelman, A. Oberg, and F. Smith. Portsmouth, N.H.: Heinemann.

Lévi-Strauss, C. [1955] 1973. A Writing Lesson. In *Tristes Tropique,* by C. Lévi-Strauss. Translated by J. Weightman and D. Weightman. New York: Atheneum.

Luria, A. 1976. *Cognitive Development, Its Cultural and Social Foundations.* Edited by M. Cole. Translated by M. Lopez-Morillas and L. Solataroff. Cambridge: Harvard University Press.

Mead, G. H. [1934] 1962. *Mind, Self, and Society.* Edited by C. W. Morris. Chicago: University of Chicago Press.

Ong, W. 1982. *Orality and Literacy.* London: Methuen.

Scheman, N. 1983. Individualism and the Objects of Psychology. In *Discovering Reality,* edited by S. Harding and M. Hintikka. Boston: Reidel.

Shields, M. 1978. The Child as Psychologist. In *Action, Gesture, and Symbol*, edited by A. Lock. New York: Academic Press.

Shields, M. 1984. Dialectics, Dialogue, and the Social Transmission of Knowledge. Unpublished manuscript.

Stern, C., and W. Stern. 1907. *Die Kindersprache. Eine Psychologische und Sprach-Theoretische Untersuchung.* Leipzig: J. A. Barth.

Tannen, D. 1983. Oral and Literate Strategies in Spoken and Written Discourse. In *Literacy for Life*, edited by R. Bailey and R. Fosheim, 79–96. New York: Modern Language Association.

Trevarthen, C., and P. Hubley. 1978. Secondary Intersubjectivity. In *Action, Gesture, and Symbol*, edited by A. Lock, 183–229. New York: Academic Press.

Vygotsky, L. S. [1930] 1978. *Mind in Society.* Edited by M. Cole, V. John-Steiner, S. Scribner, and E. Souberman. Cambridge: Harvard University Press.

2 Images of Student Writing: The Deep Structure of Teacher Response

Louise Wetherbee Phelps
Syracuse University

In composition practice, problems have been defined and tackled in a characteristic way. First, a situation arises where teaching breaks down in ways that don't yield to trial-and-error solutions. In these circumstances, the educational system shares with its popular critics the tacit assumption that pedagogy is both responsible for the problem and capable of solving it unilaterally. So crisis generates methodology, or more accurately, a babble of competing methods, each defended by passionate adherents. (This was the situation, for example, in the 1960s when Albert Kitzhaber described freshman English programs.) As it becomes clear that this debate will not yield definitive solutions, research begins, with the goal of comparing methods to discover empirically which is most effective and why.

When this approach proves equally inconclusive, researchers call for more fundamental inquiries into the constituent processes and activities that underlie surface behavior or its products. The scholars construct theories and models of these processes, often by borrowing or adapting basic research from other fields. At some point, they look beyond behavior per se to define the underlying conceptual schemas that shape the attitudes and choices of both teachers and students. Ultimately theories are brought into more comprehensive networks of meaning, and metacriticism develops to evaluate the methods, assumptions, conclusions, and roles of the researchers themselves. At this point it is likely that theoretical frameworks may effect radical, even paradigmatic, changes in practice.

I've just outlined what I call the "arc" from practice to theory and back (the PTP arc, for short). Although theory is often thought of as rarefied and in the stratosphere, I shall reverse the metaphor and illustrate theory as an underlying "deep structure" for teaching practice. The concept of an arc posits that explicit theories of practice evolve normatively in the direction of greater depth, as suggested in the sketch in Figure 1. The end node of this arc represents the point at which the problem no longer exists, at least as originally framed. This point marks the beginning of new practices, new problems, and new arcs.

Something like this is probably a very common pattern in applied fields that, responding to compelling immediate needs, seek rational bases for practical action. In composition, we can trace movement along the arc (to varying levels of theoretical depth) in any number of cases where practical problems have defined research topics: sentence combining, heuristics, revision, and cohesion, to name a few. It's not unusual to find collections like this one that, by juxtaposing different phases of the arc, clearly reveal its dynamic (for example, Olson's 1984 volume on writing centers).

In this essay I want to explicate the PTP arc as it applies to the topic of responding to writing. Research on this newly problematic practice is gathering momentum (Brannon and Knoblauch 1982; Griffin 1982; Purves 1984; Sommers 1982). Behind the recent attention lies a history of research about evaluation that did not directly address the issue of teacher response, as well as scattered early studies categorizing such responses or studying their effectiveness (see Horvath [1984] for an annotated bibliography and Knoblauch and Brannon [1981] for a critique). If we grasp all this literature as fitting into different phases of the PTP arc, we will be in a better position to judge the various contributions and to plan future research.

An important purpose of my discussion is to point out the dangers of terminating the arc at a relatively shallow depth. There are tendencies

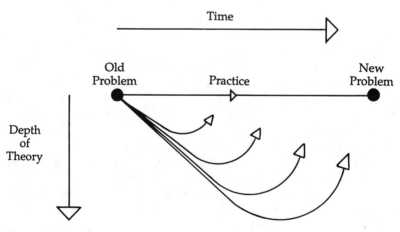

Figure 1. PTP Arc

in the work on teacher response, as in composition generally, to short-circuit theory development because of the pressure to solve urgent educational problems. This pragmatic attitude expresses the misconception that problem solving is a matter of choosing wisely among familiar alternatives. But fundamental inquiry is actually a process of reconstituting the question itself, making these familiar answers irrelevant. This fundamental inquiry changes the way we perceive and value information, the way we frame questions, the connections we make among phenomena and concepts. As a result, our concept of the original situation is so transformed that even the goals of teaching practice may change.

The structure of my essay is somewhat unorthodox, consisting of a series of analogies. The first section lays the groundwork by defining four phases of the arc at increasing theoretical depth. This analysis abstracts a pattern common to studies on many topics of modern composition. Then I will use some of my own work as a "representative anecdote" (Burke [1945] 1969, 59–61) for the development of that arc with respect to "pedagogical hermeneutics" — my term for the complex pattern of interpretive practices that links teacher reading to student writing. My starting point is a set of categories representing different attitudes that teachers can adopt toward student writing. In the thematic part of my essay, these categories have a straightforward descriptive meaning: they are presented as a possible contribution to thinking on the deep structure of response. The next section, however, returns to a metathematic level; in order to give concrete meaning to the phases of the PTP arc, I will reexamine teacher attitudes from the perspective of several interpretive gestalts. Through these perspectives I will read the categories variously as suggesting (1) stages in the development of a teacher's personal expertise; (2) temperamental or situational options in a repertoire of reading approaches; (3) a reflection of historical change in the understandings of written language; (4) a typical example of the recurring PTP cycle in composition research; or (5) a paradigm for the development of composition toward a more sophisticated relationship of theory and practice.

Exploring the PTP Arc

In this section I want to sketch the PTP arc as a hypothesis about the development of inquiry, arising from practical needs in the classroom (and perhaps generally in other praxis settings). This hypothesis needs to be tested in ways that are beyond the scope and purpose of my essay, where the PTP arc is not validated empirically but interpretively, through a set of analogues. But the familiar course of composing process studies may serve as an implicit test case.

In distinguishing abstract phases of the arc ("moments" in the useful phenomenological term), I do not mean to imply that they are necessarily discrete or consecutive. As we will discover in the alternate readings of my own research, such moments have historical interpretations, but do not represent or predict the chronology of actual events. All these phases may exist simultaneously in the field through the work of different individuals; examples of each may occur early and late in the progress of research on a given topic. My claim is simply that over a period of time, the *shared* conceptions that dominate research tend to evolve in the direction of deeper and more comprehensive modes of understanding.

Phase One: Methodology

In modern composition, research has typically originated in the effort to discover a more effective teaching method or to advocate one as superior to others. Formal research, which usually grows out of informal experimentation with new methods, attempts to prove those methods' efficacy by carefully controlled comparisons of results (a mode of inquiry typified by the standard research study in *Research in the Teaching of English*). "Results" typically mean the features (e.g., length, quality) of written products produced by students under each pedagogical system. As research becomes increasingly "scientific," studies become more distanced and neutral, sometimes employing elaborate statistical apparatus (Hillocks [1986] draws conclusions from a large body of such research through meta-analysis). But the modes of analysis do not change; they consist of observation, categorization, and comparison, often involving construction of a taxonomy. Many studies seek to isolate crucial, single variables that influence teaching outcomes.

In this first phase, researchers study mainly teaching behaviors at an observable, surface level of description: assignments, classroom activities, evaluation and response to texts, and (less superficially) the information, ideas, and techniques presented to students. Sometimes expert styles and strategies used by experienced teachers are contrasted with those of novices (e.g., Siegel [1982] on teacher commentary). More commonly, researchers think of differences in teaching as inherent in a "method" (a notion found in numerous articles on heuristics, conferencing, peer tutoring, and other techniques). But in these studies, focused ostensibly on what teachers do, the notion of pedagogical method actually incorporates and conflates methods by which students learn (imitation, freewriting, reading, analysis of texts), and methods by which students write effectively (planning, outlining, revision). Failing to distinguish among the theories of teaching, learning, and composing behaviors, or to account for their interaction in practice, many experiments unwittingly present a mixed causal analysis.

Phase Two: Transition

The second phase is a transitional one, in which a number of important changes set the stage for the truly philosophical thinking necessary to undergird powerful theories. These changes may occur both consecutively and simultaneously and are interdependent in complex ways. Researchers begin to note the limitations of purely methodological and behaviorist studies, which take for granted virtually everything that is interesting in both writing and teaching. They call for studies of the constituent processes of behavior, interpreted now more liberally to include cognitive events not physically observable. This reorientation, which occurred in composition as part of a general restructuring of the field, acted as a catalyst for intensive empirical research into composing processes, using methods adapted from other fields such as case studies, protocol analysis, and simulation (Emig 1971; Hayes and Flower 1983; Bereiter and Scardamalia 1983). For other methods, see Mosenthal, Tamor, and Walmsley 1983.

At its inception, research on composing carries over many of the assumptions and analytical modes of the first stage, while conceiving the *topic* of study at a more fundamental level. First, we might note what the new object of investigation actually is. The change of focus is not from student texts (these had been studied only incidentally, as teaching outcomes) to student writing processes. Rather, it is from evaluating teaching methods to studying the nature of the writing process in some ideal sense. This new goal produces comparisons of "expert" writers to "novices," initially emphasizing the same kinds of taxonomic descriptions and univariate causal analysis as the former studies of teaching methods. Texts still play an important role in determining the success of outcomes, but now good prose results from better composing processes instead of better teaching methods.

The second element necessary for the transition is the development of explanatory concepts. The possibility of powerful explanatory concepts does not reside in any one phase. They are often incipient in taxonomies, and it is what the researcher does to develop and extend them that determines whether they function to explain or merely classify. What happens in the arc's transitional second phase is that such concepts begin to function more actively in the design and interpretation of empirical research and to be elaborated into networks and systems by theorists. Attention to more basic aspects of the subject matter provokes such thinking, along with the influence of inquiry in other fields. In this phase, thinkers often turn to other disciplines for concepts and patterns to help them organize their data. A primary example is protocol research, which drew on generative concepts from cognitive psychology (e.g., planning, constraint, knowledge structure) to build the first cognitive models of composing (Hayes and Flower 1983; Flower and Hayes 1980).

The second phase sees a progressive development of concepts in terms of their power, scope, perspicacity, and linkage within larger networks. As in all development, it may be hard to decide exactly when the transition is complete and the third phase achieved, since the passage is a mixture of gradual and discontinuous, sharp change. But second-phase thinking produces, on the whole, fairly limited models and theories that do not restructure thinking. They tend to be confined to specific subareas of inquiry and to illuminate or confirm without surprising. Their implications are fairly local. One factor is simply that the cumulative thinking of the field has not reached a critical mass, the point at which (often suddenly) ideas begin to cut across previous boundaries and remap the territory, tying together many phenomena that had previously been studied separately and treated as independent.

In composition, one feature of second-stage research is that it focuses strongly on the writer and tends to be psychologistic. It also treats composing, reading, teaching, oral language, texts, and social contexts as relatively discrete phenomena, studying each in a different "school" of research with methods thought appropriate to that kind of entity or event. These biases, of course, work against forming explanations for the relationships among these elements of language use and language learning; conversely, the biases mean that discourse is not yet conceived as a multiplistic, multidimensional, and constantly changing feature of human life. Such conceptual limits are evident in, for example, research on coherence that regards it as a solely textual phenomenon; studies of composing that treat it as a decontextualized, short-term event; and theories of teacher reading that focus on response rather than comprehensive hermeneutical transactions.

A further, critical symptom of second-phase thinking is treating discourse events, objects, and their qualities as unambiguously observable. Shifting to the cognitive level of behavior (as in the case of composing) does not immediately problematize the observation process. Rather, the researcher may acknowledge that much cannot be observed directly, but believe that what is observed is fact (and, in some cases, that those facts represent cognition itself). There are two problems with this attitude. The first is that it treats the discourser as a natural object rather than a person, whose activity is a "process" like any other the researcher might observe in the nonhuman world, where events are not self-interpreted. The second is that it idealizes the researcher's own processes of perception, cognition, and discourse as transparent to the truth of phenomena rather than as constructive and interpretive. This is to operate on one hermeneutical level, that of the observer, whose privileged framework remains tacit and unquestioned.

Phase Three: Theory

In the third phase of the PTP arc, there paradoxically may be a return to the phenomena themselves in a search for more precisely tuned and suggestive ways of construing facts. From this source and from the development of reworking of concepts from earlier phases, composition research in this phase builds comprehensive and implicative networks of concepts — that is, constructs true theories. Just as process replaced (teaching) method as the object of study in the second phase, in the third phase the writing process as a psychological, behavioral phenomenon broadens to discourse as a highly contextualized, transactional human activity.

Susanne Langer (1967) has characterized mature science (what I am calling third-phase, fully theoretical thinking) as philosophical, "because it is concerned with meanings rather than facts, and the systematic construction of meanings is philosophy" (52). In composition, the invention and extension of what she calls "logically negotiable, intellectually fertile" concepts seem to coincide with attention to interpretive frameworks, i.e., structures of meaning in which activities are performed or understood. Here we see the first systematic effort to characterize what people do in terms of the underlying beliefs or attitudes that motivate them and serve to explain behavioral choices and differences. We can see this maturation into third-phase research in the work of Flower, Hayes, and their colleagues, whose cognitive models of composing put increasing emphasis on the knowledge of writers (Flower and Hayes 1984; Flower et al. 1986) at the same time as they build more and more comprehensive networks of concepts sensitive to relationships between cognition and context.

Questions about interpretive frameworks introduce, for the first time, into composition the "double hermeneutic" that characterizes the human sciences. The double hermeneutic refers to two layers of interpretation involved in understanding human activities. The first layer embraces the perspective of the participants themselves, the insider's view of events. "The social scientist studies a world, the social world, which is constituted as meaningful by those who produce and reproduce it in their activities — human subjects. To describe human behavior in a valid way is in principle to be able to participate in the forms of life which constitute, and are able to be constituted by, that behavior" (Giddens 1982, 7). Third-phase research in composition considers the cultural and personal frames that organize people's participation in discourse as a purposeful and socially grounded activity. (Purves and Purves [1986] articulate this shift in an elegant critique of exclusively psychologistic conceptions of writing, arguing against the term "process" in favor of "activity" and exploring cultural influences on the understanding of writing and textuality.) The cultural frames of participants may differ considerably from those that researchers construct to analyze the same activity — the second layer of the double hermeneutic. In this disjunction lies the catalyst for a move into the fourth phase of the PTP arc.

Phase Four: Metatheory, Metacriticism

Because of the double hermeneutic, metatheoretical thinking occurs in a human science almost simultaneously with philosophical thinking about its subject matter. This is in contrast to the development of natural science, where, because the objects studied did not think or talk, the interpretive nature of research itself remained tacit for a long time. In a human science like composition and rhetoric, the study of frames underlying people's behaviors causes researchers to recognize that they themselves construe facts in terms of preestablished meaning structures that determine what they notice and value. Their work is an interpretive practice carried out within a particular discourse community. That being so, it is impossible for researchers to treat their own constructions of events as absolutely privileged. Thus, knowledge formation and knowledge itself become problematic and subject to inquiry.

In this phase, then, models of activity are placed consciously within the larger thematic frameworks — cultural, historical, and philosophical — which motivate and organize these models. The scholar applies these frameworks to analyze metatheoretically all previous levels and their relationships and to view her or his own knowledge, methods, and allegiances critically. It becomes clear that alternate approaches to discourse, teaching, and inquiry represent conflicting ideologies, each with its own history and enduring value. At this point, the research community may go beyond celebrating its own theoretical advances to recognize that even prior phases of the PTP arc cannot be thought of as simplistically progressive. Instead, different moments of the arc may now serve to limit and criticize one another, and all may be played against practice itself.

To summarize, the arc passes through these stages:

1. a purely pragmatic phase aimed at establishing the most effective teaching methods;

2. a transitional phase in which constituent processes are described and largely psychologistic models are constructed, using limited explanatory concepts;

3. a fully theoretical phase in which interpretive frames are studied, the double hermeneutic discovered, and theories broadened to account for social activity and to incorporate multidisciplinary perspectives; and

4. a metatheoretical phase in which studies are placed within comprehensive cultural networks and metacriticism required.

As shown in the figure at the beginning of this chapter, the arc is not a simple movement from a practical to a theoretical orientation followed by an application. Rather, practice continues without pause, no matter what line of thinking and investigation research is pursuing. To varying degrees in different circumstances, inquiry continually affects practice. The relationship between theory and practice at *any* point is not a simple one-way influence, but a dialectic. Theoretical ideas filter into practice and are in turn affected by it. What distinguishes the terminus of the arc is that at some depth, theory (explicit formulations of deep structures) acquires the power to counter strong tacit assumptions with new conceptions. At this moment the original problem has become moot, or uninteresting, or simply transformed beyond recognition, replaced by other concerns. This rhythm of the arc has the universal act form described by Langer (1967) as a sequence "where the subsiding phase, or cadence, of one act (or vital element) is the up-take for its successor" (323).

Characterizing Teachers' Frameworks of Response

In the rest of this essay, I want to interpret the arc image concretely in terms of research on teacher response. First, I need to indicate briefly the phase levels of contemporary research on this topic and propose a more comprehensive conception of the object of study. (For surveys, see Knoblauch and Brannon 1981; Griffin 1982; and Horvath 1984.)

With few exceptions, the early research on evaluation, including commentary on student writing, represents phase-one research (Arnold 1964; Jerabek and Dieterich 1975). More recent efforts to discriminate types of teacher response are transitional and thereby quite mixed. For the most part, they attempt to categorize different types of response in various terms such as goal, style and content of commentary, features responded to, and so on (Lees 1979). A number of researchers begin to address the topic at a more fundamental level than commentary itself: Purves (1984), who distinguishes readers' roles; Gere (1980), who contrasts two views of language underlying evaluation; or Sommers (1982), who, along with Brannon and Knoblauch (1982), addresses the issue of ownership of the text when response affects revision. These studies, however, are primarily descriptive taxonomies, offering concepts that are suggestive but isolated, not yet elaborated or inserted into networks. What places them at this level is that the concepts introduced ("ideal text" in Brannon and Knoblauch, formative vs. summative evaluation in Horvath, appropriation in Sommers) refer only to response/evaluation and do not directly address the activity of the teacher in constructing textual meanings. Their focus implicitly treats commentary or the judgment it expresses as primary, rather than the process of understanding, which bears a complex relationship to the articulated response.

Scattered here and there in the literature are studies that deal with what Griffin calls "orientations," that raise questions about the structures of expectation and belief underlying teacher response (Emig and Parker 1976; Nold 1978; Knoblauch and Brannon 1981). Contemporary studies of error, starting in 1977 with Shaughnessy (see also Bartholomae 1980; Kroll and Schafer 1978; Williams 1981) have also focused attention on the processes and premises of teacher reading from a different perspective. These studies, along with others in progress which begin to set teacher response in the context of contemporary theories of reading and literacy in literature, hermeneutics, cognitive science, education, and linguistics (Freedman 1985; Anson, this volume), set the stage for research on pedagogical hermeneutics to address all the topics and levels of the PTP arc.

In the research discussed in this section, I chose to examine the interpretive frameworks that underlie and organize teacher readings of student texts.[1] My analysis is based on phenomenological accounts written by teachers about their acts of reading student writing. Teachers were asked to describe their reading as an experience and to explain the conceptual basis for their approaches. The teachers were primarily graduate students, some first-time teachers and others with extensive experience. When they wrote the accounts, many were beginning to study theories of reading and rhetoric, so I was interested in the changes in their thinking while under the pressure of learning and writing about interpretive processes. (Some of the data consists of the teachers' later annotations to the accounts and of interviews taped some time afterwards.) My long-term goal was to develop a hermeneutic theory for the special case of reading student texts, characterized as being read in-process and within a reciprocal teaching-learning relationship. Such a theory would address processes of meaning-construction, frameworks for interpretation and response, technical and ethical problems in reading writing-in-process, and a number of other issues. As I will explain in the third section of this essay, this notion of a pedagogical hermeneutics has become even broader as my work continues. Here I will concentrate on characterizing the interpretive frameworks that teachers bring to these readings.

Here is what I mean by interpretive frameworks in this context, where they constitute the deep structure for reading and responding to student texts. Insofar as reading is a purposeful and consciously directed activity (and this is true despite the importance of tacit or unconscious processes in any such act), teachers practice it in terms of a network of concepts that "frame" it as a particular kind of act (Goffman 1974). Such concepts represent or ground answers to questions like these: What am I doing when I read a student paper? Why am I doing it — what are my goals? What is the nature of the text I am reading? How do I read? How is my reading related to other actions? For whom do I read? How is my reading (and related actions) interconnected with the student's actions as a writer? What, after all, is writing? How do students learn to write, and what does my reading of student texts have to do with it?

I could go on: the concepts most directly related to the reading act are woven into a dense web of ideas about writing, reading, and teaching. I am concerned with that knowledge structure insofar as it is expressed in teachers' own explanations of what they do — that is, to the extent that it is a more or less consciously accessible set of beliefs and values constituting a "theory" of how to behave. (The accounts showed clearly, although to varying degrees, that teachers were able to discover through introspection and various modes of observation, including protocols, things they had not "known" about

their own ideas and practices. In the most thoughtful analyses, provoked by prolonged self-study, theoretical readings, and group discussions, teachers compared what they had thought they believed,
what they "really" believed, and what they did in actual reading acts.
These teachers almost all reported changing both their views and their
reading practices as a result of these reflections.)

An individual teacher's concepts about the activity of reading student
texts tend to be correlative: that is, they cluster in ways we can call a
globally coherent "attitude" toward the task. Such conceptual clusters
are value-laden: they express ideas not only about what acts and
objects *are*, but about what constitutes "good" writing, "good" answers
to assignments, "good" responses by teachers, and so on. These general
frameworks translate into specific conceptions of a given reading
situation and the technical and ethical demands it makes of a reader.
For the individual teacher, this specific conception is the way that
fundamental assumptions, largely tacit, manifest themselves focally.
Depending on the participants' theoretical sophistication, introspective
sensitivity, and depth of commitment to the inquiry, teachers' written
accounts or talk about their teaching will make the underlying global
attitude more or less overt, but where it is less so, the interpreter can
find its traces in the particular description of a given reading.

What Is "Text"?

Because of the clustering properties of interpretive networks, one way
to describe them is to take up a single concept and find its correlates.
In this analysis I will take the concept of the student *text* as my entry
to the conceptual cluster and attempt to define four possible attitudes
toward the reading act. In the closing section I will discuss the status
of these attitudes as ideal possibilities and as concepts formulated in
a hermeneutical research method.

The concept of text itself is complex enough that we need to focus
the discussion in two steps. I am interested in characterizing the object
that teachers believe themselves to be reading. Specifically, how is it
bounded and distinguished from other entities? I will begin by taking
these images of text on the level of a linguistic unit and asking how
teachers circumscribe that unit. Decisions at this level, because of the
correlative principle, distinguish three different attitudes toward the
reading task, along with one variant. To get at the more amorphous
fourth attitude, the second step will be to consider metaphorical
boundaries that have to do with such issues as the distinctness of
written text from the discourse surrounding it and the source and
ownership of its language and meanings.

Although there are many senses in which the text is an object of the reader's analysis, most simply it is a unit of written language which is composed and inscribed in some physical medium (handwriting, typewriting, computer printout or disk) that is available for reading and rereading. Text is a unit because it is treated as such by the writer, the reader, or both. I will make the simplifying assumption that it is teachers who determine how a text is circumscribed for their reading purposes: for example, a student may be required to turn in a series of drafts read successively or a portfolio that is read all at once. Teachers often control length and, to some degree, other boundary features such as how the text is titled or introduced and concluded.

Teacher-readers make several choices that set bounds for the textual object, choices that discriminate the first three attitudes. One is a decision about the temporal stability of the text, and thus its continuity or discontinuity with past versions of the "same" text and with potential, future revisions. Another choice concerns the separability or discreteness of the text from other writings produced by the same author. Finally, the third choice allows teachers to regard one student's writing as individual and unique or as an element in a collective class text.

The choices facing teachers in circumscribing text are not mutually exclusive, but can be combined in many patterns. Taken purely, however, each offers the possibility of enlarging the object that is being read by extending its spatial or temporal boundaries. Here are the ways this extension can work. (1) The text read by the teacher at a given sitting is regarded as a historical object that readers encounter as a series of forms replacing one another over time. The teacher reads the current form of this object as a cumulative record of the composing process. (2) The text read by the teacher at a given sitting is a sample from a corpus of writing produced by a student-author in the class setting. Often, that corpus or a large portion of it is read continuously as a single text, as one might read chapters in a novel (whether at one sitting or not). (3) The unit read by the teacher is the entire body of writing produced by a class in response to an assignment or occasion for writing. In the three attitudes and variation that I will explore, these ideas of text as object are correlated with a range of ideas about the reading act, evaluation, response, writing, and learning. (More precisely, correlates are a range of ideas compatible with and coherent with others in the network: I will be describing typical possibilities.)

Evaluative Attitude, Closed Text

Let us begin with the *closed* conception of the student text. Here the reader treats the inscribed text as self-contained, complete in itself.

Though there may be a history of previous drafts or even the expectation of future revision, the reader addresses the text as a discrete discourse episode to be experienced more or less decontextually. The paradigmatic case is that of holistically scored examination essays. Biographical and other contextual information is not merely irrelevant, but deliberately withheld, so the text is cut off from the ongoing thought of the author. The text has neither past nor future, only present; it stands independent of other writings with which it might be thought continuous.

Correlated with this concept of text is a view of reading as evaluation, almost entirely suppressing the interpretive foundation of judgment. Readers who treat a text this way in the classroom situation speak of "grading" a "stack" or set of papers; the testing situation is even more overtly comparative. As with any judgment, the text is classified through comparison and contrast to other texts of the same type, or more systematically through reference to general "rubrics." The only really functional rubrics are those derived more or less consciously from the analysis of particular assignments as raising certain issues, calling for certain forms, and so on.

Insofar as this attitude is associated with traditional styles of teaching composition, one might expect it to be quite error-oriented, with judgments focused on the surface or language of the text. That is possible, but not necessary. Other types of judgment are compatible with a closed view of the text and its reading. A particularly clear case is the reading of an essay in the subject-matter classroom, where the evaluation focuses on content. Here, of course, the teacher is concerned that the writer display knowledge about a particular topic. Comparably, in the writing classroom the teacher who treats the text as closed is focusing on the way in which the text displays the writer's ability to write. In such cases the reader may define strengths and weaknesses in the text at any level of description. In the accounts I've gathered, the evaluation is commonly comprehensive, including content, style, and mechanics.

The evaluative emphasis of this attitude leads readers to project the writer's competence from the text. The notion of competence here is relatively fixed, either as a kind of talent or ability, or as a level of knowledge and skill. The text, a performance, is taken as isomorphic with, or unambiguously reflecting, the writer's competence, often defined relative to expectations developed through comparisons with other writers in a set. The teaching style associated with such evaluations depends on presenting to the writer a critical standard: this text is good or bad in such and such respects, and would be improved if it had such and such qualities (e.g., were clearer, more detailed). These qualities are translated into general writing skills which the writer is thought to possess, lack, or need to improve. Correspondingly, it is assumed that learning occurs when the writer generalizes principles of good writing from commentary that identifies critical standards.

Formative Attitude, Evolving Text

If the first attitude is adopted in a writing classroom, it provides no basis for the concept of writing as a process at all, since the text has been detached from its own history and future. In the second attitude, the object acquires historicality as an *evolving* text. Let us consider first the weak version of this position, which is the most commonly held. Here the text being read is one of a set produced during a composing process. The teacher understands the text in relation to other members of the set, sometimes literally read in conjunction, but more often brought to bear through memory and anticipation of previous and later drafts. This view of student writing corresponds to a notion of composing as occurring in a sequence of relatively fixed stages. Even in this formulation, which preserves the literal distinction between successive texts, the stability of the draft being read is shaken, and the reader begins to experience difficulties distinguishing (especially for the sake of judgment) the actual text and its achieved meanings from the potential ones he or she envisions. The text becomes less important for itself than for what it may point to in the way of unrealized intentions — a fact that considerably changes the interpretive task of the reader.

We can see the correlates of the second attitude more clearly, however, if we explore it in its strong form, which represents an ideal possibility that most readers only partially articulate and act on. (From this point of view, the weak version represents a transitional state between the two attitudes.) Here, instead of thinking of a series of related texts, we think of a single text in the process of evolution. Ontologically, this language unit exists ambiguously between the writer's mind and the collection of inscriptions through which it takes form. What the reader sees in looking at any single draft — or for that matter, at lists, notes, and outlines — is a particular state of that continuity of text. (This is exactly analogous to seeing an individual from day to day. The person may look different, grow, and change, but his or her identity continues.) Together, all the related inscriptions that a writer produces in converging on a final text form the objective correlate of the composing process. Most of these, of course, the reader has no access to; but the teacher who does read and respond to some inscription short of the final text cannot help but enter into and influence the composing process itself.

Reading addressed to such a shifting and volatile object takes on a very different character. (I don't mean to imply here that the idea of text is prior to its correlates. The concept of text is a convenient starting point for analysis, but one may just as well say that it follows from a notion of the composing process as vice versa.) The major difference lies in what the reader is trying to understand. In this attitude, the text becomes more saliently a sign than a symbol. The text in its extended sense (which the reader now contemplates as a continuity, either literally or in imagination) points beyond itself to a process of composition. The reader's effort to understand is directed not primarily at the text language, but *through* it to a field of incompleted action.

This point, however, leads us to reconsider the first attitude in these terms and to understand better an ironic conflict that exists in it. The reader who closes the text also reads through the text to something beyond. The difference is that the "something beyond" is, in this instance, the inferred achieved skill or knowledge of the writer, taken as a product to be evaluated. Because this position does not lead to a well-developed teaching strategy (although it is appropriate for certain kinds of judgment), readers who practice it in the classroom are constantly drawn to find in student texts the esthetic experience that literature offers; they speak of wanting to be "lost in the text." In other words, such readers desire the student text to transcend the situation which their pedagogical role constructs, releasing them from the necessity for judgment and from the teaching consciousness itself, which always focalizes the deficit between what the text is and what it could be.

In contrast, the second attitude foregrounds not the reader's experience, but the activity of analysis. Readers begin asking "why" questions: "Why does this point or this sentence work, or not work?" "Why has the writer made a particular choice?" Such questions logically lead the reader into conversations, written and oral, through commentary, tutorial sessions, or class discussions. In this context, judgments become the effort to translate specific problems with reading a text into a writing problem which the writer confronts at some particular moment in composing. The comparison of texts with those of other students, against professional standards, even against the requirements of the assignment, tends to be bracketed in favor of helping the individual writer to work out the potentials dimly sensed by the reader in the evolving text.

This attitude locates learning largely in the actual composing process. However, it logically implies extending that process into an oral and written dialogue, not only with the primary teacher-reader but also with other readers, usually peers. In this respect both composing and reading broaden their scope by becoming social, not merely cognitive, actions. At the same time, reading (like the text and composing process) extends itself in time. Teachers, and other readers including the writer, can "read" the textual meanings at various stages of their development into discursive form; indeed, the distinction between actual inscription and the trying out of ideas in conversation tends to break down. The writer and the readers become "co-writers" through these varied interactions, as some teachers remark.

Developmental Attitude, Portfolio of Work

The third attitude extends the text in a different direction. Whereas the first group of teachers read a "stack" of papers and the second read collected bits, scraps, and drafts of the composing process, the third reads a "portfolio" of work by one student. Again, many readers adopt this position without following its radical possibilities. In the transitional or weak form of this attitude, teachers continue to read and grade individual papers, attempting to help students perfect each one, but they "keep in mind" the whole body of the writer's work, and focus on how it displays improvement. But the true correlate of the portfolio as an extended text is reading from a *developmental* perspective. In this attitude, the text itself blurs as an individual entity; unless it takes on special value because of a writer's commitment, it is treated simply as a sample excerpted from a stream of writing stimulated by the writing class, part of the "life text" each literate person continually produces.

The reader's function in this kind of reading is again analytical and represents the foundation for later pedagogical decisions and actions. The reading is through the text to the writer's developing cognitive, linguistic, and social capacities as they bear on writing activities. The set of a single writer's texts to which the reader has access, either literally or through memory, is the corpus from which the reader tries to construct a speculative profile of the writer's developmental history and current maturity. This picture, which might include ideas about the writer's language resources and ability to use them, style of composing, or conceptions about writing and reading, would need constant updating. Since the picture is almost entirely inferential, it requires testing against the writer's own perceptions and even theories of his or her own problems and progress. From this picture, student and teacher together can attempt to diagnose more specifically the problems that confront the writer in particular writing situations.

Reading in both the second (process) and third (developmental) attitudes presses the teacher to make and update models of the processes, events, and objects that are part of hermeneutical exchanges. Readers need to constantly develop, and confirm or negotiate with writers, shared images: of the textual meanings, actual and potential; of the course of composing in a given case and the problems that confront the writer in beginning or continuing it; of an individual writer's development and the ways that particular assignments, purposes, and texts challenge her or his growth. In none of these cases does the reader deal with a static entity: texts, the writing process, reading itself, the writer's development, and all other aspects of the teaching situation are changing rapidly and interactively. As I noted earlier, for teachers themselves the process of thinking, talking, and writing about reading activities is a catalyst for changing the relatively stable conceptual frameworks within which they construct such images.

Another choice facing teachers, between focusing on the individual or the class, may be thought of as creating a variation or supplement to the other attitudes, rather than a dominant stance toward student writing. Here the teacher treats the class papers on a particular topic or occasion as constituting one giant text authored by the class as a whole. The teacher approaches this text diagnostically, in the sense of attempting to build a picture of the class's response to an assignment. The teacher is reading through the text to the writing and especially to the learning processes, now conceived not as unique from one individual to another, but as a range of responses to teaching initiatives. The reader is creating from this range of responses a global picture of the writing class as a sustained learning event, with particular components, rhythms, highlights, turns, and so on, improvised from day to day within some more or less well-articulated, long-term plan. The reading of texts provides the teacher with feedback for making the more detailed local plans, for new assignments, class activities, and so on. For some teachers, this process seems almost equivalent to an esthetic act, constructing a drama of learning (Coles 1978).

Contextual Attitude, Text as Context

In my own teaching and the hints I pick up about the reading strategies of other teachers, I am beginning to perceive a new attitude toward text that did not appear in any of the accounts (running from 1981 to 1984) on which this analysis is primarily based. I am not prepared to characterize this new attitude with any authority, and I am even more unsure of its correlates. If in the second attitude the text stretched out in time and in the third it expanded into an aggregate text of one author's writing, in the fourth attitude it becomes interfolded with context until it has no determinate edges. From the first to the second and third attitudes, authorial language was extended in time and scope, but it was still psychologically bounded by a reader's attributing its language to the student-writer, along with control of its intended or possible meanings (note many current arguments for "students' rights to their own texts"). The fourth attitude seems to doubt this notion of ownership, with its implied hermetic seal on a text as sole product and property of a single author: a notion that combines capitalism with a Romantic view of the creative artist. New, more socially oriented notions of construing text seem to raise a different kind of boundary question, not of circumscription but of semiotic autonomy. How much is a text self-authored? How much is it coauthored (quite literally) with the teacher or other readers who influence choices during the composing process? (This question differs from what is asked about the co-construction of *meanings* by readers working with texts cut loose from their authors' composing processes.) To what degree does the student-writer actually incorporate the language, and thus meanings, of others into the text — in quotations, cliches, remembered phrases?

These questions suggest that the teacher must "read" a text — however it appears bounded, temporally or spatially — as embedded in and interpenetrating many other discourses. That is, she or he must read a *situation* as fully as possible, attending to the issues of authorship, the permeability of the student's writing to its context, the embedded mixture of languages that the student is struggling to control. Among the extensions of "text" in this perspective are the teacher's assignments (fragments of which often appear in student writing), commentary on drafts or remarks in conference or workshop, the sources that a text incorporates through quotation or paraphrase, and a host of other more indirect contributions to authorial language and meaning.

Without being able to detail this attitude, especially as a reading practice, I can point to a few examples where compositionists seem to be raising such questions and reading in this highly contextualist vein, where the text is defined and redefined through its relationships to a *context* or field of discourse.

Many compositionists nowadays are investigating the social nature of language, and especially the emergence of students into new discourse communities as they enter the academic environment. David

Bartholomae (1986), reporting on the way he reads freshman placement exams, describes the discrepant and mixed, conflictual languages of these student texts as their writers try out roles and voices in the new discourse community. In his reading, Bartholomae is concerned with "the difficult, and often violent, accommodations that occur when students locate themselves in a discourse that is not 'naturally' or immediately theirs." He describes his bias as a reader this way: "I was looking to see what happened when a writer entered into a language to locate himself (a textual self) and his subject, and I was looking to see how, once entered, that language made or unmade a writer" (12). Bartholomae's view of these texts correlates with different purposes in reading, different articulations of composing problems (for example, he rejects notions of egocentricity and writer-based prose), a different conception of learning to write. He constructs a network of concepts representing an ecology of discourse — for example, authority, enabling fictions, commonplaces, appropriation, the textual "I" — that replaces emphases on ownership, individuality, originality, and the writer's mind as a private world. He remarks, for instance, that "learning . . . becomes more a matter of imitation or parody than a matter of invention and discovery" (12). This is a radically different attitude toward student writing, not encompassed in the previous three models I have described. (It may be thought of, though, as a transformation of the developmental attitude by a contextualist perspective: development as a writer becomes here analogous to the social construction of the self.)

Another instance in which I discern reading in the fourth attitude is the effort to apply Bakhtin's theories of language to reading student writing. An example is an essay by John Edlund (1985) that attempts to analyze the writing of international students as incoherent through the intermingling and cross talk of two voices in their texts, representing American cultural values against those of various Asian societies. This is a variation of what Bakhtin (in his theory of the novel) calls "heteroglossia" — the incorporation of *"another's speech in another's language"* (1981, 324). Edlund interprets the voices in these ambivalent texts as creating largely uncontrolled and unconscious dialogues between the languages, specific meanings, textual meanings, and underlying ideologies they incorporate. In order to answer his questions about these texts, Edlund had to "read" a broader situation (heteroglossic and dialogic in Bakhtin's more encompassing sense) to discern the forces working for and against the univocal identity and authorship of each text. His interpretation focuses on the way that, for these students, acquiring English meant having to entirely restructure their conceptual systems. In this case, as in the other example, reading focuses on the dissolution of boundaries, the diversity of sources and influences for both language and meaning in a given text, and the conflicts endemic to textuality.

In thinking about the loss of semiotic autonomy apparent with the fourth attitude, it is impossible to separate the control of language from issues of meaning. Students continually assimilate languages and specific genres of discourse from the communities they encounter in television, film, books, magazines, newspapers, and conversation. This process shows up in student texts with particular clarity, because assimilation is incomplete, difficult, often strongly resisted. Thus teachers can identify the bits and pieces of native and alien voices coming into uneasy dialogue. As Bakhtin points out, this dialogue is ideological, because languages are saturated with the value-laden meanings of different social groups (270–72). When student texts echo the words and phrases of teachers, textbooks, secondary sources, the writers are not merely, neutrally, acquiring useful vocabulary. The point is even clearer when their language defies assimilation and perpetuates their own sociocultural commitments (to generation, class, gender, ethnic group, region, etc.) and their own discourse genres, often strongly oral.

This insight from an incipient fourth attitude toward reading forces us to take another look at the others with respect to the ownership, attribution, source, and conflict of *meanings*, an issue I bracketed in order to focus on the more basic one of circumscription. The three attitudes defined by differences in the objects read (the closed text, the historical text-in-process, the corpus of writing) need to be reexamined in terms of changes in teachers' conceptions of the location, nature, and provenance of meaning. I will leave this matter for future consideration, with this comment. In the passage from the first to the second attitude (by far the most salient today among rhetorically educated teachers), the transactional nature of reading comes into view, accompanied by a great deal of baggage in the form of multiple theories and models for the co-construction of meanings through the interrelations of writers, texts, readers, language codes, and ecologically defined contexts. There is no question in my mind that sensitive teachers are beginning to explore the significance of these conceptions of reading for their own activities. But research has not even begun to consider seriously the implications of the differences between the two cases: reading relatively fixed public texts with absent or even dead authors, as with the literary canon; and reading an unstable, evolving student text, embedded in and highly interdependent, even as language, with oral and written metacommentary. The implications and ethical consequences of these differences are vast enough to call for a new hermeneutic to explicate the reading and criticism of writing-in-process.

The third (developmental) attitude also takes on different meanings when development (conceived as progressive growth or maturity in an individual) comes under the social critique underlying the fourth attitude. At this point, it seems to me that our concerns cross from the negotiations of *situational* meanings and intentions (associated with specific writing occasions) to the negotiations that maturing individuals and their communities conduct over identity, socialization, individuation, and *cultural* meanings. The fourth attitude thus problematizes both transactional reading (directed through the text to a composing process) and developmental reading (directed through an expanded text to the writer's developing powers of literacy). First, it requires teachers (and researchers) to examine critically the part a teacher-reader plays in the evolution of textual meanings, in the case where a composing episode is enfolded with hermeneutical acts. And, second, it demands that we address explicitly the nature and ethics of literacy education as an unfolding dialogic relation between the authorship of the self and the appropriation of socially grounded languages, meanings, and norms of interpretation.

The attitudes and text images I have defined are summarized here along with the phases of the PTP arc, in anticipation of my strategy in the next section.

Reexamining Teacher Attitudes

Research on pedagogical hermeneutics is in the transitional phase where everything is up for debate, including the nature and scope of its subject matter and founding concepts. Part of my purpose here is to suggest how its enormous promise may be realized in future research by following the path of the PTP arc. In the absence of the full complement of phases in the research itself, we can find an analogue in practice, in the teacher attitudes I have described. Let us interpret these habits of thinking from a number of different perspectives that reveal the complex correspondences and mutual influences between theory and practice.

The first possibility I would like to consider is that these attitudes form a progression in the maturation of individual teachers as they become more experienced. There is suggestive evidence in my accounts that teachers become dissatisfied with reading closed texts and begin

Table 1

Summary of Attitudes and Phases

	Attitudes toward Student Writing		Phases of PTP Arc	
	Attitude	*Object of Reading*	*Phase*	*Object of Inquiry*
1	Evaluative (summative)	Closed Text	Methodological	Teaching Methods
2	Process (formative)	Evolving Text	Transitional	Processes
3	Developmental	Corpus of Writing (portfolio)	Fully Theoretical	Activities and Their Frames
4	Contextual	Text/Context (situation, field of discourse)	Metatheoretical Metacritical	Research, Theory, Knowledge

to move into the transactional, process-oriented attitude. A few were reading in a primarily developmental attitude. And I know of a few who subsequently began to introduce into their reading practices contextualist and metacritical themes that point to a fourth attitude. However, these changes are obviously not inevitable in teachers' development. They are probably stimulated by many external factors including (as I suggested earlier) self-study, discussions with other professionals, exposure to theory, and so on. Teachers also have temperamental and situational reasons for making these choices, even after they become aware of them.

Nonetheless, I think experience itself presses teachers toward increasingly generous and flexible conceptions of the text and the reading task. The teachers who break out of the narrowest conceptions of evaluative reading (in one case, a novice teacher wrote that he carefully avoided reading the texts so that he could grade them more efficiently) are simply the ones who critically observe what is happening between them and their student writers. While provoked and assisted by formal theories, these changes grow most fundamentally out of teachers' own practice of thinking seriously about the meanings and consequences of their own actions and, as a result, modifying their previously tacit conceptions.

Besides impressions gathered from the writers of these accounts, I would argue this position on the basis of my own experience. When

I finished my analysis I was immediately struck by the parallels with my own development, enough so that I studied my records and writings from the last twenty years to check my memory. It would make an interesting case study, which I can't undertake here. But let me summarize the trends in my reading modes, which are closely tied to and motivate increasingly fundamental theoretical investigations.

1. Overall, my reading attitudes move from the grading of a closed text (teaching high school in the 1960s) through process-oriented readings of drafts (in a writing lab) to developmental reading of portfolios (university teaching). It is still primarily developmental in the strong sense, but also situationally flexible and more pluralistic.

2. My notion of the text object I am reading has broadened correspondingly. My master's thesis (Phelps 1976) records my reconceptualizing text as a structure that evolves over time and can be read at any stage from list or word cluster to print. After a long period of exploring this notion and its connection with the teacher's role as "cowriter" of text, I began to read not "papers" but a corpus of writing from a single author. During these two phases I rarely wrote commentaries on text at all. I am now focusing my reading on dialogues among groups of writers and extending text in various ways to a holistic discourse situation that includes my own oral and written "texts." I am thus looking at student writing as interpenetrating and interacting with the language of sources, critics, and interlocutors. When I do comment directly on student texts, I foreground and attempt to problematize my interpretive processes and their relation to writers' composing acts and literacy development.

3. Another way to put this is to say that my interests have moved from texts as performances or displays, to underlying processes of discourse and literacy development, to the frameworks and contexts for these activities, including teaching itself.

I would like now to step back from the idea that these attitudes toward reading represent a progression from primitive to sophisticated, or novice (poor reader) to expert (good reader). A developmental taxonomy does not need to make that assumption. Instead, each mode of reading can be seen as adding a new competence. We might compare reading attitudes to the three systems of representation that Bruner (1973) describes for infant development: enactive (motor), iconic (perceptual), and symbolic (linguistic) (327). He regards each of these as a new and increasingly powerful technology that amplifies intellectual abilities. Each supplements rather than replaces the others. These systems of representation constitute a repertoire of competences that can be brought to bear by the individual separately or together, according to need and temperamental preference. Along these lines, I suggest that the attitudes distinguished here provide a set of increasingly powerful choices for teachers, which they can adapt and mix to fit their own purposes and varied reading situations.

One conclusion I would draw from thinking about reading habits in these first two perspectives is that deep structure is not something introduced by the PTP arc, which represents explicit theoretical thinking. Deep structures — images of student writing and correlates of those images — underlie all practice. They run all the way to the bottom, to the most fundamental level, and the deeper they are, the more significant to teachers' decisions. They are normally tacit. Many teachers, however, myself among them, are impelled by experience to examine these deep structures critically, make them more precise, consistent, and connected, and therefore open to transformational change. This thoughtful reflection is the essence of true "teacher research," which is not just the collection of data in the classroom but the careful observation of meanings in behavior and its consequences.

Clearly, however, these understandings and changes in teacher attitudes do respond to the progress of thinking in the profession. Changes in reading practices reflect a series of specific historical developments in the way theorists conceive texts and discourse activities. Once the profession asserted a stage model of composing and emphasized revision as important in good writing, it became inevitable that teachers' reading should focus on drafts. In this respect, some initial efforts to study response (Sommers 1982; Brannon and Knoblauch 1982) reflect certain commitments of process theory in their emphasis on students' rights to their own texts. This notion (which is very appropriate in context, where they are looking critically at teacher reading in the first attitude) nevertheless has a mentalistic ring that sounds strange to anyone thinking about reading student writing from the perspective of avant-garde literary criticism and philosophy. In fact, contemporary composition is moving away from narrow process theories. The attitudes toward student writing that I have described correspond with rough accuracy to shifts in the emphases of rhetorical theory, from text forms to psychological process to activity in context; from psychological to social; from composing as writing to reading as composing to the convergence of the two in negotiations over meaning (Petersen 1986; Langer 1986). The whole range of attitudes is available in practice because these ideas are in the air, though theories of teacher response lag behind.

It is interesting that the development of pedagogical hermeneutics (as explicit theory) does not just pick up where composing process theories are now, but stands near the beginning of the PTP arc. This brings me to my last two interpretive gestalts, in which the sequence of teacher attitudes may serve as an analogue for the development of the arc in two senses. First, the arc may be thought of as a cycle repeated with every new problem in the field. Knowledge about fundamental thinking in other areas does not permit one to avoid all the naivete of early research, much less to skip some phases of inquiry. Joseph Williams (1983) has made a comparable point regarding the stages of intellectual growth identified by William Perry (1968). Williams uses himself as an example. On the one hand, as an adult he has presumably achieved the higher stages of development in Perry's scheme (where one can tolerate ambiguity and uncertainty in knowledge, view even one's own beliefs critically, yet make commitments). On the other hand, despite his experience and his conscious knowledge of this mature attitude, Williams points out that he recapitulated Perry's stages in mastering the computer and studying cognitive psychology. Thus it makes sense that pedagogical hermeneutics should follow its own course of phased development, despite the advances in writing theory that precede and accompany it.

On the other hand, there is a sense in which the profession grows up as a whole. There are some areas of investigation where the PTP arc has progressed far enough to have transforming effects — for example, I have suggested that this is the case with composing process theory, which is now placed fairly firmly within comprehensive philosophical networks keyed by notions of context and community (Phelps 1988). Once this work reached the metalevel of thinking, it became (unlike earlier process theory) truly paradigmatic and generative. Because of its comprehensive scope and influence, such a theoretical deep structure undergirds the whole field, and any problem, old or new, is reconceived within it. This, I think, changes the arc while it does not obviate the need to pass through each phase. It may, perhaps, compress the arc so that phases are more simultaneous and interactive, rather than sequentially motivating one another. The phases become more clearly moments in a pluralistic inquiry that is concept-driven at all levels. This is my hope for research in pedagogical hermeneutics within a contextualist paradigm for composition.

Moving toward a More Complete Understanding

One of the characteristics of mature theorizing is to recognize that one's own categories are fictions. I therefore want to acknowledge that the images and attitudes toward text I have presented in this essay are, on the one hand, interpretations and, on the other hand, idealizations. They are interpretations because they were developed essentially through text analysis and no doubt reflect both my theoretical biases and my own practices (which I have tried to display sufficiently so that readers can make their own judgments). They did not pop out of the data, but were the product of difficult decisions about where to draw lines and how to correlate different beliefs and feelings. They are idealizations because I am interested in the logic of conceptions. If we begin with any particular concept, such as the textual object of reading, we find empirically that certain ideas commonly cluster with it in people's practices. At the same time, empirically it is always possible, and often actually true, that people act on the basis of idea clusters that are inconsistent and illogical, or that there are discrepancies between their stated beliefs, their underlying assumptions, and their behavior. What I have done is to rationalize these clusters by considering the logical possibilities inherent in the concept of text object — in some cases, possibilities that may not yet be fully actualized as frameworks for action. Finally, as developmental hypotheses, these attitudinal categories are undoubtedly as flawed as all stage theories — and I have put them forward in this aspect very weakly.

The PTP arc and its phases have all the same kinds of limitations as the characterizations of conceptual frameworks for reading (one reason they can interpret one another). I had an even harder time trying to locate the cleavage lines between the categories and struggling with an image that didn't always say iconically what I wanted it to. I think it is very important to remember that any such analysis divides up a constantly-shifting reality in one of many possible ways. (Cf. Bereiter and Scardamalia [1983] for another view.) However, interpretive categories are not arbitrary and are intended to capture some aspect of that reality as truthfully as possible. Together, my conception of the PTP arc and taxonomy of teacher attitudes point to the crucial significance of deep structures for practice and suggest gaps in our understanding that need to be addressed in future research.

It became obvious to me in writing this essay that, in my own research, I had entirely skipped the process phase of inquiry (although some of my reading accounts provide some insights into the phenomenology of the reading event), and I hope that this line of investigation will be taken up. Molecular models of reading texts-in-process, comparable to cognitive models of composing and phenomenological descriptions of reading literature, are necessary to support research into responses and their impact on writing. The study of response itself is unique to pedagogical hermeneutics, because overt response here is a mediating link between authorship and interpretation. Unlike most literary criticism, response in this context participates directly in a wider field of dialogic exchange between student writers and their readers. One conclusion I drew from this work is that I was not paying enough attention to student writers' views of what teachers were doing and saying. What is going on here is not simply one-way reading, but a whole circle of reciprocal and interlocking interpretations: teachers of texts and students and situations; students of assignments and commentaries and class discussions and conferences; writers of their own writing; and so on. This is truly a hermeneutic situation because it rests on the possibility, and frequent actuality, of misinterpretation. Beyond that, there is the appropriation of and resistance to other discourses that show up in the heteroglossia of student texts, underlying which are all the ecologically situated issues of literacy, acculturation, and power.

The study of pedagogical hermeneutics as a field where students and teachers engage in dialogue and conflict has the same radical potential for enlarging our horizons that we felt in early composing process research. To realize this potential, we must resist the temptation to close the PTP loop prematurely because of the misconception that theory isn't practical. Theory — the deep structure of all teaching activity, whether we know it or not — is the only thing that is.

Acknowledgments

I would like to thank students in the Rhetoric, Linguistics, and Literature Program and teaching assistants at the University of Southern California for their sensitive and detailed accounts of how they read student texts.

Note

1. I have collected written accounts by teachers, starting in 1981. The thirty-five-plus accounts so far represent a range of teaching experiences and theoretical expertise, from first-year teaching assistants (novices) to a very few professional colleagues. The majority had substantial experience in teach-

ing writing, but little theoretical background when they wrote the initial accounts, which were annotated in many cases a semester later, and in some cases followed up with taped interviews. I am continuing to collect and study such accounts as part of my work in pedagogical hermeneutics and welcome any from readers of this essay.

References

Arnold, L. V. 1964. Writer's Cramp and Eyestrain — Are They Paying Off? *English Journal* 53:10–15.

Bakhtin, M. M. 1981. *The Dialogic Imagination: Four Essays.* Edited by M. Holquist; translated by C. Emerson and M. Holquist. Austin: University of Texas Press.

Bartholomae, D. 1980. The Study of Error. *College Composition and Communication* 31:253–69.

Bartholomae, D. 1986. Inventing the University. *Journal of Basic Writing* 5:4–23.

Bereiter, C., and M. Scardamalia. 1983. Levels of Inquiry in Writing Research. In *Research on Writing: Principles and Methods,* edited by P. Mosenthal, L. Tamor, and S. A. Walmsley, 3–25. New York: Longman.

Brannon, L., and C. H. Knoblauch. 1982. On Students' Rights to Their Own Texts: A Model of Teacher Response. *College Composition and Communication* 33:157–66.

Bruner, J. S. 1973. *Beyond the Information Given: Studies in the Psychology of Knowing.* Edited by J. M. Anglin. New York: Norton.

Burke, K. [1945] 1969. *A Grammar of Motives.* Berkeley: University of California Press.

Coles, W. E., Jr. 1978. *The Plural I: The Teaching of Writing.* New York: Holt.

Edlund, J. 1985. Bakhtin and the Social Reality of Language Acquisition. Paper presented at the meeting of the Conference on College Composition and Communication, March, New Orleans, La.

Emig, J. A. 1971. *The Composing Processes of Twelfth Graders.* Urbana, Ill.: National Council of Teachers of English.

Emig, J. A., and R. P. Parker. 1976. *Responding to Student Writing: Building a Theory of the Evaluation Process.* ERIC Document Reproduction Service ED 136 257.

Flower, L. S., and J. R. Hayes. 1980. The Dynamics of Composing: Making Plans and Juggling Constraints. In *Cognitive Processes in Writing,* edited by L. W. Gregg and E. R. Steinberg, 31–50. Hillsdale, N.J.: Erlbaum.

Flower, L. S., and J. R. Hayes. 1984. Images, Plans, and Prose: The Representation of Meaning in Writing. *Written Communication* 1:120–60.

Flower, L. S., J. R. Hayes, L. Carey, K. Schriver, and J. Stratman. 1986. Detection, Diagnosis, and the Strategies of Revision. *College Composition and Communication* 37:16–55.

Freedman, S. W., editor. 1985. *The Acquisition of Written Language: Response and Revision.* Norwood, N.J.: Ablex.

Gere, A. R. 1980. Written Composition: Toward a Theory of Evaluation. *College English* 31:44–58.

Giddens, A. 1982. *Profiles and Critiques in Social Theory.* Berkeley: University of California Press.

Goffman, E. 1974. *Frame Analysis: An Essay on the Organization of Experience.* New York: Harper.

Griffin, C. W. 1982. Theory of Responding to Student Writing: The State of the Art. *College Composition and Communication* 33:296–301.

Hayes, J. R., and L. S. Flower. 1983. Uncovering Cognitive Processes in Writing: An Introduction to Protocol Analysis. In *Research on Writing: Principles and Methods,* edited by P. Mosenthal, L. Tamor, and S. A. Walmsley, 206–20. New York: Longman.

Hillocks, G., Jr. 1986. *Research on Written Composition: New Directions for Teaching.* Urbana, Ill.: National Conference on Research in English.

Horvath, B. K. 1984. The Components of Written Response: A Practical Synthesis of Current Views. *Rhetoric Review* 2:136–56.

Jerabek, R., and D. Dieterich. 1975. Composition Evaluation: The State of the Art. *College Composition and Communication* 26:183–86.

Kitzhaber, A. R. 1963. *Themes, Theories, and Therapies: The Teaching of Writing in College.* New York: McGraw-Hill.

Knoblauch, C. H., and L. Brannon. 1981. Teacher Commentary on Student Writing: The State of the Art. *Freshman English News* 10:1–4.

Kroll, B. M., and J. C. Schafer. 1978. Error Analysis and the Teaching of Composition. *College Composition and Communication* 29:242–48.

Langer, J. 1986. *Children Reading and Writing: Structure and Strategies.* Norwood, N.J.: Ablex.

Langer, S. 1967. *Mind: An Essay on Human Feeling,* vol. 1. Baltimore: Johns Hopkins University Press.

Lees, E. O. 1979. Evaluating Student Writing. *College Composition and Communication* 30:370–74.

Mosenthal, P., L. Tamor, and S. A. Walmsley, editors. 1983. *Research on Writing: Principles and Methods.* New York: Longman.

Nold, E. W. 1978. *The Basics of Research: Evaluation of Writing.* ERIC Document Reproduction Service ED 166 713.

Olson, G. A., editor. 1984. *Writing Centers: Theory and Administration.* Urbana, Ill.: National Council of Teachers of English.

Perry, W. G., Jr. 1968. *Forms of Intellectual Development in the College Years: A Scheme.* New York: Holt.

Petersen, B. T., editor. 1986. *Convergences: Transactions in Reading and Writing.* Urbana, Ill.: National Council of Teachers of English.

Phelps, L. W. 1976. The Development of a Discourse Model for Composition: Recursion in the Teaching Process. Unpublished master's thesis, Cleveland State University, Cleveland, Ohio.

Phelps, L. W. 1988. *Composition as a Human Science.* New York: Oxford University Press.

Purves, A. C. 1984. The Teacher as Reader: An Anatomy. *College English* 46:259–65.

Purves, A. C., and W. C. Purves. 1986. Viewpoints: Cultures, Text Models, and the Activity of Writing. *Research in the Teaching of English* 20:174–97.

Shaughnessy, M. P. 1977. *Errors and Expectations: A Guide for the Teacher of Basic Writing.* New York: Oxford University Press.

Siegel, M. E. A. 1982. Responses to Student Writing from New Composition Faculty. *College Composition and Communication* 33:302–309.

Sommers, N. 1982. Responding to Student Writing. *College Composition and Communication* 33:148–56.

Williams, J. 1981. The Phenomenology of Error. *College Composition and Communication* 32:152–68.

Williams, J. 1983. Cognitive Development and Rhetorical Form. Paper delivered at the Penn State Conference on Rhetoric and Composition, July, Pennsylvania State University, University Park.

3 Transactional Theory and Response to Student Writing

Robert E. Probst
Georgia State University

We can't agree fully even on the simplest of terms. Or rather, we can agree, but we do so without understanding one another fully, without coming to total unanimity, complete correspondence between what you mean by a word and what I mean. The word *dog* will mean one thing to someone whose experience has been with friendly puppies, another to someone who has been mauled by a rabid mongrel; one thing to someone who raises Irish wolfhounds, and another to someone who has a pet dachshund. It's true, of course, that we all know, more or less, what the word means, but in that *more or less* there is a great deal of latitude. Within the domain of meaning marked out by a word there is room for infinite variations and gradations.

There is, in other words, no direct connection between the word and what it signifies — the connection is made in the mind, both the individual mind of one person and the collective mind of the group that shares the language. Language has both social and idiosyncratic dimensions. That is to say, speakers of a language have come to agree, roughly, on what a word may and may not represent, but within that range individuals will differ in their understandings, depending on their experience. Although they are part of a community, and thus share a common language, they inevitably develop concepts — understandings of terms — with unique and individual shadings.

Transactional theory respects this fundamental fact: meaning resides in the person rather than in the dictionary. A word comes to mean something to us through our repeated experiences with it in various circumstances; it is the sum, or the residue, or the abstraction of those experiences that constitutes the meaning of the word. When we read, then, we bring those meanings with us to the text. As Smith (1979) has said, "What we already have in our head is our only basis for both making sense and learning more about the world" (78).

Rosenblatt, describing the reader's transaction with a literary work, argues that we must acknowledge and respect what the student brings to the work. It is only by relating the text to prior knowledge that the student can comprehend what is read:

> In order to share the author's insight, the reader need not have had identical experiences, but he must have experienced some needs, emotions, concepts, some circumstances and relationships, from which he can construct the new situations, emotions, and understandings set forth in the literary work. (Rosenblatt 1978, 81)

Consequently, whatever meaning there is in literature resides not on the page, but in the transaction between reader and text. Until the reader addresses the page there is no meaning; there is only the potential for meaning:

> A novel or poem or play remains merely inkspots on paper until a reader transforms them into a set of meaningful symbols. (1978, 25)

What becomes of that potential depends upon not only the text, but also its readers — who they are; what they know; what they call to mind, either intentionally or inadvertently; what purpose they have in reading; and what they are able or willing to do as and after they read. The transaction between reader and text is characterized by this mutual influence, by the active engagement of the reader — not the writer alone — in the process of creating meaning by bringing the newly confronted text together with past experience, both in and out of texts.

Transactions with Student Papers

So it is with the student's paper. It, too, is only a collection of inkspots on the page until the teacher comes along, and, with his or her unique background and biases, transforms it into meaning. The meaning that the teacher makes of the paper will depend upon who that teacher is, just as the meaning any reader makes of a literary work depends upon who that reader is.

Roth (1983) acknowledges the uniqueness inevitable in any reading — of either literary text or writing assignment. Commenting on the apparent obtuseness of some students, and the consequent difficulty in understanding their reactions to literary works and their responses to writing assignments, she remarks:

> When we complain that students do not read the material, we are often incorrect. Except for those who actually do not read the words on the page, literally do not open the book, students are, in fact, reading — typically in a highly individual . . . fashion, based primarily on personal associations. Such "reader-based reading," to extend Flower's term, has yet to be revised in the context of the course as interpretive community. And each course, each instructor and group of students, structures a unique interpretive community. (212–13)

The student's perceptions, in other words, have yet to benefit from the shaping and honing that discussion with others will enable. Here Roth offers an interesting concept of response that relieves teachers of the burden of attempting to represent some absolute standard of good and evil in responding to student writing. The teacher here is not judge and executioner, but is rather the manager of a small interpretive community — the class — and the representative of a larger one — the discipline of language and literary studies. The teacher's role, then, is to initiate students into those communities, to engage them in the dialogue necessary to produce knowledge. In so doing, the teacher presumably must stimulate talk within the class about the thinking and writing its members are undertaking, and must bring to that talk knowledge of the broader intellectual community. But still, though the teacher holds the authority that derives from responsibility for the class and from knowledge of the discipline, he or she must respect the individuality of the students and involve them in the tasks of thinking, writing, and evaluating — not simply presenting to them, ex cathedra, the pronouncements of an unchallengeable authority. To do so would exclude them from the community into which the teacher is charged with bringing them. It is to treat them as outsiders.

The teacher's task, then, is not that of providing a final judgment upon the work, or of identifying all its failings, but rather that of helping the students to re-see and re-think within the context of an interpretive community. In other words, the teacher serves as a reader attempting to understand the text — coming to the student's paper as a participating member of a society and a discipline, and responding to the writing accordingly. Implicit in this view is the notion that both reader and writer are in pursuit of meaning. It is a shared commitment — they are not opponents sparring in a linguistic ring, the student attempting to slip confusions and inadequacies past the teacher, and the teacher attempting to catch, label, and castigate all the flaws.

Although the composition teacher's situation is, in some ways, analogous to that of the reader of literature, sharing the uncertainties and ambiguities transactional theory suggests, it is unique in at least one important way. The writing teacher has a text to confront and can see it only with her or his own eyes, but the author is also there to assist. With the writer present, authorial intention can become a principal concern. Dealing with a literary text, we grant that the writer's intention is beyond our grasp. We may speculate about it, but there are other ways of making meaning out of a text, and in the long run they may be more productive. In the writing classroom, however, we can sit down with the writer, explaining what we inferred, asking what was intended. With the student text we can productively discuss intentions, and perhaps help by doing so.

Roth seems to suggest that the classroom is a microcosm of, first, the community of scholars who pursue the discipline under study, and second, the society as a whole. As such, it should function according to the principles of that discipline and that society. In the academic community, at least as it is now conceived by many of its members, knowledge is forged out of an ongoing dialogue, an endless sequence of transactions between reader and text, and between one reader and another. Each of these transactions is characterized by active and creative involvement in the making of meaning, each the activity of an individual with a unique background, with particular biases, preferences, purposes.

Influences upon the Transaction

As the culture evolves through these transactions, defining and redefining its knowledge, so might the writing class. But it seems to be a complex process, one that does not reduce easily to formulae. Ruth and Murphy (1984) have analyzed the complex transactions that occur during an assessment of writing, demonstrating convincingly the potential for confusion. First, the writer of an examination question reads and interprets the text of the question or assignment prepared for the student. Second, the student reads the question and interprets. After this, the student writes and then may read the paper, interpret, and revise. Finally, the rater, who probably is not the same person who prepared the prompt, reads the paper and interprets. There are at least three, perhaps four, transactions here, each with the characteristics transactional theory suggests. That is to say, to each transaction the reader brings a unique, individual history, and thus a personal understanding of the words employed and the concepts relied upon by the question and by the answer. There is much room for straying, many forks in the road where readers may choose different paths:

> Our own constructivist model for interpreting writing tasks pro-
> poses that the readers of the topic (both the student-writers and
> the teacher-raters) choose rather freely among cues embedded in
> the text of the topic, both honoring and ignoring elements which
> may enable them, with varying degrees of success, to match the
> test-maker's intentions and expectations. The topic functions as a
> springboard — a prompt. Thus the "meaning potential" of any
> given task is relative to the linguistic, cognitive, and social rever-
> berations set off in the respondents. Both the language of the
> topic and the general knowledge of the participants interact in a
> writing test to determine what meanings the topic may elicit. (413)

And there may be other elements that influence the meanings made
from a text. Jensen and DiTiberio (1984), for example, have begun to
consider the significance of psychological type in shaping writing
processes and influencing the interaction between teacher and writing
student. Using the Myers-Briggs Type Indicator to characterize students,
they have observed interesting correlations between students' psychological type and their patterns for writing, and have begun to speculate
about the possible problems that might arise when a student of one
type encounters a teacher of a different type:

> The Myers-Briggs [test] characterizes personality on four bi-polar
> dimensions, each of which represents opposing psychological
> processes: Extraversion-Introversion (ways of focusing one's en-
> ergy), Sensing-Intuition (ways of perceiving), Thinking-Feeling
> (ways of making decisions), and Judging-Perceiving (ways of
> approaching tasks in the outer world). (286)

Individuals tend to have a preference for one or the other of each of
these pairs, and consequently seem to develop that preferred mode of
interacting more fully, and earlier, than they develop its alternative.

Writing processes, Jensen and DiTiberio report, seem to correlate
with personality traits. For instance, extroverts, who "focus their energy
outward toward interacting with people and things," tend to write
quickly, without a great deal of planning, to benefit from such techniques as freewriting, and to enjoy talking about their topics. Introverts,
who "focus their energy inward through consideration and contem-
plation," tend to plan more carefully and reflectively, to work alone,
and to pause often to reconsider their direction (288–89). Similar
differences were observed on the other three dimensions.

From this research, the authors speculate that

> teachers in general may tend to advise students to write as they
> (the teachers) do, instead of adapting their advice to the needs of
> different students. We further suspect that a lack of match between
> writing teachers' preferences and those of their students is not

the most critical variable; lack of understanding of the richness and usefulness of individual differences is, we believe, of more profound importance regardless of one's type. (298)

Jensen and DiTiberio are encouraging teachers to acknowledge and accept individual differences in ways of dealing with the world and with the task of writing — with differences, in other words, in ways of transacting with experience and texts. The understanding they are recommending to teachers is much the same as that suggested by Ruth and Murphy, and by Rosenblatt. They point out that "the conceptual system of Jung and Myers can probably tell us a great deal about how teachers evaluate writing" (299). And, presumably, teachers aware of the system, and of the nature of reading, would be better able to govern themselves as they evaluate student writing, so that they do not penalize students whose patterns are different from their own, either by grading them more harshly or by failing to see how, as teachers, they might help their students develop.

As Jensen's research points out, there may well be much that is unconscious in determining the role we play as readers of student papers. We need to take into consideration, too, the conditioning offered us by our profession, which may encourage us to adopt roles that are not as productive as they might be. As teachers, our vision may well be obscured by the purposes we set for ourselves, and our reading of student papers consequently less adequate than it would be if we held a different notion of our responsibility to the student and the text. As Sommers (1982) describes the situation:

> The problem is that most of us as teachers of writing have been trained to read and interpret literary texts for meaning, but, unfortunately, we have not been trained to act upon the same set of assumptions in reading student texts as we follow in reading literary texts. Thus, we read student texts with biases about what the writer should have said or about what he or she should have written, and our biases determine how we will comprehend the text. We read with our preconceptions and preoccupations, expecting to find errors, and the result is that we find errors and misread our students' texts. (154)

In other words, not only do we bring to the texts our natural biases, those resulting from the uniqueness of our personalities, our abilities and experiences, but we compound the problem by adopting a severely limited conception of the teacher's role. In describing in detail the various roles a reader of texts may take, Purves (1984) identifies the "common reader," the "copy editor/proof-reader," the "reviewer" or "gatekeeper," the "critic," and the "diagnostician/therapist" (260–62).

Sommers's research has indicated that when we adopt the role of the "copy editor/proof-reader" — the hunter of errors — errors are what we find. And perhaps little else.

Teachers as Readers

Teachers might profitably reflect on the roles they adopt in reading papers and might consciously try to conceive of their role as that of the common reader, as Purves suggests — one who reads without the narrow focus implicit in the roles of editor or diagnostician. Teachers might read student papers with the same purpose they bring to other texts — the purpose of making meaning. In such a role — which is not so much a role but a shedding of roles in favor of direct, honest encounter — the teacher may be better able to serve as assistant in the student's own efforts to make meaning. As a real reader, the teacher may model the strategies necessary for the student to adopt while writing.

There is, after all, a great similarity between the activities of the reader and the writer. Rosenblatt's description of the transactional nature of reading could as well be a description of writing:

> As the reader submits himself to the guidance of the text, he must engage in a most demanding kind of activity. Out of his past experience, he must select appropriate responses to the individual words, he must sense their interplay upon one another, he must respond to clues of tone and attitude and movement. He must focus his attention on what he is structuring through these means. He must try to see it as an organized whole, its parts interrelated as fully as the text and his own capacities permit. From sound and rhythm and image and idea he forges an experience, a synthesis, that he calls the poem or play or novel. Whether for a nursery rhyme or for *King Lear*, such an activity goes on, and its complex nature can only be suggested here. The amazing thing is that critics and theorists have paid so little attention to this synthesizing process itself. . . .
>
> In the *teaching* of literature, then, we are basically helping our students to learn to perform in response to a text. (1978, 279)

Rosenblatt speaks here of reading as a creative process, describing it in language that we might more readily expect to see explaining the act of writing. Selecting, focusing, structuring, forging, synthesizing — these are the tasks of the writer as well as the reader. Both writer and reader are participants in the process of shaping meaning.

But we must help the student keep clearly in mind that our purpose in reading and writing is the making of meaning, because that purpose is easily lost. Writing can be easily reduced to a pointless exercise in error-avoidance, or in guessing the expectations of the teacher, as suggested in Sommers's research on responses to student writing:

> Teachers' comments can take students' attention away from their own purposes in writing a particular text and focus that attention on the teachers' purpose in commenting. (1982, 149)

When that happens, students are no longer engaged in real writing, but only in an exercise, an empty simulation of writing. Failing to recognize that their own reading of the student's text is circumscribed by all the constraints Rosenblatt's transactional theory describes, teachers may ignore the limitations of their own vision, ascribe to themselves a crystalline objectivity that they can't possibly possess, and thus may make it more, rather than less, difficult for the student to see what he or she is accomplishing or failing to accomplish in the prose.

White (1984) points out that this inevitably unique reading is not a misreading as the New Critics would have viewed it; that is, as a corrupted or error-ridden failure to discern a truth that lies in the text. The New Critical assumption that meaning is to be ferreted out of the text in which it hides leads us into problems:

> If we are limited to what the student puts on the paper, we tend to be literalists, putting aside our intuitions of what the student meant to say or our predictions of what the student *could* say if he or she followed the best insights of the text. This formalistic misreading of student writing, which pretends to be objective, demands that the student believe that *our* concept of what was written is what is "really" there. By comparing the student text with what Nancy Sommers calls . . . our "ideal text," we appropriate the student's text, deny the creative impulse that must drive writing, and turn revision into editing. (191)

Implicit in White's analysis is the notion that we must abandon the illusory goal of objectivity in our teaching of writing. It is both fraudulent and dangerous: fraudulent because knowledge cannot exist independent of someone to do the knowing, and thus cannot escape subjective elements; dangerous because it leads us to deny the fundamental fact of writing, which is the effort to make something of significance out of human experience.

The Student's Responsibility

Much that we do, especially in the assessment of writing, leads us to strive for this objectivity. Holistic scoring systems, useful when speed and efficiency are desirable, are intended to produce a rating of the compositions rather than to provide advice and assistance to the student-writer. Analytic scales and primary trait analysis are more likely to generate information about specific elements in a composition, and thus to provide information for the student. Both, however, imply that the judgments appropriately come from outside the student. The rating that comes from a holistic scoring is clearly *given* to the student by an evaluator. The scores on analytic scales are — or can be — somewhat less absolute. They can be discussed, with reasons offered for scores given, inviting the student to respond, but they may as easily be seen as absolute, the final judgment passed by the one in whom power resides.

What is important in the teaching of writing, however, is to transfer that power to the student. The responsibility for making judgments about the quality of their work must become the students'. They are the ones who must feel the rightness or wrongness of their statements, because, ultimately, they are responsible for what they write. If, as Rosenblatt and those who accept her theories argue, individuals make knowledge out of their own transactions with the written word and with the world, then they must come, sooner or later, to accept responsibility for it. Our ways of responding to papers must encourage that. If our responses fail to encourage that responsibility, if they are pronouncements from on high, then instead they encourage submission and discipleship, attitudes appropriate, perhaps, for a typesetter, but not for a writer.

A writer is someone who contributes to the making of knowledge. It may be knowledge on a small scale — perhaps that of the journal writer, straightening out the details of life, imposing order on his own experience — or it may have broader significance, as in the writings of a philosopher, historian, or novelist. Regardless of personal ambition, however, the writer must have integrity, which means not unthinkingly accepting the judgments of others. Nor does it mean rejecting them out of hand. Rather, the writer must assimilate these judgments and use them in making her own judgments. The responses we make to writers at all stages of their development must encourage them to begin to take that responsibility.

To encourage that assumption of responsibility, the teacher needs to share honest responses, showing the student the effects of his or her writing, modeling the transaction between reader and text. Further, the teacher needs to provide opportunities for the student to engage in that sort of exchange with other readers. Knowledge is forged by individuals working in a community of people who hold similar interests or confront similar problems, and the classroom offers us the most convenient microcosm of those broader communities for which students' education should prepare them.

Students need responses to their writing that show them what it is like to engage in the making of meaning, and that implies personal conferences, no grades, time for the students to talk with one another, peer response, and acceptance of digression from the conventional or habitual or expected. Teachers must help their students to see both potential and problems. They must be alert to patterns developing within each student's work, and to the disruptions of those patterns. And they must guard against the temptation of believing that their own perceptions are of greater value than they actually are.

Our role, after all, is not primarily that of gatekeeper, whom Purves (1984) describes as one charged with admitting or not admitting, approving or not approving. The gatekeepers, Purves says, "act not as surrogates for the common reader, but as surrogates for various establishments" (262). As teachers we should strive not to keep our students out, but to help them get in, and we do that by participating with them in the transactional processes of making meaning linguistically.

Ultimately, students must become their own evaluators. In essence, we are asking teachers to help wean students from a simple view of the world. We want students to see teachers not as right authority figures to be deferred to, nor as wrong authority figures to be rejected, but as individuals, representing a culture and a discipline, with whom to talk. Too often our appointed role, the task of dealing with too many inadequate papers by developing students, our textbooks, and perhaps above all our gradebook, lure us into thinking that we are, in fact, authorities, armed with absolute knowledge. The Warriner's grammar and its countless simulacra, venerable with age if not pedagogic wisdom, may sometimes deceive us into speaking with authority on matters that are beyond our knowing.

For students to become effective as their own evaluators they must become skillful readers of their own writing. The act of writing inevitably demands reading. Even the most private, least recursive writing — perhaps the journal entry, inspired by an event rather than a text, dashed off in haste, filed away without rereading, without even a second glance — implies reading. Even though the writer may not look back at what was written, nonetheless, as the student writes, he draws upon an awareness of the reader and of the possibilities of reading, choosing words, organizing thoughts, producing rhythms that could work an effect upon a potential reader, even if the reader is never anyone but the writer himself. The writer moves through the material as a reader might, conscious either of the narrative structure or the developing argument or the pouring forth of emotion, selecting from the material in his mind in accordance with the same sort of expectations a reader would bring to a text such as this. Although the writer may not have a particular reader in mind, may never intend that the text reach another person, still, an awareness of reading informs the work.

If schooling leads students to expect only the hostile reader, or only the reader who serves as proofreader, or only the reader who serves as the gatekeeper, then writing will come to seem less a pursuit of meaning than a survival exercise. Transactional theory suggests that we must be tentative about our reading of student papers, not pretending to pure objectivity, but tentative and cautious about the statements we make. Teachers must model in their reading the search for meaning that they expect students to undertake in their writing.

Epistemology

The problem is epistemological — what is knowledge, and where does it come from? If writing is the act of forging knowledge out of experience, and if it is personal and unique, as it so often must be (in the realm of values at least, if not in the domain of the sciences), then the individual must be the ultimate judge of that knowledge — does it satisfy her, does it resolve matters successfully for her, does it leave her with the sense of completeness that successful writing yields? The teacher may help the student judge those matters, but the student must ultimately come to rely on herself, and thus the act of evaluation must lead in that direction. It must not be the sole responsibility of the teacher. The act of assessing must itself be a transaction, a building of meaning.

The teacher's expertise lies in the ability to assist the student with these transactions. Circumstances can be arranged in which students may work together, reading and responding to one another's work. And the teacher can offer a reading, a response — that is to say, one reader's transaction with the text — so the student may use that information in judging the success of the writing. But the teacher cannot offer a final, conclusive, objective judgment on the quality of the text. Transactional theory denies that possibility. If meaning resides not on the page, but in the reader, and if each reader is different and thus reads differently, then all the teacher can do is offer a unique, idiosyncratic reading — *a* reading, but not *the* reading.

References

Brannon, L., and C. H. Knoblauch. 1982. On Students' Rights to Their Own Texts: A Model of Teacher Response. *College Composition and Communication* 33 (2): 157–66.

Griffin, C. W. 1982. Theory of Responding to Student Writing: The State of the Art. *College Composition and Communication* 33 (3): 296–301.

Jensen, G. H., and J. K. DiTiberio. 1984. Personality and Individual Writing Processes. *College Composition and Communication* 35 (3): 285–300.

Koenke, K. 1984. An Examination of the Construct of "Reader-Text Relationship." *English Education* 16 (2): 115–20.

Purves, A. C. 1984. The Teacher as Reader: An Anatomy. *College English* 46 (3): 259–65.

Rosenblatt, L. M. 1969. Towards a Transactional Theory of Reading. *Journal of Reading Behavior* 1 (1): 31–49.

Rosenblatt, L. M. 1978a. *Literature as Exploration.* New York: Noble and Noble.

Rosenblatt, L. M. 1978b. *The Reader, the Text, the Poem: The Transactional Theory of the Literary Work.* Carbondale: Southern Illinois University Press.

Rosenblatt, L. M. 1985. Viewpoints: Transaction Versus Interaction — A Terminological Rescue Operation. *Research in the Teaching of English* 19 (1): 96–107.

Roth, P. A. 1983. Re-viewing Reading and Writing Assignments. In *The Writer's Mind: Writing as a Mode of Thinking,* edited by J. N. Hays, P. A. Roth, J. R. Ramsey, and R. D. Foulke, 211–20. Urbana, Ill.: National Council of Teachers of English.

Ruth, L., and S. Murphy. 1984. Designing Topics for Writing Assessment: Problems of Meaning. *Research in the Teaching of English* 33 (5): 410–22.

Smith, F. 1979. *Reading without Nonsense.* New York: Teachers College Press.

Sommers, N. 1982. Responding to Student Writing. *College Composition and Communication* 33 (2): 148–56.

White, E. M. 1984. Post-Structuralist Literary Criticism and the Response to Student Writing. *College Composition and Communication* 35 (2): 186–95.

4 A Horse Named Hans, a Boy Named Shawn: The Herr von Osten Theory of Response to Writing

Russell A. Hunt
St. Thomas University

Shawn

It was in 1981, at a session during a meeting of the Canadian Council of Teachers of English in Halifax, that I first learned the term "whole language" and encountered the work of a writer whom I know only as Shawn. One presentation there consisted of a series of overhead-projector transparencies which amounted to a case study of Shawn's writing development, over his first year of school. (Shawn's development has since been described more fully by Judith Newman in *The Craft of Children's Writing* [1984].)

In Shawn's class, from the very beginning, a certain amount of time every day was set aside for writing. The children could write anything they wanted to; at the outset, of course, many of them copied material from the writing which surrounded them in the classroom — bulletin boards, blackboards, posters, and so forth. In each case the teacher asked the child to read what he or she had written and then responded in writing, reading aloud as, or after, she wrote. She never corrected the child's writing; she never marked an error. She responded to what the child's writing said — or, indeed, to what the child *said* it said, for in many cases only the child could read it.

Shawn's earliest productions were pretty distant copies of language from the classroom environment; sometimes he knew what they said, sometimes not. Shawn was a child who had not grown up in a very literate environment, and his acquaintance with written language was limited. Within a few sessions, however (under the pressure, it seems probable, of wanting to make contact with his teacher), he began to produce his own statements, about things like the earache he'd had the night before or the partridge his father caught in the greenhouse. Occasionally, outside the context of that situation, these statements were virtually incomprehensible to those of us looking at the overhead. For example:

> my Father ct a prtr
> he fat it in the grenhs

His teacher, however, accepted his reading of what he'd written, and invariably wrote a genuine response to it, like this one:

> What did your father do with the partridge he caught in the greenhouse Shawn?

And eventually Shawn began responding (this, in October, was the first occasion on which he did so):

> We lat it go

As the successive overheads were displayed, we followed Shawn's growth as a user of language. We watched his "discovery" of punctuation — for instance, the grotesque and marvelous dot, a full eighth of an inch in diameter, which was his first period. We watched as the length of Shawn's utterances grew. We saw his spelling strategies develop. We watched him taking risks with his spelling, using words that he needed rather than restricting what he said to what he could spell. For instance, at one point, when he wanted to tell his teacher about the snake he'd found, he needed the words "aquarium" and "veranda" (I particularly admired the silent *e*'s, as well as the sense of story signaled by his conclusion).

> I have a snake at home
> he is in a cwareame
> and he is brawn spas
> I fad hem undr my vradae
> and my dad Pact it up
> the End

The clearest patterns in Shawn's work — patterns that jump out in even the most cursory examination of his year's worth of writing — are the increasing length of his utterances, the way he becomes more engaged with what he's writing, and the growing sophistication of his strategies for spelling, punctuation, and other "mechanical" matters.

It is important to make clear, incidentally, that this is not to say that his spelling and punctuation became more conventional; rather, the strategies one might infer from his texts were becoming more sophisticated. On March 11, for example, he produced the following text:

> todyu is Tuesday...
> I mst the Bus

today and I gat
a driv to the scuol.
I gat a driv by
mrss Mar becz my
mtr don't have the car.

To his teacher's written response ("Why did you miss the bus at
the bus-stop Shawn?"), Shawn answered:

because I dent her the Bus

The advance here is partly in the amount of thought which seems
to be involved in the spellings ("mrss" for "Mrs.," for example) and
even more in the growing complexity of the syntax, and the sheer
length of the utterance. As Newman (1984) has pointed out, Shawn's
concern for meaning shows in his willingness to take a stab at a word
to "place-hold the meaning" in order to get his idea down, even
though with reflection he might be able to spell the word conventionally
(consider the two appearances of both "today" and "because" in this
text, for instance).

Two things were profoundly illuminating to me in that presentation.
One was watching a child learning language through using language —
and learning things I'd thought would normally be learned only when
they were overtly taught. The second involved the apparent attitude
of Shawn's teacher, and the other people at the session, toward what
I might have been tempted to call Shawn's gross errors if I hadn't just
read Mina Shaughnessy's *Errors and Expectations: A Guide for the
Teacher of Basic Writing* (1977). The teachers there didn't treat errors
either as sins to be corrected or as something cute to be chuckled over;
they treated them as evidence of principled, strategic thinking on
Shawn's part, and as a promise that Shawn could continue his
constructive, rational, active learning of the principles of written
communication. They treated them, in other words, as hypotheses in
the process of being tested.

Most vividly, perhaps, besides Shawn's wonderful, graphically and
syntactically adventurous writing, I remember a man who sat stolidly
in the middle of the classroom, watching Shawn's struggles and
victories with tolerant amusement. He asked at the end a question
whose exact words I can almost remember: "This is all very interesting.
But at what point do you start pointing out his errors so that he can
understand the importance of correctness?"

At the time, I found it amazing that anyone could have so thoroughly
missed what seemed to me the main point of Shawn's (and every
child's) miracle: We don't learn language by having our errors pointed

out and corrected; we learn as a by-product of using language in order to do things we care about doing. This principle is one of the fundamental axioms underlying what has come to be called "whole language" pedagogy. It seemed clear — and has come to seem even more so since — that this principle has profoundly important implications for the way I think about what I am doing as a teacher of writing and as a teacher of literature.

Whole Language

The principles of whole language pedagogy are derived from the ideas of an eclectic assemblage of writers about language and learning, at least some of whose names will be familiar to anyone who has been keeping up with developments in research on composing, on learning to write, and on the teaching of writing. They include the reading theorists Kenneth S. Goodman and Frank Smith and the linguist M. A. K. Halliday; going further back, much seems to be based on, or to grow out of, the American pragmaticism of C. S. Peirce and his successors — most centrally, John Dewey — and the linguistic psychology of L. S. Vygotsky. Whatever their sources, however, the ideas seem fundamentally quite simple and even commonsensical; it is only as they are wholemindedly applied to practical learning situations that their implications become new, and dramatic.

Among recent publications that offer an introduction to, and overview of, what we might call the theory of whole language pedagogy is a description of a massive study called "Children, Their Language and World," by Jerome Harste, Carolyn Burke, and Virginia Woodward, which appeared under the title *Language Stories and Literacy Lessons* (1984). Another is a collaborative account of a group of whole language classrooms: *Whole Language: Theory and Practice,* edited by Judith Newman (1985). In the absence of the kind of massive empirical and anecdotal detail which undergirds the conclusions of the Harste, Woodward, and Burke report, I think Shawn's story is a good way to begin understanding the kinds of observations of children in learning situations that were involved. From the innumerable learners like Shawn observed by Harste, Woodward, and Burke, and by Newman and her colleagues, some fairly straightforward ideas emerge.

A primary principle — indeed, almost a slogan for the "movement" — is that literacy learning is a natural phenomenon. There is some difficulty, of course, with terming any element of human culture "natural"; what it seems to mean in this context is that it is a process, like the development of oral language, that occurs virtually universally in a context which supports it and, like the learning of oral language, without conscious, institutionalized cultivation.

An equally important principle is that language is learned *in use*. The pragmatics of language use motivate and shape the learning of language, both the development of first-language ability in infants and that of written-language ability in older children. That this is true could hardly be more strongly attested than it is by the work of Kenneth Kaye (1982) and others on the development of dialogue between infants and caregivers, by the observations of M. A. K. Halliday (1975) on the development of language in his son, or by more classically oriented developmental psychology, such as that of Elizabeth Bates (1976a, 1979) or Jerome Bruner (1977, 1982).

A consequence of accepting these principles is that we are moved toward thinking of language as primarily a "top-down" process. That is, those smaller units which we have traditionally thought of as the "more basic" elements of language are not in fact "basic" at all. The meaning — indeed, the very existence — of each element of language is determined by the larger elements surrounding it. This is a principle that operates through the whole hierarchy of language phenomena. Sounds within words are determined by the words (*ng*, for instance, represents a different sound in "linger" than in "singer"); the meanings of words are determined by their sentences ("bear" can be one of a range of quite different words depending on the sentence in which we find it); the meanings of sentences are determined by the discourse around them ("It's getting chilly in here" can be an observation or a request or even a command, depending on the context in which it's uttered); an entire piece of discourse can be embedded in a context that alters it utterly (Polonius's advice to Laertes sounds rather more sensible outside the context of *Hamlet*, where Polonius is presented as a pompous fraud).

This, in turn, suggests that analysis of language into smaller and smaller units, while it may be of use to the metalinguistic understanding of some patterns of language use, and may help a teacher in under-standing the way language is structured, is not likely to be very functional from the language learner's point of view. All of this forces us toward the conclusion that language needs to be experienced and dealt with in a "whole" condition in order for language learning to occur effectively. If we separate words from the contexts by which they are determined, if we pull sentences out of discourses, if we disengage discourse from the context of use and human purpose, we tend to produce something I call "textoids," synthetic fragments of language which exhibit none of the complex richness of natural language. (Beaugrande [1982] remarks the error of working with what he calls "fragmentary and inane" texts.) And it is precisely this richness that enables us to function as the miraculous learners of language we all are, to navigate as effortlessly and unselfconsciously around the hermeneutic circle of understanding as we all must in order to understand any system of signs.

What all of this amounts to is an inversion of what I had always thought of as the most commonsensical model of language and language development. Such a model entails an assumption that it is a structure built up from the bottom, assembled out of basic linguistic elements like phones and phonemes. On the contrary, what this new view would suggest is that it is human purposes, social and interpersonal — "pragmatic" — purposes, that are the basic elements of language. Perhaps even more important, it creates a model which is so rich and complex that it seems foolhardy to suggest that discursive analysis of it will facilitate learning in any simple, direct way.

The most superficial survey of the kind of work that has been done in child language development since the publication of Roger Brown's landmark *A First Language* (1973) will demonstrate the radical changes that have occurred in our view of what is "basic" about human language learning. Elizabeth Bates (1976b) has described how we have moved away from Chomsky's (1965) miraculous and mythical innate predisposition to learn grammar — the so-called language-acquisition device, posited to account for children's development of syntax, within a system whose largest allowable element was the sentence. We have come a long way toward the Vygotskyan (1962, 1978) view that meaning and intention come first, that language develops out of the patterns of social transaction between the infant and the people around the infant. And it has become more and more clear how much there is to learn about the way children begin to use their entire, richly structured social environment as a sort of scaffolding within which to build their own language. The work of Kenneth Kaye and others (e.g. Kaye and Charney 1980) on the origins of dialogue in the relations between mothers and infants has begun to build a persuasive and detailed model of just how this works.

Hans

The richness and power of this sociolinguistic or pragmatic context has been dramatized in recent years in connection with the controversy over ape language learning. The most devastating attacks on the notion that chimpanzees like Sarah and Washoe had actually learned human language were firmly grounded on the argument that the apes were not really "using language," but were responding to inadvertent extralinguistic "cues" on the part of their trainers. For example, Herbert Terrace (1979, 1981) reported on his own (unsuccessful) attempts to teach a chimpanzee — named "Nim Chimpsky" in honor, Terrace said, of a certain linguist — to talk. He also analyzed a number of films of Nim — and more "successful" chimpanzees — "talking" with their trainers. He identified example after example of such non-intentional cueing of the chimps. The "Clever Hans phenomenon" had struck again, he said.

It is through this controversy that many people have recently come to hear the name of the celebrated horse who, at the turn of this century, amazed Europe by apparently demonstrating the ability to add and subtract (see Pfungst [1911] 1965; Sebeok and Rosenthal 1981). Der Kluge Hans (Clever Hans) held forth in Berlin, demonstrating over and over that he could "think in a human way." "What's seven and five?" Herr von Osten (his owner and teacher) would ask, and the horse would dutifully tap his foot twelve times. "If the eighth day of the month comes on Tuesday, what is the date for the following Friday?" Eleven taps. "How much is two-fifths plus one-half?" Nine taps, then ten: numerator and denominator. Most people, of course, were skeptical of the horse's skill and assumed some sort of "trick," a secret cueing system, as there is with other trained animals. Adding and simple computation would have been difficult enough to swallow; such elaborate mathematics made it virtually impossible.

But for a time the situation looked as though people would have to choke it down. The problem was that if Hans's performance was a trick, no one could figure out how it was done. Herr von Osten swore that he had taught Hans actually to perform the mathematical operations, and that he was not cueing him. He agreed to have the case investigated in order to establish that, indeed, Hans could do arithmetic. And in fact, none of a panel of experts, including animal trainers and psychologists, could discover any of the systems of cues that animal trainers use to make it seem that circus animals, for instance, can think or understand human language.

What finally happened, of course, was that in a classic and exhaustive investigation whose description still makes compelling reading, the well-known psychologist Oskar Pfungst ([1911] 1965) established what the "system" was. Hans was responding to inadvertent cues so subtle as to be virtually imperceptible — reading, in other words, the body language of the people around him. Among other things, he was responding to the slight inclination of the head and body as the interlocutor (usually Herr von Osten, but sometimes others could work with Hans) began watching for the tapping to begin, and the slight increase of tension as the questioner waited to see whether Hans would stop at the correct number. Carefully separated from anyone who knew the answer to the question, the horse was unable to perform; but when he was in a situation where his interrogator knew what answer to expect, Hans could sense it, and stopped tapping when he had tapped out the appropriate number (that is, the one his questioner expected). In the end, and after great difficulties, Pfungst was able to teach himself to start and stop the horse's tapping, in the absence of any mathematical questions, by synthesizing these subtle movements.

For a traditional empirical psychologist, of course, Hans's story is a cautionary tale. Robert Rosenthal's long-standing interest in the case, for example, derives from its implications for research methodology (Sebeok and Rosenthal 1981). If the communicative relationship between animals and humans is so rich and subtle — and there have been many subsequent confirmations of the hypothesis that it is — how much richer and more subtle is that between human beings likely to be? How much of what we've "learned" about behavior in psychological experimentation is really nothing more than artifacts of experimenters unconsciously signaling their expectations, and subjects unconsciously picking up on those signals? As Rosenthal remarks in his introductory essay in Pfungst's work, "That many experimenters over the years may have fulfilled their experimental prophecies by unintentionally communicating information to their subjects may be a disquieting proposition" (Pfungst [1911] 1965, xxii). For Rosenthal, the moral of the story is this: In setting up your experiment, be cautious; try to find ways to make sure your experimenter is not unconsciously signaling the "correct" answers to your subject, or your experiment will be invalid.

Others have drawn other morals. Roger Brown (1958), for instance, uses the story as evidence that horses — animals in general — can't use language, that we should be skeptical of all claims for intelligence in animals. "The case is dramatic because our impression of Hans plummets. He had seemed to be more intelligent than most of us but has turned out to be a quite unremarkable animal. There is not even any evidence here of an ability to recognize verbal commands, let alone understand or reply to them" (1958, 175). And Michael Polanyi cites the case as a cautionary tale of yet a different kind: an instance of observers seeing what they want to see, experimenters making their results come out right (1958, 169–70).

Like any good story, the saga of Clever Hans affords many different readings, depending on who's telling it, to whom, and in what situation. The point of my retelling it here has to do with the nature of that "paralinguistic" communication between the horse and his master. It seems clear, for one thing, that the system had to operate at a preconscious level. Herr von Osten was certainly not conscious of the system; indeed, he himself appears to have believed he had taught the horse to perform the mathematical operations (he never accepted Pfungst's explanation of Hans's behavior, and indeed aborted the study when he finally understood what Pfungst was doing). Equally important, Pfungst reported that effective "cues" were extremely difficult to generate consciously and artificially; on the other hand, it was almost impossible, through conscious effort, to *avoid* cueing Hans if you knew the answer to the question he'd been asked. The cues, it seems, were a natural, organic, and inescapable part of a communication situation.

Heini Hediger, in an essay called "The Clever Hans Phenomenon from an Animal Psychologist's Point of View" (1981), has pointed out that the Clever Hans phenomenon has never been replicated. No one has deliberately *taught* a horse to respond in such a sophisticated way to cues so subtle and so natural. Clearly, however, it's not at all unusual for horses — and many other animals — to *learn* to respond to the inadvertent cues of humans in almost equally sophisticated ways in other sorts of situations. Anyone who has ridden or driven horses at all regularly, for instance, is familiar with the kind of rapport that can develop between human and horse (owners of many other kinds of pets testify to this sort of communication as well). What distinguishes the Clever Hans case, I believe, is that Herr von Osten is the only person who has ever actually *believed* he was teaching a horse to calculate. Everybody else who has engaged in training animals for such public display has known that they were teaching the animals to respond to cues, and thus their cues have been consciously manipulated and synthesized — and relatively obvious and crude.

What are the implications of Hans's story told in this context — and juxtaposed with Shawn's? It brings to the foreground, I think, the fact that a horse could use aspects of his sociolinguistic environment, so subtle that no one knew they existed, in order to learn; even more, it shows as well that he could only do so when the whole complex remained subordinate to other purposes. Herr von Osten was teaching a horse mathematics, not devising cueing systems; Hans was pleasing his master, not attending to the cueing systems which were his means of doing so. What is common to the stories of Hans and Shawn is that in both cases, virtually miraculous achievements of language learning occurred — and only occurred — when the semiotic system was in use for real purposes, and was thus "whole" in the sense that it was organically embedded in a real, functional context. The power of the systems of cues to which both Hans and Shawn were responding — to which we all respond in language-learning situations — resides precisely in the fact that they are *not* conscious, that they bypass our consciousness just as the surface features of language do (we can remember only with difficulty the exact words people have used, though we remember the gist and import of what they said with amazing facility).

What Hans's case dramatizes, in other words, is the power of the kinds of unconscious intersubjective cueing that surround the language to which we actually attend. (It is interesting, incidentally, that the growing study of pragmatics in language use seems to show us the same thing; consider, for example, the work of Erving Goffman [1974], William Labov [1972], Livia Polanyi [1979, 1985] and others on the social frames in which conversation takes place, or of Elizabeth Bates [1976b] and others on developmental pragmatics.) One thing we can learn from Clever Hans is how inextricable linguistic phenomena are from this rich context — and how, when they *are* extricated, they change utterly. The whole context — social as well as linguistic, physical as well as grammatical — is an inextricable part of any given utterance and plays as important a role in its conveying of meaning and impact as, say, its syntactic structure.

Learning

The psychology of human development explains some of the reasons human language learning — and, if there are important differences, other learning as well — is so profoundly dependent on its social situation and the wealth of subtle cues it provides. Central to this understanding are the ideas of Vygotsky (1962, 1978), whose concept of the "zone of proximal development" seems particularly relevant to thinking about the kind of learning that can occur in such situations. Basically, Vygotsky maintains that our traditional views of learning have been derived by assessing what the learner can do *in isolation,* by her- or himself, and then assigning the learner to a particular level of cognitive development. Vygotsky argues, however, that what we ought to be concerned with is what the learner can do *in a social situation,* with the assistance of the people around him or her — that in fact, such considerations define a "zone of proximal development" where learning (or, more broadly stated, significant cognitive development) is most likely to take place. His view of learning as a result of a dialectical process occurring between the individual and the context (most centrally, the social context) describes, it seems to me, exactly how Hans and Shawn learned: that is, they utilized the whole of the social context in which they were immersed in order to learn. Michael Polanyi points out (1958, 3) that in one way Hans's performance was perfectly adapted to his situation: he achieved what there was for a horse to achieve — the reward of pleasing Herr von Osten. What he learned was a system of signs. What Shawn achieved was contact with his teacher; what he learned, as well, was a system of signs.

For a teacher, then, Hans's story should be the opposite of a cautionary tale, reminding us as it does of the resourcefulness of the learning organism. Hans's skill at reading a psychosocial situation seems to me at least as miraculous as any skill at addition or calendar manipulation would have been, and what is most remarkable is that Hans may well have been, after all, "a quite unremarkable animal," whose skill might actually be quite widespread. Such a skill is no less remarkable because it's common; quite the contrary. Even more important, it is for a teacher not a danger to be avoided, but a natural phenomenon to be utilized. If a horse can be so sensitive to the social situation around him, how much more sensitive might we expect human beings to be? How much does a human learn by responding to such cues? Shawn, and all his compatriots, offer us an answer.

Far from being concerned that students may be inferring from the people around them when they're right and when they're wrong, teachers should be delighted that children have such an ability, and eager to find ways to help them utilize it more consistently and effectively. We should be excited that such skill can be invoked in the service of — for instance — language learning.

As indeed it almost always is, of course. An infant learning to talk is virtually never overtly corrected, or needs to be, or ought to be. What happens is that the fantastically sensitive set of social antennae that each of us has — far more sensitive than even the most intelligent horse's — tells us when we've said something a little wrong, something that hasn't quite connected, tells us when there's noise in the system. We have a Clever Hans inside us who notices such things. What our Hans notices may be as crude as a "correct" response to an "incorrect" utterance: for instance, baby says, "Daddy go bye-bye," and mother responds, "That's right; Daddy's going bye-bye." Or Shawn writes of the snake from under the "vradae" in "a cwareame," and his teacher hesitates in reading it, or uses the conventional spelling of one of the words in her response.

Or it might be more subtle: an acquaintance's stiffening and distancing, communicated by body language and other, even less immediate and specific, responses, when you've used an expression that is perhaps a bit too familiar for the situation. Or, indeed, it may be genuine confusion resulting from misunderstanding. In each case, it seems clear that it is the Clever Hans in us that is largely responsible for the breathtaking rapidity with which we assimilate the unspeakably complex rules of our native dialect and the even more unimaginably complicated pragmatic rules which govern our conversational interactions.

What seems to me most important about this metaphorical Clever Hans we each carry around inside us is that it seems clear he doesn't need to — and perhaps can't afford to — become self-conscious; this kind of learning works by bypassing the sort of effortful, conscious apprehension and understanding we associate, for instance, with formal grammar instruction. Michael Polanyi's (1958) ideas about knowing are very important here. His theory of knowledge is organized around a distinction between knowledge that we consciously attend to (focal knowledge) and that far larger portion of what we know that we do not and usually cannot attend to (tacit knowledge). Virtually all our competence at using language lies in the realm of tacit knowledge. In his view, this is the sort of knowledge we acquire best in an apprenticeship situation, by "dwelling in" the activity involved. The more conscious many kinds of knowledge become, the less effectively they can be utilized. In Stephen Potter's (1971) memorable slogan designed to help the prospective game player win without actually cheating, "Conscious flow is broken flow."

It is at least interesting that in the introduction to Pfungst's book, Professor C. Stumpf makes it clear that Hans learned his "language" while everyone involved was attending to something else — to the principles of arithmetic or the mechanics of training the horse to tap. And, as Hediger (1981) observed, the phenomenon has, after all, never been recreated. It may be that in order to invoke your Clever Hans you have to be attending wholemindedly to something else.

This may be why language learning isn't always the easy, natural process that it ought to be if this "Clever Hans model" of learning invariably corresponded to what happens in the real world. When we study language in a conventional, institutional setting — in situations where we are deliberately learning a second language, for instance, whether a foreign language or a new dialect of our own, such as formal, academic written English — our internal Clever Hans is rarely given a chance to work, because the whole process is quite deliberately rendered conscious. Not only this; in such situations our "errors" are regularly corrected by an external authority. The more this happens, the less we can depend on — or even attend to — our internal Clever Hans. He specializes in noticing signals so subtle that they are overridden and obliterated by corrections from an external authority.

A consequence of this process of externalization of authority is that eventually our means of testing the accuracy and effectiveness of our statements moves outside us. We wait for external, overt, crude, obvious corrections. If we don't get them, we assume we're all right. Our Clever Hans, in other words, has been smothered.

A good example of this is the way students in my writing classes often responded to my written comments on their writing projects. In a typical conference, toward the end of a writing project when the issue had begun to be a little more like editing than like composing, I would typically mark a few characteristic errors, discussing the ways in which they *were* characteristic, and explicitly tell the student to find and correct similar problems elsewhere in the paper. Very often the student came back to the next conference with every error I'd marked dutifully corrected, and nothing else touched. Students knew where the authority was, and were not about to make a change on their own because, unless the authority had pointed the error out, it must be OK. I hate to think that student's Clever Hans was dead, but it was certainly one sick horse.

Why should this happen? It seems a reasonable hypothesis that Clever Hans only works in *real* situations, where people really do care about the answers to the questions. If no one in the room had been listening to the question, or cared whether Hans could add, Hans would have been as much at a loss as when they didn't know the answer. Just so, the child learning to speak needs — as everyone who has ever watched a child learn this miraculous and miraculously complex skill knows — an interlocutor (a "significant other," in Halliday's phrase) who cares about and responds to what he or she says, an audience engaged in *making meanings* from the child's utterances. If the people around that poor infant were concerned about supplying grammatical information and judging the correctness of the utterances, while caring little or nothing about their *meanings*, it seems likely that the child would end up in a remedial talking class (perhaps labeled "dysoral"). And perhaps that child would spend life talking, not fluently and joyfully with his or her awareness focused on interaction and communication, but, rather, painfully and self-consciously, with attention focused on avoiding embarrassment, choosing what to say — the way I tend to choose what to say in German, not according to what needs to be said but according to what I think I *can* say without making a humiliating faux pas. (It is worth considering the consequences of corrections and their unavoidable shunting aside of meaning. Suppose Shawn's teacher had responded to his first original writing ["Tomy has a new trucK"] by saying, "Very good, Shawn; but you've misspelled Tony's name and the *K* in truck should be lower case. C." Or suppose Herr von Osten had rewarded Hans's responses to cues rather than his [apparent] understanding of arithmetic?)

Implications

All of this adds up, it seems to me, to a set of ideas which help us to understand why so few adolescents find writing easy or comfortable, or are very competent at it. It also suggests some means by which we can create a situation in which students can begin moving toward greater comfort and competence. It is worth considering some of the ways these ideas have found practical implementation in the context of actual elementary classrooms.

Accepting, and wholeheartedly implementing, these ideas in the context of a conventional contemporary classroom entails some dramatic — one might even argue, revolutionary — changes. Details vary from teacher to teacher, of course, but some patterns are clear. Learning to read and write begins with what the children already know (Harste, Woodward, and Burke, incidentally, have shown us that children know far more than we used to think), instead of with the assumption that they are in essence blank slates. Trade books and "naturally occurring" published texts replace basal readers and other textoids assembled by committees from wordlists, according to formulas derived from "readability" tests. Reading for meaning replaces reading for demonstration of competence, especially for demonstration of isolated, "targetable" skills like phonics decoding, vocabulary analysis, "word-attack skills," and so forth. Writing develops in tandem with reading, just as speaking develops in tandem with listening, and ways are found to allow both writing and reading to be meaning- and intention-driven. The teacher's job becomes one of finding and creating occasions and situations in which writing and reading can serve real, instrumental purposes for the students. Evaluation of written work virtually vanishes, to be replaced by response to it, and (even more important) by *use of* it. Writing and reading are conceived of as tools rather than as foci of attention, and metalanguage — discourse about discourse — develops for each child, if at all, only as it is needed, rather than being the center of the curriculum. The inherent power of children's language-learning capability is freed.

As usually happens in descriptions of educational innovation, it sounds as though I'm hailing the advent of the millenium, and one might well wonder that such a revolution could occur with so little visible fuss. As with poor Lemuel Gulliver trying to figure out why Smithfield wasn't ablaze with pyramids of law books the day after his *Travels* was published, one might well conclude that my assessment of the situation is a little skewed. And certainly whole language methods, like other new educational ideas, are susceptible of being watered down and compromised until they have no effect; they're open to being implemented mechanically and without understanding, simply because they seem trendy or innovative; they require more flexibility and change than many teachers are prepared to exercise and accept; and they are going to have a difficult time competing for the dollars that are likely to be shaken out of governmental trees by cries of "back to the basics" and blue-ribbon committee calls for educational rearmament. I suspect that, like John Dewey's ideas — or Lemuel Gulliver's, for that matter — they're unlikely to be tried on a really wide scale. All this does not, however, constitute evidence that they are anything other than genuinely powerful methods based on substantial and profound ideas, or that they do not have important implications for composition classes at the secondary and post-secondary level.

What is most important and powerful about the ideas I am describing is their ability to help teachers move in *their own* ways in the new directions they open up rather than to adopt the recipes of experts. Frank Smith (1982) regularly refuses point-blank to make any concrete suggestions for applying his ideas on the development of reading to classroom situations, on the grounds that the central skill of teaching is precisely the application of theory, and that the appropriate situation is one in which every teacher applies a theory in a different and unique way to different situations. Still, because I also believe that it is possible for examples to function heuristically at least as effectively as abstract theories, I want to offer a few examples of the ways in which whole language theory can concretely change some fundamental practices in writing instruction.

Examples

I wish to do no more here than sketch one or two examples, and indicate a couple of important directions in which we might move under the impetus of these ideas, particularly with regard to the ways in which we respond — and do not respond — to student writing. We should not expect, of course, that we can work miracles of change in a sixteen- or even a thirty-two-week period. What we should be striving toward is opening a door of understanding even a crack, so the student will understand there is a door there and that perhaps light shines through it occasionally. As with so many processes in education, we are often not around long enough to see the student fling the door wide and walk through.

Perhaps the most important change might be characterized as finding ways to make writing more instrumental, attempting, if you will, to make it "real," and thus whole. The most effective way to do this is to create situations in which student writing — and the teacher's own — is read for its meaning, for what it has to say, rather than as an example of a student theme to be "assessed" or "evaluated." One way to do this is to employ writing in place of more usual pedagogical methods — instead of class discussion, for instance. One can create situations in which students write very frequent short pieces, in answer to specific questions or problems, often questions or problems arising out of previous (frequently written) discussions. The short pieces are then photocopied and distributed, sometimes to the whole class, sometimes to selected or relevant individuals. I regularly set up situations in which some sort of written response (to the ideas, not to the form) is appropriate; a written response which is often read *only* by the writer of the original. What is even more effective, however, is a *practical* response — for instance, a situation in which the reader has to use the information or ideas in order to pursue his or her own work. Two things are crucial here: one is that the *meaning* of the writing serves purposes the student understands and at least to some extent shares; the second is that the response the writing brings is not in any sense evaluative, but is, rather, instrumental.

It is also worth noting that, in general, response to the paper does not come from the instructor. I rarely read, and never evaluate or mark, this sort of writing — I participate in the process, of course, by writing and circulating my own work, but the main point about all this writing is that it is to be conceived of as a way of learning, not a performance to be judged. Because the language is being used for some real purpose, it can be whole — and because it is whole, it can function as part of a language learning experience.

Let me give a concrete example of how this has, in fact, worked. In about the third week of my course in eighteenth-century literature, I send the class to the library to read about the last third of the seventeenth century in literary histories, textbooks, anthologies and collections, and political histories, and to bring back questions raised by that reading. The only criteria are that they must think the questions answerable with a reasonable amount of effort and within a reasonable length, and the answers likely to be interesting or important. The questions are weeded by small groups, each of which selects two or three to write on the blackboard. These questions are then edited down to a half dozen or so by the whole class, whereupon small groups choose questions to answer. Questions which have been fruitful in the past have included these:

> Were there any women writers in this period and what role did they play?
>
> How much was a pound worth at this time?
>
> What was the Popish Plot?
>
> What does "Baroque" mean?

Each member of the class then goes to the library (working from a collaboratively-compiled annotated bibliography of useful research tools) and writes a short essay in answer to the question. Back in groups (sometimes in class, sometimes not), the individual pieces of writing — which I seldom see and never comment on or evaluate — are edited into one short collaboratively-written essay, which is then transcribed by a member of the group and photocopied for the class (again, I do not comment on or evaluate this writing). These photo-copied essays become a "chapter" of the course textbook.

The next stage in this cycle involves everyone in the class asking a question (or two or three) of each of the groups responsible for the separate reports. These questions are written out and brought to the next class session, where each group receives their questions, weeds them, answers (orally) those that can be answered or disposed of immediately, and organizes to research and write answers to one or two which seem particularly useful or important. These written answers are photocopied and appended to the original reports. Finally, all of this writing may form a springboard for a new cycle of research, writing, and publication.

Almost any subject about which someone might want to learn, and which it is possible to divide up into separate questions or issues, will afford this kind of activity. Descriptions, summaries, and synopses are particularly useful, especially at the beginning, because their utility is obvious to students engaging in a joint research project. An adequate abstract of an article, for example, will usually tell readers whether they need to look any further, and will often save a good deal of time. What is most important is that the students begin to think of writing as a tool, one which is useful for purposes that seem immediate and palpable to them, and begin to *use* it.

Responding to Student Writing

The implications such a model holds for current practices in response to student writing are, it should be clear, fairly radical. In the context of this sort of use of writing, traditional evaluative or analytic responses have no obvious role. Indeed, it is not clear whether responses by the course instructor are desirable at all. It's difficult, of course, at first to prevent students from responding to each others' writing the way they've become accustomed to seeing English teachers respond, with approving and condescending generalities, or corrections of grammar, style, or diction. But after a while they begin to figure out that for writing of this kind, such things matter only when they *really* matter, when they cause genuine confusion or misunderstanding. They also discover that I'm probably not going to look at many of the papers in any case — and if I do, I will not mark them — and thus they don't have to impress me with their knowledge of what constitutes "good English." As this happens, sometimes real exchanges of ideas are generated, the linguistic surface can become tacit and the meaning focal, and real language learning can begin. The language, in other words, begins to be whole.

I am aware of no compelling reason to believe that the process of language learning that college students are going through is different in any radical ways from the processes they went through as infants learning a first language, as toddlers learning a second (literacy), or as adolescents learning all the new languages — slangs, dialects, argots — needed to survive in a complex society like ours. The evidence is overwhelming that all those languages are learned through use if they are learned at all; that they are learned because the learner understands, or comes to understand, that the new language can serve her or his own real, immediate human and social purposes. When we disengage language from those purposes — when we make written language into an artifact to be analyzed and evaluated — we do something much more profound than merely making it something based on a fantasy: we take away what is most basic to language.

When language ceases to be whole, in fact, it's no longer language. It's still a complex, rule-governed behavior, but the language-learning resources which operate in Shawn, and Clever Hans, and in you and me, no longer work on it. They aren't, after all, processes that we can turn on and off at will; they are a central element of our human need to be part of a social group. They constitute a powerful force, but the only wagon you can harness them to is that need. What's wrong with offering students textoids and fragments of language, and asking them to create textoids and fragments, is precisely that, by definition, textoids and fragments cannot serve that need.

I see no reason not to embrace as a fundamental principle that any language used in any classroom should be, in the most thorough possible sense, whole. To keep language whole we need to treat it as whole — we must, like Herr von Osten, believe our horse is learning mathematics. We must believe our Clever Hanses, our Shawns, are indeed clever. They are — at any rate, the Shawns are.

References

Bates, E. 1976a. *Language and Context: The Acquisition of Pragmatics.* New York: Academic Press.

Bates, E. 1976b. Pragmatics and Sociolinguistics in Child Language. In *Normal and Deficient Child Language,* edited by E. M. Morehead and A. E. Morehead, 411–63. Baltimore: University Park Press.

Bates, E. 1979. *The Emergence of Symbols: Cognition and Communication in Infancy.* New York: Academic Press.

Beaugrande, R., de. 1982. The Story of Grammars and the Grammar of Stories. *Journal of Pragmatics* 6:383–422.

Brown, R. 1958. *Words and Things.* Glencoe, Ill.: The Free Press.

Brown, R. 1973. *A First Language: The Early Stages.* Cambridge: Harvard University Press.

Bruner, J. S. 1977. Early Social Interaction and Language Acquisition. In *Studies in Mother-Infant Interactions: Proceedings of the Lock Lomond Symposium, Ross Priory, University of Strathclyde, September 1975,* edited by H. R. Schaffer, 271–89. London: Academic Press.

Bruner, J. S. 1982. The Formats of Language Acquisition. *American Journal of Semiotics* 1:1–16.

Chomsky, N. 1965. *Aspects of a Theory of Syntax.* Cambridge: MIT Press.

Dewey, J. 1938. *Experience and Education.* New York: Macmillan.

Goffman, E. 1974. *Frame Analysis.* New York: Harper and Row.

Goodman, K. S. 1967. Reading: A Psycholinguistic Guessing Game. *Journal of the Reading Specialist* 4:126–35.

Goodman, K. S. 1983. *Language and Literacy: The Collected Writings of Kenneth S. Goodman.* Edited by F. V. Gollasch. London: Routledge and Kegan Paul.

Goodman, K. S., and Y. Goodman. 1979. Learning to Read Is Natural. In *Theory and Practice of Early Reading,* vol. 2, edited by L. B. Resnick and P. A. Weaver. Hillsdale, N.J.: Erlbaum.

Halliday, M. A. K. 1973. *Explorations in the Functions of Language.* London: Edward Arnold.

Halliday, M. A. K. 1975. *Learning How to Mean: Explorations in the Development of Language.* New York: Elsevier North-Holland.

Halliday, M. A. K. 1978. *Language as Social Semiotic: The Social Interpretation of Language and Meaning.* Baltimore: University Park Press.

Harste, J. C., V. A. Woodward, and C. L. Burke. 1984. *Language Stories and Literacy Lessons.* Portsmouth, N.H.: Heinemann.

Hediger, H. K. P. 1981. The Clever Hans Phenomenon from an Animal Psychologist's Point of View. In *The Clever Hans Phenomenon: Communication with Horses, Whales, Apes, and People,* edited by T. A. Sebeok and R. Rosenthal, 1–17. Annals of the New York Academy of Sciences, vol. 364. New York: The New York Academy of Sciences.

Kaye, K. 1982. *The Mental and Social Life of Babies: How Parents Make Persons.* Chicago: University of Chicago Press.

Kaye, K., and R. Charney. 1980. How Mothers Maintain "Dialogue" with Two-Year-Olds. In *The Social Foundations of Language and Thought: Essays in Honor of Jerome S. Bruner,* edited by D. R. Olson, 211–30. New York: Norton.

Labov, W. 1972. *Language in the Inner City.* Philadelphia: University of Pennsylvania Press.

Newman, J. M. 1984. *The Craft of Children's Writing.* New York: Scholastic Book Services.

Newman, J. M., editor. 1985. *Whole Language: Theory and Practice.* Portsmouth, N.H.: Heinemann.

Peirce, C. S. 1955. *Philosophical Writings of Peirce.* Edited by J. Buchler. New York: Dover.

Pfungst, O. [1911] 1965. *Clever Hans (The Horse of Mr. von Osten): A Contribution to Experimental Animal and Human Psychology, with an Introduction by Prof. C. Stumpf.* Translated by C. L. Rahn. Reissued with an introductory essay by Robert Rosenthal. New York: Holt, Rinehart, and Winston.

Polanyi, L. 1979. So What's the Point? *Semiotica* 25:207–41.

Polanyi, L. 1985. *Telling the American Story: A Structural and Cultural Analysis of Conversational Storytelling.* Norwood, N.J.: Ablex.

Polanyi, M. 1958. *Personal Knowledge: Toward a Post-Critical Philosophy.* Chicago: University of Chicago Press.

Potter, S. S. 1971. *The Complete Upmanship.* New York: Holt, Rinehart, and Winston.

Sebeok, T. A., and R. Rosenthal, editors. 1981. *The Clever Hans Phenomenon: Communication with Horses, Whales, Apes, and People.* Annals of the New

York Academy of Sciences, vol. 364. New York: The New York Academy of Sciences.

Shaughnessy, M. P. 1977. *Errors and Expectations: A Guide for the Teacher of Basic Writing.* New York: Oxford University Press.

Smith, F. 1982. *Understanding Reading: A Psycholinguistic Analysis of Reading and Learning to Read.* 3d ed. New York: Holt, Rinehart, and Winston.

Terrace, H. S. 1979. How Nim Chimpsky Changed my Mind. *Psychology Today* 13:65–76.

Terrace, H. S. 1981. A Report to a Committee, 1980. In *The Clever Hans Phenomenon: Communication with Horses, Whales, Apes, and People,* edited by T. A. Sebeok and R. Rosenthal, 94–114. Annals of the New York Academy of Sciences, vol. 364. New York: The New York Academy of Sciences.

Vygotsky, L. S. [1930] 1978. *Mind in Society: The Development of Higher Psychological Processes.* Edited by M. Cole, V. John-Steiner, S. Scribner, and E. Souberman. Cambridge: Harvard University Press.

Vygotsky, L. S. 1962. *Thought and Language.* Edited and translated by E. Hanfmann and G. Vakar. Cambridge: MIT Press.

II New Perspectives for Responding to Writing

5 Learning to Praise

Donald A. Daiker
Miami University

In *A Moveable Feast*, Ernest Hemingway recounts his first meeting with F. Scott Fitzgerald. One night while Hemingway is sitting with friends at the Dingo Bar in Paris, Fitzgerald unexpectedly walks in, introduces himself, and proceeds to talk nonstop about Hemingway's writing, especially "how great it was." Hemingway reports that he was embarrassed by Fitzgerald's lavish compliments — not because he felt flattered by them, but because he and his fellow expatriates "still went under the system, then, that praise to the face was open disgrace" (Hemingway 1964, 150).

The distrust of praise among American writers abroad seems to have rubbed off on composition teachers at home. In a 1985 study at Texas A&M University, Sam Dragga analyzed forty freshman essays that had been graded and marked by four randomly chosen and traditionally trained teaching assistants. They wrote a total of 864 comments on the essays, but only 51 of them were comments of praise. This means that 94% of the comments focused on what students had done poorly or incorrectly, only 6% on what had been done well (Dragga 1986). The same pattern apparently prevails in high school as well. A study of responses by thirty-six secondary English teachers revealed that although 40% of their end-of-paper comments were positive, the percentage of positive marginal comments was a meager .007% (Harris 1977).

The conclusion that college composition teachers find error more attractive than excellence is consistent with a pilot study of my own conducted in 1982 at Miami University (Daiker 1983). I asked twenty-four colleagues to grade and comment on "Easy Street," a student essay chosen because it combines strength with weakness in both content and style (see pp. 108). I asked my colleagues to mark the essay as if it had been submitted in their freshman composition course. They made a total of 378 separate markings or comments on the student essay: 338, or 89.4%, of them cited error or found fault; only 40, or 10.6%, of them were comments of praise. What may make the predominance of correction over commendation even more significant is that during the previous month, a departmental memorandum reported scholarly consensus on two matters of grading: (1) an instructor should not mark every writing error, because students cannot psychologically cope with a deluge of deficiencies; and (2) an instructor should use praise and positive reinforcement as a major teaching strategy.

Scholarship notwithstanding, composition teachers have traditionally withheld praise from papers they have considered less than perfect. A case in point is the well-known "Evaluating a Theme," published in the *Newsletter of the Michigan Council of Teachers of English* (Stevens 1958). The issue consists of twenty-five responses — twenty-one by college teachers, four by secondary teachers — to a single composition, and the issue's popularity carried it through sixteen printings. According to my figures, the proportion of criticism to praise is roughly the same as in the Texas A&M and Miami studies; the Michigan teachers identified nine errors or problems for every instance of praiseworthy writing. Just as important, fifteen of the twenty-five teachers found nothing in the paper deserving of praise. In three of those instances, college professors sufficiently skilled to ferret out thirty flaws apiece in a brief essay could not — or would not — identify a single source of strength. Their wholly negative comments reminded me of a grade-appeal procedure in which I was asked to evaluate eight compositions written for a colleague's freshman English class. I read the compositions in order, paper one through paper eight, and I read them with increasing despair — not because of what the student had written, but because in responding to a semester's worth of writing, my colleague had offered not a single word of praise. Not an idea, not an example, not a sentence or clause or phrase or punctuation mark — nothing, apparently, merited a compliment. I began to wonder why the student was appealing only a grade, and I had visions of Bartleby the scrivener at work in a dead-letter office.

Francis Christensen observed a quarter century ago that there are two sharply contrasting points of view toward the teaching of English (Christensen 1962). The first he calls the "school" tradition, the second the "scholarly" tradition. The school tradition, nourished by a view of language that regards all change as decay and degeneration, encourages instructors to respond to student writing primarily by identifying and penalizing error. Because of the school tradition, it has long been common to speak of "correcting" themes. There is no clearer embodiment of the negative and narrowly conformist values of the school tradition than the popular correction chart. The 1985 "Harbrace College Handbook Correction Chart," to take a recent example of the species, provides seventy-one correction symbols for instructors to use and students to interpret. Why are correction symbols needed? Why write "d" rather than "diction," or "frag" rather than "This is not a complete sentence because it lacks a verb"? Presumably because instructors find so many errors to mark that not enough time remains for them to use whole words or complete sentences themselves. Significantly, what the correction charts never include is a symbol for approval or praise.

To become teachers of English in a "positive, joyous, creative, and responsible sense," Christensen urges us to replace the inert, rule-encumbered school tradition with more enlightened scholarly views. For several decades now, composition scholars have reported the value of praise in improving student writing. Paul B. Diederich (1963, 1974), senior research associate for the Educational Testing Service, concluded from his research in evaluation that "noticing and praising whatever a student does well improves writing more than any kind or amount of correction of what he does badly, and that it is especially important for the less able writers who need all the encouragement they can get" (1974, 20).

Since writing is an act of confidence, as Mina Shaughnessy reminds us (1977, 85), it is not surprising that the scholarly tradition emphasizes responding with encouragement. Ken Macrorie (1968) recommends that we "encourage and encourage, but never falsely" (688). E. D. Hirsch (1977), who believes that written comments may turn out to be "the most effective teaching device of all" (159), agrees that "the best results are likely to be produced by encouragement" (161). For William F. Irmscher, "the psychology of positive reinforcement . . . should be the major resource for every writing teacher" (1979, 150). All of these individuals would support Diederich's statement that "The art of the teacher — at its best — is the reinforcement of good things" (1963, 58).

Praise may be especially important for students who have known little encouragement and, in part for that reason, suffer from writing apprehension. Writing apprehension is a measure of anxiety established through the research of John Daly and Michael Miller (1975b). According to these researchers, the highly apprehensive writer is one for whom anxiety about writing outweighs the projection of gain from writing. Because they fear writing and its consequences, "high apprehensives" seek to avoid writing situations: they are reluctant to take courses in writing, and they choose academic majors and occupations with minimal writing requirements. When they do write, they use language that is significantly less intense than people with low writing apprehension; that is, they are more reluctant to take a stand or to commit themselves to a position. They try to play it safe not only by embracing neutrality, but by saying less: in response to the same assignment, high apprehensives write fewer words and make fewer statements than low apprehensives (Daly 1977; Daly and Miller 1975a; Daly and Shamo 1978; Holland 1980). The problem for highly apprehensive writers is circular. Because they anticipate negative consequences, they avoid writing. Yet the avoidance of writing — the lack of practice — leads to further negative consequences: writing of poor quality that receives low grades and unfavorable comments.

One's attitude toward the act of writing, Daly concludes, clearly affects not only how one writes and how often one writes, but even how others evaluate that writing (Daly 1977). What may be equally important — since writing is a powerful and perhaps even unique mode of learning (Emig 1977) — is that by systematically avoiding writing situations, high apprehensives close off opportunities for learning and discovery.

But the cause of writing apprehension may suggest its cure — or at least its treatment. A major cause of writing apprehension is past failure or a perception of past failure; high apprehensives perceive their writing experiences as significantly less successful than low apprehensives. Daly says that the "highly apprehensive writer expects, due to a history of aversive responses, negative evaluations for writing attempts. This expectation likely becomes self-fulfilling" (1977, 571). These "aversive responses" include negative comments on assignments and low grades on papers and in writing courses. The connection between writing apprehension and teacher response is supported by the research of Thomas C. Gee (1972). Working with 139 eleventh graders, Gee found that students whose compositions received either criticism alone or no commentary at all developed significantly more negative attitudes toward writing than students whose compositions received only praise. Moreover, after just four weeks, students who received only negative comments or none at all were writing papers significantly shorter than those of students who were praised.

Since positive reinforcement, or its lack, is so crucial to a student's level of writing apprehension (Daly and Miller 1975c), one way of reducing apprehension is by allowing students to experience success with writing. They will experience success, of course, whenever their writing is praised. For students who do not share their writing with others — and high apprehensives fear negative responses from their peers as well as their instructors — the writing teacher is likely their only potential source of praise.

But praise, however beneficial as a remedy for apprehension and as a motivator of student writing, is more easily enjoined than put into practice. Dragga notes in his study, for instance, that the four teaching assistants trained in praiseworthy grading all experienced "difficulty in labeling and explaining the desirable characteristics of their students' writing." He concludes that teacher training must emphasize explicit criteria for praiseworthy grading. The title of this article implies that praise does not flow readily from the marking pens of writing teachers; it must be learned.

Still, an instructor's conscious decision to praise the work of students is a promising starting point. Sometimes all that's needed is a gimmick. My own method is to allow myself nothing but positive comments during an initial reading of a student paper; I lift my pen to write words of praise only. Another practice is to ask, just before moving to another essay, "Have I told Melissa two or three things about her paper that I like?" R. W. Reising's technique is even more effective: he has developed a grading form that requires him to write one to three positive comments before he even considers noting a weakness (1973, 43).

But sometimes what we need is not a gimmick but understanding. We need to understand that what deserves praise is, for a teacher of writing, a relative and not an absolute question. As Ben Jonson says, "I will like and praise some things in a young writer which yet, if he continue in, I cannot but justly hate him for the same" (1947, 617). Following relative standards, we are in no sense dishonest or condescending in praising one writer for what we might ignore or criticize in another — even within the same class. Diederich urges us to praise everything a student has done that is "even a little bit above his usual standard" (1974, 20).

After all, we follow relative standards in most of the teaching we do outside the classroom. In helping children learn how to talk or how to color or how to swim, we don't hold them up to the absolute standards of Demosthenes, van Gogh, or Mark Spitz; we don't even expect them to match their older friends or siblings. In fact, we praise them for the most modest achievements. I still remember trying to help my six-year-old daughter Pam learn how to hit a softball in our backyard on Withrow Avenue. Although I pitched the ball as gently as I knew how, trying to make it eminently hittable, Pam just could not get her bat on the ball. We tried all sorts of minor adjustments in her batting stance — hands held closer together, feet placed further apart, head turned at a more acute angle — but Pam kept missing. Despite my encouragement, she was losing heart in the enterprise. Finally, on perhaps the thirtieth pitch, Pam did hit the ball — nothing like solid contact, but still a distinctly audible foul tip. Of course, I jumped up and down; of course, I shouted, "Way to go, Pammy!"; and of course, she smiled. I praised her lots more when she managed first a foul pop, then a dribbler to the mound, and then a genuine ground ball. As a high school student, Pam started at first base for the varsity softball team.

Even with relative standards, a commitment to positive reinforcement, and perhaps a gimmick or two, most of us could benefit from some practice in praise. For that purpose, let's work with an essay written several years ago by a Miami University freshman in response to an open assignment.

Easy Street

The crowd screams and chants, as a bewildered contestant nervously jumps up and down in search of help. Excitedly, Monty Hall comments on the washer and dryer behind box number two in trade for the big curtain where Carol Marroll is standing. The contestant, with glamour and greed in her eyes; wildly picks the curtain. But when raised there stands a 300 pound cow munching on a bail of hay. Embarrassed and sad, the woman slowly sits down.

The old American ideal of hard work and get ahead had traditionally been one followed by many men. But with the arrival of the twentieth century, their seems to be a new way to get ahead. The new American ideal of something for nothing. It seems to have taken the place of honest work. In our popular television game shows, the idea of being able to win prizes and cash by just answering a few simple questions seems to thrill the average American. It is so popular and fascinating that the morning hours are consumed with five to six hours of the programs. The viewer is thrown into a wonderland where everything is free for the taking. The reason for such interest in these programs is that they show life as most of us really wish it be to be — soft, easy, free. Our society now enjoys the simplicities of life, and our television game shows exemplify that.

One of the newest of all American dreams is to win a state lottery. What easier way is there to become a millionaire with such a small investment? The state makes it as easy as just reading a couple of numbers off a card, or scratching away a secret spot. Who hasn't at least once in their life, dreamed of hitting the big one, and living off the fat the rest of their life; without ever having to work again? Our country clubs, local junior football teams, even our churches have lotteries now thriving on that dream.

In our whole vocabulary their is no word that can command as much attention as the word "free." It sums up our modern culture and feelings. Advertisers use the word as frequently as possible knowing its strong effect on the public. The idea of giving something away without the consumer having to pay for it has made many a company successful.

The old American ideal seems to have moved over for the new. No longer does a man have to work late or get up early. By just guessing the right tune in five notes; he could be ordering caviar in the morning rather than toast.

When "Easy Street" was evaluated by college instructors, grades ranged from *B* to *F,* with *C* and *C-* by far the most common. But my colleagues found much to praise even in an essay they rated average or slightly below average in quality. Their comments of praise are categorized below, according to the four levels Nina Ziv (1984) used in her study of teacher response: conceptual, structural, sentential, and lexical.

   A. Conceptual level.
      1. "Your thesis — that the new American ideal is 'something for nothing' — is strong and clear."
      2. "Your thesis is interesting and clear, and your use of particular, graphic details to support the thesis greatly aids your reader's understanding. The conversational tone of your paper also helps the reader understand you."
      3. "The content of this paper is interesting & to the point, the essay is fairly well unified, and you show the ability to use effective details."
      4. "There is much that is strong here; your sense of detail is good and your ideas are insightful."
      5. "You have provided some excellent examples which capture the essence of the 'new' American ideal."
      6. "Your ideas are brilliant, and the way you have argued your point is convincing. Keep up with original and thought-provoking ways of looking at life around you."
      7. "I like the scope of your commentary, which moves from the initial, interest-provoking example, to the statement of American ideals in paragraph #2, to the further example — of the state lottery — in paragraph #3."
      8. "You come across as being perceptive and as concerned about an important trend in our culture."
      9. "Your ideas here are strong and clear" (refers to second paragraph).
      10. "Your paper has fine unity and some precise illustrations."
   B. Structural level.
      1. "The paper is well-organized and well-focused, with some nice paragraph transitions."

     2. "Good details" (refers to next-to-last sentence of first paragraph and to middle sentence of third paragraph).

     3. "An effective opening paragraph — good detail!"

     4. "Well put, effective use of specific detail" (refers to last sentence of third paragraph).

     5. "A superb choice of topic — and a good natural organization from specific to general — from private to public — and from analysis to significance."

     6. "Effective introduction — your detailed description gets the reader interested and draws him into your analysis."

     7. "Good strategy for your opening: you caught my attention."

     8. "Good details here" (refers to opening sentences of third paragraph).

     9. "I like this" (refers to the whole of first paragraph).

   10. "I got a good first impression of this paper. You've started off well with an anecdote that gives the reader a good visual picture and gets her into your thesis."

C. Sentential level.

     1. "Good sentences" (refers to middle sentences of second paragraph).

     2. "Good parallelism" (refers to third sentence of third paragraph and to first two sentences of last paragraph).

     3. "Very nice pair of sentences — clear and concise" (refers to first two sentences of fourth paragraph).

     4. "Effective closing image. Good!"

     5. "Nice structure" (refers to last sentence of fourth paragraph).

D. Lexical level.

     1. "Good — effective word choice here" (refers to "chants, as a bewildered contestant").

     2. "You have a vigorous and full vocabulary."

     3. "Nice title."

     4. "Nice series — good climax" (refers to "soft, easy, free" of second paragraph).

     5. "Nice phrase" (refers to "with glamour and greed in her eyes").

Although these positive comments show that "Easy Street" has much to praise, instructors marking the paper more readily recognized error than they identified strengths, especially on the sentential and lexical levels. For example, many instructors pointed out the dangling modifier in the next-to-last sentence of the first paragraph ("But when raised"), but no one applauded the effective use of appositive adjectives ("Embarrassed and sad") as modifiers in the following sentence. It seems clear that we have been better trained to spot comma splices and fragments and other syntactic slips than to notice when students take risks: Only one of two dozen evaluators commended the student for "soft, easy, free," a notable instance of series variation with the coordinating conjunction eliminated. Instructors routinely called attention to the misused semicolon in "By just guessing the right tune in five notes; he could be ordering caviar in the morning rather than toast." Far fewer heard the interesting sentence rhythms created by the sophisticated use of repetition.

So perhaps we need to go back to school ourselves to learn how to recognize what merits praise in student writing. A good starting point for syntax are the chapters on free modifiers in *Notes toward a New Rhetoric* (Christensen and Christensen 1978) and in *The Writer's Options* (Daiker, Kerek, and Morenberg 1986), and the articles on coordination by Winston Weathers (1966) and Robert L. Walker (1970). But probably even more useful are sessions at conferences, at department meetings, and at workshops for teaching assistants in which we help each other learn what to praise and how to praise. But, if we listen to students, the "how" may not be all that important. At the same time that students tell us that criticism must be specific to work — a comment like "diction" or "logic" or "awkward" is almost always misunderstood unless explained in detail — they receive even vague compliments like "nice" and "good" and "well written" with gratitude and thanksgiving (Hayes and Daiker 1984). Don Murray once casually remarked at a Wyoming Conference on Freshman and Sophomore English that one of his favorite responses to student writing begins with the five words "I like the way you." He told us we could complete the sentence in any way we chose: "I like the way you use dialogue here" or "I like the way you started your paper with a story" or "I like the way you repeated the key word *animal* in this paragraph."

In his preface to John Gardner's *On Becoming a Novelist*, Raymond Carver (1983) recalls his experience as a college freshman in Gardner's creative writing class at Chico State College. Carver remembers, above all, that Gardner lavished more attention and care on his work than any student had a right to expect. Although Gardner would cross out what he found unacceptable in Carver's stories and add words and even sentences of his own,

> he was always looking to find something to praise. When there was a sentence, a line of dialogue, or a narrative passage that he liked, something that he thought "worked" and moved the story along in some pleasant or unexpected way, he'd write "Nice" in the margin or else "Good!" And seeing these comments, my heart would lift. (xvi–xvii)

It's a good bet that genuine praise can lift the hearts, as well as the pens, of the writers who sit in our own classrooms, too.

References

Carver, R. 1983. Preface to *On Becoming a Novelist*, by J. Gardner, xvi–xvii. New York: Harper.

Christensen, F. 1962. Between Two Worlds. Paper delivered to the California Association of Teachers of English, February, San Diego. Reprinted in *Notes toward a New Rhetoric*, edited by F. Christensen and B. Christensen, [1967] 1978.

Christensen, F., and B. Christensen, editors. [1967] 1978. *Notes toward a New Rhetoric: Nine Essays for Teachers*. 2d ed. New York: Harper.

Daiker, D. A. 1983. The Teacher's Options in Responding to Student Writing. Paper presented at the annual Conference on College Composition and Communication, March, Washington, D.C.

Daiker, D. A., A. Kerek, and M. Morenberg. 1986. *The Writer's Options: Combining to Composing*. 3d ed. New York: Harper.

Daly, J. A. 1977. The Effects of Writing Apprehension on Message Encoding. *Journalism Quarterly* 54:566–72.

Daly, J. A., and M. D. Miller. 1975a. Apprehension of Writing as a Predictor of Message Intensity. *The Journal of Psychology* 89:175–77.

Daly, J. A., and M. D. Miller. 1975b. The Empirical Development of an Instrument to Measure Writing Apprehension. *Research in the Teaching of English* 9:242–49.

Daly, J. A., and M. D. Miller. 1975c. Further Studies on Writing Apprehension: SAT Scores, Success Expectations, Willingness to Take Advanced Courses and Sex Differences. *Research in the Teaching of English* 9:250–56.

Daly, J. A., and W. Shamo. 1978. Academic Decisions as a Function of Writing Apprehension. *Research in the Teaching of English* 12:119–26.

Diederich, P. B. 1963. In Praise of Praise. *NEA Journal* 52:58–59.

Diederich, P. B. 1974. *Measuring Growth in English*. Urbana, Ill.: National Council of Teachers of English.

Dragga, S. 1986. Praiseworthy Grading: A Teacher's Alternative to Editing Error. Paper presented at the Conference on College Composition and Communication, March, New Orleans, La.

Emig, J. 1977. Writing as a Mode of Learning. *College Composition and Communication* 28:122–28.

Gee, T. C. 1972. Students' Responses to Teacher Comments. *Research in the Teaching of English* 6:212–21.

Harris, W. H. 1977. Teacher Response to Student Writing: A Study of the Response Pattern of High School Teachers to Determine the Basis for Teacher Judgment of Student Writing. *Research in the Teaching of English* 11:175–85.

Hayes, M. F., and D. A. Daiker. 1984. Using Protocol Analysis in Evaluating Responses to Student Writing. *Freshman English News* 13:1–4, 10.

Hemingway, E. 1964. *A Moveable Feast.* New York: Scribners.

Hirsch, E. D., Jr. 1977. *The Philosophy of Composition.* Chicago: University of Chicago Press.

Holland, M. 1980. The State of the Art: The Psychology of Writing. Paper presented at the Inland Area Writing Project's Summer Writing Conference, July, University of California at Riverside.

Irmscher, W. F. 1979. *Teaching Expository Writing.* New York: Holt, Rinehart, and Winston.

Jonson, B. 1947. Timber, or Discoveries. In *Ben Jonson,* vol. 8, edited by C. H. Herford Percy and E. Simpson. Oxford, England: Clarendon.

Macrorie, K. 1968. To Be Read. *English Journal* 57:688–92.

Reising, R. W. 1973. Controlling the Bleeding. *College Composition and Communication* 24:43–44.

Shaughnessy, M. 1977. *Errors and Expectations: A Guide for the Teacher of Basic Writing.* New York: Oxford University Press.

Stevens, A. K., editor. 1958. Evaluating a Theme. *Newsletter of the Michigan Council of Teachers of English* 5 (6). Ann Arbor: Michigan Council of Teachers of English.

Walker, R. L. 1970. The Common Writer: A Case for Parallel Structure. *College Composition and Communication* 21:373–79.

Weathers, W. 1966. The Rhetoric of the Series. *College Composition and Communication* 17:217–22.

Ziv, N. D. 1984. The Effect of Teacher Comments on the Writing of Four College Freshmen. In *New Directions in Composition Research,* edited by R. Beach and L. S. Bridwell, 362–80. New York: Guilford.

6 The Use of Rogerian Reflection in Small-Group Writing Conferences

Dene Thomas and Gordon Thomas
University of Idaho

Our students come to composition class with ways of communicating based primarily on spoken language. For this reason, a composition class that focuses on helping students internalize the strategies and processes that constitute literacy needs to connect with the familiar, and build on the students' familiarity with the spoken language to help them with written language. One of the techniques best suited for bridging this gap between speaking and writing, we will argue, is the use of Rogerian reflection — the therapeutic technique suggested by Carl Rogers — in small-group writing conferences.

Within the university system, there are actually three major settings for teaching writing: classrooms, small groups, and one-to-one conferences. In addition, there are three means — lectures, discussions, or writing practice — each of which can be used in any of the settings. The lecture method, which is certainly appropriate for communicating specific information that students need, is so limited that we will concentrate instead on the other two means and the latter two settings, which lend themselves to more learner participation and communication between teacher and students.

Psychologist Carl Rogers (1970), in suggesting that the principle of encounter groups be applied to educational settings, notes "a most desperate need for more participation on the part of learners" and "for better communication between faculty and students" (141). The question then becomes which setting or combination of settings we should use to encourage participation and communication. It is often all too easy to fall back on classroom discussion, which limits the number of participants and the quality of instruction. Instead, our choices of what to teach and how to teach should involve selecting certain aspects of the academic culture that we decide are valuable for our students to experience and deciding how we want our students to experience them. We need to make these decisions consciously, rather than letting circumstances dictate them to us.

More specifically, we need to concentrate on the teacher's role as audience and remember that communication is two-directional. Listening to students gives us a chance to respond; this is essentially what we do when we read and comment on their papers. Indeed, writing comments on a paper is part of the one-to-one setting. But to restrict ourselves to writing comments is not an efficient way to teach: it is time-consuming and limiting for us in the same way that writing is more difficult for our students than speaking. Like our students, we are hampered by the fact that writing is a "higher order abstraction," as Vygotsky describes it in *Thought and Language* (1962). It stands to reason that we can accomplish more by responding to students using both means of communication. But we must also determine the type of response to make to students (questioning, describing, telling, suggesting, etc.), the frequency of each type of response, and the setting in which we do each of these.

The one-on-one setting has much to recommend it. Communication is immediate and directed to the student's needs. Used as the only setting for talking about writing, however, it is very time consuming, especially if the conference is student-centered and the teacher is encouraging the student's involvement and problem solving, as Richard Beach advocates in the next chapter of this collection. There is also the danger that the teacher will impose suggested plans and procedures and, in effect, do the thinking for the student. Instead of being centered on the student, the conference then becomes centered on the teacher. Thomas Newkirk, in "The First Five Minutes" (this volume), demonstrates this danger and suggests ways in which the "dialectic encounter between student and teacher" can provide effective help, allowing for a discussion of possible alternatives instead of directives to be followed. One-on-one conferences have an important place in teaching, but should be used with the variety of readers and suggestions that can come from group conferences. Even as Rogers (1970) promotes groups, he suggests a balanced approach, using both the group and the one-on-one settings.

A large body of evidence indicates that learning groups constitute a powerful pedagogy and that they promote the most effective form of learning — active and experiential. David Johnson (1980) concludes a study of student-to-student interaction by claiming that

> teaching and learning do not typically take place within a dyadic relationship between an adult and a child. Students' learning

> takes place within a network of relationships with peers, and it
> is these relationships that form the context within which all
> learning takes place. (156)

Such relationships foster active learning that leads more easily to attitude change, which is the cognitive and the affective heart of all other learning objectives: motivation, problem solving, skill building, and content mastery (Altman and McGinnies 1960). Writing courses are particularly well suited to learning groups. We have only to think of the activity inside the editorial offices of many newspapers to realize that involved writers can talk about writing at any stage — before it has begun, along the way, and in retrospect — and that they seem to seek such discussion and to benefit from it. Small-group writing conferences provide specific benefits in each of these areas.

Overcoming Isolation with Small-Group Conferences

In addition, small-group conferences help some students overcome habits and attitudes they developed as solitary writers: for such students, learning really involves unlearning an isolated and perhaps alienated approach to writing. For other students, the simple learning of additional material and ideas leads to adjustments in perspectives that come more easily in discussions with others (Fraser, Beaman, Diener, and Kelem 1977). In discussions, one's concerns as a writer and a critical reader can be clarified by being articulated, and fear (anxiety) can be freely expressed. This sort of involvement leads to motivation — which is the first aim of any writing class or learning group, and also the first obstacle that many writers must overcome.

Once students are motivated, they can begin teaching themselves to solve writing problems, through involvement in the group. The teacher sets the topic and defines the conference in terms of the writer's responsibility for his or her own writing, in much the same way that Rogers (1942) suggests the counselor should do for nondirective counseling. This group then becomes a resource for exploring three objectives: (1) problem solving, which includes the approach to the rhetorical situation — writer's stance, audience reaction, subject; (2) skill building, which includes hierarchical thinking, expanding and organizing information, expanding short-term memory, style, syntactic fluency; and (3) content mastery, which includes learning the conventions of writing, such as the rules of grammar and mechanics, spelling, library use, and appropriate formats. Small-group writing conferences provide a means for the teacher to monitor the writing process, to evaluate it in dynamic progress, and to intervene immediately in appropriate ways — recognizing what the writer has just said, interpreting the writer's comments, and asking specific questions — again similar to Roger's method of nondirective counseling (1942). In an ideal situation, students and teacher can easily raise concerns; commentary is immediate; translation from word to idea is instantaneous; and neither students nor the teacher can completely escape involvement. In most actual situations, we see glimpses of the ideal.

For these reasons, we feel that the central feature of a small-group writing conference involves breaking down two kinds of isolation: speaking from writing and individual from group. First, speaking is used as a means of explaining what has been written, asking questions, and planning for future writing. Responses are oral and immediate, as well as written, both before and during the conference. Second, the writing process is carried on in the company of other writers, so that feedback comes from several sources in addition to what the writers have been providing themselves in the form of imagined feedback.

Perhaps the most important advantage of small-group writing conferences is that they use conversation to teach anticipation of an audience's needs. We base this claim on the work of Jerome Bruner (1966), a learning theorist who believes that learning begins with the familiar and moves on only after making connection with the known. Students in freshman composition come into class as conversationalists, knowing how to use the spoken language. They have difficulty — in varying degrees — as they attempt to make the transition to appropriate written language. Part of the reason for their difficulty is that often they have done very little writing before they reach college. Also, according to Lev Vygotsky (1962), the student must go through a "second degree of symbolization" for "speech that is merely imagined." Since Vygotsky's main interest was the relationship between thought and speech in elementary-age children, with inner speech providing the bridge between, he did not discuss writing, other than to note that its lack of an immediate audience contributed to poor motivation and that a lack of ability to plan using abstract thinking contributed to the differences in the rates of development between speaking and writing. Conversation about writing may provide a bridge between speaking and writing, parallel to that which inner speech provides between thought and speech.

The conference method of teaching writing, then, is important for several reasons:

1. The group gives students a chance to implement and instantiate what they already know about communication.
2. The group negotiates goals and directions for an academic essay.
3. The group negotiates whether each conversational contribution is appropriate.
4. The group functions as giver and receiver of information.
5. The group provides a chance for writers to explain their plans from thoughts to paper.
6. The group reacts immediately.
7. The group begins to develop a social framework of its own, based on past experiences of each writer within the group.
8. The group context, real or role-played, provides the elements of a rhetorical situation.

Figure 1 lists the basic experiences of an isolated writer and those of a writer participating in a group. For the isolated writer, most action is silent, moving directly from thoughts to writing. For the writer in a group, the action is oral; in addition, reactions and feedback come from others, rather than having to be imagined by the writer. Since most of the actual writing is still done in isolation, both before and after the conference, the group experience adds to and expands the individual experience.

So far, we have argued that small-group writing conferences, used in conjunction with classroom and individual settings, are an effective means of teaching writing. We will also describe what happens in a writing conference, in order to understand it in such a way that we can predict what will be beneficial to student writers, both in terms of our own responses and in terms of the responses we encourage

Isolated Writer	Writer in Group
Plans	Plans and explains plans
Uses past experiences	Uses and explains past experiences
Carries on dialogue with self	Carries on dialogue with group
Functions as reader of own text	Functions as reader and listener to other readers
Projects reactions	Receives real reactions
Imagines feedback	Receives real feedback
Gives information	Gives and receives information
Expands text through thought/inner speech	Expands text verbally

Figure 1. Group Additions to an Isolated Writer's Experiences

students to make. In this way, we can exercise the kind of control over the group process that will result in more effective teaching.

A Small-Group Conference in Action

The best way to describe what happens in small-group writing conferences is to observe carefully what actually happens in one. One of us (Thomas 1984) observed one small-group writing conference in all its meetings and tape-recorded all the sessions. By recording very elaborate transcripts of the oral interaction in the groups, it was possible to trace the effect that certain kinds of teacher intervention, particularly Rogerian reflection, seemed to have on developing the writing abilities of group members. The overall patterns of conversational interaction within the group were examined, as well as the techniques used by the teacher, student change and development, and the relationship of these factors to revisions made in student papers. Although the goals, plans, and methods of the course were specific, and the teacher and the students were unique personalities, their pattern of conversational interaction and the needs and abilities of the students were typical of freshman writers.

Before exploring what the teacher should do in a particular small-group conference, let us first consider the overall timing of such conferences. They can be held at any stage of the writing process — after prewriting, drafting, or turning in a finished product. Prewriting conferences can involve other early stages of problem solving (idea generating, jottings, rush writing, starts, lists). Their aim can be expansion of ideas and material, clarification of purpose and audience, improvement of style and tone, or correction of errors. Conferences on drafts tend to be more text-centered. The point during the writing process when conferences are most effective has yet to be established; from the scenario that we have established thus far, however, it should be clear that we consider deeper concerns such as expansion of ideas and clarification of purpose and audience to be more important than surface features (spelling, punctuation, and so forth).

For a student to accomplish the tasks of clarification and expansion, he or she must talk about writing in progress. This is important for two reasons: (1) when the writer talks, he or she can create text, plan, and judge what has been written; and (2) whoever the writer is talking to can provide an immediate response. The issue then becomes what sort of response is best. A response that appears to evaluate what the student has said will only result in that student becoming defensive.

Simply asking questions may lead the student to further exploration, but our experience indicates that when a student gets nothing but questions, his or her answers get shorter, rather than longer.

For example, the teacher in the group that Dene studied (Thomas 1984) managed in his first conference to set up an open-ended, caring, low-risk atmosphere similar to that of the therapeutic counseling session recommended for learning situations by Carl Rogers, who argues (1969) that students learn more when teachers are open than when they are judgmental. The first student to speak in the group was asked to give a "guided tour of her prewriting," and she responded with a long account of what she did — all in the past tense: "I put ... I started ... I noticed ... I said ... I felt ...." When she pauses, the teacher encourages her to keep talking, not by a direct question, but by a comment about Young, Becker, and Pike's prewriting strategy (1973), which the students had studied: "And then you have some particle/wave/field stuff here too." This comment prompts the student to give a long explanation and expansion of her prewriting.

Rogers notes (1951) that in nondirective counseling, clients are more likely to talk if the counselor's response is open and inviting and expressed as often as possible in the form of a statement rather than a direct question. A few sentences later, the teacher (Thomas 1984) continues this same technique and also manages to focus on the writing: "Tell us what you're trying to do at this point, what you're writing about right now. In terms of writing." Again the student responds, this time moving from explanations of what she has already done to plans for her paper. The open-ended statements from the instructor have considerable effectiveness in eliciting student comments.

One of the most effective responses noted in the small-group writing conferences we studied was Rogerian reflection — the technique pioneered by Rogers, in which the therapist repeats or "reflects" what the client is saying in an effort to get the client to clarify his or her feelings. Rogers recommends it as an effective form of nondirective counseling, but it has much merit as a teaching device as well. When used by the teacher throughout the conference groups that we studied, the students did more and more of it as the conferences progressed.

Using Rogerian Reflection as a Teaching Device

Rogers has demonstrated that statements of reflection are more effective than questions in encouraging responses. The accuracy of these reflections can be viewed on a scale from 1 to 5:

1. Misses the speaker's intention completely — misunderstands — a misfire.
2. Restates the speaker's meaning, but with less clarity than the speaker showed.
3. Restates the speaker's meaning using the speaker's exact words or paraphrases at the same level of clarity as the speaker.
4. Restates the speaker's meaning with more clarity than the speaker did.
5. Restates the speaker's meaning with more clarity in a way that also focuses the issue.

In counseling situations, it is important for a therapist to make a reflection that restates as accurately or (better still) more accurately what a client has just said; a response that indicates misunderstanding can be detrimental. But in writing conferences a reflection that misses the student's intent can still be very helpful. In several instances, the teacher makes remarks such as, "So you're all set now," and the student replies, "Well, not exactly." In the resulting discussion, the student will often state succinctly what is still unclear, knowing that remaining discussion time is short. Reflections that miss tend to focus the issues quickly.

Reflections in the third category, which restate with about the same level of clarity, give the writers a chance to consider their own words and ideas. Speaking and then hearing from another source makes real what previously were ideas in the mind only — forming the bridge between speaking and writing. Reflections in the last category, which provide additional clarity and focus, may appear to be the most desirable, and in fact, they often are very helpful. But they also have the danger of going beyond what the students intended, in effect, writing their paper for them.

Rogerian reflections have some characteristic beginnings:

"What I hear you saying is . . ."
"It seems like . . ."
"It seems to me that . . ."
"So . . ."
"It sounds to me like you are trying to . . ."

Reflections may also start more tersely, without these introductory phrases. But it is important to note the emphasis on listening to the writer that these statements indicate, whether that listening is literal (verbal) or refers to meaning that comes from reading the draft or paper. In each case, the response we make as readers or listeners comes from paying attention to what a student is trying to communicate. By recognizing the student's attempt to communicate, we give it *legitimacy* and increase the chances of further meaningful attempts.

As they are used in these small-group writing conferences, Rogerian reflections have five specific functions:

1. Pointing to structure

   It seems like you're having trouble deciding what your audience would want to read first.
   I hear two things . . .
   You're talking first of all . . .
   Well, that gives you a structure . . .

2. Clarifying

   So you're having trouble deciding which examples to use.
   So ironically . . .
   You're interested in . . .
   You want to focus . . .
   So it was . . . that that was the most fascinating . . .

3. Expanding (trailing endings)

   . . . for some reason.
   . . . or.
   . . . or something.
   . . . that was.
   . . . something like.

4. Recalling

   There was something you talked about earlier.

5. Summarizing

   (Individual) There's just a few simple things you want to try, as I hear you.
   (Group) So far I'm hearing Becky talk about . . . and I hear you, Amy,
   . . .

These five functions of Rogerian reflections can serve one of two purposes: to continue the discussion or to reach closure. They invite the writer to continue talking, in search of more content or a sharper purpose. Pointing to structure can function in either way, serving as an invitation to discuss organization or as a means of reaching closure.

Both Rogerian reflections and questioning techniques have great influence by functioning as pivotal interactions between readers and the writer, influencing the direction and the quality of discussion.

While the thrust of Rogerian reflections may be nondirective and the material on which they are based may originate with the writer rather than the teacher, the teacher or other students must be somewhat directive by their very selection of that portion of a student's comment that they choose to reflect.

Once students feel free to use Rogerian reflection as a result of imitating the teacher's responses, the conversation in groups picks up. When writers realize that others are actually listening and responding to them, they develop trust in the group and grow more willing to risk — more willing to share writing difficulties. The situation of readers providing reflection to other writers can even be reversed. As a reader makes a comment, the writer may make a reflection that sharpens and clarifies an idea within his or her own paper.

The patterns of verbal interaction within a small-group writing conference change over time. The source of the change is not a shift in basic personality or method of presentation of self; rather, it seems to come from two major causes: (1) the cohesive structure of the group encourages trust and risk-taking over time and with that risk-taking comes changes in communication patterns, and (2) the teacher models techniques of listening, reflecting, and questioning, which the students begin to imitate — not as a complete change of style, but as additions to their basic mode of communication. This latter technique can also be applied to one-on-one conferences of the type described by Newkirk later in this volume.

We know that rubber-stamp comments are less valuable to students than comments that show our involvement with the specific writing at hand. We know that comments will have more effect if they are made at a point when students can consider them in the course of drafting or revising. We also know that to write students' papers for them has little benefit for the students. Yet we all tend to make these mistakes over and over. For the lack of anything meaningful to say or write in response to a student paper, we fall back on our body of composition knowledge ("awkward" or "needs better organization"). For our lack of planning that allows responses at prewriting or draft stage, we make responses on the final paper, often phrasing the comments as if the student were going to revise, when we know that at best, the paper will now go into the stack of completed college work that lies under the student's bed. For the lack of knowing what else to do, and because we want to do something, we read a paper and think of how we would have handled that same subject. We then give directive advice, based on the paper we would have written, and if we saw the paper in process, the final paper may indeed be a shadow of the paper we would have written. We direct the students' learning and we take responsibility for it when we need to help students do these things for themselves. The use of Rogerian reflection can apply to papers by reducing the number of these errors on the part of the teacher.

When used to write comments on paper rather than as part of conference discussion, Rogerian reflection can be viewed as a variant of Peter Elbow's reader-based feedback (1981). As a part of reacting to a paper, we can describe what we read as we understand it. We can summarize, often paragraph by paragraph, and point to the structure as we perceive it. We can indicate where we're confused and provide the meaning as best we can interpret it. As we do so, we can see ourselves in conversation with the writer — less effective conversation than it would be face to face, but still conversation — because the writer has a real person as audience.

Describing — reflecting — has much merit as a written response technique. Often students who are good writers need an awareness of how they managed to put together an effective paper, of what worked, and of why it worked. Rogerian reflection also prevents us from participating in those witch hunts for error that students can find so discouraging. The written responses can be used as a basis for a conference, or they can simply stand alone on a sheet handed back to the student.

The way we will respond to student writers — and to their writings — is determined long before we face the stack of papers, themselves a response to an assignment we made a short time earlier. The assignment itself helps to determine our response, as does the situation we set up — a written comment made in the privacy of our office, a one-on-one conference where we discuss the paper with the student, or a small-group writing conference where our remarks combine with those of other writers. The timing of the response affects the type of response — are we commenting on prewriting, on a rough draft, or on a finished paper that will not be revised?

Before wrestling with these important concerns, we would like to back up still further — before the response, before the assignment, even before the class itself — to attitude. What do we believe about the students we are teaching to write? How controlling do we want to be? How much responsibility should we take for our students' writing? To what extent should the teaching of writing be a dialogue? We are arguing that effective composition teaching combines a positive regard for our students, an assumption that they are responsible for their own writing, and a willingness to enter into dialogue to communicate with them.

Rogers (1969) believes "that the individual has the capacity to guide, regulate, and control himself, providing only that certain definable conditions exist" (221). Those conditions, as we have defined them, include small-group and one-on-one conferences as part of a composition class. They also include listening carefully to students and responding in a way that acknowledges and interprets what they say, whether they said it orally or in writing. Rogers's technique is more than just a method; it's a way of viewing the students — an attitude toward the students.

References

Altman, I., and E. McGinnies. 1960. Interpersonal Perception and Communication in Discussion Groups of Varied Attitudinal Composition. *Journal of Abnormal and Social Psychology* 60:390–95.

Bruner, J. 1966. *Toward a Theory of Instruction.* Cambridge: Harvard University Press.

Elbow, P. 1981. *Writing with Power.* New York: Oxford University Press.

Fraser, S. C., A. L. Beaman, E. Diener, and R. T. Kelem. 1977. Two, Three, or Four Heads Are Better than One: Modification of College Performance by Peer Monitoring. *Journal of Educational Psychology* 69:101–108.

Johnson, D. W. 1980. Group Processes: Influences of Student-Student Interaction on School Outcomes. In *The Social Psychology of School Learning,* edited by J. H. McMillan. New York: Academic Press.

Kroll, B. 1981. Developmental Relationships between Speaking and Writing. In *Exploring Speaking-Writing Relationships: Connections and Contrasts,* edited by B. Kroll and R. Vann. Urbana, Ill.: National Council of Teachers of English.

Macrorie, K. 1970. *Telling Writing.* Rochelle Park, N.J.: Hayden.

Moffett, J. 1968. *Teaching the Universe of Discourse.* Boston: Houghton Mifflin.

Murray, D. 1968. *A Writer Teaches Writing.* Boston: Houghton Mifflin.

Nash, R. J., and D. A. Shiman. 1974. The English Teacher as Questioner. *English Journal* 63:38–44.

Nystrand, M. 1982. Rhetoric's "Audience" and Linguistics' "Speech Community": Implications for Understanding Writing, Reading, and Text. In *What Writers Know: The Language, Process, and Structure of Written Discourse,* edited by M. Nystrand. New York: Academic Press.

Rogers, C. R. 1942. *Counseling and Psychotherapy.* Boston: Houghton Mifflin.

Rogers, C. R. 1951. *Client-Centered Therapy.* Boston: Houghton Mifflin.

Rogers, C. R. 1961. *On Becoming a Person.* Boston: Houghton Mifflin.

Rogers, C. R. 1969. *Freedom to Learn: A View of What Education Might Become.* Columbus, Ohio: Charles E. Merrill.

Rogers, C. R. 1970. *Carl Rogers on Encounter Groups.* New York: Harper and Row.

Thomas, D. K. 1984. A Transition from Speaking to Writing: Small-Group Writing Conferences. Unpublished doctoral dissertation, University of Minnesota.

Vygotsky, L. 1962. *Thought and Language.* Edited and translated by E. Hanfmann and G. Vakar. Cambridge: MIT Press.

Young, R., A. Becker, and K. Pike. 1973. *Rhetoric: Discovery and Change.* New York: Harcourt Brace Jovanovich.

7 Showing Students How to Assess: Demonstrating Techniques for Response in the Writing Conference

Richard Beach
University of Minnesota

As the essays in this book indicate, there are a number of different ways of responding to student writing. The immediate, short-term goal of responding to writing is to help students revise and improve a particular paper. Beyond that short-term goal, the ultimate, long-range goal of response is to help students learn to critically evaluate writing on their own.

In this chapter, I will argue that evaluation alone may not achieve this long-range goal of helping students learn to critically assess their own writing. Instead, it may require the additional strategy of modeling various ways to assess one's own work during a writing conference.

A number of essays in this book argue for the need to respond to the content or meaning, rather than the form, of writing. In responding to content, teachers move away from the traditional role as "examiners" of how students write — matters of organization or style, for example — to enter a dialogue with the students about what they are trying to tell us. However, even in focusing on the content of student writing, we discover problems: Students don't have enough information; the boundaries of their topic are too broad; or they don't have a clearly defined purpose or stance. In responding to student writing, therefore, we must find ways for *students* to recognize, on their own, the sorts of problems that we experience as readers of their texts.

Teaching Students to Assess Their Own Writing

One way of teaching students to assess their writing is simply to tell them what their problems are and how to remedy those problems. Of course, by mimicking our commands, students won't learn to assess on their own. They just learn to do as they are told. We opt, therefore, for more indirect methods of evaluation, responding as in a dialogue, as a reader. For example, by giving reader-based evaluation ("After I read your draft, I wasn't sure what you were trying to say. You seemed to be trying to make a lot of different points.") we hope to imply to students that problems exist, i.e., that the draft isn't focused.

In giving such reader-based evaluation, we assume that students can (1) comprehend our evaluation; (2) pick up on our implications that certain problems may exist; and (3) apply our feedback to define their own problems and solutions.

Unfortunately, students often can't recognize our hints. They may comprehend the evaluation, but if they can't define their own problems, it is unlikely that they will be able to pick up on our implications that their papers have problems. Moreover, even if they do grasp the implications, my research on self-assessing indicates they may have difficulty making appropriate revisions (Beach 1976; Beach and Eaton 1984). In short, because students do not know how to assess their writing, much of our seemingly helpful feedback may not necessarily help them to critically assess their writing.

One option is to directly teach critical thinking skills. Composition teachers have traditionally assumed that instruction in the critical analysis of published and/or student texts will transfer to critical analysis of the students' own writing. While such text analysis may be helpful, students generally have difficulty transferring the global analysis of texts during class discussion to assessing specific problems in their own writing.

Another option is for teachers to demonstrate or model various assessing techniques, using their own writing, for the entire class. However, my own research indicates that large-group demonstrations have little effect on students' self-assessing (Beach 1985). I also found a number of problems with this method — problems that stem from trying to gear the modeling to an entire class of students who have disparate problems and abilities. The teachers in this research had difficulty determining which problems to demonstrate, because the students' problems were so diverse. Moreover, given the range of students' abilities, the teachers were uncertain whether the intellectual level of their demonstrations matched the pupils' abilities.

Demonstrating Assessing in the Writing Conference

Given the difficulty of coping with the range of individual differences in large-group demonstrations, a third option is to demonstrate assessing in teacher-student conferences (Harris 1983). By demonstrating assessing strategies in a conference, teachers (or trained peers) can diagnose each student's unique problems, discover the composing difficulties that led to them (apprehension, premature obsession with editing, lack of information, etc.), and practice the use of certain assessing and revising strategies that can overcome them.

The conference has the immediate benefit of providing a forum for students to practice their assessing with a teacher. The teacher can then note instances in which a student is having difficulty and demonstrate how to assess, instead of simply telling the student what changes to make. The student then has a concrete guide for trying out certain assessing techniques.

This more individualized approach to teaching assessing in conferences involves the following steps:

1. Determine a student's own particular difficulty by analyzing his or her use of certain assessing techniques in a conference.

2. Demonstrate the stages of assessing: describing, judging, and selecting appropriate revisions.

3. Describe the different components of the rhetorical context — purpose, rhetorical strategies, organization, and audience; show how each component implies criteria for judging drafts; and select appropriate revisions.

4. Have the student discuss problems and/or practice the use of certain strategies just demonstrated.

Demonstrating Assessment: A Psychological Rationale

Aside from the value of focusing on specific student problems, there are a number of other reasons for working with problems of assessment in a conference — particularly problems stemming from a student's psychological orientation or self-concept.

Writing Apprehension: Frustration with Writing Problems

In some cases, students are overwhelmed or frustrated by certain problems in their writing (Bloom 1985; Daly 1985; Rose 1984). Because students don't know how to deal with their problems, they may assume that they lack the potential to write and revise, as suggested in research indicating that writers' sense of their own efficacy is related to their writing ability (McCarthy, Meier, and Rinderer 1985). By demonstrating how we, as teachers and writers, might cope with such problems, we show students that writers can face and solve problems in their own writing.

Defining Roles in an Academic Context

Coupled with a lack of self-efficacy, students often have an unclear sense of their own rhetorical role or persona in writing within academic contexts (Bizzell 1978; Bleich 1983, 1986; Bloom 1985). As Bartholomae (1985) argues, students' "roles" are constituted by relatively unfamiliar discourse conventions. He notes, for example, that his students "don't invent the language of literary criticism . . . they are, themselves, invented by it" (145). Students must therefore learn to "approximate" the discourse conventions of the prose that defines their roles or persona within the classroom or wider academic context. This requires them, as Bartholomae argues, to be able to think like a critic, scientist, historian, or anthropologist by "accommodating" the discourse conventions of these different disciplines. If students have difficulty defining their role, they may also have difficulty describing the social or academic context that constitutes the meaning of their text (Brandt 1986; Fish 1980).

By demonstrating how we define our own roles as "teachers," "critics," or "researchers," and how those roles constitute certain discourse conventions, we show students the value of developing and defining their own roles.

Rigid, Inflexible Assessment

One manifestation of writing apprehension or role insecurity is a rigid, inflexible style of assessing. Through recall and think-aloud research, Rose (1980, 1985) and Harris (1985) have found that many students bring into the classroom rigid rules for assessing their writing, which in some cases create writing anxiety. For example, students may apply a maxim such as "every paragraph should have a topic sentence" to their draft, rigidly assuming that if their writing doesn't follow the rules, then it's not right. Assessing then becomes a matter of checking their drafts against a set of "correct" rules or maxims.

When we detect that students are applying rules or maxims in this rigid manner, we can demonstrate that the student needs to consider variations in the social context, avoiding the dogmatic application of such rules to all contexts. This approach also encourages students to develop relativistic attitudes toward writing which, as Anson argues later in this volume, are necessary for motivating self-assessment and revision.

Modeling itself, however, can sometimes promote a rigid orientation. Students may perceive any modeling behavior from an authority as implying that there is "only one way" — that they *must* use the same strategies, because this is the one and only way to assess writing.

One remedy for breaking this blind allegiance to the notion that the "teacher's way is *the* way" is for the teacher to demonstrate alternative approaches to dealing with the same problem. Another remedy is to encourage peers to demonstrate their own assessing strategies in small-group conferences. Students are therefore exposed to a range of different assessing strategies or styles other than the teacher's. This obviously assumes that the other students are able to demonstrate their own assessing and that the demonstrators themselves don't just mimic the teacher's assessing style.

Metacognitive Awareness of One's Own Strategies

Students not only need to be able to define their own logical or rhetorical strategies, they also need to know why they are using those strategies. This requires them to be able to reflect on what they are doing and why — a metacognitive awareness of their own rhetorical behaviors. Effective readers and writers are able to monitor their own use of strategies because they bring a schema or "intellectual scaffolding" for defining their problems in a systematic manner (Applebee 1984; Baker and Brown 1984).

By demonstrating that self-assessing is a systematic process involving, as I will discuss, a series of defined steps, we present students with a "scaffolding" that may enhance their metacognitive awareness.

Techniques of Assessing

In order to discuss ways of demonstrating different assessing techniques, I propose a model of assessing. As illustrated in Figure 1, assessing involves three basic stages: describing, judging, and selecting and testing revisions. I will briefly define each of these stages and then, for the remainder of this chapter, discuss how I demonstrate these techniques in a conference.

As depicted in this chart, each of these stages implies a subsequent stage. Descriptions of the social/rhetorical context (goals, strategies, audience characteristics, text structure or genre, and role or orientation) imply criteria for making judgments. These judgments then imply predictions for appropriate revisions.

Assessing is, furthermore, a recursive process; in making judgments or selecting revisions, writers are cycling back to their descriptions of the context, which in turn enable them to define criteria for their assessments. Or, in revising their text, they may redefine their conception of the context.

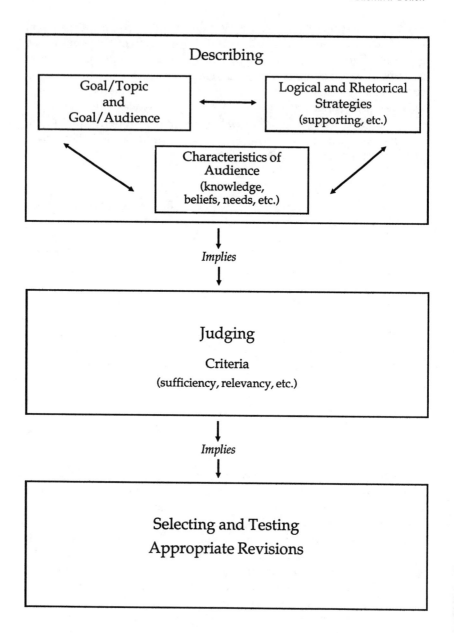

Figure 1. Stages of Assessing

In demonstrating these describing, judging, and predicting techniques, I am showing students not only how to use these techniques, but also that they are logically related. Once the students recognize these interrelationships, they begin to see the importance of considering all three techniques during assessment.

Determining Difficulties in Assessing

In order to select which technique to demonstrate, I try to pinpoint a student's difficulty in using a particular technique. I begin the conference, as both Murray (1985) and Newkirk (this volume) recommend, by letting the student set the agenda — by asking the student to give me her or his reactions to the draft, listening carefully for difficulties in describing, judging, or selecting revisions. Because most conferences are too brief to allow for adequate diagnosis solely on the basis of student comments, however, I ask each student to complete a guided assessing form (Beach and Eaton 1984) before participating in the conference. (For two additional examples of self-assessing forms, see the "Self-Evaluation Questionnaires" in Faigley et al. 1985, 234–35).

In using this form (Figure 2), students divide their draft into sections, answering the questions for each section. Students don't necessarily need to begin with the "describing" questions; they may begin by noting problems and then work back to the describing stage.

By reading over the form in the beginning of the conference and by listening to their reactions to their drafts, I try to determine students'

Describing

1. What are you trying to say or show in this section?
2. What are you trying to do in this section?
3. What are some specific characteristics of your audience?
4. What are you trying to get your audience to do or think?
5. How would you describe your organization or type of writing?
6. How would you describe your own role or orientation?

Judging

7. What are some problems you perceive in achieving 1, 2, and 4?

Selecting appropriate revisions

8. What are some changes you can make to deal with these problems?

Figure 2. Guided Assessing Form

particular difficulties in assessing their drafts. If, for example, for each
of three sections in a draft, a student has difficulty describing what
she is "trying to say or show," I might conclude that she has difficulty
inferring her intentions. The fact that this student also has had difficulty
answering my questions about goals further suggests that inferring
intentions is a problem. Many such difficulties have also been discerned
in think-aloud protocols of students' writing processes (Flower and
Hayes 1981; Harris 1985; Selfe 1986).

Next I demonstrate how I would infer intentions. Rather than using
my own writing, with which the student isn't familiar, I use the
student's writing. I adopt the student's role or persona, demonstrating
how I, from that perspective, would infer intentions. Consistent with
my concern that modeling can imply only "one correct way," I stress
to the student that while I am showing how *I* would infer intentions,
I am not implying that my approach is the only option. I also avoid
telling the student what he "ought" to be saying — for example, by
explaining what I think he is "really trying to say."

After I demonstrate a certain technique, I then ask the student to
make his or her own inferences. If the individual continues to have
difficulty, I further demonstrate that technique.

All of this requires careful attention to clues suggesting difficulties,
as well as a conceptual framework for sorting out and isolating certain
strategies. Based on my own experience and research on assessing
(Beach 1976, 1977, 1985; Beach and Eaton 1984), I will now discuss
some of the difficulties students have in describing, judging, and
selecting revisions, and some strategies I use for demonstrating techniques for each of these stages.

The Describing Stage

The describing stage consists of describing five basic elements:

goals for content (What am I trying to say?) and audience (What
do I want my audience to do or think?);

logical or rhetorical strategies (What am I trying to do: supporting,
contrasting, shifting to a different point?);

audience characteristics (knowledge, traits, needs, etc.);

text structure or genre; and

role or persona.

Describing these components of the rhetorical context is central to
assessing. Unfortunately, many students conceive of "assessing" solely

in terms of "judging." When asked to assess their writing, they begin by making judgments: "My introduction is too nebulous," "I don't have enough evidence," and so on. In making these judgments without describing the social/rhetorical context, students assess their writing in a vacuum. When they begin to consider appropriate revisions — for example, how to make their introduction less "nebulous" — they have no logical grounds for deciding on an appropriate revision.

By describing the context, writers have some basis for making judgments about their drafts. For example, one writer describes his strategy — that in the beginning of his story, he is "setting the scene in order to show what a small-town world is like." He describes his audience — the fact that the audience probably knows little about that particular setting. Now he can infer appropriate criteria for judging the setting — whether he has included enough information to convey the sense of a "small-town world" to the reader. This judgment, in turn, helps him in the final stage, selecting appropriate revisions — in this case, adding more information about the setting.

Describing Goals

Writers obviously use goals for judging whether their text says or does what they want it to say or do. Once they infer their goals, they can detect dissonance between their goals and their text, dissonance that leads to judgments about problems in achieving their goals.

This is not to imply that writers must always articulate their goals in order to assess their writing. Writers often have only a "felt sense" of their intentions without ever articulating them, but they know how to use these unarticulated intentions to determine that something is amiss and what to do about their problems.

In my research on the use of guided assessing forms, I asked students to describe what they were trying to say or show ("goal/topic") or what they wanted their audience to do or think ("goal/audience") in each of several sections of their draft (Beach 1977; Beach and Eaton 1984). Many students in these studies had difficulty stating what they were trying to say or to whom they were saying it. They would often simply restate their text *verbatim* rather than state their intended topic or idea. For example, in writing an analysis of citizen participation in the government of her hometown, a student described her draft section as saying that "a lot of citizens in the town don't vote and there often aren't enough candidates to run for local offices," almost a verbatim restatement of what she was saying in the draft. She did not go beyond that restatement to infer a point of that section, her "goal/topic" — that citizens aren't involved in town government. She also had difficulty inferring her "goal/audience," what she wanted her audience to do or think upon having read the essay. Because she had difficulty inferring these goals, she had difficulty judging her draft.

To some degree, this identification process may be difficult, particularly if students don't perceive the purpose for inferring goals — to further assess their draft. Moreover, writers in general have difficulty defining the difference between intended meanings and the meanings inherent in the existing text (Flower, Hayes, Carey, Schriver, and Stratman 1986). And they have difficulty assuming the perspective of a reader in order to construct a clear "representation" of their text (Flower and Hayes 1984), to read their own text as constituted by but distinct from their intentions.

For example, Hunt and Vipond (1984) found that the majority of college students asked to read John Updike's "A & P" adopted a "story-driven" orientation — reading the story primarily for enjoyment — as opposed to a "point-driven" orientation, reading the story for its underlying point or message. The story-driven readers were often perplexed about why certain things happened in the story, which they perceived as "pointless." In contrast, the point-driven readers could evaluate Updike's use of literary techniques, because they could relate these to a perceived point or intention. Demonstrating ways of defining goals may help students to adopt the point-driven orientation essential for judging drafts.

In demonstrating goal/topic inferences, I attempt to show students the difference between simply restating the content of a section of their draft and inferring the goal or purpose of that section. In working with the student who wrote about her local government, I first take her restatement of the text, "that citizens don't vote and there aren't enough candidates," and, playing the role of the "dumb reader," to use Walker Gibson's term, ask the question, "What's the point?" I then infer a goal statement — that the citizens aren't involved — and show the student that, in contrast to her restatement, I can use this goal statement to pinpoint disparities between goal and text.

Another problem with students' goal/topic inferences is that they are often so global they are not very useful for perceiving disparities between goals and text (Beach and Eaton 1984; Nold 1982). For example, in writing an autobiographical narrative about a series of shoplifting incidents, a student states that he was "trying to show what I was like when I was a teenager." This inference is too global for assessing what it is he wants to show about this past self. The student needs to articulate more precisely what the incidents reveal about his past.

Students also mimic abstract goals, gleaned from textbooks or instruction, about what they should do in order to produce "good writing." They will say, for example, that they want to "grab the reader in the beginning," even though they may have little idea about what achieving that goal entails.

Having diagnosed the previous student's goals as too global, I then infer, using his other comments in the conference, a more precise goal statement: "In portraying my shoplifting, I'm trying to show that I was so lonely that I would do anything to be popular with my peers." I then use this goal inference to review the shoplifting episodes, judging whether the description of the student's behavior in each episode conveys his need for friendship. In doing this, I am demonstrating the *value* of creating precisely defined goal statements.

Describing Rhetorical or Logical Strategies

In describing rhetorical or logical strategies, writers define what they are doing in their texts — supporting, contrasting, describing, evaluating, specifying, etc. In naming these strategies, writers go beyond simply summarizing what they are trying to say and begin identifying what they are trying to do, conceiving of their text from a functional or pragmatic perspective.

As suggested by current versions of speech-act theory (Leech 1983; Levinson 1983), each strategy implies certain criteria for assessing the success or failure of that strategy (Beach 1982; Beach and Liebman-Kleine 1986; Cooper 1984). By describing these strategies, writers evoke the particular criteria necessary for judging their use. They then narrow down the criteria in light of their particular goals and the characteristics of their audience. For example, the strategy "supporting" implies the criteria *sufficiency, relevancy,* or *specificity of support:* Do I have enough support; is my support relevant to my thesis; is my support specific enough? A writer may, for instance, assume that the audience knows little about his essay's topic. He may then be particularly concerned about the sufficiency of information — is there enough supportive information for that audience to understand a point? Or, in writing a memo making a request, a writer may be concerned about her power, right, or ability to make such a request, and about her audience's perception of her sincerity in making it. She then becomes concerned that the language of her request implies that she has the right to make it.

The process of describing strategies and inferring implied criteria is complicated, requiring a pragmatic perspective toward writing — that writing does things rather than simply conveys information. Constructing a model of text based on strategies means that writers read their own texts as a series of rhetorical or logical moves. Because students are often asked to read primarily for information, many simply do not read texts in terms of what a writer is doing, instead focusing mainly on what the text is saying.

Moreover, students may have little knowledge of the criteria constituting successful use of a strategy. They may be able to infer that they were "defining the concept of beauty," but may not know how to assess their definition.

It is not surprising, then, that many students in my research had difficulty describing their strategies and inferring implied criteria (Beach and Eaton 1984). When asked to describe their strategies, students often had difficulty going beyond describing what they were trying to "say" to inferring what it was they were trying to "do." They frequently restated content — "I am writing about my high school and college courses," rather than inferring their strategy — "I am contrasting my high school and college courses." Because they were merely restating the content of their essays, these writers then had difficulty making specific judgments about their texts. Students who inferred a strategy were more likely to make a judgment, because they had some basis for making it.

In demonstrating the difference between a content summary and a strategy inference, I again show how inferences about strategies can be used to imply criteria. For example, having inferred that the student is contrasting high school and college classes, I then note that "contrasting" implies, among other criteria, the need for relevant, valid evidence supporting the contrast.

Describing Characteristics of Audience

Making inferences about characteristics of the audience is also a complex process. There is much debate and conflicting evidence about how much writers actually attend to the needs of an audience (Burleson and Rowan 1985; Rubin 1984; Rubin, Piche, Michlin, and Johnson 1984).

I would argue that, rather than conceiving of audience as a unified global construct, writers assign a set of prototypical characteristics to audiences, based on what and how much the audience knows or believes about a topic and what their needs, status, power, attitudes, or expectations are (Beach and Liebman-Kleine 1986). Writers focus on those audience characteristics most relevant to the writer's immediate goals. For example, in writing a set of directions for windsurfing, a writer may conceive of her audience as "someone who knows little about windsurfing." Or, in arguing the case for nationalizing the steel industry, a writer conceives of his audience as "someone who is opposed to my belief about nationalization." These conceptions are prototypical because writers often never know, even with familiar audiences, exactly what the reader understands, believes, or needs. As Ong (1975) argues, audiences are ultimately fictitious. Writers must therefore rely on constructs derived from approximations of their audience.

Writers also derive these characteristics from their defined goals and strategies. In giving a set of directions for windsurfing, a writer knows that she needs to consider what the audience may or may not know about windsurfing, because that characteristic is particularly useful for judging the relevancy and sufficiency of information in her directions.

Inferring these characteristics also allows writers to adopt a reader's perspective, necessary for distancing themselves from their text. Having created the construct "someone who is opposed to nationalizing the steel industry," the writer can then assess the text from this new perspective, removed, for the time being, from his own interests, beliefs, and dispositions.

When we asked students to infer characteristics of their audience on their self-assessing form, most students made few, if any, references to specific audience characteristics (Beach and Eaton 1984). Most of their inferences consisted of anticipated emotional responses, such as "my reader should like this beginning" or "my audience will be bothered by this section," inferences reflecting a more subjective, story-driven orientation than a point-driven orientation, to use Hunt and Vipond's distinction.

When I sense that students are having difficulty inferring audience characteristics, I demonstrate how I infer these characteristics from my description of strategies or goals. For example, in writing about the lack of citizen participation in her hometown, the student I previously referred to began her paper by describing the town's government, noting that she was trying to "provide background information in order to set the scene." However, she had difficulty judging her use of this defined strategy — setting the scene — because she had difficulty inferring an audience.

In the conference, I use her description of the "background" strategy as a way to focus on determining how much her audience may know about her hometown. Once I've isolated the appropriate attribute — knowledge — I create the construct "someone who knows little about the town." I then use that construct to judge her descriptions of the town.

Describing Text Structure or Genre

Students also benefit from describing their writing's organization in terms of a genre or text structure (Calfee and Curley 1984; Meyer 1975). Describing the genre or text structure provides students with a blueprint or master plan for defining the relationships between their strategies. Certain genres (mystery stories, editorials, lab reports, etc.) and certain text structures (problem/solution, comparison, narrative, opinion/example, etc.) are constituted by certain strategies. For example, having defined their writing as a problem/solution text structure, students can assess the contribution of certain strategies — defining the problem, citing reasons for the problem, citing consequences of the problem — to the overall text structure. From this information, they can determine if they have excluded certain strategies typically associated with a certain structure.

However, students often have difficulty describing the logical relationships between strategies in terms of a genre or text structure. Many students, particularly those who employ little substantive revision (Beach 1976; Perl 1979; Sommers 1980), conceive of organization as a format or, as displayed in textbooks, a set of boxes to be filled in with verbiage, rather than as a structure for defining logical relationships among strategies. Or they cite a set of rules or maxims for "how to write a good lab report."

When I discern that students conceive of structure as boxes to be filled in, I show them how my description of structure reveals my use of strategies and the logical relationships among those strategies. I often draw a map or chart of the student's draft, visually showing the location of different strategies and using the representation to demonstrate how I conceived of the relationships among the student's strategies.

Describing Roles or Orientation

Writers create a role — student, scientist, critic, reviewer, devil's advocate, cognitivist, proponent — constituted by certain discourse conventions (Bartholomae 1985; Brandt 1986) and reflecting certain personality characteristics or attitudes (Bleich 1983, 1986). As Anson and I demonstrated in a study of memo-writing in role-play sessions, writers create and extend their roles *through* their use of strategies conventionally associated with or implied by a writer's conception of goals, strategies, audience, and text structure/genre (Beach and Anson 1988). For example, in writing a book review, a writer may initially assume the role of "friend and admirer" and praise the author, but then, in showing the weaknesses of the author's current book, switch to the role of "critic." The writer then assesses whether the strategies or styles used are consistent with his or her role.

Students, however, often have difficulty defining their roles, because many are learning to accommodate the somewhat unfamiliar, formal "student" or "academic" roles constituted by "academic discourse" (Bartholomae 1985; Shaughnessy 1977). For example, some students experience "role ambiguity" in switching from "expressive" writing to more "transactional" writing, which requires a more "authoritative" stance (Ronald 1986). And, if students do not have a clear sense of purpose and audience constituting the meaning of a social context, they may also have an unclear sense of their role.

When I perceive that students do not have a clear sense of their role or orientation, or that they are experiencing "role ambiguity," given what I impute to be the student's purpose and audience, I demonstrate how I would define my own role.

The Judging Stage

Having described these components of the rhetorical context, writers then judge their texts, defining obstacles to achieving their goals. In defining problems, they detect dissonance between goals and text, dissonance that serves as an incentive to revise.

In attempting to describe their goal/topic, goal/audience, strategies, and text structure, writers often create what they believe is a representation of their essay consisting of ideal goals — what they had hoped to accomplish as opposed to what they actually accomplished.

Unfortunately, as Flower, Hayes, Carey, Schriver, and Stratman (1986) point out, these ideal goals are "not a nicely-formed, idealized version of a text — a sort of Platonic template for easy comparison" (29). They often consist of a series of disparate goal/content, goal/audience, or strategy intentions. Unless students can distinguish between their text and their goals, they will have difficulty judging the draft.

Even if they can distinguish text and goals, many students in our research (Beach and Eaton 1984) had difficulty recognizing any dissonance between goals and text. If students can envision a frustrated reader whose expectations have not been fulfilled by the paper, they may be more likely to recognize the dissonance.

In order to demonstrate ways of sensing dissonance, I go back and describe goals, strategies, characteristics of audience, and text structure. I then review the text from the perspective of an audience member with one of these characteristics — for example, as "someone who knows little about book publishing" — and cite instances in which I, as reader, didn't have enough background information to understand the draft. Given the writer's goal of informing the reader about book publishing, she or he begins to recognize that, from the reader's perspective, something's amiss.

Beyond Detection: Defining Reasons for Problems

Once writers sense the dissonance, they need to specify the reason for the problem, why something is amiss. Students do find it awkward to make explicit their reasons for problems, because they are accustomed to subconsciously applying tacit knowledge of conventions. One purpose of assessing in the conference is to help students make explicit their assessing processes.

Without specifying reasons for problems, students have difficulty selecting appropriate revisions, the next phase in the process. Writers may often simply detect a problem, sensing that some difficulty exists — "something's not right here," "this doesn't sound good" — but fail to explain the problem by citing specific reasons for it. These judgments don't point toward any predicted solutions, because they are too vague. In contrast, judgments such as, "I don't have enough examples to support my thesis," imply some specific remedies: add more examples.

This is not to suggest that writers necessarily must articulate a reason for the problem in order to revise. Writers may sense that something's wrong, and then, employing a "detect/rewrite strategy" (Flower, Hayes, Carey, Schriver, and Stratman 1986), simply rewrite texts according to the same set of propositions, or gist. Simply restating or recasting the same semantic content, however, may avoid dealing with larger problems of meaning affecting the draft.

In order to demonstrate the process of moving from initial detection to defining of reasons, I try to show students that the act of detecting problems, alone, is not sufficient to help them predict appropriate revisions. I take a reaction such as "this doesn't sound right," and try to use it to specify possible solutions, showing the student that it leads me nowhere. I then infer a more diagnostic reaction, for example, "Given my audience's knowledge, readers won't understand the concept of 'mindfulness' because my definition is too technical." By defining a potential audience attribute and potential audience frustration, I specify the problem in terms of a certain strategy — defining. Naming or categorizing the problem in terms of a strategy, I can then draw on what I know about defining to predict appropriate revisions. I show the student that by specifying reasons for problems, I evoke or activate my knowledge of strategies in order to predict appropriate revisions.

Specifying Criteria

Students also need to specify criteria that imply appropriate revisions. They may have difficulty specifying their reasons, because they may not understand — or know how to apply — criteria such as sufficiency, relevancy, validity, clarity, appropriateness, or coherence. For example, one student thinks there is a problem with her extended illustration of an ineffective teaching technique, but she can't define the reason for the problem. First I show her how to define a reason for this problem. Having defined her strategy, *giving examples,* I infer implied criteria — relevancy, sufficiency, or clarity of the information in terms of illustrating the point. I then ask, given her goals and audience characteristics, is this a problem of relevancy, sufficiency, or clarity? I note that from my perspective as reader, the illustration is too long. This suggests that sufficiency of information serves as a useful criteria for selecting and testing appropriate revisions. The student will then begin to recognize the value of specifying criteria in order to make revisions.

However, judgments cannot be made in a vacuum. To judge their draft using these criteria, students need to cycle back to the description phase. Given their descriptions of goals, audience, strategies, and text structure, they can then judge their draft.

When students begin to make judgments but fail to cycle back to their descriptions, I again demonstrate, using their descriptions, how to judge sufficiency, relevancy, and so on, according to their perceptions of the rhetorical context.

Selecting and Testing Appropriate Revisions

Once writers have defined a problem, they select and test those revisions that will best solve it. A writer may select a certain revision strategy — adding, deleting, modifying, rewording, truncating, reorganizing — and/or formulate the content involved in using that revision strategy ("I will add more information about the appearance of the house"). In selecting strategies and/or content, writers are also selecting a certain "level" of revision. The "level" of revision refers to the extent to which they may primarily retain their semantic content, employing a "detect/rewrite" strategy (Flower, Hayes, Carey, Schriver, and Stratman 1986), or whether they want to change the semantic content by making more substantive revisions.

For example, a writer may decide simply to delete a sentence that says the same thing as a preceding sentence, a revision that primarily retains the meaning of the text. Or the writer may decide to reorganize a report according to a different set of categories more familiar to the audience, recasting information but communicating the same meaning. At a higher level, she may apply a different perspective to the text, discovering a different goal, changing her role, or reconceiving her relationship with the audience. In selecting these "high level" revisions that change meaning, the writer must cycle back and redefine her context.

Thus, making "high level" revisions involves more than simply changing text. It involves changing meaning, realigning one's conception of the social context and relationship with audience. In adopting a different perspective, a writer might realize that while initially he was placating the audience, he may now be threatening that audience. In deciding whether such realignment is appropriate, the writer must rely on his own attitudes or beliefs, as illustrated in one of Sommers's (1978) case-study subjects, who noted that he deleted all expressions of his own personal opinions to avoid making waves.

Difficulties in Selecting Revisions

Just as writers' descriptions imply judgments, their judgments imply appropriate revisions. If their information is irrelevant, then they need to delete that information or make it more relevant. However, when students in our study were asked to answer the question on the form, "What are you going to do about your problem?" many had difficulty identifying possible revisions, because they hadn't clearly defined the problem or reasons for the problem (Beach and Eaton 1984).

In these instances, I go back to the judging stage and demonstrate how specifying problems and reasons for problems implies revisions. For example, having judged a part of a text as irrelevant, I show students how that judgment implies different options or levels of revision.

Testing Optional Revisions

Once students select a revision, they are often satisfied that it is appropriate, but they fail to consider why or how it works in light of their goals, strategies, and characteristics of audience. For example, in writing about police corruption, a student notes that he wants to add some more examples of police corruption, but he doesn't know *why* he's adding the examples. I then show him how to review the revision in terms of his goals, strategies, or audience characteristics. The student soon realizes that the additional examples help bolster his charge — his central point — that police corruption exists in all areas of society. Having reaffirmed his goal, he can test whether each additional example suppports his contention that "corruption is everywhere."

In showing students how to justify their revisions by considering their goals, strategies, or audience characteristics, I illustrate that assessing is recursive — that writers must continually cycle back to (and redefine or reaffirm) their conceptions of the rhetorical context.

From Modeling to Student Comprehension and Application

Those, then, are some of the techniques of assessing that I demonstrate in the conference. In most cases, I demonstrate no more than one or two of these techniques in any one conference. Otherwise, as several contributors to this volume aptly caution, I end up dominating the conference rather than having the student practice his own assessing. After I complete my demonstration, I ask the student whether he understands the technique I demonstrated. If the student hasn't understood the technique, I repeat the demonstration until I am confident that she not only conceptually grasps the technique, but can also use it in assessing her own writing.

In subsequent conferences, I often find that my demonstrations have benefitted students who are able to use these techniques on their own, either in the conferences or on the guided assessing forms. To evaluate the influence of the demonstrations, I studied one teacher's use of demonstration with a group of eight college freshmen enrolled in a remedial composition course (Beach 1977). I analyzed (1) the transcripts of conferences and the students' assessing forms for evidence of students' use of assessing techniques, and (2) the students' revisions from the beginning to the end of the course. Over time, most students demonstrated marked changes, particularly in their ability to describe goals and strategies and to use those descriptions to judge their drafts and make revisions that improved their writing.

If learning to assess drafts is central to learning to revise and improve writing quality, then demonstrating these assessing techniques assumes a central role in composition instruction. In addition, because these techniques are merely formalizations of what skilled writers do when they assess their own or someone else's writing, showing students how to use the techniques helps them to view written discourse as the embodiment of intentions within the context of real social and pragmatic purposes.

Acknowledgments

An earlier version of this chapter was published in *College Composition and Communication,* February 1986, 37:56–65.

References

Applebee, A. 1984. *Contexts for Learning to Write.* Norwood, N.J.: Ablex.

Baker, L., and A. Brown. 1984. Cognitive Monitoring in Reading. In *Understanding Reading Comprehension,* edited by J. Flood, 21–44. Newark, Del.: International Reading Association.

Bartholomae, D. 1985. Inventing the University. In *When a Writer Can't Write,* edited by M. Rose, 134–65. New York: Guilford.

Beach, R. 1976. Self-Evaluation Strategies of Extensive Revisers and Non-Revisers. *College Composition and Communication* 27:160–64.

Beach, R. 1977. The Self-Assessing Strategies of Remedial College Students. Paper presented at the annual meeting of the American Educational Research Association, New York.

Beach, R. 1982. The Pragmatics of Self-Assessing. In *Revising: New Essays for Teachers of Writing,* edited by R. Sudol, 71–87. Urbana, Ill.: National Council of Teachers of English.

Beach, R. 1985. The Effects of Modeling on College Freshmen's Self-Assessing. Unpublished research report. University of Minnesota.

Beach, R., and C. M. Anson. 1988. The Pragmatics of Memo Writing: Developmental Differences in the Use of Rhetorical Strategies. *Written Communication* 5:157–83.

Beach, R., and S. Eaton. 1984. Factors Influencing Self-Assessing and Revising by College Freshmen. In *New Directions in Composition Research,* edited by R. Beach and L. S. Bridwell, 149–70. New York: Guilford.

Beach, R., and J. Liebman-Kleine. 1986. The Writing/Reading Relationship: Becoming One's Own Best Reader. In *Convergences: Transactions in Reading and Writing,* edited by B. Petersen, 64–81. Urbana, Ill.: National Council of Teachers of English.

Bizzell, P. 1978. The Ethos of Academic Discourse. *College Composition and Communication* 29:351–55.

Bleich, D. 1983. Discerning Motives in Language Use. In *Composition and Literature: Bridging the Gap,* edited by W. Horner, 81–96. Chicago: University of Chicago Press.

Bleich, D. 1986. Cognitive Stereoscopy and the Study of Language and Literature. In *Convergences: Transactions in Reading and Writing,* edited by B. Petersen, 99–114. Urbana, Ill.: National Council of Teachers of English.

Bloom, L. 1985. Anxious Writers in Context: Graduate School and Beyond. In *When a Writer Can't Write,* edited by M. Rose, 119–33. New York: Guilford.

Brandt, D. 1986. Social Foundations of Reading and Writing. In *Convergences: Transactions in Reading and Writing,* edited by B. Petersen, 115–26. Urbana, Ill.: National Council of Teachers of English.

Burleson, B., and K. Rowan. 1985. Are Social-Cognitive Ability and Narrative Writing Skill Related? *Written Communication* 2:25–43.

Calfee, R., and R. Curley. 1984. Structures of Prose in Content Areas. In *Understanding Reading Comprehension,* edited by J. Flood, 161–80. Newark, Del.: International Reading Association.

Cooper, M. 1984. The Pragmatics of Form: How Do Writers Discover What to Do When? In *New Directions in Composition Research,* edited by R. Beach and L. S. Bridwell, 109–21. New York: Guilford.

Daly, J. 1985. Writing Apprehension. In *When a Writer Can't Write,* edited by M. Rose, 43–82. New York: Guilford.

Faigley, L., R. D. Cherry, D. A. Jolliffe, and A. M. Skinner. 1985. *Assessing Writers' Knowledge and Processes of Composing.* Norwood, N.J.: Ablex.

Fish, S. 1980. *Is There a Text in This Class?* Cambridge: Harvard University Press.

Flower, L., and J. Hayes. 1981. The Pregnant Pause: An Inquiry into the Nature of Planning. *Research in the Teaching of English* 15:229–43.

Flower, L., and J. Hayes. 1984. Images, Plans, and Prose: The Representation of Meaning in Writing. *Written Communication* 1:120–60.

Flower, L., J. Hayes, L. Carey, K. Schriver, and J. Stratman. 1986. Detection, Diagnosis, and the Strategies of Revision. *College Composition and Communication* 37:16–55.

Harris, M. 1983. Modeling: A Process Method of Teaching. *College English* 45:74–84.

Harris, M. 1985. Diagnosing Writing-Process Problems: A Pedagogical Application of Speaking-Aloud Protocol Analysis. In *When a Writer Can't Write,* edited by M. Rose, 166–81. New York: Guilford.

Hunt, R., and D. Vipond. 1984. Point-Driven Understanding: Pragmatic and Cognitive Dimensions of Literary Reading. *Poetics* 13:261–77.

Leech, G. 1983. *Principles of Pragmatics.* New York: Longman.

Levinson, S. 1983. *Pragmatics.* Cambridge: Cambridge University Press.

McCarthy, P., S. Meier, and R. Rinderer. 1985. Self-Efficacy and Writing: A Different View of Self-Evaluation. *College Composition and Communication* 36:465–71.

Meyer, B. 1975. *The Organization of Prose and Its Effects on Memory.* New York: Elsevier North-Holland.

Murray, D. M. 1985. *A Writer Teaches Writing.* 2d ed. Boston: Houghton Mifflin.

Nold, E. 1982. Revising: Intentions and Conventions. In *Revising: New Essays for Teachers of Writing,* edited by R. Sudol, 12–23. Urbana, Ill.: National Council of Teachers of English.

Ong, W. J. 1975. The Writer's Audience Is Always a Fiction. *Publication of the Modern Language Association* 90:9–21.

Perl, S. 1979. The Composing Processes of Unskilled College Writers. *Research in the Teaching of English* 13:317–36.

Ronald, K. L. 1986. The Self and the Other in the Process of Composing: Implications for Integrating the Acts of Reading and Writing. In *Convergences: Transactions in Reading and Writing*, edited by B. Petersen, 231–45. Urbana, Ill.: National Council of Teachers of English.

Rose, M. 1980. Rigid Rules, Inflexible Plans, and the Stifling of Language: A Cognitivist Analysis of Writer's Block. *College Composition and Communication* 31:389–401.

Rose, M. 1984. *Writer's Block: The Cognitive Dimension*. Carbondale: Southern Illinois University Press.

Rose, M. 1985. Writer's Block: Thoughts on Composing-Process Research. In *When a Writer Can't Write*, edited by M. Rose, 227–60. New York: Guilford.

Rubin, D. 1984. Social Cognition and Written Communication. *Written Communication* 1:211–45.

Rubin, D., G. Piche, M. Michlin, and F. Johnson. 1984. Social Cognitive Ability as a Predictor of the Quality of Fourth-Graders' Written Narratives. In *New Directions in Composition Research*, edited by R. Beach and L. S. Bridwell, 297–308. New York: Guilford.

Selfe, C. 1986. Reading as a Writing Strategy: Two Case Studies. In *Convergences: Transactions in Reading and Writing*, edited by B. Petersen, 46–63. Urbana, Ill.: National Council of Teachers of English.

Shaughnessy, M. 1977. *Errors and Expectations*. New York: Oxford University Press.

Sommers, N. 1978. Revision in the Composing Process: A Case Study of College Experienced Adult Writers. Unpublished doctoral dissertation, Boston University.

Sommers, N. 1980. Revision Strategies of Student Writers and Experienced Adult Writers. *College Composition and Communication* 31:378–87.

8 Responding to Student Journals

Toby Fulwiler
University of Vermont

Journal writing tells teachers more about what students know and don't know than more formal assignments designed specifically to find these things out. In fact, the personal, expressive language of journals reveals not only student knowledge, but how students construct that knowledge, and how they feel about what they've constructed. For teachers interested in both the product and process of learning, journals are the most comprehensive writing assignments available. At the same time, the informal, subjective, self-expressive nature of this rhetorical form makes it the most undervalued, misunderstood, and seldom used of the major modes of academic discourse, in virtually all subject areas of the curriculum.

While journals may promote personal learning, they also promote some anxiety on the part of teachers who would incorporate them smoothly into classroom settings: What ground rules govern the use of classroom journals? How do they relate to other course assignments? What direction should teachers provide when assigning journals? When and how should they be read? And, once read, how should teachers respond to or evaluate them? Journals are important, but as academic assignments go, they're also pretty slippery.

The Tradition

Most modern writing assignments are based on traditional rhetorical principles, many dating back to the classical era of Aristotle, Cicero, and Quintilian. Such rhetoric pays relatively little attention to personal forms of discourse, emphasizing instead the public modes of "argumentation, exposition, description, and narration" (Corbett 1971), modes that reemerge in the school curriculum as essays, term papers, and literature reviews — each defined by its own set of formal expectations. Until quite recently, formal training in writing meant learning variations of these fairly mixed formulations of language (Knoblauch and Brannon 1984). While exceptions existed in the remarkable books of Ken Macrorie (1970), James Moffett (1968), Peter Elbow (1973), and a few others, most rhetorics and handbooks written for college freshmen continue to emphasize the public modes, most often reducing the personally expressive to something rather nebulously called "prewriting."

However, the work of James Britton and his colleagues at the University of London has placed expressive modes of discourse at the very center of the rhetorical world. Britton (1970), drawing upon the work of Sapir, Vygotsky, Gusdorf, and others, describes expressive discourse as "what runs through our minds" (169) and expressive writing as "the earliest forms of written down speech" (174). Britton considers expressive language the matrix from which the other two modes, transactional and poetic, arise.

Recent surveys (Applebee 1981; Britton et al. 1975) which look at the kind of writing assigned in secondary education reveal that remarkably little attention is being paid to expressive writing, especially outside the English class. These surveys raise certain questions about the role of discourse in American schools and colleges, where so many of our attitudes toward language are shaped. If we know that when we use language, we generate thought, why do the generative uses of language — which here I will simply call expressive — play so insignificant a role in secondary and higher education, where the business of the day is learning and learning to think? Could it be demonstrated that expressive discourse, the central feature of contemporary rhetoric, should likewise become a central feature in contemporary education?

Notes toward an Alternative Curriculum

The minimal role played by expressive discourse in American education recently led me to reconsider how I assigned, responded to, and evaluated writing when I taught college literature classes. When I teach literature to undergraduates, especially to freshmen and sophomores, my primary job is to help them learn about, learn from, and appreciate literary art. In other words, it is their attitude, understandings, and learning that I care about first; other things, including their reading, writing, and speaking skills or their knowledge of terms, come second. Yet when I reviewed my own stated objectives in light of my assignments, I encountered what I would now call a major discrepancy:

traditionally I assigned several short papers, a midterm and final exam, and a journal. Typically, I counted the short papers and the exams as about 90% of a student's grade, and the journal 10%, if that. While I believed that I valued — and therefore emphasized — the *process* of learning, my assignments suggested that I really valued the *product* of learning — the demonstrations of skills and knowledge in the formal papers and examinations. The journal, in which the students and I wrote daily in class, and which I collected and read three or four times a term, hardly counted for anything when it came to assessing or measuring student learning.

Is it consistent to ask students to become independent learners in their journals, and then to turn around and measure them according to their ability to replicate a few limited and fixed forms of discourse? At best we give a mixed message; at worst we teach caution, conformity, and obedience.

So I stopped teaching this way. I abandoned all fixed-format and formal writing assignments. I no longer required the out-of-class essays and reviews, and I stopped giving examinations of any kind. In their place I asked students to keep what I called "dialogue journals," hoping to promote an ongoing course-long conversation between the students and their ideas and between me and the students. They would write as they felt; I would respond as I liked.

On the first day of class I explained how the course would work, allowing time for drops and transfers: (1) students would be expected to write in the journals daily, both in class and out; (2) periodically I would collect, read, and respond to the journals; and (3) at the end of the term I would assign each journal a grade (Fulwiler 1979). Good journals, I pointed out, would be long, frequently used, and thoughtful. As the course progressed, we talked further about what those characteristics meant. Among other things, these assumptions meant that the journal constituted all the written work in the course. (In subsequent years, partly in response to student recommendations, I added back a take-home or open-book final exam which counted about 20% of each student's final grade.) began to emphasize and "count" journal writing for two reasons: First, I wanted to rectify a contradiction between what I said and what my assignments said; second, I felt quite certain that I would learn more about both the quality and quantity of student learning from the journals than from the formal writing. Now I would have to make this difference clear to the students — and before I could do that, I would have to articulate the difference more carefully to myself.

The Mind at Work

I used journals heavily in those literature classes, asking for two to three times the amount of writing I had ever assigned before. We used journals as many teachers of writing across the curriculum have learned to use them: to respond to questions and readings in the course, to connect personal experience with class content, to reflect on anything related to literature, to monitor the students' own learning, and to carry on a dialogue with me (Gere 1985; Thaiss 1982; Wotring and Tierney 1981).

Some samples of journal writing will illustrate more precisely how journals promote learning. I have selected three entries from the journal of a former student, written for an introductory class in American literature. Margaret was a fairly quiet first-year student, taking English as an elective, planning to major in business. She wrote the following entries in response to my standing assignment to record each of her encounters with the authors we read in the course — in this case, three modern American poets. Margaret's writing is more typical than not of first-year college writers. Consider first her response to Robert Frost's poem, "Mending Wall," and notice the features that typify journal writing. (This passage and the two following have been segmented for ease of reference; the actual entries had no paragraph divisions.)

> October 30
>
> "Mending Wall" is literally about two neighbors mending a wall between their two yards. One of the neighbors, who happens to be a poet, is wondering why they mend the wall every year when all they are separating [is] only pine and apple trees. He doesn't want to tell his neighbor that he doesn't think it's right to keep repairing the wall. He things the neighbor should come up with it. But every year they keep repairing the wall that deteriorates somehow along the way. He says sometimes it could be that the ground swells in the winter or that when the hunters go looking for rabbits, they are reckless. There is also "something" that he says makes the wall deteriorate but he doesn't know what it is.
>
> A confusing part in the poem is when he talks about elves. I don't really understand what he means by that. It obviously doesn't have much to do with the literal interpretation of the poem. It could have some symbolic meaning, which it probably does, but I don't know what it is. Also, the "something" that I mentioned before is confusing. It symbolizes something too, probably.
>
> Maybe this poem is talking about how people build walls between themselves and Frost is telling people about it. He is questioning

> why people do this and maybe he's telling how some people do too but they may just go along with tradition or past experience or whatever it may be called. People just don't have the guts to speak up about some things and maybe he's saying that they should. I think he wrote it to tell people not to build walls between each other when actually they serve no purpose.

In this journal entry, Margaret does not write a formal interpretation of "Mending Wall," but rather tries to make sense of the poem. We can readily identify her methodical, survey-like approach: First she explains what the poem says on the surface, looking for language she's familiar with; next, she writes about language she's not familiar with, where she's confused; and finally, she generates a hypothesis, telegraphed by the word "maybe," which tentatively explains that the poem is "about how people build walls between themselves." This is an approach many of us would use to solve a language problem — exactly what poetry represents to so many students.

In helping her to solve problems, Margaret's writing is fairly ego-centric, full of first-person references, especially in the middle passage where she writes "I don't really understand" and "I don't know what it is." In fact, these lines show her doubt and confusion, admitted here as she talks out loud to herself, on paper; but they also tell us something about the writer herself. We learn, for example, that she is a careful reader and a methodical thinker, as well as a good problem solver — and that she's not afraid to share momentary confusion with a trusted teacher. Moreover, we see some familiarity with previous literary instruction when she guesses that certain words probably "have some symbolic meaning." Her knowledge that poetry is often symbolic leads to her tentative hypothesis about walls. She also reveals something of her own personal values when she talks about people not having "the guts to speak up" and about walls "serv[ing] no purpose." And, of course, we learn that she is not afraid to reveal ignorance or ask questions, which implies that she trusts her reader not to exploit these admissions of uncertainty.

Modes of Response

From our own analytical perspectives, we can make many interesting observations about Margaret's journal writing. But what would we write back to her? I might, for instance, (1) applaud her separation of the literal from the symbolic in the poem; (2) question her about her previous experience with "symbolic meaning" which, judging from her language, was perhaps a rather confusing one; (3) discuss "elves" with her; or (4) ask about the elements in the poem she ignored and ask why. Above all, I would attempt to carry on a critical dialogue with her, applauding or disagreeing with her interpretation if I felt like it, but not "correcting" it. The journal has done its work by providing the place, time, and context for deliberative, interpretive thinking.

In this case, I wrote no response to Margaret's individual entry on "Mending Wall," since we discussed all the student journal entries the next day, in class. I asked Margaret and her classmates to share their written reactions to Frost's poems with each other in small groups for a few minutes, then we discussed the various problems raised by the poems — including "elves" and "symbolism." The response to Margaret's journal writing in this instance was made by her peers in the context of the class discussion. As it turns out, I did not actually see Margaret's individual thoughts on "Mending Wall" until several weeks *after* we had discussed it, when I collected the journals to read. Though I wrote comments on some of the entries in her journal, I felt that the class discussion of "Mending Wall" had been thorough, and I chose not to comment on opinions which Margaret herself had by then changed.

Consider another of Margaret's entries, this one written the next day, after reading W. H. Auden's poem, "The Unknown Citizen."

> Oct. 31. I read the Unknown Citizen. I like this poem a lot. It seems to be so true. At first when I read the last two lines, I didn't understand them but after I read them again I understood what he was trying to say. It seems to be true that everyone wants to be the perfect person and cause no trouble or be different. The author considers this good when everything is normal, nothing unique or showing the citizen's personality. They don't want any problems.

> But then the poet asks if he was happy? How could he be when he never really did anything according to the records. He must have lead a very boring life. He couldn't have been free either because all he did was follow the norms of society. He didn't want to differ from being normal so he was always a slave to these roles and expectations of others. When there was war, he went to war, as was expected of every good American. When the country was not at war he was keeping it that way. He didn't want to show any radical ideas.

> It is true that humans don't want to differ from the normal because I was reading my sociology and some experiments they do show it. Like if everyone else in a group picked a line that was obviously shorter than the others and said it was the longest, the next guy would agree outloud even though he didn't really agree. No one wants to be different . . . .

In this entry, we see Margaret struggling with a satirical poem, in which Auden apparently criticizes the government's attempt to keep quantitative records on its citizens, pointing out that such records are rather empty documents when it comes to revealing anything about the quality of citizens' lives. In writing about the poem, Margaret reveals that she does not fully understand Auden's satire; such understandings will have to wait for further reading or class discussion. But look further at the nature of her thinking, as well as the subtle relationship she establishes between herself as writer and us as readers.

Because this is a journal entry, it would be inappropriate to comment on the vague pronoun reference, grammatical slips, missing active verbs, overly colloquial language, misspellings, and inappropriate punctuation. Nor would we need to comment on missing scholarly apparatus such as titles, subtitles, footnotes, references, or bibliographies. While conventional or academic aspects of writing are important — in their place — they have little to do with my understanding of Margaret's understanding — which is my primary day-to-day business as a teacher. At other times, or in other courses, my business might be to pay attention to those other things, but not now.

I learn here about Margaret's initial encounter with Auden. She likes his poem immediately, though she is somewhat confused about the last two lines. She reads the poem in light of her personal values, noting that the life led by this statistical manikin seems to her quite "boring," and, in its thorough normality, is also slave-like.

As a liberal arts instructor, I am also pleased that she uses concepts learned in another class — sociology — to make sense out of related material in my class. At the same time, I notice that she introduces this outside information in an overly generalized manner and that she expresses too much rote confidence in the sociological knowledge ("It is true that . . ."). But note that the journal gives me this information in a mode that does not threaten the student because she won't be graded on it here; later, looking at the whole journal, I will grade — but not during the term and never on any one entry. Together we can talk about how she discovers what she knows and how she approaches what she doesn't know. Margaret does not need to impress me, and I do not need to correct her.

In this case, I wrote a brief note to Margaret about her mention of the sociology class, asking whether she thought that Auden might be making fun of the kind of statistical truths that both governments and sociologists generate. But that was the end of our exchange there, as far as I ever knew. I used the journal as the excuse to plant some ideas of what I thought the poem was about, but again, I believe the class discussion on Auden had already added to her interpretation of this poem.

In another of Margaret's entries, written a few days later, she tries to come to grips with Gwendolyn Brooks's contemporary short poem, "We Real Cool."

> Nov. 5 The poem We Real Cool by Gwendolyn Brooks is kind of neat. The structure is interesting. They don't write one whole sentence on one line, but they separate the sentences by putting we on one line and the rest on the next. I don't know if that's supposed to mean anything but it is different and just about any reader would probably notice it. It seems like its grammatically wrong but there's only a couple of sentences that aren't. Like we real cool and we Jazz June which must mean something because those words are capitalized. It could mean any number of things, though. Its pretty straight forward except for this line.
>
> It says that these boys are neat because they dropped out of high school. They stay out late and they know how to shoot pool well. They're always talking about sin, swearing and stuff, although they do have to water down their booze, but then Jazz June doesn't make any sense and why do they die soon? Maybe just because they get into so much trouble they're going to end up in jail or something. I can't figure out that one line. Maybe they just live it up, jazz it up in June and are really going to make a nuisance of themselves then. I really don't have any ideas about that line. I still wonder what the structure of the poem has to do with anything. Maybe we is an important part of the sentence and it should be separated in the poet's opinion. Maybe he wants you to know that the boys stick together through thick and thin.
>
> Actually it doesn't even have to be boys. All it says is the Pool Players, Seven at the Golden Shovel. There could be girls in this bunch too. Our stereotypes just don't let me think that girls hang around somewhere playing pool. Why is it that girls it seems, don't ever play pool? Is it not feminine or something? I used to play all the time and so did my sisters but we never played anywhere other than at home. That's kind of weird. But anyway, maybe the poem is trying to tell us not to drop out of school because all kinds of problems could come out of it. That's what actually started the poem, they had to leave school because they were too cool for it and then their troubles started. Maybe that's the underlying meaning here. I can't see any other possibilities right now.

Here, Margaret works hard to wrest meaning from a poem alien to her personal experience in both voice and subject. She wonders about the structure, the word combinations, the street-talk rhythm, the capitalization of certain words, and the moral of it all. As she does this, she pays little attention to propriety in her own writing and actually mistakes simple pronoun references: at different points she calls the author of the poem "they" and "he." She makes these slips thoughtlessly — without thinking — because her mind is focused on the language of the poem rather than on the language in which she writes about the poem. I have little doubt that she could straighten out her references to the author if that were important; in the journal, at this moment, it is not. In fact, at this moment, the writer's linguistic resources actually include pronoun miscues; in the journal we can ignore or applaud them; in formal writing we would do neither.

Notice how Margaret uses the word "maybe" to trigger certain thoughts: to try something out, make a guess, formulate a hypothesis. "Maybe" signals this student's willingness to risk untested thought, witness what it looks like, and discover whether it might warrant further support or development. Note, too, how after one such "maybe" (last section), she moves to an "actually," a word that triggers her awareness of sexist assumptions: "It doesn't even have to be boys." In this digression we witness, graphically, the power of writing to promote insight and self-consciousness, for had she not already written at length about the poem, it is unlikely that she would have witnessed her own biases so clearly. Finally, look at her frequent expression of doubt: "I don't have too many ideas about that line." She continues to feel free to articulate her confusion; in several cases, the very process of articulation helps her unlock that confusion.

This journal entry actually served as the springboard to an extensive and only mildly digressive discussion in class about the nature of sexist assumptions in authorship and readership: Margaret mentioned her concern that "it doesn't even have to be boys," a position some students supported and others questioned. I let the discussion go for a while — not having any real answer myself anyway. In this instance, the class response rewarded Margaret's journal writing; later that week when I again collected journals, I wrote this to her:

> Margaret — It's wonderful to watch you shifting around in this entry. Do you realize that at times you call the author "they" and "he"!! I know how that happens when you read really hard and actually enter into the poet's world. It's a strong poem — and you're right, they *could* be girls in that bunch — I'd never thought of it until you raised the issue in class.

My own responses to these several journal entries, ranging from nothing to a few words to a personal note, illustrate the freedom that journals provide the teacher-responder. Since I commonly use the journal as a springboard to class discussion, I feel that the class itself provides the most vivid and concrete response to each journal writer, including me, since I too read my entries out loud with the students and hear their reactions to what I wrote. When I do respond to journals, every few weeks when I collect samples from the class, I comment on those entries that still interest me and those in which I feel the student most invested. And I respond differently to different students, though I am always basically positive and honest in what I write back.

The Structure of Restless Minds

Kenneth Burke (1950) argues that every statement human beings make falls into a pattern that can be analyzed: "Given enough industry in observation, abstraction, and classification, you can reduce any expression (even inconsequential or incomplete ones) to some underlying skeletal structure" (65). Burke suggests that each emergent form of expression has its own structure, its own dignity. In other words, we do not need to see journal writing as *bad* expository writing, nor *undeveloped* theme writing, nor *failed* referential prose.

When teachers use journals to monitor or assess student knowledge, they tacitly agree to pay considerable attention to the student's own structure of knowledge — a structure more loose, imprecise, and idiosyncratic than that traditionally preferred by teacher or textbook, but a structure nonetheless. In journals, the writer's ideas actually generate their own form, as the writer formulates, shapes, and reformulates them in the process of composing. When composition researcher Linda Flower (1979) studied "writer-based prose" (writing for the writer), she discovered that the "internal structure of the data" actually dictated "the rhetorical structure of the discourse" (28). Literary scholar Morse Peckham (1951) discovered something quite similar in the writing of nineteenth-century Romantic poets and called the structure "organic." From the ridiculous to the sublime? Perhaps — but let's give credit where due: The exploring mind expresses its own structure; journal writing, like Romantic poetry and many modern forms of discourse, structures itself as necessarily, usefully, or playfully as it pleases. The literary scholar might say that form follows content; the rhetorician might say that mode shapes itself according to the needs of audience and purpose.

In other words, the writer's emerging ideas create an organic structure, with strong associational and digressive patterns, as one shade or nuance gives rise to the next. Or as Knoblauch and Brannon (1984) put it more globally: "Making verbal discourse, then, is a process of asserting connections among the ideas, impressions, images, bits and pieces of recollection or research, insights, fragmentary lines of reasoning, feelings, intuitions, and scraps of knowledge that comprise a person's experience of some subject" (68–69). In her text, Margaret initially makes a holistic generalization, then surveys the entire poem from beginning to end, working from what she knows to what she doesn't, asking questions along the way. She also freely associates, allowing one idea or word to suggest the next; still other times she writes rather deliberately in circles, as she returns again and again to the central problem of meaning in the poem — a pattern she also repeats with individual words and lines. While the patterns seem loose, they are far from random or arbitrary; Margaret structures the piece as she thinks it through, purposefully and methodically. This "idea-logical" structure makes the information easy to follow and understand; at the same time it retains the spontaneity and liveliness of good conversation. Such writing is, more than anything else, an individual's own structure of learning, revealing the preconditions, rough edges, emotional entanglements, and all the starts and stops of thought. If we accept the informal structures found in journals as different from, but not necessarily inferior to, more formal structures, then we have laid the foundation for considering journals as serious written documents, worthy of study in their own right.

In describing what happens when writers compose essays, Ross Winterowd (1965) also provides us with a marvelous insight into journal writing: "The communicative act, as Cicero has so well demonstrated, is not simply a matter of formulae and rules. Rather good essays reflect *restless minds*, minds that enjoy turning ideas over, taking them apart to see what makes them tick, and explaining them to others" (93). Good journals, even more than good essays, provide wonderful glimpses of "restless minds."

For my purposes, Margaret's journal is as finished a document as it needs to be (or as unfinished as any document really is). This does not mean she is finished explicating or even understanding Frost or Auden or Brooks or the class or herself. Her understanding will continue to develop from class to class, from course to course, year to year. Nor does it mean, however, that her writing does not need to be "rewritten" or "transformed" or "transitioned" to some other form, format, or formality in order to prove that she possesses a certain kind of literary knowledge. Of course, she could stop her journal writing at any time and craft a formal essay on one of these poems; were she to do that, she would simply learn *different* — not necessarily *better* — things about the poem and herself than if she devotes that same amount of time to more journal writing. I believe the author of these journal entries is, in fact, a fair writer of formal prose. I see evidence of her composing skill through her problem-solving approach to these puzzling poems, her methodical reading ability, her fluent conversational style, and her command of language conventions. Her several superficial errors are *not* errors of ignorance, sloth, or rebellion, but the results of intense concentration as she focuses on meaning — assumptions, self-doubts, and all — rather than on conventions or style.

The Problem of Response and Evaluation

If Margaret's freshman journal makes a convincing case — or even just an intriguing one — about the nature of expressive communication possible through journals, why do so few academics "count" that communication? The answer, I think, is directly related to what journals do best: create personal engagement. Many teachers feel that the learning in journals is too private to witness and too subjective to measure in any way. At least part of this assertion is true: Journals do imply subjectivity, privacy, and even intimacy; they also imply, for the writer, license to think, react, speculate, evaluate, and try things out — freely, without fear of penalty, censorship, or negative commentary of any kind. As soon as outside readers enter the picture in an evaluative role, the nature of the journal inevitably changes, a situation no less troubling for the reader than for the writer.

But while the journal does necessarily change as it moves from a strictly private to semipublic document, it still remains personal, talky, tentative, and loosely structured — difficult to use when impersonal, formal, fixed grades must be determined. If it can't be counted, neither teacher nor student will use or value it. If anything, teachers have been schooled to discount it.

Academics know, of course, how to respond to and measure the discourse modes asked for in the academy, be they narrative, descriptive, persuasive, or argumentative. Regardless of the risk-taking variations often found on the pages of *Esquire, Time,* and *The New Yorker* — not to mention nonfiction bestsellers — such writing in colleges and universities must be clear, precise, coherent, correct, organized, illustrated, and well documented. Despite the difficulty and questionability of writing such prose, English handbooks prescribe it, English professors teach it, and instructors across the curriculum measure student worth, in large part, according to the student's ability to write it (Ohmann 1976, 133–71). The criteria are fairly clear and the tradition deeply rooted — conditions that make variation in mode, or other modes, suspect. If journal writing is ever to achieve some measure of academic respectability, it too must be, to some extent, describable and understandable. In other words, how teachers respond to journal writing will depend on how well they can identify exactly what it is and does — and that identification has yet to be systematically made.

An Alternate Style

Looking at the work of recent language theorists who have studied the general category of personal, expressive discourse, together with our own observations about journal writing, we can begin to describe some language uses and features that the traditional texts say little about.

Britton et al. (1975) describe expressive writing as language close to the writer's self, more particularly: (1) "thinking aloud on paper"; (2) explorations of "the writer's feelings, mood, opinions, preoccupations of the moment"; and (3) cases in which a writer may "actively invoke a close relationship with his reader" (89).

James Kinneavy (1971), thinking primarily about "public" expressive writing, nevertheless identifies semantic features similar to Britton's: (1) "highly subjective" referents; (2) imagistic; (3) "connotative rather than denotative"; (4) "a heavy preponderance of . . . superlatives"; and (5) the clear emergence of an "authentic I" (432–33). In addition, Kinneavy points out that the language often has "the associative rhythm of ordinary speech" (436) and the "situational context" must be explained (438).

Linda Flower (1979) calls expressive discourse "writer-based prose," which she describes as "verbal expression written by a writer to himself and for himself" (19). Flower identifies three principles that characterize such prose: "Its underlying focus is *egocentric;* and it uses either a *narrative* framework or a *survey* form to order ideas" (25). In other words, she defines further what Britton might have meant by the term "relatively unstructured," and gives us more specific criteria to look for in the kind of writing most often found in journals.

Finally, Winston Weathers (1980) identifies a long tradition of "Grammar B" — he calls it an alternate style — that is also more personal and less structured than the more formally organized language of "Grammar A." In making this case, Weathers considers published works from *Tristram Shandy* to *Leaves of Grass* to *The Electric Kool-Aid Acid Test*. While Weathers, like Kinneavy, focuses on deliberately crafted, published prose, his description of useful but unconventional language features includes "crots," "lists," "labyrinthine and fragment sentences," and "language variegation" — which he defines as "pressing against the walls of ordinary/orthodox vocabulary, a playing with words/ word forms to achieve a certain kind of lexical texture — a reading surface that is exciting and rebellious all at once" (14–34).

The Rhetoric of Journals

Putting the general observations from rhetorical theorists together with our specific knowledge of journals leads us to describe some features of expressive discourse in a positive and concrete way. After several years of collecting photocopied student journals, I separated the *A* and *B* journals from the *C* and *D* ones; I then made detailed after-the-fact analysis. Consequently, what I found is basically what I looked for: criteria to help us correlate successful journal writing with successful subject matter learning.

In order to recommend that journals be taken more seriously by the academic community, I have compiled a list of features to use in making judgments on — and in guiding specific responses to — the contents of student journals. In the practice of actually reading journals, it is not useful to take them apart as I have done here; it is useful, however, to compare this alternative rhetoric to traditional modes. The characteristics are divided into three general categories: (1) language features, (2) cognitive activities, and (3) document features.

Language Features

Journal writing is commonly characterized by informal language, similar to that in speech, letters, personal essays, and some journalism and fiction. These features include the following:

Personal voice: The frequent use of "I," suggesting the writer in the active voice, using him- or herself as agent or referent, authority or questioner, and sometimes, giver of answers. In an academic journal these personal pronouns often precede speculations or observations about ideas, data, and personal experience. Look for phrases such as "I think," "I believe," "I wonder," and "I feel" — phrases that indicate the writer's own involvement in a given subject (see Kinneavy 1971, 433).

Conversational tone: An informal attitude toward language, recognized by a variety of shortcuts and expressions common in casual conversations among friends. Journal writing is usually the recording of first utterances; when we write, we typically utter first in language that is most accessible and comfortable for us to use. James Britton et al. (1975) describe such writing as "speech written down." Look for colloquialisms, contractions, generalizations, sentence fragments, and grammatically awkward constructions.

Informal punctuation: Frequent use of shorthand symbols to speed the writing and, perhaps, an absence of formal punctuation and precise reference documentation. Writers commonly refer to books without underlining titles, to articles and poems without using quotation marks, and to authors without documenting sources. In journal writing abbreviations work well; the writer needs just enough to establish meaning at the time — perhaps a little more if the teacher is to be let in, too. Look for frequent dashes, few semicolons, and no footnotes.

Bound context: References in the journal entries that are unexplained and not clear to anybody except the writer or someone very close to the writer — which may or may not include the teacher. Such references indicate a desirable preoccupation with ideas rather than audience. Journal writing should be "close to the self," to use Britton's term. Margaret's references to "my sociology" in her Auden entry and "my sisters" in her Brooks entry might be examples of such relatively unexplained references. They belong there, but the details are not entirely clear to external readers. (See also Kinneavy 1971, 432.)

Experimentation and play: Evidence of poems, songs, sketches, drawings, doodles, imitations, and playful spelling, grammar, and punctuation. The journal is a place to try things out in language. In other written forms this experimentation might count against the writer, suggesting something less serious, more like fooling around. However, these "qualitative" features indicate the writer at work or play with either language or ideas; in journals one must take, expect, even encourage the good with the bad and the ugly. As Kinneavy writes: "The individual who does not revolt against conventional language does not really discover himself" (430). Look for attempts to write in another voice, imitate a certain style, and deliberately eschew punctuation or capitalization. Look also for dialogue, drama, description, verse, or graffiti. (See also Weathers 1980, 30–40.)

Emotion: The presence of words or phrases that convey strong feeling. In formal academic prose, we commonly encourage writers to edit their work carefully, deleting unnecessary editorial words, which often overly color a situation. We also often encourage writers to hold their personal feelings at bay while they explore an idea or concept in an "objective" or "rational" manner. In journal writing we would do neither. A journal devoid of emotive adverbs and adjectives may even raise doubts about the writer's involvement in the subject. In a journal, then, we expect to see the writer using "superlatives": emphasizing, overemphasizing, and revealing biases (see Kinneavy 1971, 432). Furthermore, expressing such biases on paper is one of the best ways to see what they are, how substantial they are, and to what degree they will withstand rigorous scrutiny. Look for words that indicate some feeling, such as "really," "very," "wow," "nuts," and expletives of all sorts.

Scribal error: Mistakes in spelling, punctuation, and grammar; incorrect references; or incomprehensible handwriting. I list this item with tongue only partly in cheek. I still remember one student showing me his neat, carefully written but overly cautious entries of the first several weeks, then flipping to the messy, loosely written, but far bolder entries written ten weeks later: "See, I'm thinking faster than I can write and so my handwriting can't keep up!" Though I laughed at the time, I have since seen many instances where carelessness in transcription results not from ignorance of conventions, but from speed of recording thought. Of course, in formal writing these same features connote unwarranted haste, neglect, or ignorance, and thus result in penalties for the writer. Look for simple errors such as writing "to" for "too" and "right" for "write," subject-verb agreement, stretches of illegible penmanship, and confused pronoun references.

Cognitive Activities

While journals are likely to contain any or all modes of symbolic thought that can be written, sketched, or diagrammed, they are especially useful for encouraging the very modes of thought most valued among academics. The following list is necessarily partial, incomplete, and suggestive; it will, however, indicate the kind of thinking journals encourage.

Observation: Writers record what they see in the most useful language at their command. The simplest observations are sensory experiences, primarily visual, but also aural, tactile, and the like. More complex observations try to capture whole experiences or events. In any case, the key to good observation is being there, finding words to capture what is witnessed, and being able to re-experience it again through reading. In the sciences or social sciences, such observation is often the heart of the scientist's work; journals — or logs or notebooks — allow the scientist to speculate on close observations of data for later use. In the fine arts, observation often plays a similarly significant role. Once they are recorded, the writer can observe and interpret his or her observations, the essential act of the conscious learner (Berthoff 1978, 12). Look for details, examples, measurements, facts, analogies, and descriptive language (color, texture, size, shape, movement, etc.), along with observations about the same.

Speculation: Words or phrases that show the writer wondering "what if?" Speculation, in fact, is the essence of good journals, perhaps the very reason for their existence and importance. Don Murray (1978), who has written extensively about the process of composing, characterizes true composing as "searching for meaning" (86) — the essence of speculation. While speculation is characteristic of other prose forms — critical essays, for example, or the discussion section of laboratory reports — it is risky during exposition, argumentation, or examination. But journals allow the writer to speculate freely, without fear of penalty. Bad speculation and good. Silly as well as productive. Because the bad often clears the way for the good, and the silly sometimes suggests the serious. Look for writers telegraphing their speculations with key words such as "maybe," "perhaps," and "actually," or with phrases such as "what if" and "I wonder."

Confirmation: Evidence from the journal that the student's ideas are being supported or reinforced by the class or teacher. In such cases, students feel good when they write about ideas on their own, then later find those same ideas cropping up, independently, in class discussions or teacher presentation. In fact, this experience generates a sense of learner confidence difficult to plan for, but important to happen. Journals prove to be one of the few ways for students to monitor this occurrence consciously — far more reliable than occasional after-class conversations, for instance. Used in this manner, journals invite planned preclass rehearsal of ideas and so create a climate in which such confirmatory experiences are likely to occur. Look for such recordings, especially in entries written after class on the days in which significant class discussion occurs.

Doubt: The writer doesn't know or isn't sure about something and records that uncertainty in the journal. The journal is one of the few places in the academic world where — in writing — such frank admissions of ignorance have a place. It is all right for a student to admit orally, in or after class, that he or she doesn't know an answer or doesn't understand something; it is another thing altogether to admit that on an examination or in a formal essay. In the journal one expects to write about what one does not know as well as what one does. Another name for a journal? A doubt book. (See also Kinneavy's notion of self-confession [1971, 436], an activity characteristic of expressive discourse.) Look for phrases such as "What's that supposed to mean?" and "I just don't get this."

Questions: Evidence of curiosity in written language. Good thinkers ask lots of questions, perhaps more than they are able to answer. Questions indicate that something is happening — in this case, that there may be some disequilibrium or uncertainty in the writer's mind, and that he or she is willing to explore it through language. Again, the ability to *see* one's questions certainly helps sharpen, clarify, and understand them better. The frequency of questions in journal entries is one of the best indicators of overall quality. The mere fact that the questions are raised is more important than whether subsequent journal entries lead to answers. Look for lots of question marks.

Self-awareness: Words and phrases that indicate the writer is conscious of him- or herself as a learner and thinker. Self-awareness seems to be a necessary precondition to both higher-order reasoning and mature social interaction. In describing the active mind as a "composer," Berthoff (1978) claims that "there's something to be learned by observing it in operation" (12). Journals are places where writers can actually monitor and witness the evolution of this process — and the teacher, looking over the writer's shoulder, looks too for each writer's effort to achieve insight (Dixon 1968). Instructors can encourage or nourish self-awareness by asking frequent questions: "What did you learn in class today?" or "What have you learned so far?" Look for phrases such as "actually," "I think," "I just realized," and "wait a minute."

Connections: Evidence that writers see ideas or material from one course in relation to another course or to other events in their personal lives. Journals encourage such connecting, because no one is insisting that writers stick to one organized, well-documented subject. Connections can be loose or tight, tangential or direct; nevertheless, they are connections made by the writer, not someone else. As Knoblauch and Brannon put it, "the business of making connections . . . is the essence of composing" (1984, 69). Look for references such as those Margaret made about sociology in her Auden entry.

Digressions: Indications that the act of writing has caused the writer to wander away from the subject about which he or she began to write. Sometimes this results in what Peter Elbow (1973) calls "garbage"; however, he would also remind us that "meaning is not what you start out with but what you end up with" (15). Digression is new thought in unpredictable directions; it is one of the clearest positive things that happens when people freewrite or write in journals. Digressions, which are characteristic of good conversations and good reading experiences alike, suggest that the writer's mind is mixing academic matters with personal ideas or experience — or simply that the writer's mind is active and the writer is capturing a record of that activity. The value, of course, is that digression indicates exploration initiated by the act of writing — exploration that may be internal, into one's own head; or external, out into the world of sights, sounds, objects, and symbols. Digressions are positive in journals, but negative in every other type of formal academic writing. Look for references to the writer's family, friends, or personal experiences (such as Margaret's free association about playing pool while reading the poem "We Real Cool").

Dialogue: The writer using the journal to write directly to the teacher, expecting a response. When journals are assigned by instructors in academic settings, there is an explicit contract between teacher and student that entries related to the subject matter of the specific course will be shared. Such journals are "dialogical." I do not expect complete candor of writers who know they must share their observations with an outsider who will eventually grade them; after a few weeks, however, I am surprised if some frank dialogue does not take place through the medium of the journal. Look for direct questions and observations addressed to you.

Information: References to the subject matter of the course. Ironically, unlike a class notebook, such evidence is often the least interesting for writers to write and readers to read; however, such "Cliff Notes stuff," as one freshman called it, usually serves the writer more as a record than anything else — and these same references supply the teacher with the kind of evidence otherwise discoverable primarily in daily quizzes or homework. Look for names, dates, formulae, ideas, outlines, summaries from books, lectures, or class discussions, but don't dwell on them.

Revision: Has the writer looked back in the journal and changed his or her mind on a subject written about earlier? If so, this suggests the writer is conscious of his or her thought and is making some effort to reexamine, modify, and change it — which is, of course, evidence of some intellectual growth. Berthoff (1978) advocates what she calls a "double-entry notebook," in which writers return periodically to reflect upon previous entries — her idea, in other words, is to build opportunities for revision into the journal itself. An additional kind of revision occurs when the writer takes a journal entry and forges it into a full-fledged formal paper, an idea nicely articulated by Ken Macrorie (1970), among many others. Look for words and phrases that indicate reconsideration or reflection, such as "I just realized," "Back in September I wrote," or "When the course began."

Posing and solving problems: The writer examining an issue and redefining it in his or her own terms — perhaps answering it as well. Good journals will give some evidence of both activities. It matters little whether the problem is posed well, or whether the solution actually works. (If the problems are consistently ill-defined and the solutions always off-base, that does matter; but here, the journal will

be invaluable in another way, as an early clue to the student's difficulty.)
According to Paulo Friere (1970), individuals must articulate problems
in their own language in order to experience authentic growth —
journals are, perhaps, the best place in the academic world in which
to do that. Evidence of posing and solving problems — whether literary,
social, scientific, or mechanical — suggests that there is life in the
writer's mind, original thinking, and care enough about the subject.
Look for examples of questions treated in a careful or extended manner
and subsequent attempts at answers.

Document Features

Some indicators of quality in journals are formal; that is, they derive
from the very form, structure, and nature of the journal as a written
document — which, of course, allows for anything. But we can make
some comments of a practical nature in this area as well, so long as
we don't turn them into prescriptions.

Frequent entries: How often the students write in their journals.
Regular writing is one of the best indicators that the journal is being
taken seriously; sheer quantity is a sign that the student has spent
time writing, which in turn increases the likelihood that the journal
will be useful to the writer. When someone asks me what a good
journal is, I often answer, "a long one." Count the number of entries —
or ask students to do so before they hand in the journals. Also look
for patterns of use by noting dates during which writing activity was
heaviest.

Length of entries: Does the writer write a paragraph? Several paragraphs? A page or more? The longer a student writes at a given sitting,
the more likely that some useful insight or thought will develop. (I
suggest that my students write at least a page at each sitting; one
night one student wrote forty pages, using the journal to keep herself
company while she camped alone in a field.) Long entries suggest that
the writer is giving the journal writing the maximum chance to
encourage understanding and comprehension. Estimate words per
entry — or ask students to do so before handing in the journals.

Self-sponsored entries: How often the writer initiates a journal entry
without a cue or prompt from the teacher. Such entries indicate
students' seriousness in attempting to use language to explain their
experience to themselves. Monitor, in your own journal, the specific
entries you assign in and out of class; keep track of how often students
choose to write on their own — or ask them to keep track.

Chronology: Dates recorded for each entry. Journals are written
records of thought through time; the essential hallmark of a journal

is the date recorded at the beginning of each entry, which provides the chronological record. Journals may often have other evidence of accurate documentation, such as notations on the time of day, place of writing, and weather conditions.

Unity: A coherence embracing the whole document. Formal academic papers are more likely to be "theme bound," with each element in each piece supporting a unified, coherent, documented, and developed whole. However, journals, as whole documents, will exhibit multiple themes and rather random patterns of development, with little coherence or documentation. Unity can be found in journals, but obliquely rather than directly; for example, unity might be evidenced through (1) minor structural features, (2) a generally consistent personal voice, (3) recurrent references to particular concerns (themes?), and, perhaps, (4) a frame such as that provided by an introduction, conclusion, and table of contents — this latter only when one calls a particular journal volume complete for the time being.

Clippings: Newspaper articles, drawings, artifacts, and photographs the writer has somehow included in, or attached to, the journal. These suggest extra effort to make connections to personal interests and life. My own journal is full of sketches and notes from my ten- and fourteen-year-old daughters, poems from my wife, business cards from old friends, and old ticket stubs from John Prine concerts.

Guidelines for Responding to Journals

In each course where I used journals exclusively, the students wrote with a fervor I had not seen before, most journals averaging well over one hundred pages. Students wrote this way in part because the journals counted so much (I don't kid myself here), but they also wrote because they had never before had the freedom to learn in this way. In other words, once they understood that such writing served a purpose and was valued, they too began to value it. At the end of the term it was remarkably easy to see who had learned what, easy to assign grades, and easy on me as a reader. Never once did I face a stack of class journals with the same reluctance I often faced term papers, critical essays, and exams. I expected more lively writing and more personal engagement, and I usually received it.

I even asked my students to help me identify the qualities of "good" journals so that, together, we could understand them better and see how they worked. It turned out, of course, that they valued as writers the same things I valued as a reader. For example, they called journals "dull" which contained too much "Cliff Notes stuff." So did I. And they were excited about personal insights and connections brought about by writing in the journals. So was I.

I have waited until the end of this chapter to articulate anything approximating "guidelines" for responding to (or for evaluating) student journal writing. Though one can list the things that journals in general do well, one cannot prescribe what they ought, ultimately, to be composed of, look like, or be held accountable for. That said, however, I believe there are certain things instructors can do that increase the probability of journals being a successful assignment for the classroom, as well as for the individual student.

1. Ask students to keep looseleaf notebooks with dividers to separate academic sections (your class and others) from personal sections. This allows you to collect sample entries from their academic sections, which you can collect every few weeks. It also allows students to keep private and personal entries private and personal. You will know from samples and class participation which students are working hard and which are not.

2. Count, but do not grade, the fact that students keep journals. You can count the number of entries, length of the whole journal, or just the evidence that a journal has been kept. You can give open-journal exams to add credibility, or raise grades by one-half for "good journals" (i.e., long ones, with frequent entries). But if you want students to feel free to try out ideas, don't hold them accountable for the quality of individual entries.

3. If you do assign grades because the journal is a substantial amount of the total coursework, publish that fact in advance to the class, along with the qualitative features (such as the ones I've listed here) on which you intend to base the grade. Base your grade on a holistic reading rather than performance on any individual entries.

4. Whenever you ask students to write in their journals, be sure to write in yours with them; when you ask for sharing, be willing to share yours, too. These acts give credibility to the writing, which is important since you are not grading it in the traditional sense.

5. Whenever you ask for journal writing — at the beginning of class, at the end of class, as a special focusing activity, as homework — *do* something with it. Ask students to share ideas from the journal with each other in small groups, to volunteer to read aloud to the whole class, to share a few lines with a neighbor. The best response to journal writing is the student's

discovery that the writing leads her or him to more knowledge and more courage to share that knowledge with the classroom community.

6. When you do write in response to selected entries or in a paragraph at the end of a bunch of entries, write positively and honestly in pencil. Treat the shared journal entry as you would a letter from the student, kindly, and sometimes ask for a response back. In other words, treat the journal as the student's turf, on which you intrude carefully and with respect.

7. Finally, share copies of good journal writing — yours and your students' — with the class. Make overhead transparencies of entries relevant to the day's work (e.g., contrastive views on Frost's poetry) and project these to the class to demonstrate the energy and ideas possible in good journals — things which good journals, in turn, make possible. This activity usually opens up the class for more sharing and more frank appraisal of what journal writing can be and, at the same time, advances the business of your class. The real trick to responding to journals is to offer opportunities for daily response from as many people in your classroom community as possible.

I believe that journals are more useful than formal papers, because writers remain free to respond to their educational world as they see fit; the very nature of expressive discourse implies risk, experimentation, and failure. Too often in my own journal I've sat down to write profound material and turned out drivel; too often I've started to write silly, ego-gratifying entries and had them turn into useful insights. Use your own writing as your best guide and read with an open mind and a large measure of tolerance. Look for patterns, trust your impressions, don't worry about a few omissions or occasional silliness — they come with the territory.

You will note that some of the characteristics I find in "good" journals — personal or emotional voice, self-doubt, digression, and error, for example — run directly counter to traditional notions about appropriate academic discourse. However, all of the scholars I have cited in this piece make a common plea, asking the academic world to notice the great variety of rhetorical purposes language serves in the contemporary world and to use it likewise in the academy. The writing found in student journals is an alternate style, not an inferior one; furthermore, if we allow, it can teach us much. In the world of writing, as in the worlds of art and science, the most interesting work is often outside and beyond conventional formulas, traditional wisdom, and established paradigms. Right now, journal writing is outside and beyond; let's bring it in and take a closer look.

Acknowledgments

I wish to thank my colleagues Richard Sweterlitsch, Mary Jane Dickerson, Tony Magistrale, and Robyn Warhol for helping me to clarify the three categories of features for the analysis of journals.

References

Applebee, A. N. 1981. *Writing in the Secondary School.* NCTE Research Report 21. Urbana, Ill.: National Council of Teachers of English.

Berthoff, A. E. 1978. *Forming, Thinking, Writing: The Composing Imagination.* Rochelle Park, N.J.: Hayden.

Britton, J. 1970. *Language and Learning.* Harmondsworth, England: Penguin.

Britton, J., T. Burgess, N. Martin, A. McLeod, and H. Rosen. 1975. *The Development of Writing Abilities (11–18).* London: Macmillan Education.

Burke, K. 1950. *A Grammar of Motives.* Englewood Cliffs, N.J.: Prentice-Hall.

Corbett, E. P. J. 1971. *Classical Rhetoric for the Modern Student.* 2d ed. New York: Oxford University Press.

Dixon, J. 1968. Creative Expression in Great Britain. *English Journal* 57 (6): 795–802.

Elbow, P. 1973. *Writing without Teachers.* New York: Oxford University Press.

Emig, J. 1977. Writing as a Mode of Learning. *College Composition and Communication* 28:122–28.

Flower, L. 1979. Writer-Based Prose: A Cognitive Basis for Problems in Writing. *College English* 41:19–37.

Friere, P. 1970. *Pedagogy of the Oppressed.* New York: Herder and Herder.

Fulwiler, T. 1979. Journal Writing across the Curriculum. In *Classroom Practices in Teaching English 1979–1980: How to Handle the Paper Load,* edited by G. Stanford, 15–22. Urbana, Ill.: National Council of Teachers of English.

Fulwiler, T. 1984. How Well Does Writing across the Curriculum Work? *College English* 46:113–25.

Gere, A. R., editor. 1985. *Roots in the Sawdust: Writing to Learn across the Disciplines.* Urbana, Ill.: National Council of Teachers of English.

Hairston, M. 1982. The Winds of Change: Thomas Kuhn and the Revolution in the Teaching of Writing. *College Composition and Communication* 33:76–88.

Kinneavy, J. L. 1971. *A Theory of Discourse.* Englewood Cliffs, N.J.: Prentice-Hall.

Knoblauch, C. H., and L. Brannon. 1984. *Rhetorical Traditions and the Teaching of Writing.* Upper Montclair, N.J.: Boynton/Cook.

Macrorie, K. 1970. *Telling Writing.* Rochelle Park, N.J.: Hayden.

Moffett, J. 1968. *Teaching the Universe of Discourse.* Boston: Houghton Mifflin.

Murray, D. 1978. Internal Revision: A Process of Discovery. In *Research on Composing: Points of Departure,* edited by C. Cooper and L. Odell. Urbana, Ill.: National Council of Teachers of English.

Ohmann, R. 1976. *English in America: A Radical View of the Profession.* New York: Oxford University Press.

Peckham, M. 1951. Toward a Theory of Romanticism. *Publication of the Modern Language Association* 66:5–23.

Thaiss, C., editor. 1982. *Writing to Learn: Essays and Reflections by College Teachers across the Curriculum.* Fairfax, Va.: George Mason Faculty Writing Program, George Mason University.

Weathers, W. 1980. *An Alternate Style: Options in Composition.* Rochelle Park, N.J.: Hayden.

Winterowd, W. R. 1965. *Rhetoric and Writing.* Boston: Allyn and Bacon.

Wotring, A., and R. Tierney. 1981. *Two Studies of Writing in High School Science.* Classroom Research Study 5, Bay Area Writing Project. Berkeley: University of California.

9 The Writer's Memo: Collaboration, Response, and Development

Jeffrey Sommers
Miami University

Writing teachers should teach students to escape the "house of self-consciousness," to learn how, in Mandel's words, to "lose one's mind" when writing (1980, 375). There comes a time, however, when it is crucial for students to "regain their minds" — after they have completed a written draft. As Susan Miller (1982, 182) has suggested, this calls for a "post-rewriting" stage in the composing process — a stage of metacognition, of examining and reflecting on the completed cognitive process of writing a draft. When Murray (1982) recommends that writing teachers recruit students' "other selves" to assist in their development as writers, he too is supporting the idea that students engage in such an act of metacognition.

Because the other self is an authority on the writer's composing process, it ought to be consulted — and respected. Brannon and Knoblauch (1982) have argued cogently that writing teachers must recognize students' rights to their own texts, must acknowledge students' authority in speaking about what they have tried to do. Unfortunately, what Brannon and Knoblauch call the "transfer of responsibility" for development, from the teacher to the student, is more easily encouraged than practiced: "Our concern has been only secondarily to show how it can be done, and primarily to argue that it should be done" (165).

In this chapter, I would like to make primary their secondary concern, by describing a teaching method that engages students in metacognition through facilitating a shift of responsibility for writing development, from the teacher to the student. This method, the "writer's memo," has a number of salutary effects which can lead to students' development as writers — effects that also address a number of pressing needs in composition pedagogy, chief among them the role and nature of response in the writing class. After briefly describing the writer's memo, I will devote most of this chapter to considering the effect this response method has on the teacher as collaborator, and on the student as developing writer.

The Writer's Memo

The best way to make contact with students' other selves may be through writing itself; the best way to get students to provide answers we would like about how they compose is to ask them direct questions. Requiring students to write a memorandum to their teacher-reader, answering specific questions about how they composed a written draft, can produce the written response of the "other self." Beaven (1977) describes a similar technique and comments that "as students analyze their own creative processes and compare them with others, they begin to recognize various strategies they might try" (144). The use of such self-evaluation, she adds, promotes "self-reliance, independence, autonomy, and creativity" (147).

From the perspective of response, however, the writer's memo accomplishes more than simply helping students become more effective readers of their own writing. By creating opportunities to make explicit the sorts of transactions that Robert Probst advocates in Chapter 3 of this collection, teachers can adopt a constructive role as respondents, rather than judges, while guaranteeing the students' rights to their own texts. Further, by encouraging metacognition, this method assists students in developing their own written voices, teaches them to write reader-based prose (Flower 1979), and helps them to decenter (Kroll 1978).

In introducing the writer's memo to their classes, instructors typically distribute a memo assignment sheet, which accompanies a regular writing assignment. The memo assignment sheet includes a series of questions that deal with the process of writing the assigned paper and with the students' feelings about the finished draft. Questions on the writing process, for example, ask students to recount how they selected a topic, how they generated ideas for use in the paper, or what problems they encountered in organizing their thoughts. Some questions deal with the students' composing choices; for instance, one might ask students to explain which other organizational patterns for their ideas they considered before making the final decisions about the structure of their writing. Other questions compel students to evaluate their own work by asking them to point out and explain their essay's greatest strength — students can be asked to select their single best sentence or paragraph or transition, which can have the further benefit of bolstering students' confidence, simply by helping them to locate parts of their writing worth praising, even while the draft is still quite rough. The students can also be asked to compare the effectiveness of the draft to one of their earlier pieces of writing, or to identify weaknesses of the draft. Still other questions can be used to reinforce ideas about writing or techniques covered in class or in a textbook, and to suggest various new approaches to the writing process.

Finally, students can be asked to provide the instructor with needed assistance in effectively responding to the draft. Questions about audience and purpose are useful ones to pose, as well as those that allow students to direct their teacher's responses to their individual needs as writers: "What questions would you like me to answer about your draft?"

When the memo questions are distributed with an assignment, the teacher should explain that the memos are required and that papers will not receive comments until the memos are completed. At the same time, the instructor stresses that the memo itself is a tool for both student and teacher, and will not be evaluated or graded. (Making it clear to students, right from the start, that the writing in their memos won't be criticized is important, because anticipating such criticism may inhibit students when they respond to the memo questions — and such inhibition is counterproductive to metacognition.)

The memo questions can usually be placed on the same sheet as the essay assignment, making it easy for students to see the connections between the two writing tasks. Over the course of the term, questions need to be varied from assignment to assignment in an effort to keep the memos from becoming a rote-like chore and to tie the questions as closely as possible to each given assignment. By asking students to share their memos with each other or to read them to the class — or by writing a memo to the class about one of his or her own drafts — a teacher can show the range of responses possible and say something about the importance of metacognition in the writing process.

Writer's memos can also be used when students turn in revised versions of earlier drafts. Questions can ask students to explain and justify the changes they have made in their work from one draft to the next. This is particularly useful in responding to the revised paper, because it guarantees that the teacher will be focusing on the conceptual concerns — or specific parts of the essay — about which the student is most interested in receiving some response. It is also possible to ask students to review their memos, including the revision memos, at the end of the term and then use them, collectively, as the source of an essay examining their own experiences and growth as writers. One year, one of my students chose to write about the value of memos in his own revising process, arguing that the memos provided a "bridge" between himself and his reader, between his early drafts and his subsequent ones. He asserted that writing the memos actually constituted his first step in reconceiving and rewriting his work. His essay, titled "Bridge Over Troubled Waters," effectively demonstrated the power that the student-teacher memos can have in encouraging metacognition through a simple response technique.

The Teacher as Collaborator

Recent work focusing on how teachers respond and on alternative ways of responding to student writing argues that the most effective role for the writing instructor in the process-based course is that of guide or fellow explorer or editor. Nancy Sommers, Donald Murray, Lil Brannon, and others suggest, for example, that teachers should begin collaborating with student writers instead of merely judging them. But doing so can be risky and troubling, especially for instructors who have grown used to the comfortable and powerful role of judge, or for young teachers insecure about their own authority in the classroom. It is quite easy to feel "dumb."

As Gibson (1979) has explained, however, writing teachers cannot help being "dumb" so long as they are not privy to the writer's intentions before reading the work. That sort of "dumbness" may well be what the world beyond the classroom is like when we read: picking up a novel or a newsmagazine requires us to muddle through, without knowing much about the writer's intentions beforehand. But it is difficult to imagine an effective editor or collaborator attempting to read an author's work in such ignorance. If writing teachers are to become collaborators rather than judges, they simply must have prior information about the writer's intended audience and purpose.

A clinical specialist in critical-care nursing, with whom I have collaborated in the past, recently sent a manuscript to her editor at one of the professional nursing journals for which she writes. She included a cover letter, part of which read as follows:

> The section, "Assessing the organ system," could become quite cumbersome since multisystem failure can often occur with Toxic Shock Syndrome. I plan only to write a paragraph summing up the assessments needed for each system and to try to place the large body of knowledge in some type of chart or figure. Paragraph 2 is my first attempt at consolidating this information. I am

interested in how well I have managed to present the information
in this section.

Her request for focused editorial assistance produced the desired effect:
Her editor commented specifically on the very passages and strategies
she had mentioned in her letter ("I'm especially thrilled with your
multi-system assessment chart and your use of nursing diagnosis. All
of these fit together very well"). Thus, the nurse was able to continue
her writing, confident that she was on the right track for the particular
audience she was addressing.

Just as the nurse's letter enabled her editor to avoid being a "dumb
reader" of the work, so the writer's memo can enable writing teachers
to avoid being "dumb readers" of student writing. By discussing the
importance of audience, teachers have attempted to increase students'
awareness of the significance of the rhetorical situation in any given
writing task. They also have tried to devise assignments that incorporate
an imagined audience — as in the case method — so every student
paper is not necessarily addressed to "The Teacher." But when teachers
devise such assignments, or when they encourage students to independently select, analyze, and write to a suitable audience, they create
more problems for themselves as readers: It becomes increasingly likely
that the teacher will not be the primary audience for the text. How,
then, can teachers respond intelligently? The answer, I think, is that
unless teachers find out who the writer's intended readers are and
why they are being addressed, the teachers *will* remain dumb readers,
largely incapable of responding intelligently enough to function as
either guides or collaborators.

The writer's memo addresses this problem by asking students to
describe the audience they have selected for a given piece of writing
and to explain their purpose in writing the paper. One student in a
literature and composition course answered such questions this way:
"My purpose in writing . . . to Mr. Ionesco is to give my opinion on
how he could improve his play." The play to which she refers is *The
Lesson*, an absurdist farce which completely befuddled her. The memo
also asked the student to explain whether she had considered moving
any of the sections of her letter from one place to another, in case she
had had any second thoughts about its organization. She responded
by discussing her organizational strategy in terms of her stated purpose
and audience:

> This is a letter criticizing Mr. Ionesco's play and not many people
> take criticism very well so I wanted to be sure to say something
> positive. At first I was going to write all the praise in the first
> paragraph and then go into my criticism but I opted for mingling

the two. In the first three paragraphs there is something positive
said as well as negative.

A sensitive editor responding to this writer's work would not voice
objection to the consistently weak praise of Ionesco that appears
throughout the student's letter. The writer has made it clear in the
memo that she feels it important to include "something positive" to
make her negative comments more palatable to her reader, Ionesco
himself. Yet without this information, many teachers might be inclined
to suggest that the faint though sincere praise either be strengthened
or eliminated, neither of which the writer is willing to do, given her
purpose.

The writer's memo can further help teachers assume the role of
collaborator by requiring students to compose specific questions that
they want answered by their teacher-reader. The memos thus virtually
require a collaborative response from the teacher, as the nurse's letter
did with her editor. Toward the end of her memo about Ionesco's play,
the student demonstrates how to elicit such a collaborative response.
She writes: "In para. 1, I say I liked the basic theme; in para. 2 I say
some parts are funny; in para. 3, I say the end was a surprise. I think
all of these are praises but if you had written this [play] would you
see them or only the criticism?" This writer knows what she wants
from her editor, and a question as specific as the one she has posed
insures that she will get it.

If each teacher is to become a Maxwell Perkins to his or her student's
Scott Fitzgerald, as Butturff and Sommers (1980, 104) urge, then the
teacher must have access to such basic information as that provided
in this writer's memo. Instructors have learned the dangers of responding prematurely to a student paper during a first reading: the comment
"oops" in the margin too often becomes necessary after asking a
question about the text only to find the answer on the very next page.
It may be equally dangerous to read a student paper without first
reading the accompanying memo.

Being informed in this basic manner not only encourages teachers
to read and respond as editors, but also protects the students' authority — what Brannon and Knoblauch (1982) call the "composer's
right to make statements in the way they are made in order to say
what he or she intended to say" (165). Several advocates of the
conference method of teaching writing, such as Carnicelli (1980), are
equally concerned with protecting students' rights by always granting
them the "first say" about their work. The writer's memo gives students
the "first say," whether the instructor responds in writing or in
conference.

In short, the writer's memo helps teachers to adopt a productive role as responders to student writing. Additionally, for teachers who prefer to hold conferences with students about written work, the writer's memo can serve as a catalyst for these meetings, providing both teacher and student with ample material to structure the dialogue and give it the sort of direction that Newkirk (this volume) demonstrates in his analysis of student-teacher conference sessions. Finally, for teachers who comment on every paper in writing, or even on cassette tapes, the writer's memo offers a focus for response and thus makes the responding process more efficient and more effective.

The Student as Developing Writer

Earlier, I referred to Murray's suggestion (1982) that teachers should enlist the assistance of students' "other selves" in encouraging the development of their students' writing abilities. Murray hypothesizes that perhaps

> we can also help the other self to become articulate by having the student write, after completing a draft, a brief statement about the draft. That statement can be attached on the front of the draft so the teacher can hear what the other self says and respond, after reading that statement and the draft, in writing. (146)

Murray goes on to suggest that face-to-face conferences are likely to be more useful than written dialogue, because the teacher can "listen with the eye" by observing body language, pauses, and reflection. It is, of course, possible to combine the student's written statement, which parallels in a less guided way the memos I have been describing, with an oral response by the instructor. Murray's central argument against this approach, however, is that something valuable is lost if the students respond in writing rather than orally in front of the teacher.

I would like to argue just the opposite: something is lost if these kinds of responses are restricted completely to the oral mode. Why not, as much as possible, use writing itself to improve writing? I asked students who had used the writer's memos which kinds of questions on the memos proved most difficult to answer, and why. Two responses, which were typical, are worth considering. In one, the student wrote, "Why?!!! P.S. — I'm not asking you why, I'm saying that was the most difficult question." In another, the student circled the question "Why?" on the evaluation sheet, and wrote, "That's the question. It is very hard to really understand one's own writing, but that question helped most." Answering the question "why," in writing, requires a process in which the student reflects on the purpose of the writing or on the composing process itself — and this, in turn, leads to discovery. For example, one student wrote, "When writing the memos I would discover things about my paper that I hadn't realized." Using writing itself as a means of discovery, as Murray himself consistently and persuasively argues, is one of the true benefits of writing, and the memos provide opportunities for students to realize and discover this benefit.

Additionally, having students write these memos addresses a related concern, one articulated by Murray (1983) in his response to being the subject of a think-aloud protocol analysis: "I'm a bit more suspicious now than I had been about the accounts that are reconstructed in a conference days after writing. They are helpful, the best teaching point I know, but I want to find out what happens if we can bring the composing and the teaching closer together" (170). From comments written in the memos I have examined, as well as from class response to their use, it is clear that students routinely compose the memos immediately after writing a draft. The memos are thus "fresh" accounts of the composing process. Whether the teacher reads the memo hours after it has been written or days later becomes irrelevant; the memo remains a permanent record of the writer's initial response, and the composing and responding are thus brought more closely together.

Murray is not alone in questioning the use of protocols in research on composing; there is much concern, for example, that imposing metacognition during the act of writing may well distort the natural composing process. However, the possibility that writing the assigned memos might affect the writing processes of students, if they keep them in mind *while* writing, is actually an argument in favor of their use. In explaining why some questions on the memos were difficult for her to answer, for example, one student wrote:

> Because I often really did know the answer — but *gradually!* I came to keep the questions in mind when I was actually writing — they became essential for 'behind the paper,' and actually began to make the writing easier — because I thought about them and made decisions before actually writing.

For this student, the memos became part of the recursive process of composing as she referred to the questions before, during, and after producing a draft. Another student wrote that "writing memos always got me to start thinking about a way I should start my paper." Still another said, "They didn't take a lot of time but a lot of thinking." The product of all this thinking is to encourage students to see writing as a process, one that includes not only drafting, prewriting, and rewriting, but also discovery — at all stages during composing.

Because students continue to learn more about themselves as writers over the span of a course, the memos do not seem to wear out their welcome as the term progresses. In fact, the length of the responses often increases. But this increased length is also a product of the collaborative relationship growing between writer and reader — a relationship the memos are designed to cultivate. The students begin to feel comfortable writing to the teacher, more relaxed and honest, and the memos begin to display authentic voice.

And, of course, the voiceless quality of student writing — a product of the students' lack of awareness of audience when writing — persists as a major problem in freshman composition courses. The teacher is an audience, of course, but not a "real" one. Advocating a kind of writing replicated by the student-teacher memo, Elbow (1981) claims that

> you don't write *to* teachers, you write for them. You can feel the difference vividly if you write a regular essay assigned by your teacher and then go on to write something directly *to* him: . . . [like] a letter . . . . You will find [such] writing refreshing and satisfying compared to regular assignments — even if harder. It's a relief to put words down on paper for the sake of *results* — not just for the sake of getting a *judgment*. (220)

In writing their memos, students become real writers writing to a real audience — the teacher-reader — with a real purpose in mind — to communicate information about how the essay being submitted came to be written. And they seek real results: useful editorial comments from their reader.

Students learn quickly that the memo is a different form of communication from the papers they are assigned. Said one student in her evaluation, "From the student's point of view it's nice to have the chance to communicate to you their feelings about the assignment, their paper's content, and why they feel the way they do about those things." Such a comment implies that students begin to use the memos for their own purposes, beyond the teacher's stated one of making reader response more effective; students begin to use the memos to converse with the teacher.

Classroom discussion, lectures, and analyses of written passages simply do not demonstrate the importance of audience as vividly as the act of writing to a real audience, someone who will *respond*, actively, to the writing. Instead of the "writer-based prose" so many freshmen write (Flower 1979), the memos are examples of reader-based prose, true transactional writing which comes about as the students grow in awareness of their audience. One student, composing a letter, shows in her memo this increasing sense of audience, indicating her efforts to write reader-based prose: "A problem now may be that since I accept it as a letter to someone I think to myself, 'how much of this would he really want to know?'" Later in the course, this student chose to write a letter to herself in an effort, as she explained in her memo, to escape the problem of audience completely. But since the letter was really intended to be read by others including her teacher, she sadly acknowledged in the same memo that "there is no escape from audience."

This student, then, is beginning to decenter, and to understand the difference between writing directed inward to the self and writing directed outward to a reader. Again and again, students remark on their assessments of the memo method that it helps them to look more closely at their writing as someone else might — in the words of one student, to learn "what questions to ask myself as a reader and writer," and, in those of another, to see the paper "from a reader's point of view."

Occasionally, in a moment of true metacognition, a student will comment on this issue of decentering — and on the difficulty in making the transition from writer-based to reader-based prose. One student, for example, wrote:

> In writing this and all my papers, I've found it difficult to tell you exactly what I'm trying to say. I mean, I know what I want to say, I know what the paper says, but does someone reading know? They all seem to yet I always, always have doubts . . .

This student's genuine puzzlement, expressed authentically and naturally, comes across poignantly in his repetition of "always," counterbalanced against his prior comment that his readers "all seem to" know what he's saying. Having these doubts, however, is a sign of true progress, a sign of a writer making crucial discoveries about his own writing. Written spontaneously, without reference to any of the questions on the memo assignment, a comment like this one also demonstrates in and of itself the process of decentering. This student has seen that even within rigidly organized school contexts there is a place for "real" communication and response.

But perhaps the most important benefit the memo method holds for student development is its way of urging students to think of themselves less as students and more as writers. Practicing writers ask their colleagues, friends, and editors for specific assistance. By asking students to do what writers do, teachers can create and reinforce the idea that students are writers — young, perhaps inexperienced — but writers nonetheless. All of the memo questions, those that probe the composing process as well as those that ask for self-evaluation of the completed draft, are based on an unspoken assumption that students are truly writers, writers whose texts are serious in their intentions to communicate or explore ideas. The students' written assignments are not treated as exercises intended to demonstrate proficiency in using certain stylistic devices; they are treated instead as proposed solutions to problems presented by rhetorical situations. By asking students to consider what they have done as they attempted to solve the rhetorical problems they had posed for themselves, writing teachers imply that the students *are* writers. The memos encourage every student's "complex, internal growth into the character of an Author" (Miller 1982, 182) through the implicit assumptions teachers make about their classes when they assign these memos. Teachers begin to treat their students as writers — and, in turn, students begin acting the part.

Because the students communicate as writers to their teacher, the teacher begins to communicate back as a reader. So when the student writing about Ionesco asked if the reader was likely to overlook her praise and only notice her criticism, I responded by telling her that as a writer myself, I tend to notice, at first, only the criticism. Eventually I get past the criticism and the hurt long enough to observe and appreciate any praise. In other words, I did not reply as the writing teacher might have ("Certainly the balance of praise and criticism will make your piece of writing more acceptable to your reader"), but instead responded as myself, as a person — or to borrow the term David Bleich uses in the opening chapter of this collection, as a "correspondent" in an exchange about language. Since the memos vividly present the authentic voices of student writers, they invite the teacher to respond in his or her own authentic voice as a reader, editor, fellow writer. The interchange of purposeful comments between real people keeps the memos alive for both student and teacher, preventing them from becoming a dry, automatic activity akin to marking off boxes on some master checklist for revision. Ultimately, the writer's memos change not only the student but also the teacher, freeing both from their academic roles and encouraging both to assume the more productive roles of writer and reader.

Conclusion

Recent investigations into what student writers really learn (Rubin 1983) showed that students acquire an ability to read their own work critically before they acquire the skills necessary to implement revision based on that critical reading. Rubin concluded that making students more aware of their composing processes does help them develop as writers, even though they cannot always demonstrate their development immediately when they write. Research on students' self-assessing processes (Beach 1976; Beach and Eaton 1984) similarly argues that making students more aware of their composing processes does help them to develop as writers by encouraging them to revise more copiously. It is this inquiring and reflecting — this looking back into the process leading to a completed draft, and reflecting on both it and the final product — that constitute the essential value of the writer's memo. All the other benefits grow out of increasing the student's awareness of the composing process — an awareness ultimately creating in the writer the capacity for internal response, for communication between the writer and the self.

But the memos do this without the need for an elaborate mechanism. They simply ask students to do what *we* do when we write: use the composing process to our own advantage so we can achieve our purpose in communicating to the specific audience we have in mind as we write. The memos encourage students to think about their readers and to communicate with their most present reader — the teacher. And by doing all of these things, the memos lead to maturity in writing: in sensitivity to audience, purpose, and voice. Most important, they lead students to maturity *as writers* — in helping them to take over the responsibility for their own continued development. In a surprised tone, one student wrote in a memo: "Sometimes I think these memos help me as much as they help you."

That's one student who is getting the point.

References

Beach, R. 1976. Self-Evaluation Strategies of Extensive Revisers and Non-Revisers. *College Composition and Communication* 27:160–64.

Beach, R., and S. Eaton. 1984. Factors Influencing Self-Assessing and Revising by College Freshmen. In *New Directions in Composition Research*, edited by R. Beach and L. S. Bridwell, 149–70. New York: Guilford.

Beaven, M. H. 1977. Individualized Goal Setting, Self-Evaluation, and Peer Evaluation. In *Evaluating Writing*, edited by C. Cooper and L. Odell, 135–53. Urbana, Ill.: National Council of Teachers of English.

Brannon, L., and C. H. Knoblauch. 1982. On Students' Rights to Their Own Texts: A Model of Teacher Response. *College Composition and Communication* 33:157–66.

Butturff, D., and N. Sommers. 1980. Placing Revision in a Reinvented Rhetorical Tradition. In *Reinventing the Rhetorical Tradition,* edited by A. Freedman and I. Pringle, 99–104. Conway, Ark.: L & S Books.

Carnicelli, T. 1980. The Writing Conference: A One-to-One Conversation. In *Eight Approaches to Teaching Writing,* edited by T. Donovan and B. Mc-Clelland, 101–32. Urbana, Ill.: National Council of Teachers of English.

Elbow, P. 1981. *Writing with Power.* New York: Oxford University Press.

Flower, L. 1979. Writer-Based Prose: A Cognitive Basis for Problems in Writing. *College English* 41:19–37.

Gibson, W. 1979. The Writing Teacher as Dumb Reader. *College Composition and Communication* 30:192–95.

Kroll, B. M. 1978. Cognitive Egocentrism and the Problem of Audience Awareness in Written Discourse. *Research in the Teaching of English* 12:269–81.

Mandel, B. J. 1980. The Writer Writing Is Not at Home. *College Composition and Communication* 31:370–77.

Miller, S. 1982. How Writers Evaluate Their Own Writing. *College Composition and Communication* 33:176–83.

Murray, D. M. 1982. Teaching the Other Self: The Writer's First Reader. *College Composition and Communication* 33:140–47.

Murray, D. M. 1983. Response of a Laboratory Rat — Or, Being Protocoled. *College Composition and Communication* 34:169–72.

Rubin, D. 1983. Evaluating Freshman Writers: What Do Students Really Learn? *College English* 45:373–79.

10 Response in the Electronic Medium

Geoffrey Sirc
University of Minnesota

I would like to begin this discussion of how the computer both does and can respond to student writing by invoking an incident from "The Jetsons," the old cartoon show that projected a technologically sophisticated future. In this particular incident, George Jetson, citizen of the future, is preparing supper. He goes to the "Food-O-Matic," a machine whose push-button menu offers instantly prepared hot meals that appear in an opening at the bottom of the machine. In this episode, George desires "saturnian steak"; he punches in the choice but receives no food. He then resorts to banging on the machine, frustrated that the Food-O-Matic is on the blink.

I begin with this incident because I think "The Jetsons" version of how future technology will aid in food preparation can illuminate contemporary thinking about how current technology has been and can be used to aid in responding to student writing. In this chapter, I will provide a brief overview of the forms computer-assisted writing response take, chart what I perceive to be their limitations, and discuss alternative ways in which to conceive the undertaking. In particular, I will argue that whenever we have our machines talking directly to students (through preprogrammed words or phrases activated by some sort of textual input) in the hope of providing useful writing instruction, we limit our pedagogy. The computer, I suggest, so far can only serve effectively, in terms of a general pedagogical tool, as a *medium* for response rather than as a respondent.

The Goals and Problems of Computer Response to Writing

Currently there are three main forms of computer-aided response used by teachers of writing and their students: programs that allow a teacher's paper grading and commentary to be done on a computer;

programs that analyze a student's text for certain kinds of surface errors; and programs that respond, in preprogrammed dialogue, to the writing of a student-user.

The development of these types of programs owes, generally, to three seemingly compelling aspects of the computer: its speed, its ability to recognize keywords, and its interactivity. Since computers can perform routines quickly, it is thought they will be able to take much drudgery out of the task of writing and its teaching. Marling (1984), for example, desires to transfer his paper grading to a computer because, as he states to his school's director of computing, "I never want to write another definition of a comma splice, or of how to correct it." He adds that "it was the repetitive drudgery I wanted to eliminate" (797).

The machine's speed, as well as its ability to identify preprogrammed words or phrases, is crucial not only to the production of computerized grading programs, but also to text-feedback programs, which identify the appearance of stylistic infelicities (such as "to be" verbs) in student text. The machine's "interactive" nature is its ability, through onscreen prompts, to provide a kind of dialogue situation with students. Nold (1975) describes the appeal of the interactive (and personal) environment:

> [T]he hallmark of interactive computing is the response — both intellectual and muscular — of the student to the computer's words and the incorporation of the student's response into the computer's next question or topic. . . . Computer programs can call forth creativity because they provide a fertile environment: privacy of communication and time. When students use good computer programs well, the computer provides a patient and non-threatening, fluid and provocative backboard against which to bounce ideas. (269–71)

Computer-assisted response programs have proven immensely popular and are described in glowing terms by their developers. Even such a scholar as Sommers (1982), who has devoted much study to the question of evaluating student writing, seems pleasantly struck by the new technology for response:

> Within a few minutes, the computer delivered editorial comments on the student's text, identifying all spelling and punctuation errors, isolating problems with wordy or misused phrases, and suggesting alternatives, offering a stylistic analysis of sentence types, sentence beginnings, and sentence lengths, and finally, giving our freshman essay a Kincaid readability score of 8th grade which, as the computer program informed us, "is a low score for this type of document." The sharp contrast between the teachers'

> comments and those of the computer highlighted how arbitrary
> and idiosyncratic most of our teachers' comments are. Besides,
> the calm, reasonable language of the computer provided quite a
> contrast to the hostility and mean-spiritedness of . . . teachers'
> comments. (149)

Despite how slick these programs appear, the basic question with
which to begin an inquiry into the way computers presently respond
to student writing is, why would one want a student's paper, the
potentially fragile first steps of a developing writer, to be "read" and
"responded to" by a medium that can't read? Indeed, computers
currently do a great deal of responding to our students, but what do
they say? What do the current promoters of computer-aided instructional software appear to want the machines to say?

Answers to these questions must, of course, be understood within
the context of our general infatuation with technological domination —
an infatuation that has saturated our culture since well before the
days of the Jetsons. We have a Spielbergian faith in machines to deliver
us from our mired condition — to take us into a brave new world of
power and freedom. Before we proceed, it may be worth summarizing — to act as a kind of framework for our own response to computer
response — the thinking which (probably rightly) holds that technology
offers a revolutionary environment in which to learn.

Papert (1980) has one of the most lucid, informed arguments on
this subject. His central concern is the passive/aggressive dichotomy
prevalent in the use of computers in education. Rather than the child
using the computer, the computer, in effect, uses the child; the machine
teaches or programs the child, not vice versa. Papert sees this either/
or dichotomy extending throughout most of education: children are
either right or wrong. In Papert's scheme, the computer will not be
used aggressively to teach a passive child how to "get it," but rather
as a medium to allow students aggressive mastery of ideas. Papert
uses the phrase "object-to-think-with" (23) to capture this notion of
the computer as a medium for cognitive growth. What the computer
can provide, as Perkins (1985) has suggested, is an epistemologically
powerful environment for learning, rather than simply a mechanically
slicker delivery system for the standard pedagogy:

> By reducing onerous mechanics, the new symbolic technologies
> may free us to attend in new ways and aspire to new levels of
> cognition. One might put it this way: The written word extended
> the reach of thought by helping us to circumvent low-level
> limitations of human short-term memory. Information-processing
> technologies might further extend the reach of thought by helping
> us to circumvent the low-level limitations of human computational

ability, including not only computation with numbers but with
words and images. (12)

Unfortunately, our love for and belief in technology can degenerate
into guilty obsession, fixated on the mechanical means rather than the
intellectual ends. Such fixation is, according to Papert, endemic to the
development of technology; the example he uses concerns the manner
in which we have stayed with the "QWERTY" keyboard (designating
the first six letters of the second-from-top row of a typewriter) — even
when we found it functioned poorly — because of its achieved status
as norm:

> QWERTY has stayed on despite the existence of other, more
> "rational" systems. On the other hand, if you talk to people about
> the QWERTY arrangement they will justify it by "objective"
> criteria. They will tell you that it "optimizes this" or it "minimizes
> that." Although these justifications have no rational foundation,
> they illustrate a process, a social process, of myth construction
> that allows us to build a justification for primitivity into any
> system. And I think we are well on the road to doing exactly the
> same thing with the computer. We are in the process of digging
> ourselves into an anachronism by preserving practices that have
> no rational basis beyond their historical roots in an earlier period
> of technological and theoretical development. . . . The computer
> revolution has scarcely begun, but it is already breeding its own
> conservatism. (1980, 33–34)

The principle Papert is suggesting has important implications for any
review of programs designed to respond, in one form or another, to
student writing. We must avoid being captivated by the often attractive
and impressive features of instructional computer programs, instead
looking beneath their surface to the underlying pedagogical assumptions they force us to adopt and take responsibility for.

Trends in Computer Response

To illustrate some basic trends in electronic response, I have selected
some representative programs. By no means is this an exhaustive
survey or even a review of specific software; such discussions are
available elsewhere. I am more interested in providing a theoretical
overview and critique of the methodology.

Marling (1984) and Kotler and Anandam (1983) provide examples
of computerized grading programs which, judging from the literature,
are the most uncommon form of computer-assisted response. Marling's
program, called Writer, Grader, and Reader, consists of three parts: a

text editor for the students' writing, a grading program to do what Marling calls the "repetitious, rule-driven tasks" (798), and a translation program to provide commentary. The text editor, a customized version of a generic product, does not directly concern us. The Grader software consists of three components: class setup, in which data on the class and assignments are entered; a maintenance program, to add or delete students and to review comments, grades, and error totals; and the grading program itself, which uses the eighteen function keys of a Digital Equipment Corporation microcomputer to correspond to eighteen of the most frequently perceived errors. The grading program is described by Marling:

> [T]he student's essay scrolls up into a grading window that occupies the top two-thirds of the screen. Below the window are running error totals in the eighteen error categories. The student's text occupies about half the screen — the extra space at the right is for mnemonics and commentary. The teacher reads the essay by pressing the line feed key, which puts new lines on the screen. When he sees an error he moves the cursor to it, then presses the auxiliary keypad key labeled with the error. The error turns reverse video — black on a white square — and a mnemonic, such as "AGR," appears in the right margin. Any position can be marked multiply, as, say, the source of a comma splice, wordiness, and misspelling. . . . Marginal commentary is inserted in the same fashion — press the Comment Key to move out to the margin, write out as long a comment as you desire, press the key again to move back to where you were in the essay. Comments and mnemonics can be mixed, comments giving sharpness to a general mnemonic such as "AWK." And comments can be as long as necessary . . . and I tend to write more of it than I do on traditional papers. (799–800)

The student using the Reader program discovers grammar-book information regarding the highlighted errors. By focusing the textbook commentary on the student's specific errors, Marling sees this program's advantage over simply giving students a handbook and letting them find the information for themselves. He also claims that, although transferring the grading process to the screen initially requires more time, the preservation of all the error codes and commentary for each student's paper aids conferences on student progress, and he feels the program's use results in a decrease of the codable errors.

Kotler and Anandam's RSVP (Response System with Variable Prescriptions) Feedback Program for Individualized Analysis of Writing also allows teachers to code and keep track of errors made by students and to print out, for students, "personalized letters discussing their writing problems on as regular a basis as the teacher wishes" (361).

This program has the option of adjusting commentary according to the student's writing ability: primary, basic, intermediate, and superior. The letters provided to students consist of the same commentary in Marling's program: instructional material and examples like those found in a grammar handbook. For Kotler and Anandam, the benefits are obvious:

> Given a detailed letter of the type shown here, along with some brief comments (or even symbols) on the paper, students can identify — with a peer tutor's, paraprofessional's, or teacher's help, if necessary — the weaknesses of their writing and correct them next time. (365)

Though the authors stress that these letters are "personalized," and "individualized," they are acontextual in regard to the student's own writing; the letters' individualization lies in the extent to which the stock, preprogrammed phrases correspond to the surface errors the student actually made in the paper.

Similar to these grading programs that direct students' attention to their writing's surface are text-feedback programs, such as Bell Laboratories' Writer's Workbench. It really is a composite of many separate programs, each identifying certain features of a student text. Kiefer and Smith (1983, 1984) have been most active in reporting on the use of Writer's Workbench, which they claim "speeds learning of editing skills by offering immediate, reliable, and consistent attention to surface features of their prose" (1983, 201). Among the programs available within Writer's Workbench are: Organization, providing a first- and last-sentence outline of an essay, allowing a check for coherence; Development, counting words per paragraph and comparing them with an average; Findbe, identifying incidences of that particular linking verb; Diction, highlighting various undesirable word choices; and Suggest, offering alternatives for those undesirable words. There are also programs to check spelling errors, homonyms, punctuation, grammar, passives, nominalizations, and more. Kiefer and Smith find these programs "indispensable" (1983, 210), not only for sharpening editing skills, but for stimulating students' feelings about writing. The benefit over other kinds of editing instruction lies in the programs' analysis of a student's own writing. The response the student receives (1984, 74–75) is either precise numerical information ("sentence info: no. sent 13 no. wds 301, av sent leng 23.2 av word leng 4.29") or a message such as this one, given by the Abstract program:

> In this text, 2.8 percent of the words are abstract. Psychological research shows that concrete texts are easier to read, easier to

use, and easier to remember. Generally, the lower the abstract index, the better. Your percentage of abstract words given above, however, is higher than the usual limit, 2%. Have you illustrated each of your points with fully developed specific details? If not, do so before handing your paper in.

Cohen and Lanham (1984) have a similar type of stylistic analyzer called HOMER, which responds in a more jocular manner: "'1 sentence contained 'to be' verbs. I see you avoid 'to be' verbs — how delightful!!'" "'1 sentence contained 'wooly' words. I'm glad you haven't pulled the 'wooly' words over my eyes" (88–89).

The last form electronic response currently takes involves dialogue programs that question students and then respond to their answers. Burns and Culp (1980), widely recognized pioneers of these programs, transferred classical invention heuristics to the screen in the form of prompts designed to elicit student information. After the program cues a user to supply the essay topic, it leads the student through a systematic exploration of that topic, with questions such as "What objects do you associate with *your topic*? How might they be included in your theme?" (8). After the student answers these questions, the computer-generated dialogue responds to the student's writing with positive feedback and, often, requests for more writing: "That's the idea Walt. Give me some more info now." "Super, Walt! Anything else?" (8). As Burns and Culp see the benefit of their program:

> The resulting interaction [between user and program] would first bring to the conscious level what was *already* known about the subject being explored, and, second, this interaction would help the writer discover what he or she did *not* know about the subject, thus generating some felt difficulty, some dissonance, and prompting the student to articulate the particular problematic situation which the computer-cued interaction uncovered. (6)

Selfe's Wordsworth II (Selfe 1984; Selfe and Wahlstrom 1982) works similarly, with dialogue loops designed to assist a student in writing common freshman assignments such as narration, description, and persuasion. The modules give a student assistance in both the early and later stages of writing. Wordsworth II's onscreen prompts include instructional material ("You know, Shawn, the special challenge in writing a narration is to recreate the scene for your reader. You have to bring the situation to life by providing very vivid, explicit details that document what happened and how it happened" [1984, 176]); questions to test a student's mastery of that material ("Now, Shawn, which paragraph *shows* you what happened? Type in the number" [178]); and cues designed to generate content ("Got any ideas? Let's try listing them" — and after the student has typed in a list of seven ideas — "Well, Horatio. That's a good start, but you could probably use a few more ideas on your brainstorming list" [1982, 9]). Selfe and Wahlstrom find the program valuable because it "forces students to engage in various predrafting, drafting, and postdrafting strategies that are useful in any composing situation" (10).

Computer Response and Underlying Pedagogy

It should be acknowledged from the start that developers of most computer programs for writing instruction have a sincere interest in aiding students through the writing process. However, to extend Papert's earlier example, those who hold strongly to the QWERTY keyboard probably do so out of a sincere desire to ease the typing process. These electronic response programs simply do not show enough respect for individual students; if they did, they could not affirm that "forcing" a student "to engage in various predrafting, drafting, and postdrafting strategies" is "useful in any composing situation."

Recent research on the composing processes (Bridwell, Johnson, and Brehe 1987; Bridwell, Sirc, and Brooke 1985; Selzer 1983) teaches us to respect the differences in writing behaviors, according to individual writers and specific tasks. Some writers plan visually, some verbally; some mentally, some on paper; of those who work on paper, some use lists, some actual prose. And these behaviors may vary according to different genres and contexts. Some writers, like the engineer studied by Selzer, engage in communal brainstorming and do little or no revision. Our computer-assisted writing programs must respect the broad range of learning styles in our classroom communities or, as Elias (1984) warns, echoing Papert, "the computer revolution in writing classes may be dead before it really gets underway" (3).

The traditional two-way relationship in a writing class — teacher to student, and back — has broadened to accommodate a cybernetic third party, but the kind of thinking that results in these computerized response programs may reduce the interaction to one between the computer and student, making more real Papert's fear of the computer "programming the student." The notion that the computer can replace the teacher in certain crucial response situations, as seen in Marling's comments about the tedium of comma splices or Kiefer and Smith's idea (1983, 210) that Writer's Workbench can sensitize a student to language, needs a great deal of elaboration and proof (or more revolutionary hardware and software) if we are to believe it. What is more important in the classroom writing situation than feedback? Why is this an area we would even want to put in the hands of a medium that cannot read? As Robertson (1986) has recently claimed, "As much as anything we can do, responding to the content of student papers can help our students to write sincerely" (91). And, as Hirsch (1977) has noted:

> To make comments on a student's paper is to build upon productive schemata which the student already has, and to encourage their expansion and improvement. Because the comment method is so direct and so widespread in all forms of practical instruction, we can reasonably assume that it has the highest importance in composition teaching. (159)

How can the parameters of what makes a successful paper — in what is, by definition, an individual situation — be delineated in a fixed, non-writer-, non-situation-, and in many cases non-genre-specific program? When can a preprogrammed generic response (even one based, perhaps, on keywords or length) tell anything significant about a specific student text, except coincidentally? When can a fortune cookie ever tell you anything about your life, except accidentally? Consider, for example, Burns's (1984) report of a student who entered wisecracks instead of exploratory discourse on his topic while using Burns's program:

Computer: What special experiences made you select life as your topic?
Student: Don't get off the subject pal, you tell me what life is all about!
Computer: Fine, Glenn. Write some more.
Student: You don't know what the [expletive deleted] I'm writing anyway. (25)

Burns claims Glenn "did not understand how the program could help him" (26). Perhaps Glenn understood that the program could not help him.

Computer response programs that stress prewriting procedures raise a serious problem with invention in general. As seen in these interactive dialogue programs, teachers have begun to prescribe invention wholesale, regardless of individual learning styles. In a short time we have gone from Young (1978) bemoaning invention's absence in pedagogy to prewriting's unfortunate reification in the writing process. Invention heuristics are in danger of becoming the Valium of the writing profession — no matter what your writing problem, they can help. Hashimoto (1985), in a strong critique of structured heuristics, claims their use is both "optimistic" and "oversimplified" (73). Citing exhaustive evidence from cognitive psychology, he delimits the value of invention heuristics in a writing class:

> With limited knowledge about how writers think heuristically, teachers must be careful not to oversimplify both the procedures and insights they offer to students. They cannot, for instance, offer one or two heuristic procedures to students without helping students to understand the limitations and specific applications of such procedures. They cannot expect to teach their students to discover interesting things, abundant things to say about all subjects. (And they cannot grade their students on their ability to discover interesting, abundant things to say.) They cannot expect their students to change their perceptions easily or quickly or to recognize unique solutions to problems. (78–79)

As Hashimoto suggests, heuristics have no respect for individual cognitive styles. To cite a personal example, one of the learning-disabled students I currently work with had major problems writing a narrative for me. After much labor and many unsatisfying drafts, he burst into my office with a breakthrough version of the paper. He was proud to tell me how he finally came up with a good text: "I think best in flow charts," he told me, "so I just started looking at the incident as one point in the flow chart, then started looking backwards." This student, I suggest, had to escape from a verbal to a more formal, visual mode to write his paper. Writing answers to preprogrammed questions would have helped him about as much as talking to me and his classmates for three weeks did. And, as Elias (1984) has observed, these structured response programs can exclude the serendipity that can occur in a looser style of prewriting.

There is a related problem in the persona, an extension of the teacher, that comes on the screen in many computer-assisted response programs. Citing time away from the teacher as a requisite for worthwhile student invention activities, Emig (1971) worries that there is "no place where a student can be alone, although all accounts of writers tell us a condition of solitude is requisite for certain kinds of encounters with words and concepts" (99). Similarly, the use of current dialogue invention programs might be another way of denying the student opportunities for solitude that might be needed for invention; we may not be gaining as much as we think by having an iconic teacher come on and "guide" a student's process of inquiry. In discussing the programmed persona — the unflaggingly cheery, supportive personality in which many of these programs respond — Jobst and Wahlstrom (1984) wonder if such genial anthropomorphism is actually conducive to learning; they cite age as a factor to consider when using these programs and have announced research undertaken on "the effect of [a] neutral or even hostile persona on the learning process ('You mean you still don't know how to use the semicolon? Okay, dummy, let's get started.')" (5).

Taken as a whole, computer response programs announce an unfortunate return to a pre-process paradigm, emphasizing form and surface correctness, at the possible expense of our student's own writing processes. From Emig's railing over the "Fifty-Star Theme" (1971, 97) and Perl's (1979) significant discoveries about how obsession with editing (for students, "primarily an exercise in error-hunting") can warp a student's composing behavior by "intrud[ing] so often and to such a degree that it breaks down the rhythms generated by thinking and writing" (333), we now have both a program (Wresch 1984) for generating five-paragraph essays and Writer's Workbench, which epitomizes the text as a surface product to be measured according to arbitrarily privileged criteria. Response programs that give knee-jerk demands for the user to enter more text, despite the powerful writing that user already may have done, seem wrongheaded in terms of providing an effective environment in which students can work; they give a response based solely on quantity rather than quality. How can the programs accommodate the student who knows after only four or five entries what she wants to write about? She still will have to work through the program in order to reach the next section. That might produce a sense of frustration and tedium — writing, even the generation of a six-item list, can become drudgery, a chore, almost a kind of punishment. What student, receiving only a fourth-grade or sixth-grade reading level analysis from the computer, is going to be happy when other papers in his class receive a high-school reading level? When is information about a paper's reading level, as such, ever necessary for students?

We have come quite far from Nold's fearful, trembling humanist who finally approaches the computer, convinced of its "non-threatening" status. One would think, like Papert, we would want to use the technology, in this instance, to evolve the process paradigm full-blown, to further empower our writers in developing their processes of written language production, of making meaning for themselves and for readers. Current response programs head back in the direction of the end product, a direction one would have thought had been eliminated by advances in composing process theory. Whence will the new relationships with knowledge come, if the focus of thinking takes us back to discarded metaphors?

Even if this kind of program would help an already-mature writer practice the editing of drafts, we should think twice about introducing an intense surface-level focus to our students. Writing cannot be conceived of as a board game, where all we have to do is hope that we get our prepositions down to the mystical number, eliminate as many "to be" verbs as possible, reduce the number of nominalizations, and get that high maturity index. Scholars studying the use of text-feedback programs must determine not that the programs effectively teach editing skills, but that they do something other than reinforce the epistemology of the "error-hunt." Checking for prepositions is fine for some writers who want or need that information, but computer-assisted exercises for students may become such an easily exportable curriculum (both to screen and classroom) that we lull ourselves into thinking they will teach powerful ideas about writing. For those who would claim that the use of such feedback programs actually improves editing skills, I would cite Perkins's claim (1985) that such "low-road transfer" of skill (e.g., from editing with a text-feedback program to editing without it) has been found to require *"extensive, varied* practice." Substitute "editing" for "programming" in the following observation:

> By this formula, only years of programming experience on a variety of programming tasks should yield higher level skills suitable for a range of programming tasks. Consistently with this, Mawby . . . reports a crucial observation about very skilled young programmers: Without exception, several interviewed disclosed enormous time on task. No instances of overnight wonders have surfaced. (Perkins 1985, 14)

When one asks the computer itself — its mechanics — to respond, that response will be unsatisfying. Emig (1971) had to remind us that "persons, rather than mechanisms, compose" (5). And, to extend her idea, it is persons, rather than mechanisms, that respond. All the computer can do is count and identify keywords it's been told to identify. We do better to conceive of the computer as a medium, a *means* for response, rather than, in its mechanics, as an end. What computerized response offers, by definition, is non-commentary as commentary, uncommentary. Teachers who develop and use computer-assisted response programs refer to glowing student surveys as proof of the programs' effectiveness; perhaps students are responding so positively not to the pedagogy, but to the medium in which they are working.

The Computer as Response Medium: Toward Rich Pedagogy

Computer-assisted response programs that utilize the computer's power as medium rather than delivery system, programs that allow writers, whether naive or experienced, to respond to each other, hold the most promise for the increasingly computerized writing classroom. I will close this article by discussing several computer-mediated response programs, focusing on the two I use in my own classes. Schwartz (1984) pioneered popular use of the computer as medium with her SEEN program, which, though limited by preprogrammed questions, allows students to comment on each other's writing and exchange this commentary. Schwartz realized that, rather than a series of stock, non-discourse-specific comments, what would help a student writer is an environment in which "the student can discourse with peers to refine ideas and learn about audience needs" (46). Preprogrammed, open-ended question prompts, used to help develop a writer's hypothesis, make up the first part of the program, but what makes SEEN revolutionary is the electronic bulletin board the program mimics. Here, student writers can read each other's ideas (those developed in the first part) and comment on them. A simple notion, to be sure, but *real* response from *real* writers is a sorely needed element in response programs. The program is a controlled, limited, but important way to expose a novice writer to the world of discourse.

Currently, we are seeing the emergence of other programs allowing the computer to be used as a very sophisticated medium for discourse. It should be mentioned at the outset that these types of programs are wholly new and untested in writing, but what they offer seems intriguing enough to warrant further study. PROSE, designed for the Macintosh, allows a teacher to comment onscreen about a student's paper (much like Marling's program), giving the teacher the ability to "mark" a paper, the marks corresponding to canned grammar-book information which is then read from an onscreen window by the student. What distinguishes PROSE, however, is its ability to allow the teacher to write his or her own comments in a similar window. PROSE, then, is a slick version of the old marked-up student paper. PROSE has another, more questionable feature: its ability to direct "forced revision." The teacher can arrange onscreen response so that the student *has* to revise before proceeding any further through the graded paper. The benefits of response-as-hostage seem slight.

Another similar, more flexible version of such a program is For-Comment. Word-processed files can be "imported" into this program (used primarily in the business environment) in order for users to read, review, and offer specific comments and suggested revisions. The program allows the writer to mark passages to which she wants reviewers to pay particular attention. The program allows a multiplicity of reviewers to read and respond to a given text, so, like Schwartz's program, the student writer can draw on the benefits of a community of readers, rather than the monolithic reading of one teacher. Like PROSE, ForComment operates in a windowed environment and allows the reviewer to type comments and possible revisions in the windows. In ForComment, the suggested revisions can actually be "swapped" into the file itself, to see how various suggested revisions will look: It seems an ideal method to teach post-structuralist notions of authors and texts. And, using a dialogue feature, the writer can answer his reviewers, allowing increased practice in metalanguage.

The above programs demonstrate the interest in computer-assisted response; if the computer is a powerful tool to aid writing, then by extension, it may become an equally powerful medium in which to respond to writing. The computer's ability to store, manipulate, and collate data, when brought to bear on textual commentary, may ease a student's bewilderment about how to use commentary and help guide the student's attention and allow the commentary to visibly affect the writing. To scrawl "awkward" in the margins of a student's text is one thing; the computer's value as response medium can be seen in a program like ForComment, in which a teacher can now mark an awkward passage with a special prompt, enabling the student to pull down a window that explains why the passage is awkward and suggests a smoother syntactic choice. Grading becomes almost three-dimensional; reading a corrected paper may become a kind of mini-tutorial rather than just a quick scan to check the grade. Obviously, the amount of time spent grading papers in this mode may outweigh the actual benefits of such a program. Perhaps, until the time problem is solved, such a computer-assisted response may be used once or twice a term or for students with special needs.

I have been using other forms of computer-assisted response for a few years now and will conclude this chapter with a brief discussion of them. One method I use was derived from my composing process research, using a keystroke-recording program developed at the University of Minnesota, under the auspices of a FIPSE grant (Sirc and Bridwell 1988). Briefly, the program overlays a commercial word-processing package (WordStar), intercepts the keystrokes as they go into memory, saves them, and allows them to be played back onscreen in real time (see Bridwell, Sirc, and Brooke 1985; Bridwell, Johnson, and Brehe 1987; Sirc and Anson 1985). I had been looking for ways to use this program for pedagogical as well as research purposes. In thinking about how the onscreen playback of a composing session could be used as a teaching tool, I had the image of the art teacher who watches a student draw, sees a struggle to achieve an effect, and models for the student the drawing process which he or she uses as an artist, tracing over the rough parts, showing the student one way the effect could be achieved.

I began, then, by asking students in my classes if they would like to watch me revise their papers onscreen. Many do, but I stress that this is purely voluntary, open to any students who feel they could benefit from the session. I take their texts and, with the recording program saving my keystrokes, begin to revise. Then my student and I watch a replay of the revision unfold together, discussing ideas about form and content while I explain my choices and while my student surfaces issues in his or her original draft. I tell students places where I'm still not happy, where I didn't capture a meaning well enough. And then they join me in the revising process, making further suggestions. This procedure builds on, to use Hirsch's phrase again, the "productive schemata which the student already has." My faith in the medium is such that I use a program that wasn't even designed for what I'm doing with it.

I offer my method as something that can be done with technology that I think has humane ends, and can help instantiate thinking about writing as constraint juggling, problem solving. Like the developers of PROSE and ForComment, I believe that sometimes actual revision is the best response writers, especially basic writers, can use. By replaying the real-time record of my revision, we can watch not only writing unfold, but we are able to discuss the theoretical issues involved in writing as well. A student can watch me expand her ideas, or more clearly focus or organize them. Students respond well to having these broader notions personalized through their own texts. Listening to a student talk about his own writing, and my revision of it, affords me as a teacher more insight into the student's conceptualization of writing, what is and is not understood. He or she can also see where I totally misread a passage and perhaps realize the inability of that text to reach a reader properly.

Talking about the difference between this kind of real-time revision and marginal comments that ask for more detail, one of my students said, "You try to think 'more detail,' and you can't think of anything." She wanted a printout as a kind of model to refer to, telling me that remembering how I extended her details might help her when she goes blank. To be sure, Burns (1984) cites this as one goal for the next generation of computer response programs: "Second-generation pre-writing software should allow students to explore and better define their own cognitive styles" (32).

"I like how you took my ideas," another of my students added. "It's kind of like opening up the page to an idea. Like one idea you might have added two more pages to. I like that, the whole aura around it, it's kind of like what I was looking for. It's kind of like reading a book right beside the writer. It's good." I liked hearing I was "opening up a page" to her. That was one purpose of my computerized response, to make it a kind of process revision, marginal and end comments given life. I am not advocating — nor do I use — the foregoing method of computer-assisted response for all students. Time would prohibit it, and some might not learn well this way. So I show those writers interested a process response for one or two papers.

The other method of computer-assisted response used in my classes is a utility program that runs on a local-area computer network. This utility program mimics a CB radio; all (or any subgroup of) the student writers on a network can "discuss" (in writing, since they have to type the messages they send over the network) their papers on the same channel. Once they type in a comment, they send it over the network and that comment, along with the sender's name, is seen by all writers on the channel. I break my classes up into four- or five-person conference groups, each group on a different channel, and they use the network for their peer-group conferences. Again, it must be stressed that the power of the computer in this response setting is merely to provide a medium of exchange between human users; actual texts are discussed by actual readers. The computer also provides the capacity to store transcripts of these conversations; my students print these out and use them to guide revisions. A sample transcript will illustrate this type of computer response:

Paul: well lets hear it.
Joe: Over all I liked it except in the first Paragraph I was a little confused about what you were trying to conquore [sic].
Michelle: I really liked it. I wasn't aware of the strong male passion for motorbikes.
Paul: Does it seem to apply to the young male adult?
Joe: yes
Andrew: Joe is right, How about starting out "Motor cycles are great the women love them . . ." and then explain other benefits of cycling also explain what dangers there are right off
Paul: I like that, that's not bad, I will take that under consideration.
Michelle: I think you got your point across well as far as them not being as cool as you had thought. But because of the title I expected to hear more about the "ups" of motorcycles along with the "moral" of the story. I don't know much about them so I would

like to hear how fun they are. I'm just curious — how badly did you get hurt?

There is nothing really revolutionary about this: it is a peer-group conference, simply conducted in writing (though the benefits of that, yet to be shown, may be powerful indeed). Issues of title, purpose, and audience come up; Paul, the writer of the paper under discussion, has a better sense of what he should do in a revision. All the students, through articulating their commentary, have also had practice in developing a metalanguage, a self-reflexive discourse that will aid them in "owning" the process of writing.

My uses of computer response, then, are those that put the focus on the computer as enabler. Computers per se have nothing to tell my students. But I have much to tell them, and they have much to tell themselves; if computers can aid in this endeavor, so much the better. I am not interested in a computer acting as a faceless arbiter for my students' writing. I distrust response programs that center on writing as deficient, as absent of quality, as an error field to be charted. These programs use the sophisticated power of the machine (to a human, the embodiment of perfection) to institutionalize students' deficiency. Marling (1984), in conference with a student, becomes the man behind the curtain in Oz's palace: Silently and skillfully he manipulates the buttons and levers of his awesome engine, invoking the specter that will humble the quivering Dorothy.

> [Grader] also made conferences with students about their "progress," or lack thereof, incredibly direct. I could scroll through the error total for a series of papers without saying a word, letting the student judge his "progress." Sometimes he left muttering "Jeez, I've got to do something about that . . . ." (806)

The programs I use are much less glamorous than the others I've discussed, but they allow students' work to be treated as serious writing, worthy of response. Computer response programs are best when they liberate students to write and talk about their writing. In so doing, we as educators are willfully freeing ourselves from the conservative bias Papert tells us is inherent in new technologies:

> The first use of the new technology is quite naturally to do in a slightly different way what had been done before without it. It took years before designers of automobiles accepted the idea that they were cars, not "horseless carriages." (36)

We have come a long way in writing theory, and with the growing amount of recent thinking from other disciplines infusing our own, our future looks ever more interesting. We must, then, resist retreating into conservative pedagogy with our use of computer-assisted response, simply feeding students the same surface-based criteria on which they were poorly nourished for years, only now with a sugar coating. I am reminded, again, of the old Jetsons episode, in which technology has provided not a glorious, undreamed-of "astro-future," but simply the same impoverished realities disguised with the prefixes and suffixes of innovation. The Respond-O-Matic will always go on the blink.

References

Bridwell, L., P. Johnson, and S. Brehe. 1987. Computers and Composing: Case Studies of Experienced Writers. In *Writing in Real Time: Modelling Production Processes*, edited by A. Matsuhashi. New York: Longman.

Bridwell, L., G. Sirc, and R. Brooke. 1985. Computing and Revising: Case Studies of Student Writers. In *The Acquisition of Written Language: Response and Revision*, edited by S. Freedman. Norwood, N.J.: Ablex.

Burns, H. 1984. Recollections of First-Generation Computer-Assisted Prewriting. In *The Computer in Composition Instruction: A Writer's Tool*, edited by W. Wresch. Urbana, Ill.: National Council of Teachers of English.

Burns, H., and G. Culp. 1980. Stimulating Invention in English Composition through Computer-Assisted Instruction. *Educational Technology* 20:5–10.

Cohen, M., and R. Lanham. 1984. HOMER: Teaching Style with a Microcomputer. In *The Computer in Composition Instruction: A Writer's Tool*, edited by W. Wresch. Urbana, Ill.: National Council of Teachers of English.

Elias, R. 1984. Will Computers Liberate the Comp Drudge? Paper presented at the spring conference of Delaware Valley Writing Council and Villanova University's English Department, February, Villanova, Pa. ERIC Document Reproduction Service ED 224 954.

Emig, J. 1971. *The Composing Processes of Twelfth Graders*. Urbana, Ill.: National Council of Teachers of English.

Hashimoto, I. 1985. Structured Heuristic Procedures: Their Limitations. *College Composition and Communication* 36:73–81.

Hirsch, E. D., Jr. 1977. *The Philosophy of Composition*. Chicago: University of Chicago Press.

Jobst, J., and B. Wahlstrom. 1984. How "Friendly" Should Effective Software Be? *Computers and Composition* 2:5.

Kiefer, K., and C. Smith. 1983. Textual Analysis with Computers: Tests of Bell Laboratories' Computer Software. *Research in the Teaching of English* 17:201–14.

Kiefer, K., and C. Smith. 1984. Improving Students' Revising and Editing: The Writer's Workbench System. In *The Computer in Composition Instruction: A Writer's Tool*, edited by W. Wresch. Urbana, Ill.: National Council of Teachers of English.

Kotler, L., and K. Anandam. 1983. A Partnership of Teacher and Computer in Teaching Writing. *College Composition and Communication* 34:361–67.

Marling, W. 1984. Grading Essays on a Microcomputer. *College English* 46:797–810.

Nold, E. 1975. Fear and Trembling: The Humanist Approaches the Computer. *College Composition and Communication* 26:269–73.

Papert, S. 1980. *Mindstorms: Children, Computers, and Powerful Ideas*. New York: Basic Books.

Perkins, D. 1985. The Fingertip Effect: How Information Processing Technology Shapes Thinking. *Educational Researcher* 14 (7): 11–17.

Perl, S. 1979. The Composing Processes of Unskilled College Writers. *Research in the Teaching of English* 13:317–36.

Robertson, M. 1986. "Is Anybody Listening?": Responding to Student Writing. *College Composition and Communication* 37:87–91.

Schwartz, H. 1984. SEEN: A Tutorial and User Network for Hypothesis Testing. In *The Computer in Composition Instruction: A Writer's Tool*, edited by W. Wresch. Urbana, Ill.: National Council of Teachers of English.

Selfe, C. 1984. Wordsworth II: Process-Based CAI for College Composition Teachers. In *The Computer in Composition Instruction: A Writer's Tool*, edited by W. Wresch. Urbana, Ill.: National Council of Teachers of English.

Selfe, C., and B. Wahlstrom. 1982. *The Benevolent Beast: Computer-Assisted Instruction for the Teaching of Writing*. ERIC Document Reproduction Service ED 234 398.

Selzer, J. 1983. The Composing Processes of an Engineer. *College Composition and Communication* 34:178–87.

Sirc, G., and C. M. Anson. 1985. What Writers Say: Analyzing the Metacommentaries of College Writers. *Forum in Reading and Language Education* 1 (2): 59–74.

Sirc, G., and L. S. Bridwell. 1988. A Computer Tool for Analyzing the Composing Process. *Collegiate Microcomputer* 6 (2): 155–60.

Sommers, N. 1982. Responding to Student Writing. *College Composition and Communication* 33:148–56.

Wresch, W. 1984. Questions, Answers, and Automated Writing. In *The Computer in Composition Instruction: A Writer's Tool*, edited by W. Wresch. Urbana, Ill.: National Council of Teachers of English.

Young, R. 1978. Paradigms and Problems: Needed Research in Rhetorical Invention. In *Research on Composing: Points of Departure*, edited by C. R. Cooper and L. Odell. Urbana, Ill.: National Council of Teachers of English.

III Studies of Response in the Instructional Context

11 Response to Writing as a Context for Learning to Write

Martin Nystrand and Deborah Brandt
University of Wisconsin–Madison

For several years we have conducted research, funded by the National Institute of Education, examining the effectiveness of peer conferencing in college freshman writing instruction at the University of Wisconsin–Madison. From this research, it is clear that students who write for each other not only learn to write better, but also that they learn to write differently than students whose sole audience is the instructor. Specifically, how both groups of students learn to write is significantly related to the kinds of response they get from their readers and, as a consequence, how the writers come to view their readers.

In this chapter, we first review research that examines the general benefits of intensive peer review. Then, to gain a more precise sense of just how talking about writing can affect writing, we show how revisions that several students make in their papers can be traced to discussions of their drafts. Examining revisions in light of the discussions that give rise to them sheds considerable light in a wholly unobtrusive way on the motivations for the revisions, and thereby provides insight into the composing process of writers.

Peer Conferencing in the Writing Studio

The "Expository Writing Studio" is a student-centered method of teaching expository writing, successfully introduced by Nick Doane and developed at the University of Wisconsin–Madison over the past six years. Students meet regularly in groups of four or five, and the same groups meet three times a week over the course of the term for the purpose of sharing and critiquing one another's writing. The instructor assigns few topics and gives students no checklists to use in monitoring their discussions. Rather, students keep journals and prepare pieces of exposition from these notebooks for presentation to classmates at every class meeting. Students are required to prepare a new paper or a substantial revision for each class. They are instructed to consider the extent to which the author achieves his or her purpose; they are to avoid discussing spelling, punctuation, and usage; and they are required to provide each member of their group with a photocopy of their work. Periodically the instructor collects the best papers from each student for evaluation, but does relatively little direct instruction; teacher intervention in these groups is minimal.

Much recent research supports the effectiveness of intensive peer review. Peer work is found to contribute to gains in critical thinking, organization, and appropriateness (Lagana 1973); to revision (Benson 1979); to attention to prewriting and increased awareness of one's own writing processes (Nystrand 1983); and to writer confidence (Fox 1980). Moffett (1968) explained the effectiveness of peer conferencing in terms of the regularity and sustained quality of feedback. Research on writing groups has recently been summarized in Gere (1987).

Our experience corroborates all these conclusions. We are particularly impressed with the effective way that intensive peer review conditions writing as a communicative act. Intensive peer review works largely because it establishes reciprocity between writer and reader as a condition of discourse. In so doing, it heightens writers' awareness of the balance their texts must strike between their own intentions and their readers' expectations. Intensive peer review accomplishes this, moreover, in a way that is not always possible or as fully possible when students write exclusively for the teacher. For practical reasons, teachers are unable to give useful feedback to all their students' writing every class day. Even less are they able effectively to respond to student papers as actual texts. By this we mean that, though teachers may judge papers for the effectiveness of their persuasion, explanation, etc., the actual effects of the paper in persuading, explaining, etc., are rarely at issue for teachers. As Gere and Stevens (1985) point out, teachers evaluate papers not as actual texts, but as ideal texts. The focus of peer conferencing, Gere and Stevens conclude, is "an actual text, one which communicates the meaning students find inherent in the text presented," whereas teacher response is more concerned with "an ideal text, one which possesses certain abstract features of writing quite independently of any meaning. . . . [W]riting groups unconsciously assume that the purpose of writing is rhetorical, that it is meant to have some influence or effect on a reader/listener" (103).

Largely as a consequence of this difference in textual orientation, groups tend to deal with errors more functionally than do instructors.

Groups, more consistently than teachers, work with errors as evidence of what the writer is trying to say. Very few writers are able to compose more than a simple note without striking a word or line. Typically the process of composing takes a rather bumpy road, and as much as writing, the writer is engaged in scratching and rewriting. In writing, students not only say what they mean, but also discover having said things they didn't intend. These mistakes or inadvertencies are in effect troublesources (discrepancies between what the writer has to say and what the reader knows and expects to find), many of which are detected and repaired by the writer in the form of scratch-outs, deletions, insertions, and rewrites. Indeed, drafting may be defined as this very sort of problem solving, and actual composing is as filled as talk (more so than one might think) with starts and stops, misstarts and repairs (see Halliday 1988). Other problems are detected only when someone else reads the completed text. It is these problems — these mistakes and difficulties — of course, that are the focus of effective feedback which writers require if they are to learn to write. The effectiveness of intensive peer review lies largely in its efficacy in defining true troublesources — not discrepancies between the writer's text and some ideal text, but mismatches between what the writer actually has to say and what the reader actually needs and expects to find.

Experience in identifying and resolving such troublesources is unquestionably essential to learning to write. Consequently, the problems writers address as they compose and revise shape just what they learn about writing. But just what constitutes a troublesource? What do students — whether rescanning and reworking their own draft or reading someone else's text — regard as a problem? If pressed, most readers tend to regard *mistakes in spelling, capitalization, punctuation,* etc., more categorically as problems than difficulties with *organization, development, and tone.* Whether the latter prove troublesome for any given text will vary a great deal from reader to reader, for example, according to readers' expectations of a certain kind of discourse (Is this meant to be informal or formal? Is this a draft or the final copy?), and also according to how much individual readers know about the topic: Knowledgeable readers will more consistently query ambiguities, whereas unknowledgeable readers will more consistently query abstruseness (Nystrand 1986, Chapter 5). Readers also will register problems — with diction, tone, abbreviations — related to the character of the discourse (Is this an informal note or something to be published? Where will it be published?). And finally, whether any of these items does, in fact, prove troublesome depends upon the relative status of writer and reader (see Ochs 1987). For example, students probably have a higher tolerance for ambiguities in the published texts of "important scholars" than professors have for ambiguities in the papers of their students.

To gain some understanding of student writers' awareness of troublesources, especially as it affects what they learn about writing, we have conducted a number of studies. In these studies we have focused on students' revisions and their ideas about revision, since what writers say about revision and actually change in their texts reveals a great deal about their ideas of troublesources. Furthermore, by comparing students who write exclusively for the instructor with those students who write mainly for their peers, we have investigated the respective roles that these two different audiences play in affecting students' revisions and their ideas about revisions.

Study One: The Effects of Peer Conferencing on Premises about Composing

In one study (Nystrand 1986, Chapter 8), students were asked to write about how they generally write papers. They did this once at the start of the term and once again at the end. These descriptions showed clear and significant differences in students' ideas about revision, depending upon whether they had written exclusively for the instructor or whether they had written substantially and extensively for their peers. Students who wrote mainly for the instructor saw their readers chiefly as judges, for example, and increasingly saw revision as a matter of editing and tidying up texts ($r = .23$; F $[1,113] = 6.586$; p $< .01$); their focus was mainly on lexical and syntactical concerns.

The peer-conferencing sections stood in sharp contrast to their counterparts. Whereas students writing solely for the instructor increasingly treated revision as a matter of editing (start of term: no significant difference; end of term: F $[1,105] = 15.99$; p $< .001$), students writing for one another increasingly viewed their readers less as judges of their writing and more as *collaborators in a communicative process* (start of term: no significant difference; end of term: F $[1,105] = 7.55$; p $< .007$). Increasingly these students treated revision as a matter of reconceptualization (start of term: no significant difference; end of term: F $[1,105] = 4.931$; p $= .029$).

In other words, students who regularly wrote for each other increasingly saw their texts not as something to be judged, but rather as the functional means and their best chance for balancing their own purposes as writers with the expectations of their readers. Finally, this study showed that students' attitudes toward writing became increasingly more positive to the extent that they wrote for each other (start of term: no significant difference; end of term: F [1,105] = 3.465; p = .065).

Study Two: The Effects of Peer Conferencing on Revision

As follow-up to this research, we examined the revision processes and actual revisions of studio and nonstudio writers. To do this, we elicited and collected drafts on set argumentative topics in all sections of the course, which included both studio and nonstudio (more conventional settings in which the teacher was the exclusive audience) classes. One week later, we asked students to revise these drafts in class. In the same session that students wrote the initial drafts, we also asked them to explain in a brief written statement what they needed to do to revise their essays into final copies; in the final session, we asked them to assess both the strengths and weaknesses of their revisions. These drafts and revisions, as well as revision-needs statements and self-assessments, were then read for the traits shown in Figure 1. Two trained graduate students read each paper blind; the interrater reliability, computed as a Pearson product-moment correlation, was r = .72; F [1,306] = 327.05; p < .00001. Statistical analysis of these traits then allowed us to examine some general differences in revision practices and revision premises, both within and between studio and nonstudio classes.

In these analyses, we found three essential differences between studio students' and nonstudio students' revisions. First, studio students' revisions were of higher quality than those of their counterparts. In addition, studio and nonstudio students expressed very different views of what is required to effectively revise their papers. Finally, the expressed premises of studio writers more closely related to the revisions they actually made than did those of their counterparts, which is to say, studio writers have more insight into their writing. We now look more closely at these findings.

Writing Quality

Revisions were read for clarity of topic and commentary, and mastery of genre features such as diction, tone, organization, and presentation of evidence. The very best papers were judged "crystal clear" both in topic and commentary and demonstrated "clear mastery of the possibilities of the essay genre." A multivariate analysis of variance, comparing studio and nonstudio sections in terms of all these features,

I. Evaluate the essay for the following:

   1. *Topic:* To what extent is it clear what the piece is about?

1	2	3	4	5	6
Unclear	Occasional Questions	Adequate		Very Clear	Crystal Clear

   2. *Comment:* To what extent is it clear what the writer has to say about this topic?

1	2	3	4	5	6
Unclear	Occasional Questions	Adequate		Very Clear	Crystal Clear

   3. *Genre:* To what extent is it clear that this text is an essay?

1	2	3	4	5	6
Wholly Inadequate	Blurred Genre	Adequate	Clearly an Essay		Mastery of Genre

II. To what extent does the writer's own statement of strengths and weaknesses match your own rating of the revision?

   1. At the level of *topic:*

1	2	3	4	5	6
Not at All		Some		Quite a Bit	Completely

   2. At the level of *comment:*

1	2	3	4	5	6
Not at All		Some		Quite a Bit	Completely

   3. At the level of *genre:*

1	2	3	4	5	6
Not at All		Some		Quite a Bit	Completely

III. Is the revision different from the original? How much?

   1. At the level of *topic:*

1	2	3	4	5	6
Not at All	A Little			Some	Very Much

   2. At the level of *comment:*

1	2	3	4	5	6
Not at All	A Little			Some	Very Much

   3. At the level of *genre:*

1	2	3	4	5	6
Not at All	A Little			Some	Very Much

Figure 1. Reader Evaluation Form

Figure 1 (*continued*)

IV. To what extent do the changes made in the revision match those identified in the revision-needs statement?

1. At the level of *topic:*

1	2	3	4	5	6
Not at All	A Little		Some		Very Much

2. At the level of *comment:*

1	2	3	4	5	6
Not at All	A Little		Some		Very Much

3. At the level of *genre:*

1	2	3	4	5	6
Not at All	A Little		Some		Very Much

showed significant differences between the two groups (post hoc F [1,91] = 1.79; p = .04).

Revision Premises

We found several revealing and significant differences between the two groups when we compared the revision-needs statements of the two groups. Studio students (1) had more to say than their counterparts about their revision needs, (2) were more specific about these needs, (3) explained more clearly what their revisions were to accomplish, (4) were more openly critical of their drafts, (5) more clearly particularized their revision needs to a rhetorical situation, and (6) discussed their revision needs in a more coherent and integrated manner. Comparing the two groups on these and other factors shown in Table 1, a multivariate analysis of variance showed the two groups were altogether different.

Relationship between Revision Premises and Actual Revisions

One of our assessments examined what students said they were going to revise. We then correlated these goal statements with expressed premises about revision. Studio students, more than their counterparts, accurately estimated the strengths and weaknesses of their papers as judged by independent readings, and the accuracy of these estimates correlated with the students' explicit emphasis on rhetorical goal-setting in their statements of revision needs. This emphasis by studio

Table 1

Multivariate Analysis of Variance on Premises of Revision

Studio Effect: F (8,84) = 6.78; p = .000

Studio vs. Nonstudio Univariate:

| | Means | | | |
	Studio	Nonstudio	F	p
(a) Number of words in statement of revision needs	75.42	45.63	31.78	.000
(b) Author is specific about revision needs*	2.72	1.87	11.91	.001
(c) Author discusses revisions explicitly in terms of reader needs*	1.57	1.21	2.97	.088
(d) Author clearly explains purpose of revisions*	2.47	2.05	4.52	.036
(e) Author accurately identifies strengths in draft*	1.00	1.24	7.94	.006
(f) Author's motivation for proposed revisions is obligatory or functional*	3.21	2.08	17.45	.000
(g) Revision-needs statement is coherent, showing evidence of reasoning and reflection*	3.01	2.24	9.73	.002

N = 95
*Judged on 6-point Likert scale

students on rhetorical goal-setting was also apparent in their statements of what they proposed to do to improve their original drafts. By contrast, nonstudio students merely said they needed to "elaborate more."

Study Three: Relationship between Revisions and Group Discussions

We have attempted to account for the revision styles of studio students in terms of the classroom context in which they write and revise. Because these students experiment with the resources of written language while engaged in an ongoing, reciprocal relationship with their readers, they can connect their choices as writers with the functional effects of those choices. As a result, text revisions tend to be more specific, more explicitly related to readers' needs, and more clearly embody a particular rhetorical situation.

This part of the chapter takes a closer look at the context itself to see how conversations in peer writing groups motivate and stimulate revision. For an entire semester, we videotaped the conversations of five college freshmen enrolled in a studio section of expository writing at the University of Wisconsin–Madison. In addition to videotaping their meetings, we collected all drafts and revisions done by the five-member group. The videotaped discussions, along with the actual texts, provided access to the contexts that motivated revisions. As a result, we were able to gain insight into the relationship between discussions and revisions. And we were able as well to trace the intricate interrelationships of the revisions themselves.

Experimenting with Text

To demonstrate these processes, we now consider the first and second drafts of an essay written by a college freshman named Alice. The essay, entitled "Description," is about the time Alice was accidentally knocked unconscious by a baseball bat. She reads the rough draft to her writing group. It begins this way:

> Storytelling is a true art. A good storyteller can describe a moment so that his audience will actually experience the event being described. The storyteller will use descriptive words to trigger similar memories of his audience. Following is a true story of an event that happened to me when I was about nine years old.

After the group discussion, Alice revises her draft. The new version begins this way:

> Last Saturday as I watched "The Road Runner Show," I saw Wile E. Coyote get cracked on the top of the head with an anvil. This happened when his well planned scheme to capture the elusive road runner backfired as usual. As I watched, stars appeared and began to dance around his head. This sight triggered a memory of something that happened to me when I was about nine years old.

Alice's revision is substantive and, we could agree, fortuitous. The second introduction more clearly and conventionally announces the essay as a narrative and, in fact, enacts the functions of storyteller that Alice only refers to abstractly in the first introduction. What motivated this revision? Transcripts of the conversation that takes place after Alice reads the first draft indicate that her writing group focused directly on two sources of trouble: What kind of text is this, and what is this text about? The group then began to rehearse new possibilities for beginning the story:

Amy: Why do you start off by saying storytelling is a true or a good storyteller can just . . . Why do you start out talking about stories?

Alice: Well, 'cause I didn't know . . . because this is real details, you know. This is . . . this story . . .

Alan: It sounds like she's going to start talking about storytelling.

Alice: This story, see, this is the name of it, "Description," and a good . . . storytelling is an art. And good stories can describe.

Amy: Well, if you named it "Description" . . . "Description" just kind of summarizes that, you know. You don't really need that because that's not part of your story. And you don't go back to it, you know. Maybe you should go back to it.

Alice: Maybe that's how I could end it. I don't know how I would open it if I didn't , you know. What's going to make someone interested in this? What's going to make someone pick it up and read it?

Kristen: I thought it was neat here about [Kristen refers to a passage in Alice's story that relates her sensations immediately after being struck by the bat. The draft reads: "What my eyes beheld was remarkable! On a vivid black velvet background shone five perfect, bone white stars. Each was perfectly shaped, and had five points. They all moved slowly in a circular, clockwise motion."] You could start out with that.

Mike: Yeah, that's a good idea. Something like that. That's what I was thinking when you . . . when I read that . . .

Alice: That's how I should start it?

Kristen: Anything can happen in a cartoon. You could get . . . what you felt like . . . who is the guy on "Bugs Bunny"?

Alan: OK. What do you think? Me and the Coyote have a lot in common. Back when I was in ninth grade . . .

Mike: I used to sit and watch cartoons when I was younger. And one day I had a similar experience . . . be compared to somebody.

Alice: It's funny because you'd think that, you know, that's just cartoons. And all of a sudden you're laying there and you're seeing these stars.

Thus, Alice's new introduction clearly is motivated (in fact, inspired) by the discussion with her peers, who alert her to a serious problem in the first draft: the opening does not fit the conventions of a narrative. Her introduction scrambles the signals, so alternatives must be found. But it is also through issues of genre *conventions* (the opening doesn't fit) that Alice clarifies her *intention*, both in terms of finding an appropriate way to make readers interested in her story and in terms of her own realization that getting hit on the head was like a cartoon. Experimenting with text occurs within this context of intention, convention, and reader response.

In examining eleven sets of discussions and subsequent revisions, we began to conceive of conversations and revisions in terms of "entry points." That is, we asked: At what level of text did the peer group "enter" a draft under consideration and, likewise, at what level of text did the writer "reenter" the text during revision? We used a framework developed by Nystrand (1986) that views writer-reader interactions as a constant, reciprocal negotiation among the following three levels of text functioning: What kind of text is this (genre-level)? What is this text about (topic-level)? What is being said (commentary-level)? These concerns pertain equally and reciprocally to writers and readers. Writers, as they compose, continually and appropriately elaborate elements of genre, topic, and commentary. When understanding is threatened or potentially threatened, they may repair understanding by revising at the level of genre, topic, and/or commentary. Readers likewise monitor the text in terms of these three levels as part of successful comprehension. Communication occurs when a writer's elaborations mesh with a reader's expectations.

This model has several obvious conceptual advantages for the purposes of our study. First, it was not only applicable to revised texts but also directly applicable to the discussions themselves, as we were able to trace the extent to which the group discussed a draft in terms of its genre, topic, and commentary. Thus, the model allowed us to seek relationships between the discussions and subsequent revisions. And, perhaps more important, it allowed us to relate text changes to their *function within a particular text*. Past revision studies have primarily focused on the structural nature of text revisions (word, phrase, clause, etc.) or have catalogued abstract operations such as deletions or substitutions (Bridwell 1980; Sommers 1980). But these systems do not provide the means to investigate the functional impact that revisions have, either on the text or on the reader-writer context. The Nystrand model considers revision in relationship to function, meaning, and context.

Results of Analysis

Three major findings emerged from our analysis of the relationship between discussion and subsequent revisions.

1. *A direct relationship existed between the group's "point of entry" during discussion and the author's "point of entry" in subsequent revisions.* As we watched the videotapes of students discussing rough drafts, we could reliably predict the sorts of revisions that would grow out of particular discussions. In a very basic way, the *extent* of the discussion predicted the extent of revision. If a discussion was short, perfunctory, or focused on surface correctness, subsequent revisions were typically

perfunctory and limited to surface changes. On the other hand, extended talk typically led to more revisions, and talk that focused on clarifying and elaborating specific points in a draft more predictably yielded revisions at the level of genre, topic, or commentary (and sometimes at all three).

The discussion of Alice's story is typical in this regard. Discussants entered her text primarily at the level of genre, and this discussion gave Alice a specific place to reenter her text during revision. In fact, the revisions Alice went on to make to the draft as a whole, not just to the introduction, continue to buttress the essay at the level of genre (see the appendix, page 228, for full texts of her first and second drafts). Alice tightened the chronology of the story and paid more explicit attention to some of the conventional features of narrative, including setting, complication, climax, resolution, and evaluation. We see in this pattern yet another way that intensive peer review can lend specificity to revision: giving writers a specific problem to sit down with during the revision process. Instead of the generic direction to write a second draft, studio students have the chance to begin each revision with a specific direction.

We say "chance" because not all the discussions we examined provided such direction. Five of the eleven cases involved minimal discussion, or to put it another way, in five cases the group "entered" texts in only superficial or "obligatory" ways. Three of these cases focused exclusively on isolated commentary-level concerns (for example, "Explain a little bit more what 'runner's high' is"), and the other two focused on what we call "obligatory" genre concerns, involving spelling, punctuation, or word form (e.g., "Should it be 'hanged' or 'hung'?"). In all but one of these cases, revisions likewise were limited to surface changes, bringing no discernible changes at the levels of genre, topic, or commentary.

This direct relationship between discussion and revision bears both cheerful and cautionary implications for teachers committed to intensive peer review. On the one hand, these case studies suggest that students do indeed *listen* to their peers. They do return during revision to the sources of trouble identified in discussions, often, as in the case of Alice, with good effect. On the other hand, unless the discussion is functional — that is, unless the discussion addresses readers' particular needs and expectations in concert with the writer's particular intentions and goals — then revisions themselves will tend not to be functional either. Functional revisions seem to depend on functional discussions. This is not to say, however, that students revised *only* the aspects of their drafts identified as troublesome during peer review. This point is addressed by the second major finding of our analysis.

2. *Changes at one level of text tended to implicate changes at other levels of text.* In one sense, this is an obvious finding. But actually, very little attention has been paid in revision studies to how changes at one level of text have an impact at other levels — how, for instance, elaborating commentary (what is being said about something) can actually alter what the writer and reader perceive as the topic, or how changes in topic might create new constraints on a writer's choice of genre. Revision studies' lack of attention to these interrelationships of textual changes is especially unfortunate given the fact that the spiral of repercussions which can be set off by just one choice during composing is an intuitively salient — and most challenging — characteristic of the writing act.

The need to consider how changes at one level of text may pressure changes at other levels is also especially pertinent when observing learning writers. Unlike expert writers, learning writers may lack the technical proficiency to control and realize intentions through the resources of written language, so that in a very real way, their texts can "get away" from them as they attempt to revise. Likewise, certain revision choices can create problems so technically demanding that an inexperienced writer may abandon (or simplify) an intention or plan in order to accommodate those choices.

Before considering the specific pressures we saw occurring in these students' revisions, we should consider first what we mean by the interrelationship of text revisions. In a deep sense, of course, a change at any level of text can and usually does affect meaning at other levels, so that to assign a revision to the category of genre, topic, or commentary is simply to name the primary aspect of a text that is being addressed by any one revision choice. For example, in the earlier case of the narrative essay, the writer was motivated to revise the introduction in terms of genre. The expository opening in the original draft threw her readers off; they did not know what to make of it in light of the narrative nature of the rest of the essay. While the point of entry appeared to be genre, however, the revision also implicated the topic of the introductory paragraph, as the second draft shifted away from the ostensible and distracting topic of "storytelling" to the topic of the story itself.

In the case of Alice's paper, in other words, "storytelling" was discarded as a topic as part of her decision to abandon the expository opening for something more conventionally appropriate to the form and meaning of the story. But in other cases, these multiple-level revisions appeared more explicitly orchestrated, as elaborations at one level called for reproportioning of text at other levels. In the following example, for instance, we see how the decision to elaborate a text at the level of commentary "crowds out" the original topic of the writer's draft; in fact, commentary and topic seem to reverse roles. Here, a student named Mike has written a rough draft called "Colosseum," which, in the introduction at least, attempts to draw parallels between spectator sports of ancient Rome and modern America. The draft begins this way:

> Recently I attended a football game between the Wisconsin Badgers and the Ohio State Buckeyes. There were over seventy thousand in attendance. The screaming fans were cheering the accomplishments of the two teams combating on the field. I was impressed by the massive spectacle. In Rome two thousand years ago, similar "games" were held by the Romans in the Colosseum. Today, after the contest the opposing teams shake hands and go about their normal lives, but in Rome the defeated was left dead in the sand.

The draft goes on to describe the seating arrangements in the Colosseum, the nature of gladiator fights, chariot races, battles with animals, and the attitude of the crowds, mentioning briefly that the games "tied in with religious celebrations." Mike concludes by surmising whether future generations will regard football in the same way we regard the Roman sports, as "barbaric" and "uncivilized."

In the group discussions that met this rough draft, no explicit attention was given to Mike's apparent aim to draw parallels between Roman and modern attitudes toward sports. Instead, the group simply wanted more factual information about Roman spectator sports. One student said she wanted to hear more about the religious angle and why the Romans grew more bloodthirsty toward the end of the empire. The group did center on some ambiguity at the level of commentary, but the discussion ended with Mike's long oral elaboration about the brutalities that occurred in the Colosseum.

The influence of this discussion registers in the paper that Mike eventually turned in to the instructor. He now had so much to say about the Colosseum itself that he began with it directly, setting the scene of a typical fight. Here is the revised version (whose title eventually became "Roman Spectator Sports"):

> The scene is a hot, Sunday afternoon in Rome. Two men face each other, poised for battle as the crowd looks on. One is armed with a long, broad sword, while the other brandishes a long spear and a shield of shiny metal. As the signal is given, the men begin to fight. Each exchange lunges and blows until finally, one is left

lying in the sand, helpless. The victor then looks to the Emperor who is seated on the royal podium, for the signal to either spare the life or not. The judgement is death, so the victim buries his sword deep into the heart of the defeated.

Although this may sound like a passage from a fiction novel, it is not. Events similar to the one described went on every day in Ancient Rome in the Colosseum. These "games," as the people called them, were the entertainment the populus attended. They were much like modern day baseball games.

In this revision, we see a direct shift of the original topic (games then, games now) into commentary ("They were much like modern day baseball games"), as the growing elaboration about the Colosseum itself elevates it to the topic level. Hence, revision at the commentary level implicates the topic. Yet we could also say that the group's request for factual elaborations puts pressure not just on the topic, but maybe even on the genre as well. Mike originally had the potential to write a more analytical piece about the nature of spectator sport. But in accommodating his readers' desire to know more about the Colosseum and the games, he ends up with a descriptive essay, much like an encyclopedia entry.

Although genre is not the ostensible point of entry for either the discussion or the revision of "Colosseum," we were surprised to find the amount of explicit attention this group of students gave to issues of genre and how deeply implicated genre was in many of the revisions they undertook. In fact, this was the third major finding of our analysis.

3. Students in this study devoted a significant amount of attention to genre, and genre appears deeply implicated in both the motivations and effects of their revisions. An earlier investigation of the conversations of peer writing groups (Brandt 1985) showed that approximately 25% of the conversational turns recorded in ten meetings of introductory writing students pertained to issues of genre (compared to 50% of the turns given to commentary and the other 25% given to topic). Much of this talk involved considering what was "allowed" or "required" by a certain genre — what parameters or obligations writers felt constrained by or what expectations a choice of genre set up in readers. We discovered similar concerns among the students in this study. Of the eleven episodes analyzed, four took genre as the point of entry (five discussions entered at the comment level and the remaining two entered at the topic level). In two other cases, although it was not the point of entry, genre did become directly implicated in the revisions.

The following excerpt exemplifies a conversation that takes genre as its point of entry, again primarily in terms of readers' expectations and confusions about what they perceive as two somewhat contradic-

tory impulses in the paper. Mike has just read aloud his draft of a
paper called "The Wind," whose topic has been inspired by several
teacher-assigned readings that treated the wind from perspectives
ranging from scientific to poetic. In responding to the draft, the group
essentially asks if the paper is supposed to be funny or scholarly:

> *Alice:* I was wondering if you might want to kind of make the wind sound
> like kind of a like a practical joker? You know, blowing the plates
> and trapping the people underneath the tent and blowing out the
> fires, and all that stuff.
>
> *Alan:* I think it's got humor now and it still has . . . it's a scholarly paper.
>
> *Mike:* I didn't mean it to be humorous, really.
>
> *Alan:* But it has a couple, you know . . .
>
> *Alice:* Well, it's funny because we can relate to this stuff.
>
> *Amy:* You just talk about [the wind] going off on a rampage. "The wind
> would always blow all the napkins, paper plates, and plastic knives,
> spoons and forks." That's hysterical 'cause the way you were saying
> it. You just sounded so desperate.
>
> *Alice:* Now that's funny. That makes it funny.
>
> *Mike:* It happens.
>
> *Alan:* Have you ever tried to do a picnic? It's impossible.
>
> *Mike:* Do you think I could make a paper out of this? . . .
> [A few minutes later]
>
> *Alan:* I liked it the way it is. It sounds scientific. Maybe you'll have to
> footnote it.
>
> *Mike:* I don't have . . . this isn't . . . this isn't a scholarly paper. I've written
> three already. This is just a paper . . . this is just a paper to make
> people think about . . . how they . . . how the wind isn't so good.

This exchange tells much about how writers — and readers —
explore the impact of certain text choices on the comprehension of
genre. And some of the most interesting discussions we examined had
students considering how a preliminary, expressive piece of writing
(begun as a journal entry) could be turned into a more transactional,
public form. Alice, for instance, brought to the group an expressive,
impressionistic piece on the history of Bascom Hill, the oldest section
of the Madison campus, and sought advice on how the preliminary
draft might be turned into a scholarly, historical essay. One of her
group mates suggested she delete a paragraph that explained, "I found
out most of my information in a pamphlet put together . . . ," noting
that such information could be put in a bibliography instead. The
same group member also suggested that Alice delete such phrases as,
"Our university has been around so long that I'm sure there are an
unlimited number of tales to be discovered," and "All it takes is a
little bit of digging and a lot of curiosity," because, in the student's

words, "That's personalizing it too much." Alice also expressed concern about the line, "I'm not a history major, but I find the history of our college intriguing." In such discussions of genre, the students resembled people in an unfamiliar social situation attempting to puzzle out the parameters of acceptable behavior.

But on other occasions we found genre implicated, perhaps unwittingly, as student revisers ran into trouble at other levels of text. That is, as discussions revealed to writers the need to rebalance their intentions with the interests of their readers, the original genre often gave way, unable to accommodate the pressures created by the demands of the revision. Quite literally, as writers perceived their tasks as more complex or problematic than originally estimated, something had to give way — and frequently that was genre.

We saw this tendency in Mike's essay on the Colosseum, which in accommodating demands on the commentary level, "downshifted" from analysis to report. A similar result occurred with an essay written by a student named Alan and originally entitled "A Particular Spot." The point of the original draft was that college students frequenting campus-area bars are "fake," and he supported his contention by describing the various social behaviors affiliated with various bars — to enter a certain bar was to take on a certain persona. But in discussions with his peers, Alan soon learned that his choice of the word "fake" was problematic, because it carried sweepingly negative connotations for his readers. During the discussion, group members continually pressed Alan for a definition of "fake," a call for elaboration at the level of commentary. But Alan's solution to the challenge was to rehearse less controversial assertions, arriving at: "There's a different group of people at every bar."

This strategy stuck in the revised essay, renamed "Bars at Their Finest," which asserted that "bars on campus offer something to everyone." But as the topic-commentary structure shifted, so did the genre, from argument to report. The shift was comparable to moving the essay from the editorial page to the travel section: a guide to Madison's attractions.

Observing these revisions underscores the extent to which genre, topic, and commentary all implicate or constrain each other; a shift in one can have implications for the others. And this interrelationship of constraints is obviously at play during the revising process. While the "entry point" of a revision may be at any level, implications occur at all levels. In Alan's case, the commentary in his original draft most thoroughly upset the expected balance between writer and readers.

But once the old commentary was abandoned and the new commentary embraced, the genre itself had changed.

Finally, as we suggested before, the multilevel pressures of revision hold special concern for less experienced writers and for teachers interested in understanding their writing development. It is a well-known fact about learners that the cognitive load created by new and unfamiliar demands frequently causes a sort of conservation of energy in order to accommodate the new demands. This often can result in backsliding, as some previous skills temporarily recede. Recalling the cases of Mike in the "Colosseum" essay and Alan in the "bars" essay, both students had available as writers the generic frameworks for undertaking analytical or argumentative writing, for their early drafts made efforts in these directions. But *under the particular configuration* of genre-topic-commentary operating in a particular reader-writer context, they did not sustain these genres, settling instead for less demanding reporting. Given different contextual and textual constraints, the writers might have chosen to retain their original genres.

Conclusion

Results of these studies, then, confirm a direct relationship between the functional concerns taken up in peer review and the functional concerns taken up during revision. Specific responses provide writers with specific directions for revising, and ongoing feedback allows them to connect textual choices with the effects of those choices on readers. From this, we may say that revisions are text hypotheses of sorts, and that learning results when writers are able to test their efforts in the crucible of reader response. The special value of intensive peer review is that in their experiments with the resources of written language, writers are never far removed from a functional writer-reader context.

These studies also point up the need for much better understanding of revising processes themselves. Methods of analysis need to be developed and applied that will connect text changes to their functional role in the specific communicative act that is unfolding between writer and reader. Such an analysis also must capture the interrelationship of revisions; it must account for how changes at certain levels of text set up pressures at other levels of text. Recent useful attempts have been made to classify text revisions as either "meaning changing" or "meaning preserving" (Faigley and Witte 1984). Such conceptions represent an advance in linking revision to meaning and function within a particular text. However, our study reveals that changing meaning at one level of text can actually preserve meaning at other levels of text. (In her narrative essay about the baseball bat episode, Alice changed meaning in her introductory paragraph in terms of its topic. But in doing so, she actually preserved meaning at the level of genre.) The complex interdependence of text features must be adequately accounted for in any theory of revising.

More sensitive methods for revision analysis would also prove valuable in understanding writing development. Looking at revisions (or the lack of revisions) simply in quantitative terms, or in terms of generic sorts of operations or as evidence of "novice" behavior, cannot go far in explaining why students do what they do when they revise. Such approaches can mask or overlook what is significant in the patterns of revision and the ways that any revision represents a writer's interpretation of how, *on this particular occasion,* the resources of written language could be managed appropriately.

Acknowledgments

The research reported in this chapter was supported by a grant from the Wisconsin Center for Education Research, 1025 W. Johnson, Madison, WI 53706. At the time of this research, WCER was supported in part by Grant No. NIE-G-84-008. The views in this paper are not necessarily those of the National Institute of Education or the Department of Education.

The authors thank Joyce Melville, Dennis Rinzel, Anita Gallucci, and Jean Walia for their invaluable assistance.

References

Benson, N. 1979. The Effects of Peer Feedback during the Writing Process: Performance, Revision Behavior, and Attitude toward Writing. Unpublished doctoral dissertation, University of Colorado, Boulder.

Brandt, D. 1985. Orchestrating Literacy: Writing, Reading, and Talking about Texts. Paper presented at the annual meeting of the National Council of Teachers of English, Philadelphia.

Bridwell, L. S. 1980. Revising Strategies in Twelfth Grade Students' Transactional Writing. *Research in the Teaching of English* 14:197–222.

Faigley, L., and S. Witte. 1984. Measuring the Effects of Revisions and Text Structure. In *New Directions in Composition Research,* edited by R. Beach and L. S. Bridwell, 95–108. New York: Guilford.

Fox, R. 1980. Treatment of Writing Apprehension and Its Effect on Composition. *Research in the Teaching of English* 14:39–49.

Gere, A. R. 1987. *Writing Groups: History, Theory, and Implications.* Carbondale: Southern Illinois University Press.

Gere, A. R., and R. S. Stevens. 1985. The Language of Writing Groups: How Oral Response Shapes Revision. In *The Acquisition of Written Language: Response and Revision,* edited by S. W. Freedman, 85–105. Norwood, N.J.: Ablex.

Halliday, M. A. K. 1988. Spoken and Oral Modes of Meaning. In *Comprehending Oral and Written Language,* edited by R. Horowitz and S. J. Samuels. New York: Academic Press.

Lagana, J. 1973. The Development, Implementation, and Evaluation of a Model for Teaching Composition which Utilizes Individualized Learning and Peer Grouping. Unpublished doctoral dissertation, University of Pittsburgh.

Moffett, J. 1968. *Teaching the Universe of Discourse.* Boston: Houghton Mifflin.

Nystrand, M. 1983. Increasing Student Awareness of Their Own Composing Processes. Unpublished final report to the National Institute of Education.

Nystrand, M. 1986. *The Structure of Written Communication: Studies in Reciprocity between Writers and Readers.* New York: Academic Press.

Ochs, E. 1987. Input: A Sociocultural Perspective. In *Social and Functional Approaches to Language and Thought,* edited by M. Hickmann. New York: Academic Press.

Sommers, N. 1980. Revision Strategies of Student Writers and Experienced Adult Writers. *College Composition and Communication* 31:378–87.

Appendix: Draft and Revision of Alice's Essay "Description"

Draft 1

Storytelling is a true art. A good story teller can describe a moment so that his audience will actually experience the event being described. The story teller will use descriptive words to trigger similar memories of his audience.

Following is a true story of an event that happened to me when I was about nine years old.

As I stood under the [word missing] of the school I scanned the schoolyard.The day was warm with a cool breeze that pulled at my hair. The grass was a dark vivid green (and leaves of the old oak tree). I spotted a group of three girls. One of the girls a full head taller than the other two. Jeanette! Suddenly I remembered something very important I needed to tell Jeanette. I started running toward the group. The group of girls was about 100 feet out in the yard under the old oak. They, and the grass surrounding them, were dappled with sun and shadow from the sun shining through the leaves of the magnificent old oak. As I quickly moved toward the group I noticed how the top of the mighty oak swayed in the breeze. The only sound audible was the wind whipping past my ears. Coming up behind the group I noticed Jeanette had a bat poised over her left shoulder. To avoid the bat, I ran to her right side. At that split second I saw the white ball seemingly hanging in the air moving toward us in slow motion. I knew what was to happen next & tried to stop my forward motion. It was too late. In the silence of my panic the next thing I would see would be the hard wood of the bat. Jeanette swung with all her might, missed the ball, but continued her follow through to bring the bat squarely into contact with the bridge of my nose with a crack.

For what seemed like an eternity I felt as if I were floating on air. The next sensation to enter my brain was the impact of my body crashing to the ground. Oddly it felt as if I had fallen back onto a comfortable bed for a much needed rest. Then, in the silence I felt the cool dampness of the grass on the backs of my bare arms. Sound began to return. My whole body seemed numb; I was engulfed in silence. I smelled a "tinny" smell — like metal against metal or the smell of an electrical fire — which burned throughout my head. What my eyes beheld was remarkable! On a vivid black velvet background shone five perfect, bone white stars. Each star was perfectly shaped, and had five points. They all moved slowly in a circular clockwise motion.

And a piercing pain shot through the bridge of my nose straight through each eye and around the top on my head. The darkness dissolved and my eyes found sunny blue skies and the upper halves of people's torsos gazing down on my crumpled body. I was relieved to find my sight had returned, but not as happy to also experience the accompanying pain. As I lay there in tortured agony with those piercing eyes invading my privacy, I longed for the numb, quiet darkness and those five perfect stars to return.

Draft 2

Last Saturday as I watched The Road Runner Show, I saw Wile E. Coyote get cracked on the top of the head with an anvil. This happened when his well planned scheme to capture the elusive road runner backfired, as usual. As I watched stars appeared and began to dance around his head. This sight triggered a memory of something that happened to me when I was about nine years old.

One eventful day, as I stood under the veranda of my school, I scanned the school yard for one of my girl friends. The day was sunny and warm with a cool breeze that pulled at my hair. About 100 feet out, on a plush carpet of green, was a small group of girls, one of the girls a full head taller than the others. Jeanette! Suddenly, I remembered a very important secret that needed to be relayed to Jeanette. I started running toward the group.

The girls were under a huge oak tree. They, and the grass surrounding them, were dappled with sun and shadow shining down through the leaves. As I moved toward the group, the only sound audible was the wind whipping past my ears. Coming up behind them, I noticed that Jeanette had a bat poised over her left shoulder. To avoid the bat, I ran to her right side. At that split second I saw the soft ball, seemingly suspended in mid-air. I knew what was to happen next and tried to stop my forward motion. It was too late. In the silence of my panic, the next thing I saw was the hard wood bat. Jeanette swung with all her might, missed the ball, but followed through to bring the bat squarely into contact with the bridge of my nose. Inside my head, the sound of the impact was like the thud of a heavy rock falling into moist earth, followed by a high pitched ringing in my ears.

As the impact of the bat knocked me off my feet, I felt as if I were floating on air for an extended moment. The next sensation was the impact of my body crashing into the ground. Oddly, it felt as if I had fallen back onto a comfortable bed for a much needed rest. My whole body felt numb as I was engulfed in silence. I smelled something tinny — like friction of metal against metal, or the smell of an electrical fire, which burned in my sinuses. But the image in my mind's eye was remarkable! On a vivid, black velvet background shone five perfect, bone white stars. Each star was perfectly shaped, and each had exactly five points. They all moved slowly in a circular clockwise motion.

Then, in the black silence, I felt the cool dampness of grass on the backs of my bare arms. Sound began to return, and a piercing pain shot through the bridge of my nose straight through each eye, and around the top of my head. The black velvet began to dissolve away to sunny blue skies. For a moment I was disoriented, then I realized that I was lying on my back. I was relieved to find my sight had returned, but the pain that accompanied it was not as welcome.

Next I perceived the faces. It seemed that every student from my small school was crowded around, gazing down on my sprawling body. I was stunned from the blow and could not move. It hurt just to think, let alone try to get up. I was helpless to do anything but lie there and experience every pulse of the throbbing pain, while the faces watched on. It felt as if the pain would grow greater and greater until it consumed me, then my life would end. All of those eyes staring down on me, witnessing my desperation, were draining me of what dignity I had left. They were all observing my weakest and most vulnerable moment. I longed for the numb, quiet darkness and those five perfect stars to return and shut the faces out.

I waited for all to go black again, but I never lost consciousness. Just then I caught sight of my teacher rushing to my aid. Surprisingly, the mere sight of her brightened my outlook on the situation. It was comforting to see a figure of authority — someone who might be able to do something about the sad state I was in. She took me in her arms and carried me away from the faces.

As it turns out, all I got was a slight concussion and a very swollen, bruised face. This, in turn, made me the center of attention at school for the following week. I loved it, and would relate my harrowing tale to anyone who would listen. So, needless to say, I lived to tell about it!

12 The Student, the Teacher, and the Text: Negotiating Meanings through Response and Revision

Cynthia Onore
City College of the City University of New York

The changes brought about through theory and research on composing are just now having their full impact, an impact that extends well beyond the boundaries of assignments, evaluation procedures, and response techniques. We have discovered, for example, that a fully realized process pedagogy requires a change in the relationships among students, and between students and teachers in the classroom. Collaborative learning within a workshop setting is more compatible with teaching writing as a process than, say, the isolation of students from one another while the teacher lectures about rhetorical forms or rules of usage. Donald Murray (1982) suggests that his change from teaching while standing to teaching while sitting resulted naturally from the changes in his ideas about composition teaching. Other changes have followed naturally from the process pedagogy, too: using holistic rather than atomistic evaluation procedures; construing writing as a mode of learning, and not solely as a way of displaying learning (Applebee 1981; Britton, Burgess, Martin, McLeod, and Rosen 1975; Emig 1977).

There is, however, yet another concomitant change inherent in the move from a product to a process pedagogy, and that is our way of conceptualizing both the development of writing abilities and the development of an individual text. But reconceptualizing writing development cannot and will not occur without reexamining the classroom authority structure and perhaps even redefining the purposes for the composition class. In traditional classroom settings, the authority of teachers and of textbook precepts prevented student writers from asserting ownership over their writing. Text appropriation by teachers, in particular through their commenting practices, has been well documented (Brannon and Knoblauch 1982; Knoblauch and Brannon 1981; Sommers 1982). As long as judgments of what may be "better" or "worse" — that is, of what constitutes improvement in writing — remain the province of teachers alone, then the writer cannot fully and authentically engage in choice making and problem solving. And without the authority to make choices, the writer can never understand how central are the consequences of any meaning-making activity in writing.

If the composition classroom is to be a context for exploration and risk-taking, for finding and solving problems — in short, for learning — then power must be shared. Such changes, of course, imply that teachers and students alike might be able to swim against the whole tide of their personal and cultural histories — a monumental task, to be sure. Nonetheless, challenging the tradition of teacher- and textbook-dominated learning is necessary, since otherwise teaching and learning may be doomed, Sisyphus-like, to repeat endlessly the same endlessly unproductive efforts.

Perhaps without realizing that it focuses on such an end, the composition class can become an embodiment of what Friere (1970) calls "co-intentional education," since meanings cannot be given to writers, but must be intended by them in response to a personal need to express something. Personally expressive meanings are then offered for the individual and collective transactions of a community of other readers and writers. The relationship of a writer to her text, then, is one of ownership and authority, a slippery balance between personal autonomy and social responsibility.

In arguing for a process pedagogy, we are arguing at the very least for a writer's right to his own texts and not so subsidiarily for the right of the classroom community to interpret and feed meanings back to the writer. Paradoxically, while a focus on meaning-making requires individual ownership of a text, it simultaneously requires that a writer negotiate with that community his or her intended meanings so that neither pure idiosyncracy nor tyranny results. The power relationships within the classroom are thus fundamentally altered: language and learning are not commodities to be deposited in one writer or another, a process Friere terms the "banking concept" of education. Rather, the classroom community becomes a "problem posing" environment in which meanings must be exchanged — made and shared — with other members of the community so that the full impact of one's own words can be fully felt. The process, then, cannot be linear but must be an ongoing negotiation between writers, their own texts, and other readers in the class.

The context I am defining here, the one Friere would term "problem posing," may also be termed a context of inquiry. A curriculum based on inquiry, according to Hedley (1968), requires that the student must confront a decision-making situation, analyzing what is involved in making choices and what each potential choice might mean. The teacher-reader's role must be to express what is implied for him or her in the choices made, and perhaps offer alternatives. The student may accept the implications of meaning as these are mirrored back to him or her. If not, then the writer must reenter the process of meaning-making and negotiation. For a writer, the latter decision would propel reentry into the composing process, even though such reentry implies withholding closure and entertaining a whole new set of options and alternatives. The process may then be repeated indefinitely. Only the constraints of due dates, or boredom, or resignation, or even the inability to "tolerate chaos" (Berthoff 1981), would obviate the desire or ability to thus prolong involvement in composing.

The traditional classroom, with its rigid authority structure and its ready-made forms and meanings, tends to inhibit genuine inquiry. Questions of meaning and structure have been answered independent of and prior to a writer's intentions. If questions are posed at all they tend to imply a single, right answer. By reifying both questions and answers, the classroom becomes a "one context variety" (Shuy 1984). Latitude in choice making is thus so limited that inexperienced writers may be unaware that choices exist. Paradoxically, then, the traditional classroom determines much more than questions and answers; it creates and sustains the illusion that universal definitions of improvement for writers and text can be formulated. Indeed, reifying the "one context variety" is the implicit or explicit purpose of both traditional rhetoric and virtually all composition textbooks and handbooks.

As long as teachers hold sway over student writers' meanings, writing abilities may develop in ways that are obscured from view. Worse still, when teachers control meanings, writers may not develop at all. Since responses to writing are a very visible form of expressing the classroom power relationship, commentary on writing plays a central role in altering the classroom context, in establishing a forum for real inquiry into meanings and relationships, in redefining improvement.

Much as we would like to say that embracing this new pedagogy and its attendant authority structure will automatically produce classroom results much more satisfying than those of the more traditional pedagogy, it is my belief that as long as we retain our longstanding view of what improvement in writing looks like, we will not be able to see it when it exists nor foster it when it does not. If we insist on a linear model of growth — a model perfectly compatible with viewing language and learning as commodities to be traded — then we can certainly expect to be disappointed by students' attempts to explore and expand their linguistic and intellectual repertories. It seems unlikely that students will improve their writing if we simultaneously demand new insights and new text options. If, on the other hand, we wish to teach writing as a process, then we must reenvision its central metaphor — "growth" — to include textual performances that show both occasional gains and frequent losses. Perhaps more importantly, we need to understand what writers are gaining through the process of inquiring and composing — and that means understanding what they are gaining through their losses.

Typically, we assume that if our students are really learning to write and really practicing their craft, their texts will get better and better and their successive drafts will improve. This view, however, does not fully embrace the thrust of current research, which suggests that growth in writing can be more internal, less "visible." The difficulty then becomes recognizing the signs of growth we can rely on. It may even be necessary to recognize that writing ability is *not* developing even when the text becomes more effective.

In the remainder of this chapter I will present the findings of my study on teacher commentary and student growth in writing. I will argue that a recursive, developmental model is compatible with teaching writing as a process and viewing meaning-making as a mode of negotiation in language.

A Case Study of Response and Revision

This chapter reports on a study that was based on a set of assumptions which does not fully match those detailed above. What has emerged as the central flaw of this study was the mistaken belief that altering the nature of teacher commentary alone would have a fundamental effect on the nature of learning to write. I assumed that students' writing would improve if comments were facilitative and meaning-centered, inviting students to reconceptualize their texts. Because these assumptions were not supported by the study, I have attempted to reconstrue the events of the classroom, to reinterpret the commentary and the relationships and roles that teacher-reader and student-writer played, in order to understand more fully the context-dependent nature of responding to student writing.

Design of the Study

Dan, Alex, and Miranda, the three case-study participants, were undergraduate students enrolled in a required expository writing course at New York University. Alex and Miranda were first-semester fresh-men, while Dan was a second-semester sophomore. All three had been educated in New York City public schools.

I was both their classroom teacher and the principal investigator for the study. These students participated in the regular instructional context and followed the same assignments as other members of the class. Each student drafted his or her texts, shared first drafts with peer groups for oral and written commentary, shared second drafts with the teacher for written feedback, and submitted a final draft. Students collected their writing throughout the semester and chose three of their seven essays to be evaluated at the end of the term.

Twice during the semester there were differences between the procedures the three participants followed and those for the rest of the class. On the third and fifth assignments, I collaborated with two other experienced teachers of writing to produce comments for the participants' second drafts. One goal of this procedure was to avoid idiosyncrasy in commenting. We commented, independently, then met to share the comments we had generated, and finally constructed collectively a comment that I would copy onto the students' papers. During the process of reaching a consensus, we negotiated with one another about what we perceived to be the writer's purposes, where confusions centered, and which possibilities we thought the writer might entertain in reformulating the text. Our goal was to be nondi-rective, facilitative, and meaning-centered in our feedback.

While we attempted to disengage the writers from relying on already established forms and meanings in order to encourage continued exploration and even the reformulation of ideas, we simultaneously sought to support the writers' authority over their own texts. We wished the writers to own their writing, to be free to choose which options to pursue. In order to achieve this, we asked only what Searle (1969) calls real questions, those for which we did not have answers but assumed the writers did, rather than exam questions, where the questioner wishes only to see if the respondent has the answer which the questioner already has. The tension between, on the one hand, questions that assume writers' authority over their own writing and, on the other hand, comments designed to offer alternative worlds of meaning to the writer, and perhaps in the process to undermine a coherence already achieved, is acute. Nonetheless, we sought to achieve a balance between these two poles of tension.

In addition to the commentary devised for the participants, another procedure was different for them than for other members of the class. During their composing/revising of all drafts in the series produced for the two assignments under investigation, the participants were asked to report in (Onore 1983) to a tape recorder whenever they reached a natural resting place. Reporting-in is a variation of composing aloud. It allows the writer to choose when to pause in order to describe what he was doing and thinking about, what choices he was making and why. In addition, each writer was asked to react to the commentary on draft two, to explore its meaning and impact.

After each assignment was finished, the students were interviewed about the papers, their choice-making activities during composing, their feelings about the comments they received, and their assessments of their successes and failures with these writing tasks.

At the completion of the study, the drafts in a single text series were blind scored on a holistic scale by three raters, in order to judge the relative effectiveness of the drafts in a series. (A writer was measured against him- or herself and not in relation to the work of others.) The raters were asked to perform two other tasks: to comment on their evaluations of the texts, and to compose a macroproposition (van Dijk 1980) for each text. A macroproposition is an assertion that conveys the gist of a text. By comparing macropropositions, I could determine how the writer's revisions from draft to draft had affected the meaning of the text. Since the teacher commentary had been designed to foster reformulation and reconceptualization (global concerns) and not just internal consistency (local concerns), the construction of a macroproposition was one way to evaluate the overall thrust of the writer's revisions.

Findings

Alex's work was consistently judged to have improved almost linearly from first through final draft, the final papers being judged superior to first or second drafts. The raters unanimously concurred in these judgments. Dan's drafts improved over successive attempts in one instance and declined in the other. For both Dan and Alex, a single macroproposition for all drafts in a series was generated by the raters, a result unconnected to the perceived quality of the texts. Only Miranda's work consistently declined in quality, according to the raters. When macropropositions were compared, it was discovered that Miranda's texts alone had generated different macropropositions for the texts in a single series. The three raters also concurred in this judgment.

The results of the ratings of these texts by outside readers led to a host of questions: What had Alex been able to do that Dan and Miranda could not? Was it safe to say that Alex had gained the most as a writer during this writing workshop and that Miranda had profited least? What role did a shift in macromeaning play in the quality of the text? While the commentary was designed to foster reconceptualization, was reconceptualizing a good idea for unpracticed writers, since it sometimes seemed to produce less, rather than more, effective texts? What were comments for, if not to help a writer improve a text and to apply what had been learned to a new piece of writing?

On the basis of the texts alone, it was not possible to answer these questions. A careful examination of the texts, the transcripts of the interviews, and the reporting-in protocols makes it possible, however, to draw inferences about the developmental processes these writers went through and to define the role of meaning-negotiation in a writer's drafting and revising.

Negotiating Relationships: The Shifting Role of Commentator and Writer

If meanings were exchanged through a one-directional process of interaction between readers' comments and texts, then the responses of the research participants to the written commentary would be somewhat predictable, and their texts would all "improve" from draft to draft. All participants in the study would have taken on the role of passive recipients of instructions for revision, and the teacher-reader would have consistently acted as the director of learning.

But "meaning is a form of negotiation in language" (Bruner 1985), and the exchanges of meaning that occur through response to writing and revision are a transactional process (Rosenblatt 1978). The writing workshop is a forum for curricular negotiation, too (Boomer 1982). Therefore, though the intentions of the comments remained stable, no matter who the writer was or which text we were dealing with, the writer construed the comments variously. The writer's perception of the teacher-reader's role, then, varied enormously from occasion to occasion and writer to writer. Comments, even those which take advantage of the best information about composing and revising that is available, are limited in their potential to produce predictable results since their interpretation cannot be fully controlled; neither can the ways in which writers respond and react to them. In a negotiation, in a manner congruent with Rosenblatt's definition of a transaction, each entity is simultaneously "conditioned by and conditioning" the other (Rosenblatt 1978, 17). It should not be surprising, then, that the writers in this study played very different roles, interpreted the teacher's role differently, and generated texts with a wide range of characteristics.

Discussions of the Case Studies of Three College Writers

Alex: How to Resist Negotiation and Still Improve Your Texts

Alex entered the class writing confidently and competently. As a result, his case raises important questions about the composition teacher's responsibility to an already proficient writer and the role, within that responsibility, of teacher commentary. A focus on the goal of "better" writing, on the quality of written products in isolation, does not allow us to learn much from Alex, since each time he revised, each time he responded to the commentary he received, his texts became somewhat more effective (see appendix for samples of Alex's writing). The alteration of a word here or a phrase there certainly did improve the quality of his texts. But the fact that the raters created the same macroproposition for each of the texts in a series suggests that Alex's real success lay in polishing the surface of an already constructed, non-negotiable text. Each rater noted, additionally, that even though Alex's final drafts were superior to earlier drafts, the differences from draft to draft were minimal. More importantly, however, the raters commented on their perception that the writing seemed to lack voice, that though the texts were competent, they were also perfunctory. The writer's intention, then, his stance toward his text, did not figure much at all in the evaluations of these experienced teachers of writing. These evaluative readings suggest that judgments of quality may be divorced from writers' intentions. A text may be getting better at the same time that writing ability remains static.

During interviews with Alex, he described his composing process as a stable set of procedures upon which he had learned to rely. He envisioned a "format" when he created a first draft, and this format was his anchor to composing. No matter what meanings Alex made, they always fit neatly into place within his formats. I asked what he would do if his first-draft format didn't work, and he replied that this had never happened to him.

We can infer that the context out of which Alex developed these successful strategies was one in which the purpose for writing is to get it right, to be successful no matter what. To view meaning as negotiation in language, then, is to step outside the borders of the communicative contexts with which Alex is familiar, comfortable, and successful. To make such a step is to reconstrue the purposes for writing in the first place. Unfortunately for Alex, there were no messages being communicated to him — with the exception of the message of the commentary on his texts — that would support him in risking the coherence of his text.

Is it then the obligation of the teacher-reader to invite Alex into the inquiry process, to negotiate with him? With a focus on the process of writing alone, a focus which suggests that the highest good lies in revising and reformulating just because that is what experienced writers do when they compose, then Alex is deficient, despite the proficiency of his writing. If the purpose of the writing class and the teacher's commentary is to facilitate the writer's engagement in the process of composing in the face of every and any text produced, be it competent or incompetent, then neither Alex nor his teacher-reader performed as they should.

Such an analysis of Alex and his writing fail, however, because they foreground the process of composing so much that the most important reason for writing — to learn about something — is lost. If a writer learns as she writes, learns about writing and/or about the topic at hand, then she has been successful. To impose revision for revision's sake is so narrowly to define the process pedagogy that we may forget why we are writing in the first place. Such a line of reasoning does not go far enough, however, for the reverse is just as limiting. A focus on products alone also will always obscure some issues, in particular the issue of growth. Only through reenvisioning the purposes for teaching writing can we then suggest what the purposes of teacher commentary might be. The achievements, as well as the failures, of a good writer like Alex can then become more apparent.

The growth of a writer should be a lifelong developmental process. Alex can still learn that we can use writing to create new knowledge, and in so doing that there are many more options available to him. Perhaps the real question raised by Alex's case is the purpose for commentary. If comments are for better texts, then they achieved their purpose with Alex. If, on the other hand, the comments are for the exploration of new ideas, if they are for learning, then they failed.

If we examine Alex's achievements from the framework of inquiry and negotiation, we gain a richer understanding of the role of commentary in the composition classroom. In part, Alex is able to do something his peers cannot. He can follow his reader's interpretations without violating the form that he shapes at the initial point of utterance. He can skillfully connect what's already there with what his teacher suggests he do to "improve" it. He can assimilate the comments, in Piaget's terms, and the text can assimilate new information without the integrity of either one being destroyed. In other words, accommodation, the process by which reconceptualizations occur, is blocked.

By contrast, negotiation requires that the writer owns what he says, that he trusts the reader and her interpretations, that both writer and reader are learners and teachers. The power relationship between the student-writer and teacher-reader, therefore, forms the core of this negotiation process. So, too, does the intention to inquire. Inquiry demands commitment, seeking, exploring, risk-taking on the part of all participants. The teacher's role is that of inquirer too: What is the writer really trying to say here; I would really like to know more about what she is saying; here's how I see her meaning. Inquiry on the student-writer's part requires that: She wants to know what she knows and so she must write; she wants to find out more about the subject and writing is one way of doing that; she wishes to know how others understand her meanings; she wants to negotiate those meanings so she may be satisfied with the interpretation of her message. Not only are the processes of the classroom altered through inquiry and negotiation, but so is the content. In such a context, meanings are continually modified and written language is the primary enactment of modification.

In light of this explication of the roles writers and readers can play with one another, it may be easier to see anew the successes and failures of students, as well as our own. Returning to Alex, then, and reinterpreting him as a writer, we see that he could not negotiate his meanings with the reader; nor could he inquire into his subject, because it was not his wish to inquire, because to inquire opened the possibility of scrambling his format, and because he was unaware of wanting to know anything new. In resisting the process of negotiation and inquiry, Alex substituted assimilation and regurgitation. If chaos is generative (Berthoff 1981), it is because it must result in the reorganization and reformulation of materials. Learning is a natural consequence. Inquiry is not possible without contraries, conflicts, and tensions. Chaos, then, is a categorical feature of the inquiry process just as it is a categorical feature of the composing process. Perhaps, too, inquiry and composing are not opposites, as they have traditionally been seen; they may be parts of the larger process of being in the world. Being in the world, the essence of problem-posing education, is essential for learning.

Dan: How to Remain Alienated from Your Own Texts

If Alex may be stereotyped as the good writer with serviceable strategies for school-sponsored writing, then Dan may be characterized as a nonfluent and anxious writer who has never developed functional strategies for any sort of writing, be it school- or self-sponsored. His work was judged to have exhibited losses through the drafting/

feedback/revising process (see appendix for samples). But to characterize Dan thus, and to conclude that he is like so many other unpracticed writers who have no history of success on which to depend, who edit too soon, and whose writing is either unaffected by teacher commentary or affected negatively, would allow little opportunity to learn from Dan's experiences. That he was simply unable to make language choices on paper that reflected either rhetorical control or control of his meanings would surprise no one familiar with recent research on teacher commentary and its effects on the inexperienced writer. However, if we reexamine Dan's work from the perspective of inquiry and meaning-negotiation, a different picture of his situation emerges.

There is a ubiquitous "she" to whom reference is continually made in Dan's reporting-in tapes. This person, his teacher, serves the role of arbiter of meanings and formal choices, even though she is not physically present. Her supposed likes and dislikes are considered, her questions about the text at hand are translated into rejections of that text. The reader over Dan's shoulder is not the reader I, as teacher, wished to be; certainly it was not the reader we intended to dramatize through the commentary. This reader was an all-knowing authority, the one who judged the text and whose opinion mattered most. Perhaps figuring just as prominently here is Dan's own heartfelt inability to express what he wished to say in his writing. Over and over, in order to circumvent having to make intentional choices about his writing, Dan would remark, "I'll just put this down and wait and see what she says about it." Dan neither took responsibility for his choices nor owned them. As a result, when asked about his purposes in writing Dan could never state what they were.

Here is a situation in which all the necessary preconditions to negotiation and inquiry are absent: the power relationship between writer and reader is unequal, the writer does not seek to know anything, the writer does not discover what he knows, the reader does not support and share in his explorations. Stated differently, Dan cannot entertain the chaos inherent in inquiry and composing because he never feels that he controls what he writes and thinks. To require a writer like Dan to reinvest his text with new meanings only exacerbates the anxiety he feels, since he has yet to invest a text with anything that he owns. All that Dan is learning from his writing and revising, and perhaps especially from the written commentary he receives, is that he is lost. How can he explore a *new* path when he is afraid to explore *any* path? The tension between the process of composing and the content of composing which Dan's case reveals is enormous. In a very real way, Dan has not chosen, controlled, or read his texts, and thus has not really composed at all.

I can think of no worse strategy to have used with Dan than to eliminate the possibility of ownership of a text and simultaneously to ask him to reformulate. Though seemingly facilitative, the commentary Dan received was counterproductive. Dan needed many starts at composing, many opportunities to see writing as something that was his, like breathing or thinking or speaking. He needed to become fluent before he should ever have been expected to re-see his texts in all of their potentialities.

The conditions for negotiation were not just absent; they were being violated by the context in which this exchange of meanings was taking place. There is no set of comments that I believe would have changed this situation, as long as the effect of those comments was to further distance Dan from his writing and shatter a coherence which he could hardly achieve. Only a celebration of Dan's meanings could have established a context inside of which real inquiry might have been possible. And celebration would have worked for precisely the reasons that comments designed to foster revision could not. A celebration and appreciation of Dan's work, like a parent's expansion of a child's early utterances, might have reinforced and sustained the process of meaning-making. Celebration might have altered the relationship of authority and ownership. The utterances would have been Dan's because he would have felt they belonged to him. His desire to explore would have been nurtured. In short, Dan would have found himself negotiating meanings with a trusted and interested reader. What sort of negotiation would it have been? The sort where one learns to see one's utterances through another's eyes, that is, to affirm them or perhaps to engender the intention to modify them, to shift perspective or to reassert them in a new way. But to suggest that something is unclear, that the topic might be viewed another way, or any of a host of (out of this context) potentially supportive and facilitative commentary would thrust Dan further into the chaos of his own inchoate meanings.

One thing Dan and Alex have in common, despite the marked differences in their writing ease and abilities, is their deference to authority. Throughout their schooling they have learned, we may assume, that no matter what teachers may say, they are still the final arbiters of quality (and not so incidentally, the final judges who give the grades.) Teachers hold the power in the classroom in other ways, too. Their suggestions are, for example, interpreted as orders; if there is something they deem as a possibility, that possibility is really an actuality in disguise. Additionally, of course, they have all the answers, which makes knowledge into a thing and learning into transmission and regurgitation.

In this context, students are not seekers after knowledge; they believe that if they just sit by passively, knowledge will be given to them. They are neither negotiators nor inquirers either, because to be these requires that students share the power in the classroom, that their needs may be freely felt and expressed, and that those needs, when superimposed on the non-negotiable aspects of the curriculum (state-mandated tests, districtwide requirements, school grading policies), may be dealt with honestly. Teacher and student may struggle together against the forms of oppression which have been imposed. But they may also negotiate what learning they seek and how they may go after it.

Without the student in the role of seeker, learning is not empowering. No inquiry need take place. Whatever it is necessary to know the teacher will provide, reinforce, and judge. Dewey (1933, 29–33) has suggested that the learner's attitude is of critical importance to successful inquiry. It is not enough, he maintains, for the teacher to use the method of inquiry. The student must be openminded, responsible, and wholehearted in his or her negotiations.

The teacher's comments were infelicitous (Searle 1969) for Dan and Alex because their intentions misfired. The resulting textual performances are somewhat predictable, then, given the writing abilities with which these writers entered the course. The commentary thrust the writers into familiar relationships with their own writing, thereby undermining the potential for growth. Secure in a past history of success, Alex could comfortably continue to be locked into his formats. And Dan could continue to be uncomfortable with his language, his ideas, his topics. In a real sense, a condition of stasis was established and preserved through the written responses to these writers' texts. They did not grow as writers even if, on occasion, their texts were judged to have improved from draft to draft.

To assert that the writing abilities of Dan and Alex had developed, it would have been necessary for each of them to locate some generalization about writing that they could apply to new writing situations — that writing is learning or thinking, that drafts are not graven in stone, that chaos can be generative. But none of these generalizations were fostered by the writing pedagogy.

Miranda: How Acting Like a Writer Can Be Hazardous to Your Text

Thus far I have argued that a necessary precondition to growth in writing abilities is that the writer act in the role of authority (it is no accident that the words *author* and *authority* have a similar root) over her writing. The situation is, however, even more complicated because the condition is not simultaneously sufficient to produce better texts. In other words, while a writer must be an inquirer, a participant in meaning-negotiations with readers, any particular piece of writing will not necessarily improve when he plays such a role or assumes such a stance.

Miranda's work may be distinguished from the writing of the other two participants in this study according to two attributes: On the one hand, the quality of her writing was judged by the raters to have declined from first through final draft in a given text series; the raters also generated two and sometimes three separate macropropositions for the drafts in one of Miranda's series (see appendix). In the case of Alex and Dan neither of these things happened. Further, it is from Miranda that we can retrospectively reinterpret the data from Alex and Dan. Paradoxically, Miranda acted more authoritatively, revised according to a coming-together of her own and the teacher's meanings, inquired deeper into her self-selected subject matter, in short, did all that we might wish an inexperienced writer to do, and still her texts declined in overall quality from draft to draft.

I am now standing on the edge of saying that we can separate process from product, since Miranda engaged in a process which resembles that of more experienced and accomplished writers but produced written products which were disappointing. This is only somewhat true. In fact, Miranda's writing exhibited gains and losses as she reconsidered her meanings in light of the commentary she received. The gains and losses, when judged holistically by raters, resulted in a net loss. When analyzed more closely, however, we discover that the losses are those of rhetorical control, while the gains consist in deeper and more sophisticated exploration of her subject matter.

Miranda wrote at the outskirts of her already attained abilities. In doing so she found herself in a state of disequilibrium or chaos. But in that state she was able to generate new meanings. She continued, draft after draft, to thrust herself into uncertainty and trusted that she would find a way out of it.

In the paper about her friend Phil (see appendix), Miranda began by telling a simple story of Phil's graduation from high school, his parents' goals for him, and how Phil disappoints them by dropping out of college. The story has a happy ending because Phil eventually discovers something he would like to do, and he succeeds at it. Miranda concludes the first two drafts of this paper by asserting banally:

"College isn't for everyone." When we read Miranda's paper, we were struck by Phil's struggle while trying to learn to be independent from the wishes of others, and so we wrote the following response to her paper:

> The real issue raised by your first two paragraphs is the nature of Phil's dependence on parents and teachers to tell him what to do with his life and how to do it. His realizations came about as a result of his making his own decisions. I want to know how his parents responded to this. Phil's emergence as a successful student and worker in his independently selected field point to quite a different conclusion than the one in your last paragraph. Try to explore these concerns when you revise Phil's story.

Miranda construes these comments as a wholly new way of seeing her own text. She enters into a negotiation with her reader and herself as reader to view the text in a new light. In composing draft one, she finds that she is uncomfortable with the way the principal characters in the story sound on paper. Phil comes out sounding like a "pushover," she asserts, and he really isn't. His parents emerge as pushy, but they are really "nice people." She is ambivalent about these people and her ambivalence asserts itself, despite her efforts to control it and to make her friend and his family sound like ideal characters. When she composes draft two, the one on which she received feedback from the teacher-reader, she simplifies the story, attempts to further gloss over these ambivalent feelings, and writes what she sees as a simple story of how Phil's expectations for college were not fulfilled.

Our commentary, then, can be seen as an exacerbation of the conflicts Miranda had attempted to gloss over since, despite her efforts at concealment, her reader-responder sees conflict between the characters in the story and between the narrator's supposed support of these people and her feelings of disapproval. Rather than bury more deeply her ambivalence, Miranda chooses to confront it head on. In doing so, a number of transformations occur. One transformation involves this narrative becoming a piece of exposition. The story is backgrounded while the writer's commentary is foregrounded. The narrative, in other words, becomes an illustration of a point within a deductive framework, whereas in the first two drafts, it had created a point or gist inductively. According to Miranda (and her readers and raters concur) the final draft is about how Phil "had matured, gained his independence, and set a direction for his life." In order to do this, she eliminated what she describes as "insignificant details" from the story and "added more about his relationship with his parents." In so doing, Miranda inquired more deeply into the character of Phil. She discovered, for example, that Phil is really as domineering with her as his parents are with him, an insight gained through reconceptualizing the story. She perceives Phil's treatment of her in a new way because she has viewed the relationship through a negotiated framework, a convergence of her view and the reader's view of her perspective.

There are, then, transformations in the content and in the formal schemata of Miranda's paper (Dillon 1981). The text, however, is problematic. It was judged by all three raters to be the least successful of the three drafts in this series. The final draft is not satisfying, in part, because Miranda has difficulty creating a coherence that will support her newly discovered meanings.

To blame the commentary for being inappropriate or for demanding from the writer more than she was capable of doing is overly simplistic. To blame Miranda for attempting to do something beyond her own rhetorical repertoire is also to gloss over the real significance of her experience. Even to suggest that if Miranda had just continued to draft this piece, which she did not, she would have eventually gotten it right is also to miss the point here. The point is that if we value the growth of an individual text (a performance) over the growth of a writer, we may unnecessarily inhibit the development of writing abilities. But to avoid such a pitfall it is necessary to redefine improvement in writing. It is clearly not either a text-based or a writer-based phenomenon. It is the empowerment of a learner to assert, revise, and judge her learning by seeking new knowledge, by re-seeing her knowledge through negotiation with others, by authoring her own work. It is the ability to see chaos as generative, to strive to work on the borders of our understandings rather than to work safely within the confines of what we already know.

A teacher's response to student writing is an inducement to reformulate, a celebration of meanings perhaps inchoate for the writer. Miranda told me in her interview that she had lost interest in her piece about Phil between drafts one and two, but that her interest was revitalized when she attempted to respond to the commentary she received. If we adhere to a deficit model of the development of writing abilities, then Miranda's writing is missing many important features. Through the lens of a rich developmental model, however, Miranda's writing has improved. More significantly, she has engaged in a partnership with a co-learner, a mutual transaction, and has experienced the benefits of negotiating, of seeking and finding new understandings and sharing those understandings with a reader.

Implications

I would like to be able to close this small-scale study with a set of guidelines for responding to student writing, some foolproof formula for commenting. But the message here seems to point in another direction entirely. Instead of a prescription for responding, what emerges is a thoroughgoing reconceptualization of the roles of teacher-readers, student-writers, and their transactions. In order for them to share in cointentional education (Friere 1970), which is a prerequisite for learning in general and learning writing in particular, teachers must allow students' inquiries to empower them to learn. Empowerment, in other words, is caused by and realized in inquiry. Only within a context where an inquiring learner comes together with an inquiring teacher, where both persons negotiate, exchange meanings, and share and modify intentions, can empowerment occur. Without empowerment there can be no significant purpose for responding to writing.

The school context for teaching and learning writing will always be somewhat artificial. That artificiality need not, however, be the focus of the instructional context. We know that a curriculum has non-negotiable constraints (see Boomer 1982). It is the responsibility of teachers to acknowledge honestly those issues over which they and their students have limited control. But there are also many facets of the curriculum that are negotiable, that are open to inquiry and change. These, too, must be openly acknowledged so students can explore and extend themselves in the areas open to negotiation. Perhaps in this way the gap between school-sponsored writing and self-sponsored writing will be narrowed.

Improvement

Genuine participation in learning consists in generating the modes and means of evaluating learning, too. So long as practicing writers learn within a context in which writing itself is valued over writers, then growth in writing may be hidden from view much of the time. Growth must be defined through a coming-together of both text-based and writer-based criteria. Certainly we cannot fool burgeoning writers into believing that their writing will not be judged on its ability to convey meanings independent of them. This is a non-negotiable aspect of composing. But we cannot allow this facet of textuality to override the development of a writer's own set of criteria for judging his or her performance. Professional writers have been found to judge their best writing as those pieces from which they learned something (Miller 1982). Without foregrounding learning, which is both the content of what we write and the process by which we have written, learning about writing is at best a happy coincidence. To inquire and to seek after new knowledge, to struggle into and out of chaos, to dwell on the borders of one's powers of knowing, these inhere in authentic learning situations and must be supported by the roles that students and teachers play. They also redefine improvements in writing. If the raters of the texts of the three participants in this study had been asked to identify the most interesting writing, the most engaged voice, the most impelled concerns, then their evaluations of the best pieces of writing may have been different. Clearly, the lens through which we view individual texts reflects what we value most in writing and predicts how we define "good" and "better" writing. Some of these qualities are individual and highly idiosyncratic; many are collective and socially based. Few are impermeable.

Frank Smith (1985) has said that reading is a process of asking questions of a text. Writing, too, should be seen as an inquiry process, in which asking propels composing and answering is composing. Inquiry is thus at the core of writing just as it is the core of learning. Inquiry cannot take place within a vacuum. It can only occur within a community of co-learners.

Acknowledgments

For their valuable responses to drafts of this article, I am grateful to Lil Brannon, Nancy Lester, and John Mayher.

References

Applebee, A. N. 1981. *Writing in the Secondary School.* Urbana, Ill.: National Council of Teachers of English.

Berthoff, A. E. 1981. Learning the Uses of Chaos. In *The Making of Meaning,* by A. E. Berthoff, 68–73. Montclair, N.J.: Boynton/Cook.

Boomer, G., editor. 1982. *Negotiating the Curriculum: A Teacher-Student Partnership.* Sydney, Australia: Ashton Scholastic.

Brannon, L., and C. H. Knoblauch. 1982. On Students' Rights to Their Own Texts: A Model of Teacher Response. *College Composition and Communication* 33:157–66.

Britton, J., T. Burgess, N. Martin, A. McLeod, and H. Rosen. 1975. *The Development of Writing Abilities (11–18).* London: Macmillan Education.

Bruner, J. 1985. The Language of Education. Speech presented at the Conference on English Education, the annual meeting of the National Council of Teachers of English, November, Philadelphia.

Dewey, J. 1933. *How We Think.* Boston: D. C. Heath.

Dillon, G. L. 1981. *Constructing Texts.* Bloomington: Indiana University Press.

Emig, J. 1977. Writing as a Mode of Learning. *College Composition and Communication* 28:122–27.

Friere, P. 1970. *Pedagogy of the Oppressed.* New York: Herder and Herder.

Hedley, E. W. 1968. *Freedom, Inquiry and Language.* Scranton, Pa.: International Textbook Company.

Knoblauch, C. H., and L. Brannon. 1981. Teacher Commentary on Student Writing: The State of the Art. *Freshman English News* 10:1–4.

Miller, S. 1982. How Writers Evaluate Their Own Writing. *College Composition and Communication* 33:176–83.

Murray, D. M. 1982. *Learning by Teaching.* Montclair, N.J.: Boynton/Cook.

Onore, C. S. 1983. Students' Revisions and Teachers' Comments: Toward a Transactional Theory of the Composing Process. Unpublished doctoral dissertation, New York University.

Rosenblatt, L. M. 1978. The Reader, the Text, the Poem: The Transactional Theory of the Literary Work. Carbondale: Southern Illinois University Press.

Searle, J. R. 1969. *Speech Acts: An Essay in the Philosophy of Language.* Cambridge: Cambridge University Press.

Shuy, R. W. 1984. Language as a Foundation for Education: The School Context. *Theory into Practice* 23:167–74.

Smith, F. 1985. *Reading without Nonsense.* 2d ed. New York: Teachers College Press.

Sommers, N. 1982. Responding to Student Writing. *College Composition and Communication* 33:148–56.

Van Dijk, T. A. 1980. *Macrostructures: An Interdisciplinary Study of Global Structures in Discourse, Interaction, and Cognition.* Hillsdale, N.J.: Erlbaum.

Appendix

Alex (Draft 1)

Mark Snyder suggests that there may be clear and definite gaps and contradictions between the public appearances and private realities of the self. Judging from my own experience, I believe Snyder's hypothesis to be true. I am who I appear to be; I can not deny being a participant in the game of role playing, because depending on where I am and who I'm with, I have different personalities. I am most certainly what Snyder would define asa "high-self-monitoring" individual, one who has the ability to carefully monitor his own performances in presenting himself in social situations.

Snyder claims that high self monitors can effectively adopt the mannerisms of a reserved, withdrawn, and introverted individual and then in a different situation also can be just as convincingly, a friendly, outgoing, and extraverted personality. I have found that this theory contains much truth. WhenI go to important job interviews, I dress very neatly and I try to present myself in a refined, dignified manner. I believe this, to an employer, inspires confidence and faith in my capabilities. However, when I am among close friends and family, I tend to be just the opposite. I enjoy talking to them and I am not shy around them. So I can also be a very outgoing person in certain situations.

In my life as it is now, I am thrust into a wide variety of environments: I am a son, a brother, a friend, a student, and a musician/performer, to name a few. When I examined these roles closely, I discovered that I behaved differently in each one. For example, to my parents and teachers, I usually attempt to appear somewhat studious, though I know that this is not the "real" me. The real me always does take care of all school responsibilities but is actually quite lazy about them. Subconsciously, though, I feel that I am *expected* by parents and teachers to appear studious, the underlying reason why I do so. As Snyder states, "In order to get along and be liked, one tends to be what people expect one to be rather than anything else."

I am not a fighter or an arguer by nature. I am agreeable in most instances, and I go to great lengths to avoid conflicts. Being a musician, I am forced into an environment where I must work extremely closely with several other band members. When others are at odds, many times I am the one to help them reach a fair compromise, while simultaneously avoiding any hard feelings. Snyder's opinion affirms this characteristic: High-self-monitors do not necessarily use their skills in impression management for deceptive or manipulative purposes; most high self monitors are eager to use their monitoring abilities to promote smooth social interaction.

Snyder also states that high self-monitoring individuals prefer to live in a stable, predictable social environment populated by people whose actions consistently and accurately reflect their true attitudes and feelings. He believes that in such an environment, the consistency and predictability or others would be of great benefit to those who are adept at impression management. Thus high self monitors would prefer to have friends who avoid strategic social posturing, or who are low self monitors. Strangely enough my closest friend took Snyder's self monitoring test and his score was comparitively much lower than mine. He is a blatantly honest person, and never hesitates to let his true feelings be known to others. He does not believe in mpression management; his attitude is "accept me as I am or don't accept me at all." Though we are opposites in many ways, we get along quite well, in coincidence to Snyder's theory.

Sometimes I am frustrated because I cannot be more like my friend. I feel I should be able to allow my true feelings to be seen by more people than just intimate friends and family. Occasionally I even lose sight of which is my real self. Snyder maintains that this is not uncommon. High self monitoring orientation may be purchased at the cost of having one's actions reflect very little about one's private attitudes, feelings, and dispositions. There is not much correspondence between private attitudes and public behavior in the case of high self-monitors. In some circumstances, weare persuaded by our own appearances, and we become the persons we appear to be, especially when the image we present wins the approval of those around us.

For me having many different selves is worrysome and perplexing. How am I and other high self-monitors to know which is in actuality our true self? Until we find our true self (If, in fact, we ever do), Snyder presents us with the only logical conclusion: "I am me, the me I am right now."

Alex (Draft 2)

Mark Snyder, in his article "The Many Me's of the Self-Monitor," suggests that there may be clear and definite gaps between the public appearances and private realities of the self. Judging from my own experience, I believe Snyder's hypothesis to be true. I am who I appear to be; I can not deny being a participant in the game of role playing, because depending on where I am and who I'm with, I have different personalities. I am most certainly what Snyder would define as a "high self-monitoring" individual, one who has the ability to carefully monitor his own performances in presenting himself in social situations.

Snyder claims that high self-monitors can effectively adopt the mannerisms of a reserved, withdrawn individual and then in a different situation also can be just as convincingly, a friendly, outgoing personality. I have found that this is an accurate theory. When I go to important job interviews, I dress very neatly and try to present myself in a refined, dignified manner to the prospective employer. However, in another situation, such as meeting a prospective friend, I can be just the opposite, dressed in blue jeans, and having quite an extraverted personality.

In my life as it is now, I am thrust into a wide variety of environments: I am a son, a brother, a friend, a student, and a musician/performer, just to name a few. When I examined these roles closely, I discovered that I behaved differently in each one. For example, to my parents and teachers, "I usually attempt to appear somewhat studious, though I know that this is not the "real" me. The real me always does take care of all school responsibilities, but goes about it in a far from studious manner. Subconsciously, though, I feel that I am *expected* by parents and teachers to appear studious, the underlying reason why I do so. As Snyder states, "In order to get along and be liked, one tends to be what people expect one to be rather than anything else."

It is Snyder's opinion that high self-monitors do not necessarily use their skills in impression management for deceptive or manipulative purposes; most high self-monitors are eager to use their monitoring abilities to promote smooth social itneraction. My experiences affirm this opinion. I am not a fighter or an arguer by nature. I am agreeable in most instances, and I go to great lengths to avoid conflicts. Being a musician, I am forced into an environment where I must work extremely closely with several other band members. When others are at odds, many times I am the one to help them reach a fair compromise while simultaneously avoiding hard feelings. My monitoring abilities aid greatly in this.

Snyder also states that high self-monitoring individuals prefer to live in a stable, predictable social environment populated by people whose actions consistently and accurately reflect their true attitudes and feelings. He believes thatin such an environment, the consistencyand predictability of others would be of great benefit to those who are adept at impression management. Thus high self-monitors would prefer to have friends who avoid strategic social posturing, or who are low self-monitors.

Strangely enough, my closest friend took Snyder's self-monitoring test and scored comparitively lower than I did. He is a blatantly honest person, and never hesitates to let his true feelings be known to others. He does not believe in impression management; his attitude is"Accept me as I am ordon't accept me at all." Though we are opposites on themonitoring scale, we get along quite well, in coincidence to Snyder's theory.

Sometimes I am frustratedbecause I am not more like my friend; I feel I should be able to allow my true feelings to be seen by more than just intimate friends and family. Occasinally I even lose sight of which is my real self. Snyder maintains that this is not uncommon: High self monitoring orientation may be purchased at the cost of having one's actions reflect very little about one's private attitudes, feelings, and dispositions. There is not much corre- spondence between private attitudes and public behavior in the case of high self monitors. In some circumstances, we are persuaded by our own appear- ances, and we become the persons we appear to be, especially when the image we present wins the approval of those around us.

For me, having many different selves is worrysome and perplexing. How am I and other high self-monitors to know which is in actuality out true self? Until we solve this dilemma, Snyder presents us with the only logical conclusion: "I am me, the me I am right now."

Alex (Draft 3)

Mark Snyder, a professor of psychology, suggests that there may be clear and definite gaps between the public appearances and the private realities of the self. Judging from my own experience, I believe Snyder's hypothesis to be true. I am who I appear to be; I cannot deny being a participant in the game of role-playing, because depending on where I am and who I'm with, I have different personalities. I am most certainly what Snyder would define as a "high self-monitoring" individual, one who has the ability to carefully monitor his own performances in presenting himself in social situations.

Snyder claims that high self-monitors can effectively adopt the mannerisms of a reserved, withdrawn individual and then in a different situation also can be, just as convincingly, a friendly, outgoing personality. I have found this to be an accurate theory. I am a musician and when I am seeking jobs for a band, I can present myself in a refined, dignified manner, so that the prospective employer knows that he is dealing with a responsible, reliable person who will not disappoint him if given the job. However, in another situation, such as meeting a prospective friend, I can be just the opposite, having quite an extraverted personality, and not putting up the aforementioned facade.

In my life as it is now, I am thrust into a wide variety of environments: I am a son, a brother, a friend, a student, and a musician/performer, just to name a few. When I examined these roles closely, I discovered that I behaved differently in each one. For example, to my parents and teachers, I usually attempt to appear somewhat studious, though I know that this is not the "real" me. The real me always does take care of all school responsibilities, but goes about it in a far from studious manner. Subconsciously, though, I feel that I am *expected* by parents and teachers to appear studious, the underlying reason why I do so. As Snyder states, "In order to get along and be liked, one tends to be what people expect one to be rather than anything else".

It is Snyder's opinion that high self-monitors do not necessarily use their skills in impression management for deceptive and manipulative purposes:

"Most high self-monitors are eager to use their monitoring abilities to promote smooth social interaction". My experiences affirm this opinion. I am not a fighter or an arguer by nature. I am agreeable in most instances, and I go to great lengths to avoid conflicts. Being a musician, I am forced into an evnironment where I must work extremely closely with several other band members. When others are at odds, many times I am the one to help them reach a fair compromise while simultaneously avoiding hard feelings. My monitoring abilities aid greatly in this: I know exactly what it takes to please each member and to keep everyone happy, thus I can take control of the situation and settle it in a way suitable to all. In the process, however, my own true feelings must sometimes be cast aside.

Snyder also states that high self-monitoring individuals prefer to live in a stable, predictable social environment "populated by people whose actions consistently and accurately reflect their true attitudes and feelings". He believes that in such an environment, the consistency and predictability of others would be of great benefit to those who are adept at impression management. Thus high self-monitors would prefer to have friends who avoid "strategic social posturing", or who are low self-monitors.

Interestingly, my closest friend took Snyder's self-monitoring test and scored comparitively lower than I did. He is a blatantly honest person, and never hesitates to let his true feelings be known to others. He does not believe in impression management; his attitude is "Accept me as I am or don't accept me at all". Though we are opposites on the monitoring scale, we get along quite well, in coincidence with Snyder's theory.

Sometimes I am frustrated because I am not more like my friend; as a result of frequent impression management, my true feelings are not seen by more than just intimate friends and family. The process of impression management is a difficult one to control, and sometimes I even lose sight of which is my real self. Snyder maintains that this is not uncommon: "High self-monitoring orientation may be purchased at the cost of having one's actions reflect very little about one's private attitudes, feelings, and dispositions". There is not much correspondence between private attitudes and public behavior in the case of high self-monitors. In some circumstances, we are persuaded by our own appearances, and we become the persons we appear to be, especially when the image we present wins the approval of those around us.

For me, having many different selves is worrysome and perplexing. How am I and other high self-monitors to know which is in actuality our true self? It is confusing to me when I hide my feelings in certain situations. Perhaps I just analyze the situation and behave according to my instincts of what is best, and my true feelings *are* shown. Until we solve this dilemma, Snyder presents us with an intereting outlook: "I am me, the me I am right now".

Dan (Draft 1)

There he was sitting on his beautiful sofa in the middle of his living room remembering so vividly what had happen to him over 20 years ago. Its been a long time since then and lots more had occured. Yet, that incidence in his life continues to linger in his mind. As he took a sip out of his drink, I saw an expretion on his face that told me that though his body was there, he mind wasn't.

"I was nine years old when the most bizzare thing happen to me," he said. He then kept silence for the next few seconds — as though he was reliving that experience again in his mind. It was then that he began to tell me about that incident.

A friend of the family had just arrived in New York and was spending a few days with him, his sisters and his parents. She was a very nice lady and he enjoyed being with her very much. There was something unique about though, she very much believed in sorcery. Though he was to young to truly understand what sorcery was about, he had the idea that spirits were involved — of course, he didn't think about it then.

It was a sunday afternoon and his parents had gone out shopping with his sisters leaving him alone in the apartment. He went to his toy box and took out his play soldiers. He proceeded to set them up on his bed — putting the blue ones on one side and the green ones on the other side. It was like a regular sunday afternoon, except his parents weren't home.

About an hour had gone by and the phone rang. Before answering the phone, he threw a blanket over his toy soldiers (so they wouldn't get mixed up — today he can't figure out that logic but, thats beside the point). After answering the phone, he went to the bathroom and then back to his room.

He fiddled around the room for a while and read some comics. Everything he was saying to me seem normal. I couldn't understand why he continued to remind me that it was "the most bizzare thing" that had happen to him. I soon found out.

Getting bored fiddling around the room he decided to go back to his soldiers. He walked back to his bed and took off the blanket. The expression on his face immediately change: From a normal, cheerful looking face to a puzzled, fearful look. The soldiers were no longer under the blanet. I looked at him. Could he honestly be saying that? "He must be kidding" I thought. "Thats impossible." "Things just don't disappear". I questioned this finding. "Are you sure your not kidding me?" I asked. He assured me that he was telling the truth (the sound of his voice alone proved he wasn't lying).

At not finding the soldiers under the blanket, his initial reaction was someone must be "playing a pranck" on me. He searched the house "inch by inch": didn't find anyone, anything or"anyone"! Then a frightening thought — could it be spirits. The thought of his parents friend believing in the unknown frighten him. "Could there actually be something out there" he said. His hairs stood. He froze for a moment. What am I am going to do, he thought. Certainly no one is going to believe him: "they would probably think I was crazy". He was very confused. When his parents arrived, soon after the incidence, he mentioned nothing. This experience was going to be known by no one.

He took another sip from his drink, looked at me and smiled. "Till this very day, almost 20 years later, I still don't understand what happen." He asked me if I believed his story. I also smiled and looked at him. "Its hard for me to believe but I guess you wouldn't be lying to me" I told him.

As I was leaving his apartment and waiting for the elevator he added a comment to his story. He said that not finding the soldiers was not as unexpected as not finding anyone else in the apartment. I asked him if that incident had changed his expectations for similar events. He simply replied "No — something like that couldn't happen again." I could certainly understand why this incident is so vivid in this mind but, do I really believe him.

Dan (Draft 2)

There he was sitting on his beautiful sofa in the middle of his living room remembering so vividly what had happened to him over 20 years ago. Its been a long time since then and lots more had occurred. Yet, that incident in his life continues to linger in his mind. As he took a sip out of his drink, I saw an expression on his face that told me that though his body was there, his mind wasn't.

"I was nine years old when the most bizzare thing happened to me" he said. He then kept silent for the next few seconds — as though he was reliving that experience in his mind. It was then that he began to tell me about that incident.

A friend of the family had just arrived in New York and was spending a few days with him, his sisters and his parents. She had met his parents many years before he was born; they were good friends. She was an ordinary human being — "average american". There was something unique about her though, she very much believed in sorcery. Though he was to young to truly understand its' meaning, he had conceived the notion that spirits were involved — of course, he didn't think about it then.

It was a Sunday afternoon and his parents and sisters, along with their house guest, had gone out shopping, leaving him alone in the apartment. Normally, he wouldn't be left alone (like that) but, they had made an exception that afternoon. He went to his toy box and toook out his play soldiers. He proceeded to set them up on his bed — putting the blue ones on one side and the gren ones on the other side. It was like a regular Sunday afternoon, except he was all alone in the house.

About an hour had gone by. He was still busy playing with his toy soldiers when the phone rang. He was about to answer the phone when he decided to throw a blanket over the soldiers (so they wouldn't get mixed up — today he laughs at that logic, but thats beside the point). He answered the phone, it was his grandmother, and spoke with her for a while. After their conversation, he proceeded to go back to his room, by way of the bathroom. Upon getting into the room, he fiddled around for a while and read some comics. The incident he was describing seemed normal to me. I couldn't understand why he continued to remind me that it was "the most bizzare thing that had heppen to him. I soon found out.

Like any child of nine, he was quickly bored with his comics (he sat there almost a whole hour looking at them). He decided to return to his toy soldiers. He walked back to his bed and took off the blanket. The soldiers were no longer there! Everything else was exactly as he left it when he went to answer the phone — everything except the soldiers, they were gone. He then thought, "maybe I left them somewhere else." He then proceeded to search the house "inch by inch" in the hope of finding his toy soldiers. Unfortunately, to no avail. The toy soldiers had disappeared — gone — vanished!

"That's impossible," I said, "the soldiers have to be in that house, as a matter of act they should be on your bed, if you were all alone in the house as you claim."

"Is it really impossible Dave?" he replied.

I remainded silent, he proceeded on with his story.

After searching the house "inch by inch" the thought that someone was playing a trick on him was eliminated. (As well as not finding his soldiers, he found no one.) He was trying to figure out how the soldiers could have vanished just like that. Then a frightening thought entered his mind — spirits!

This was the first time he had ever though about spirits and it was frightening! His parents guest came into mind. His hairs stood. Then he remembered that the person who had given him the soldiers, his aunt, also believed in sorcery. "Cold there actually be something out there," he said. "There must be." "Only the spirits could have taken my soldiers." He actually started believing that his aunt and his parents friend had left spirits in the house — the spirits took his soldiers. Right at that moment he heard his parents entering the house, he ran to them to give them a cheerful welcome.

He wanted to mention his "bizzare" incidence to his parents but found that he couldn't. He was not only afriad to speak because of the "spirits" but because he thought his parents would account the incident as part of the "childs imagination." Later, though, when his parents inquired about the soldiers, he told them that he had thrown them away. His story of the "missing soldiers" was going to be his and the spirits' secret."

He took another sip from his drink, looked at me and smiled. "Till this day, almost 20 years later, I still don't understand what happen. I can't seem to find any 'logical' explanation," he said.

"How did it affect you in the long run?" I asked.

"It made me realize that there is something out there. I don't know what, Dave, but I know its there. Do you believe me?" he asked.

"I don't know, I simply don't know." I replied.

Today when I think about his words, I have some doubt about his conclucion. I don't think I would end up with the same outcome (conclucion) that he did had I been put in the situation. Well, theres one thing I know for sure. I don't want to find out!

Dan (Draft 3)

There he was sitting on his beautiful sofa in the middle of his living room remembering so vividly an incident in his life that had occured over 20 years ago. An incident, he claims, that he will remember all his life. As he sat there taking a sip out of drink, I noticed a change in his facial expression.

"I was nine years old when the most bizzare thing happened to me," he said. He then kept silent for the next few seconds — as though he was reliving that experience in his mind. It was then that he began to tell me about that incident.

A friend of the family had just arrived in New York and was spending a few days with him, his sisters, and his parents. She had met his parents many years before he was born; they were good friends. She was an ordinary human being — "average americans". There was something unique about her though, she believed in sorcery. It was the conversations he had with her concerning the unknown that conceived a notion in his mind that "spirits" could exist.

It was a Sunday afternoon and his parents and sisters, along with their house guest, had gone out shopping, leaving him alone in the house. Normally he wouldn't be left alone but, they had made an exception. He took out his play soldiers from the toy box and proceeded to set them up on his bed — placing the blue ones on one side and the green ones on the other side. It was like a regular Sunday afternoon, except he was all alone in the house.

About an hour had gone by. He was still busy playing with his toy soldiers, when the phone rang. He was about to answer it when he decided to throw a blanket over the soldiers) so they wouldn't get mixed up — today he laughs at that logic). He answered the phone and went back to his room, by way of the bathroom. Upon getting in the room he began to read comics. The incident he was describing seemed normal to me. I couldn't understand why he continued to remind me that it was "the most bizzare thing" that had happened to him. I soon found out.

After getting tired of the comics, he returned to the toy soldiers. He walked to his bed and took off the blanket. To his surprise, the soldiers were no longer there. Everything else was exactly as he left it when he went to answer the phone — everything except the soldiers, they were gone. He then thought, "maybe I left them somewhere else." He proceeded to search the house "inch by inch" in the hope of finding his toy soldiers. Unfortunately, to no avail. The toy soldiers had disappeared — gone — vanished!

"That's impossible," I said, "the soldiers have to be in that house, as a matter of fact, they should be in your bed, if you were all alone in the house as you claim."

"Is it really impossible Dave?" he replied. I remained silent, he proceeded on with his story.

After searching the house "inch by inch" the thought that someone was playing a trick on him was eliminated. (As well as not finding the soldiers, he found no one.) He was trying to figure out how the soldiers could have vanished just like that. Then he remembered the conversations he had had about the unknown with the house guest. "Could it be due to the spirits?"

The thought that spirits were responsible for the disappearing of his soldiers, puzzled him. Those conversations he had concerning the unknown had only lead him to consider the possibility of a spirit existing. Now this incident, was trying to convince him that they do. And convince him is what the incident did. He could not think of any other explanation. "Only the spirits could have taken my soldiers," he said.

For days, he searched for the soldiers in the hope of finding them, but found nothing. He wanted to mention his "bizzare" incident to his parents but couldn't. The thought of hearing "that's only the child's imagination'" annoyed him; that would be their conclucion to his story. He just didn't want to hear that. He didn't mention it to his house guest because he didn't dare to. "Why didn't you mention it to anyone else?" I asked.

"I was afraid no one would believe me." he answered. I was the first person to ever hear his story. He had never mentioned it to anyone before. "Do you believe me?" he asked.

"I don't know, I simply don't know," I replied.

Today, the only belief he has which stems from that "bizzare" incident of 20 years ago, is that there's "something out there that's unexplanable; something intangible — something stronger than man." Since nothing else had occured in the 20 years to add as evidence for this belief, I asked him why he continued to believe in that "unexplanable" something.

"It is hard for me to explain why I feel this way," he replied. "I just do. I give no reasons why." I just nodded my head in response.

The incident he told me was bizzare and I don't really know how I would have reacted had I been put in a similar situation. The only thing I know for sure is that I am in no hurry to find out.

Miranda (Draft 1)

Our little scenario starts on one bright day on the football field of Fort Hamilton H.S. The field is covered with students in long blue graduation gowns and with parents eagerly carrying instamatic cameras, forcing their children to pose. One set of parents can be spotted showering praises on their only "man child," Phil. Phil's parents were both raised in Europe, came to this country with little education, no money and have worked their way into the American lifestyle. They have raised Phil never letting him forget how hard they worked, how lucky he is to be born into a middle class American family and how they expect success and perfection in every aspect of his life. So here we are, graduation day with the proud parents and son, Phil. "My son here is going to Brooklyn College," Phil's father reports, in a heavy Italian accent, to a nearby set of parents, "He's going to be a doctor. He's a smart boy, and he works hard." (This man should be a Little League mother.")

As anyone would realize soon after meeting this trio, Phil has demanding parents who have constantly told him what to do and what was expected of him (but don't get the idea that Phil is easy to push around, or a"mamma's boy": he is just as domineering and agressive as is his father).

College and the responsibilities that accompany it were totally foreign to Phil; he just assumed it would be like high school; someone in authority would tell you what classes to take, the teachers would keep after you to do your work and with little effort, you could maintain a "B" average. With the advice of his counselor who agreed that it would be good for Phil to take a double major in Chem & Bio and minor in Math and computer science, Phil came out with a wonderful schedule. 3 days a week from 9–12 and 3–6 and 9–1 the other 2 days.

Phil was somewhat disillusioned by college. He felt that the subjects he was taking wouldn't be applicable in the real world and that he was wasting his time. Immediately after registering for his 5th semester, Phil dropped out. He'd plodded through the last four terms with C's and B's, felt he wasn't prepared for more intensive courses and was no longer sure what he wanted to do with his life.

Phil got a job with the Bd. of Ed. as a high school security guard that paid a decent salary, but his upbringing contributed to his displeasure with the job. It was a nowhere job, providing him with no chance to prove himself, as he'd wanted to do.

After a few months of that he returned to Bklyn College, this time to pursue a business degree that he felt would be more useful. He found that he had both an interest and an aptitude in finance and accounting. He'd been spoiled by working and wasn't used to not having spending money. After weighing his options he transfered to Pace U. So he could go to school and work part time in a brokerage house. He spent a year at Pace and worked full time during the summer. His boss offered him a full time job with the company, and paying his tuition if he went to school at night. Decision time again. He decided to work full time and took a class at night. After 10 months Phil was made a supervisor and then 2 months later got promoted to a job with excellent opportunities, in the front office. He is now taking classes to become a registered stock brokerage and is studying very hard really for the first time.

I think Phil's experience shows that college isn't for everybody and isn't the only vehicle for success. I have to agree with Phil that it's better to get your head together before going to college so you know what you want to get out of your education. Phil is doing extremely well now (even his parents are proud) because he's in a field that interests him, and interest is a very important part of succeeding.

Miranda (Draft 2)

Our little scenario starts on one bright spring day on football field of Fort Hamilton High School. The field is covered with students in long blue graduation gowns and their eager, camera-toting parents. One set of parents can be spotted showering praises on their only "manchild," Phil. Phil's parents were both raised in Europe, came to this country with little education, no money and have worked their way up into the middle class. They constantly remind Phil of how lucky he is, how much they've done for him, and how they expect success from him. So here we are, graduation day with the proud parents and son, Phil. "My son here is going to Brooklyn College," Phil's father reports, in a heavy Italian accent, to a passing father. He's going to be a doctor. He's a smart boy, and he works hard." Phil's mother stands by smiling and nodding obligingly.

College turned out to be a difficult transition for Phil. As he puts is, "I'd been so used to always having my parents and teacher tell me just what to do, I wasn't prepared to set my own schedules in college." He turned to his advisors for help. Together they agreed that Phil should take a double major in Chemistry and biology and minor in math and computer science. Phil's first schedule consisted of difficult classes that weren't in a good order.

Phil plodded thru school and became disinterested in medicine. He dropped out after his 5th semester to take time off to figure out what he wanted to do with his life. He got a job with the B. of Ed as a high school security guard that paid a decent salary, but he wasn't satisfied. It was a deadend job and he quit after 9 months.

He bummed around for the summer and then returned to Brooklyn College, this time to pursue a business degree. He thought that the classes he'd take would be more applicable to the real world and he discovered he had both an interest and an aptitude for finance. Working for almost a year had gotten him used to having spending money so after a term he transferred to Pace University. "Pace was a better business school and I could work part time on Wall Street in a finance related job." Phil learned quickly at work, his boss offered him a full time position and the company would pay tuition at evening classes. Phil accepted and quickly advanced first made a supervisor after 6 months and two months later he was again promoted to a great front office job. He is taking classes now to become a stock broker and is studying and working very hard with great dedication for the first time in his life. He explains his new attitude, "But I like what I'm doing."

I think Phil's experience shows that college isn't for everybody and isn't the only vehicle for success. I have to agree with him that it's better to get your head together before going to college so that you know what you want to get out of your education. Phil is doing well (his parents are even proud) because he's in a field that interests him; and "interest is a very big part of success."

Miranda (Draft 3)

Our little scenario starts on one bright spring day on the football field of Fort Hamilton High School. The field is covered with students in long blue graduation gowns and their eager, camera toting parents. One set of parents can be spotted showering praises on their only "man child." Phil. Phil's parents were both raised in Europe, came to this country with no formal education, no money and have worked their way up into the middle class, with all of its benefits — a nice car, home and vacations. THey constantly tell Phil that he is lucky to be born into a good home, that they've given him many wonderful opportunities to do well in life and that Phil owes it to them and himself to succeed. So here we are on graduation day with the proud parents and their son. "My son here is going to be a doctor," Phil's father reports in a heavy Italian accent to a passing father. He's going to Brooklyn College. He's a smart boy and he works hard." Phil's mother stands by smiling and nodding obligingly.

Their behavior irritates Phil but he's grown accustomed to it so it's become a familiar annoyance. "Shut up," he whispered into his father's ear.

Over the years the relationshipbetween father and son steadily deteriorated into an ongoing polite argument. Every moment that the two are together Joe, Phil's father, nags him. "Did you do what I told you?" "Don't do that." Phil pretends to ignore him and will insist tha he doesn't listen to his father but I've known Phil long enough to realize that he does take his father's advice very seriously. In many ways Phil has developed the traits that he despises in his father. He is always offering me advice whenever I have a decision to make, even if I don't ask him for his opinion and he getsa little offended if I am not receptive to his suggestion.

Phil had a hard time adjusting to college life where students are forced to take on more responsibilities than they had in high school. Even though he was still living at home he was unable to turn to his parents for advice. For they were unaware of the demands of Phil's new life. Their advice had annoyed him but it was difficult for him to start making decisions on his own.

Phil quit school after two years, got a job and moved out of his house. Moving out forced him to sever all ties he had with his parents. Beiing "old world," they were enraged that he would move out before he got married. They also were sure that he was doing something that he had to hide from them. Phil was supporting himself working as a security guard, a job that payed a decent salary but offered no future.

After a year Phil quit work to return to school. His upbringing influenced his decision; he'd been trained to succeed and to seek out challenges. This time when he entered Pace University he knew what he wanted from the school. He took business classes and worked part time in a brokerage house. His boss offered him a good full time job which he accepted after finishing his first semester at Pace. He did well in the brokerage house and has since received several promotions.

Phil moved back in with his parents. He had matured, gained his independence, and set a direction for his life. He no longed needed his parents advice and since they now could be proud of their son they stopped offering it — except for an occasional "Phil, get your hair cut."

13 The Semantics of Error: What Do Teachers Know?

Susan V. Wall
Northeastern University

Glynda A. Hull
University of California, Berkeley

J. M. Keynes is said to have commented that those economists who would disassociate themselves from current economic theory, claiming no need for it or admitting pure dislike, were nonetheless driven by theory — an earlier one. The same can be said, wrote Terry Eagleton (1983), of literary critics, and something similar can also be said, we hope to argue in this paper, of teachers of writing. We center our discussion on one activity in the teaching of writing — responding to student papers by identifying errors. Our aim is to arrive at some answers to the questions, "How do readers — in particular, teachers — label and interpret errors in a text?" and "How can such knowledge inform the teaching of editing?" To propose some answers to these questions, we review error studies in the context of post-modernist theories of literary criticism, and we discuss the findings from a study on how teachers from various grade levels responded to an error-laden student text.

Error: The Certainty Factor

Error and correctness in writing, as topics of research and components of language instruction, have the uneasy characteristic of being quite value-laden. We are taken aback when we recognize the vigor with which readers denounce certain usages, certain errors or constructions. Joseph Williams (1981) has pointed out that errors like *different than* or *between you and I* inspire an unexpected amount of ferocity. It is not unusual, for example, for handbooks and grammar guides to refer to the very commonplace usages of *OK* and *hopefully* and *irregardless* as examples of language use that are *detestable* and *vulgar* and *idiotic* and *oafish.* A recent survey of professional people (Hairston 1981) demonstrated that they disapprove very strongly of errors like run-on sentences, nonparallel constructions, and faulty adverb forms. Pop grammarians abound — Richard Mitchell, Edwin Newman, William Safire, John Simon — all self-proclaimed guardians of the language, ready to pounce upon deviations from conventional forms. Mitchell (1979) repeats an error from a Department of Transportation manual, "If a guest becomes intoxicated, take his or her car keys and send them home in a taxi," and comments: "It's so funny that we don't discern the failure of mind that has caused this silly mistake" (72).

The thing that strikes us about such comments is the steadfastness and certainty with which readers, experienced readers, stand their ground about what counts as an error and how much it counts. We see another version of this certainty in research on the assessment of writing skills, where the assumption is that sentence-level error in writing is a simple matter to measure. A comment by a researcher who evaluated the National Assessment data on writing mechanics is typical. Mellon (1975) warned that we ought not to give these data more attention than they are due just because "the categories can be defined, the data easily obtained." He went on to comment that "sometimes the ease of getting information leads people to overstate its value" (33). (See also Hirsch and Harrington 1981; Mullis 1984.) This attitude stands in great contrast to current thinking on the evaluation of discourse skills, where issues of validity and reliability regularly receive careful attention. (Breland [1983] provides a good review of these issues.) Sentence-level error seems to be the one part of written language upon whose nature everyone agrees. In this view, error does not need to be interpreted, but only recognized. To find another vantage point, we turn to literary theory.

Reading as Interpretation

In recent years, a revolution of sorts has taken place in departments of English in this country, a revolution that has to do with new theories on the nature of reading and literature. Broadly speaking, the new theories conceive the act of reading as an act of interpretation, or what is sometimes called the "transaction" between a reader and a text (Rosenblatt 1978). In contrast to critics earlier in the century who interested themselves in a work of literature per se, respecting its autonomy and the assumed intention of its author, post-modernist critics want to emphasize the role of context in interpretation. Thus, they no longer consider a literary work as static and fixed, containing a meaning and an intended interpretation that skillful readers are supposed to ferret out and students are supposed to memorize; they see it as fluid and changing, waiting for enactments of many meanings by readers who necessarily bring different experiences to the text and who will thereby and necessarily interpret it somewhat differently.

To characterize the reading process, the phenomenological critic Iser (1972) offers the analogy of two people looking at the night sky. He explains that the two "may both be looking at the same collection of stars, but one will see the image of a plough, and the other will make out a dipper." That is, all readers engage in certain "complementary activities of selection and organization, anticipation and retrospection, the formulation and modification of expectations in the course of the reading process" (Suleiman 1980, 23), but the performance of these activities will vary from time to time, from reader to reader; consequently, different readers (and the same reader at different times) will see different things in the same text. They will see different lines uniting the same stars. (For an introduction to Iser and phenomenological criticism, see Suleiman.) What we have wondered is the extent to which something similar might be said when the text to be read is a student composition and the reader, a teacher whose intent it is to comment on student errors. And as it turns out, a few researchers have already begun to characterize error detection and correction in ways that bring to mind the interpretative nature of reading.

Williams (1981) suggested that we find errors where we expect to find them, in student papers, for example, and demonstrated that we overlook errors where we don't expect them to appear, in scholarly articles by Joseph Williams, for example. He proposes that we categorize errors not according to systems of grammar, but according to whether a rule is violated and whether a reader responds. The interesting part of Williams's taxonomy, and the way it differs from traditional systems for categorizing error, is that he includes categories for instances in which no rule is violated but a reader responds anyway, and instances in which a rule is violated but a reader does not respond at all. His point is that errors aren't equal, that some lack practical force because their violation is rarely noticed — when a reader makes semantic structure, rather than letters and syntactic form, his or her field of attention, that is.

Bartholomae (1980) examined the case in which a reader is likely to see the most errors — when as a teacher, he or she attempts to analyze the errors in essays by inexperienced writers. Bartholomae argues that a variety of interpretations can often exist for an idiosyncratic sentence, and that this variety depends upon a reader's sense of discourse or the larger meaning provided by the rest of the text, and upon a reader's skill at predicting how a writer puts sentences together or constructs a style. He objects, then, to any easy assumption that to categorize an error, to give it a label, one need only imagine the sentence the writer would have constructed if he or she had been careful enough to write the sentence correctly from the start. Classifying as error isn't like classifying a rock or a butterfly, he argues; when reading for error, we can't avoid interpretation.

Lees (1986) offered evidence that college composition instructors see some errors and ignore others, even when their task is to locate and label all the errors in a student paper. She found considerable agreement on the presence or absence of errors in certain parts of the paper, and considerable variation in other parts. (See also Greenbaum and Taylor 1981.) Lees has identified, then, one example of what Stanley Fish likes to call an "interpretive community" — a group of readers who share common assumptions about texts and common strategies for making sense of them. However, this group did *not* share the same assumptions about what constitutes an error. Lees would argue, then, that error isn't a binary matter, either "there" or "not there" in the text.

Hull (1987a, 1987b) called into question another common assumption — that writers locate and label errors in texts by consulting rules like those found in handbooks of grammar and usage. She documented that writers engage in other sorts of activities, too, strategies like focusing on the meaning of the text or listening to how it sounds. Hull proposes, then, that we enlarge our notions of editing to include such "comprehending" and "intuiting" activities, in addition to the "consulting" of rules. And she speaks out in favor of alternate error-classification schemes, arguing that traditional taxonomies fail to capture what is salient about error detection and correction. (For a review of other recent scholarship on error and editing, see Hull 1985.)

The Present Study

Given, on the one hand, assumptions about how simple it is to quantify error, and on the other hand, current thinking about the interpretive nature of the reading process, including reading for errors, we were interested in studying further the place where the contradictions inherent in these positions most often collide — teachers' readings of students' texts, teachers' quantification and interpretation of errors in student writing. The purpose of the study was to describe how teachers at several grade levels labeled and evaluated the errors they saw in a particular text. By doing so, we hoped to learn something about the knowledge teachers do or don't share about errors and editing. Instead of assuming (as our profession has traditionally done) that teachers constitute an interpretive community in this respect, we asked if this was really the case.

We did not assume, let us quickly say, that these teachers taught by labeling errors, or that their responses to the errors in the paper we provided were indicative of their responses to errors in the papers of their own students. We did assume, however, that to address errors, most teachers do annotate their students' texts. The teaching of writing in schools and colleges and universities consists in large part of the instruction that occurs when teachers comment on students' essays. It is through such comments — the directions and admonitions and suggestions and judgments made in the margins, between the lines, over the words, and at the end of essays, stories, poems, and letters — that teachers react to the written language produced by individual students and that students learn to improve their writing.

We constructed an editing task for teachers (see the appendix, page 290) which asked them:

1. to read a student essay in order to mark and label all of its errors in punctuation, grammar, syntax, and spelling;

2. to pick out the three most serious errors from those they labeled, and to explain their significance; and

3. to comment on the overall strengths and weaknesses of the student writer.

For the editing task, we used an actual student essay (see page 291) that had been written as part of a college entrance exam. We used an actual student text and the errors that occurred naturally within it rather than one we had constructed, because it is hard to construct convincing student prose or student errors, and also because our subjects would be schoolteachers who would presumably notice the difference; we wanted the task to be realistic for them. The essay was a narrative, written about a time when the student had done something creative. It was approximately 400 words long, or about one and one-half typed pages; by our count, it contained thirty-five errors in punctuation, grammar, syntax, and spelling. We don't mean to claim that other readers ought to see these thirty-five errors, too, or that they are "in" the text. Our list of errors counts, then, as a response and also as a practical way of tabulating the responses of other readers. There was a range of errors: mistakes in punctuation, tense, spelling, and syntax. The essay contained one obvious error pattern — the omission of commas in particular places. We coded teachers' responses to the essay by setting up a data base and entering demographic data (teachers' grade level, etc.) and error data (the errors identified and labeled, etc.). This data base made it possible to access and compare data — to call up, for example, all the labels that teachers used to refer to an error in a particular line, and to sort those labels according to whether teachers worked at the elementary, secondary, or college level.

The participants in our study were twenty English teachers in elementary school (grades 1–5), twenty-five English teachers in secondary school (grades 6–12), and ten college professors in disciplines other than English. We chose these three groups because we thought they represented potentially different readers when it comes to error. Secondary-school teachers have the reputation of being sticklers for correct form, and there is evidence from a national survey that they respond most frequently to student writing by marking sentence-level errors (Applebee 1981). We don't know as much about the practices of elementary-school teachers, but we believed the range of their concerns might be different. College instructors who do not teach English represent experienced readers and writers who deal regularly with student texts but who do so outside the discourse community where concern for error is paramount. Again, we expected their range of concerns to be different. (The group we omitted is the one most often studied — college writing teachers. See, for example, Lees 1986; Greenbaum and Taylor 1981.)

Results

Analysis of Responses: Assumptions and Procedures

If teachers-readers of student writing constitute an interpretive community, then we should find that they share not only a common vocabulary for labeling the "errors" they see in texts, but also a common sense of when it is appropriate to do so. In other words, when we infer what teachers know about error from their written responses to a text, we are really asking where consensus lies among members of our profession.

Our controlling question for this research, then, was this: To what extent did the locating and labeling of errors reflect agreement among these readers about the "errors" in this text? To that end, we asked these four questions:

What places in the text — words, spaces, groups of words and spaces — were marked as errorful?

How many teachers marked each place?

What kinds of errors were implied by the labels used to mark these places?

For each place marked, how consistent were the labels used?

One of our major analytic tasks was to devise a category scheme for teachers' error labels. We classified labels according to these six categories:

> *Punctuation* (which included matters of capitalization and under-lining) and *Spelling:* These are typically what Hull (1987a, 1987b) has called "consulting" errors; in correcting them, readers call upon established rules and conventions for written discourse, even looking them up in handbooks and dictionaries.
>
> *Grammar:* These are mostly errors in the forms of those parts of speech still inflected in modern English, such as errors in verb endings or noun/pronoun agreement.
>
> *Logic/Clarity:* These reflect the reader's inability to accept the sense of the text as it is written, either because it is confusing or because the words or other symbols do not fit the overall meaning that the reader is constructing. Hull refers to these as "compre-hending" errors. We would include here not only such obvious labels as "unclear" and "doesn't make sense," but also ones like "wrong word," "omission," and "irrelevant sentence."
>
> *Style/Structure:* The main concern here is for the form of the text, e.g., sentence structure, diction. The reader seems to understand and accept what is being said, but seems to feel it could be said in a better way. These often fall into the category that Hull calls "intuiting" errors.
>
> *Unclassifiable:* These include places marked but given no labels, and also labels that are too vague, ambiguous, or strange for us to understand, even guessing from the context.

These are, at best, crude categories. Deciding how to classify errors required that we do much inferring from the context, and often the categories "leaked." Consider, for example, objections to the word *preformed* in the sentence, "At my lesson I preformed my version of Heart and Soul." Twenty-six teachers marked this as a spelling error, yet it is clearly not a spelling error of the sort evidenced, for instance, when a student writes *recieve* for *receive*. Here, *preformed* is another word entirely, the wrong word — an error, one might argue, in logic/ clarity. Readers constructing sense out of a text about practicing and playing music can easily guess that the word the writer probably intended was *performed*. But they do this more on the basis of the logical sense they are making out of the story than their sense that a word the writer intended to use is there, but orthographically misrepresented.

It was often hard for us to decide between style/structure and logic/clarity when classifying an error label, particularly when the labels were those such as "word choice," "omit," or "unnecessary." Consider, for example, the sentence beginning, "The next thing that she told my parents was that I was tone deaf. . . ." Eight teachers clearly felt confused: "What was the previous 'thing'?" Two more labeled "The next thing" as "wordy" and suggested stylistic revisions. But a third group either deleted "The next thing" (six) or labeled it "usage" (two). Are these last responses objections to a phrase that doesn't make sense, or to one that is stylistically infelicitous? We can't be sure. In each instance, we had to use our combined understanding of the text (as we read it), our sense of the errors we found there, and our acquired familiarity with error labels to try to categorize the reader's response.

In the next sections of this chapter, we present global tallies and then discuss teachers' responses to high-, medium-, and low-consensus errors; teachers' error labels; those errors judged to be serious; the effect of grade-level of teaching and of training in the composing process on responses; and what the responses don't say.

Gross Tallies

The 55 teachers whose responses we analyzed found a total of 1,800 errors, or an average of 32.73 per teacher, which is very close to the 35 errors we marked as occurring in the text. (Note that the 1,800 "errors" are a total of *all* responses, all things that were marked as errors in the text, not just the 35 items we initially identified as erroneous.) The groups fell out as follows: elementary teachers saw 575 errors, or an average of 28.75; secondary teachers saw 864 errors, or an average of 34.56; and college teachers saw 361 errors, or an average of 36.1. When we look at range, the variation is much greater. The lowest number of errors detected was 9, and the highest, 56. For elementary teachers, the range was from 9 to 56; for secondary teachers, from 19 to 50; and for college teachers, from 16 to 51.

High-Consensus Errors

When we analyzed the error markings, we considered the consensus "high" if a place in the text was marked for similar reasons by 23 or more teachers (41% or more), and "very high" if it was marked by over 60%. Twenty-five places in the text could be considered locations of such high-consensus errors.

Twenty of these high-consensus places were labeled as punctuation errors, 12 by 60% or more of the teachers, reflecting what we felt were highly shared perceptions of error patterns in this student's writing. Eleven places, in our subjects' judgments, showed a failure to punctuate clauses or long phrases at the beginning of sentences: "When I was in the fifth grade[ ] my parents decided. . . ." Four more places were felt to show the writer's lack of knowledge about the handling of song titles.

We thought it was interesting, however, that there was really much less agreement on what punctuation might be needed within or after the sentence's main clause. Forty-four teachers, for example, felt that some sort of punctuation was needed for the sentence which reads: "The next thing that she told my parents was that I was tone deaf and therefore it was out of the question for me to learn how to play the piano." Out of these 44, however, 15 teachers indicated the need for a comma after "deaf"; 2 wanted a comma after "and"; 7 called for commas both before and after "therefore"; 12 wanted a comma only after "therefore"; 1 suggested commas in all three places; and 7 more underlined the entire "deaf and therefore" chunk and simply wrote "punctuation" above, making it impossible for us to tell whether the error was the omission of one comma, two, or three.

A surprising lack of agreement about mid-sentence punctuation involved final free modifiers, a syntactical construction found in enough sentences in this paper to be considered a characteristic of the writer's style:

> My parents pleaded with her *saying that I would practice all the harder*. . .
>
> I seemed to have been progressing quite well, *learning all classical music.*
>
> But, now comes the hard part *putting in the harmony with the left hand.*
>
> This cleared up my mind *allowing me to try some new tactics.*

Forty-eight teachers accepted the comma in the second sentence without objection, but only 31 called for a comma for the third sentence, 20 for the fourth, and only 15 for the first. Another 7 teachers objected to the comma in the second sentence, and 8 suggested revising the fourth to read: ". . . the hard part *of* putting in the harmony. . . ." We can't be sure why these responses are so inconsistent. Perhaps readers were struggling with other, more puzzling problems. But perhaps, too, the evidence of the high-consensus markings suggests that placing commas after elements at the beginning of sentences has been more commonly learned, perhaps even overgeneralized to a rule, while punctuation of other parts of the sentence — involving, perhaps, less familiar constructions and labels — represents a kind of knowledge that is a lot less firm.

Medium-Consensus Errors

The majority of errors in this category were errors in style/structure and in logic/clarity. Often these were the most interesting errors to analyze because of the way they reveal readers making error judgments based on their active constructions of the text's ideal, "intended" meaning. These interpretations vary particularly where, as Hull puts it, the reader must "intuit" that something is wrong. These variations typically mean that different places in the text will be marked and different labels attached, depending upon the kind of revision the reader feels is necessary.

A wonderful example of a sentence that these teachers reconstructed in different ways is the one that begins the essay's second paragraph: "My parents pleaded with her saying that I would practice all the harder, would she please let have at least a chance at it." Some of the suggested revisions were:

> My parents, saying that I would practice all the harder, pleaded with her.... [error label: dangling participle]
>
> My parents pleaded with her. "If my child would practice all the harder, would she please...." [revision advice: change indirect to direct quotation]
>
> ...saying that I would practice all the harder if she would please.... [various labels, mostly "usage" or "omitted words"]
>
> My parents pleaded with her, saying that I would practice all the harder. Would she please let me have at least a chance at it? [change punctuation to make two sentences, add omitted word]
>
> ...would she please let me have at least a chance? [wordy or awkward structure, omitted word]

These stylistic/structural revisions address problems that readers have with the form of the sentence, but they do not question what the writer says. Problems of the latter sort, "comprehending" errors, were often, we found, problems that extended not only beyond the single word or space but beyond the sentence, indeed, to the meaning of much or all of the essay.

One such problem of clarity is the question about the tone of the whole piece. Is it a joke? Just how seriously are we to take the writer's assertions that she had great difficulty learning "Mary Had a Little Lamb," that after five years of piano practice the most she could accomplish was a variation on "Heart and Soul," and that these songs represent "all classical music"? There are hints at the essay's beginning that perhaps the story is being told in a tongue-in-cheek or tall-tale fashion, poking fun at parents who believe that talent can be acquired and who virtually dragoon their daughter into weekly piano lessons — even in face of the bad news that she is tone deaf! Some cues to a possible humorous reading are features that we associate with oral storytelling, such as sarcastic exaggeration ("enlisted" instead of "enrolled") and dropping into the present tense ("my parents decided its time . . ."). The problem is that these cues (if we are reading them that way) are inconsistent; they disappear from the text. By the end of the second paragraph, about half our readers found themselves simply confused about the experience being described: "? This is not classical music." "Unclear how this relates to a nursery rhyme." "Not exactly an 'error,' but makes no sense." The result is that by the end of the piece, the writer's claims to an achievement of "total creativity" are simply unconvincing: "Is this the lesson?" "Is 'Heart and Soul' the be-all and end-all?"

Comments like these about logic and clarity show how much readers depend on culturally established textual cues to guide them in constructing meaning. But there was another kind of problem with meaning in this case, which came from a very different source: the gap between what the writer and the reader knew about her topic. The problem involved the sentences in paragraph three, where the writer describes the techniques of her piano practice:

> Much to my surprise I was able to sit down at the piano and work on the right hand which is the melody of the song. Of course there was no problem on that hand, since that as the part of the piece well known.

Here, *hand* seems to have a different, specialized meaning: not a part of the body but a musical part — "the melody [and, we would also suppose, the harmony] of the song." Readers who either did not know this bit of musical jargon or who refused to accept the writer's definition objected not only to the confusion of "part" and "hand," revising so as to make them two different things; they objected as well to other constructions that also derive from making the two synonymous — for example, the phrasing of "work *on* the right hand." Some suggested revisions were:

> . . . work on the right hand part, the melody of the song.

> I was able to sit down at the piano and work on the right hand,
> the hand which delivers the melody of the song.

We wonder: Did the apparent absurdity of so much of the rest of the
story undermine the writer's authority here, despite her efforts to
provide a definition and head off confusion?

Finally, we ought to observe that many of these medium-consensus
error markings reflect a higher agreement than we can see just from
locating errorful places and counting markings. We need to look past
these different forms of response and interpret the overall problem
the readers seem to have with the essay. For one pair of sentences we
have discussed (about "Mary Had a Little Lamb" and "learning all
classical music"), no one place was identified by more than 38% of
the teachers as an error in logic/clarity. Yet if we take all logic/clarity
error markings for those sentences into consideration, we find that the
general consensus is much higher: 56.4% of all responses to these two
portions of the text reflected some difficulty in understanding and
accepting what the writer was saying about the nature of her musical
instruction.

Low-Consensus Errors

Of all the places marked in this text as errorful, nearly three-quarters
(74.6%) were marked by 20% or fewer of the teachers responding,
and about two-thirds (63.5%) by fewer than 10%. To these low-count
places we also add instances of labels that, even though attached to
a *place* marked by many teachers, suggest a reading noticeably at odds
with the majority of readers — a label, say, of "syntax" where most
other labels for that place suggest that the problem is verb tense. If
we take together the labels for places in the text with a low number
of marks *and* the unusual labels attached to highly-marked places, the
total figure is 31.9% of all error names. We begin to see why our range
of "errors" was so broad, when we consider that nearly one in three
analyses of the text can be considered unusual, even idiosyncratic.

Of these low-consensus responses, 35.7% seemed to refer to stylistic
problems, 23.4% to problems of logic/clarity, 16.4% to punctuation
errors, 8.1% to grammar, and 2.6% to spelling errors. Another 13.8%
of these responses were unclassifiable.

We were not surprised that many of these low-consensus errors
reflected objections to the style of the paper or to its logic, these being
the kinds of responses more determined by personal taste and individual text interpretation. But we think other factors may be at work

as well, which would account for why these responses fall into the low-consensus range. Some readers may not have considered problems with style and logic as "errors," an attitude suggested by the label, "Not an error exactly, but makes no sense." We would speculate that even if readers had problems with the sense of the paper, they might not have labeled these textual difficulties as "errors" for that reason. Some readers, too, may have felt pressured by the nature of the task itself to provide us with a label, even if they did not feel particularly expert about doing so; these could account for some of the unusual and unclassifiable responses. And, most especially, we have to take into account our understanding that, as we have already observed, many readers had difficulty with the substance of this paper, finding themselves confused by or in disagreement with the text, but that the kind of error analysis reflected by marks and labels varies depending upon the "intended" meaning being imagined. As Hull observes, these kinds of errors rarely fit neatly into "consulting" categories like "pronoun agreement" or "spelling." The fact that 59% of all low-consensus responses express problems with either logic or style (often hard to distinguish by label alone) suggests that these responses, however idiosyncratic, nevertheless are part of a general consensus about the problems this writer is having with making her meaning clear and credible.

Our results here, in other words, are ambiguous. On the one hand, we are struck by the great variety of highly individual responses to this text. Such variety underscores the validity of reader-response theory as a way of understanding what readers do with texts. But it also raises the question of whether a reader's problems with style and clarity ought to be considered as "errors" at all, rather than as responses more appropriately addressed to revision than to editing. We are not suggesting that teachers disguise problems they are having with a student's style and clarity. Rather, we suggest that as a profession, we remove the label of "error" from the second category entirely. This might give students a better sense of the kinds of responses to error that are conventional, i.e., that can be generalized to a set of rules or procedures students can reasonably expect will be shared among adult readers. At the same time, students might also better understand the distinction between these high-consensus perceptions of error and the inevitably more personal, individual responses to the style and logic of particular texts. They need to know about both if they are to be prepared realistically to write for audiences other than themselves; a crucial part of that preparation, we want to argue, is knowing the difference.

Error Labels

In analyzing the labels teachers used for high-consensus errors, we saw some labels appearing over and over: *punctuation, commas, agreement, tense, wrong word,* in particular. So, for some errors, it appeared that teachers did share a common vocabulary. Our concern, however, is the functionality such labels would have were they used on student papers. (We should remember, however, that this is hypothetical speculation, for we did not ask teachers to label errors as examples of their classroom practice, but as editors.) In many instances, these labels were used generically to refer to many different kinds of problems. For example, the label *punctuation* could be and was used to refer to needed or superfluous commas, hyphens, capitals, or quotation marks. Students might not, of course, interpret generic labels in the way that teachers intend.

Another problem had to do with areas that were high-consensus in terms of detection — that is, many teachers recognized that a problem existed — but low-consensus in terms of diagnosis — they tended to differ in their assessment of the nature of the problem. One example of this occurred in the second sentence of the essay: "They enlisted me in a musical program known as the once a week piano lesson," with the phrase "once a week piano lesson." Almost 80% of the teachers thought something was wrong here, but they differed, we infer from their labels, in what they thought the problem was. Some teachers preferred that the phrase be capitalized; others added quotation marks; others objected to wording, remarking, for example, that "weekly would be better"; others recommended that hyphens be inserted. And to return to the problem of ambiguous labels, some teachers simply commented "punctuation," which could be interpreted a variety of ways.

Our point here isn't to lobby for one interpretation of the error over another, but for the recognition that there are many gray areas where correctness and editing are concerned. Students do need to learn that there are some errors most readers see and about whose nature they will agree. But it is important also, we would argue, for students to be made aware that there are many gray areas where different readers — and teachers — will diagnose problems differently.

Another example of low-consensus diagnosis is the sentence, "My parents pleaded with her saying that I would practice all the harder, would she please let have at least a chance at it." Teachers labeled the problem having to do with sentence structure — the juxtaposition of the "would she" clause with that part of the sentence preceding the comma — in a variety of ways: *comma splice, meaning unclear, grammar error, poor word choice, dangling participle, run-on sentence, sentence structure, word order.* Clearly, the problem here is hard to diagnose, and there is no ready label to categorize it. But that is just our point. Many times errors are hard to diagnose, hard to label, and this is a phenomenon that teachers can be aware of and let their students know about. We are concerned about the fact that students often may have to learn not just to identify errors, but to see whole sets of labels as interchangeable, so that "comma splice" and "dangling participle" and "sentence structure" might all refer to the same problem. This fact, we suspect, is often hidden and unstated rather than openly acknowledged, and so perhaps feeds our students' sense that English teachers are picky and arbitrary. The variety of labels can also disguise those areas of textual problems (like certain forms of punctuation) that actually enjoy a fairly strong consensus among readers, again making teachers look more arbitrary and subjective about editing than they are.

As we said earlier, some of the idiosyncratic nature of the labels we saw may be due to the way our task asked for a label in the first place, even though the error perceived might not be of the "standard" sort that lends itself to easy identification. Nevertheless, when we analyzed labels for the medium- and low-consensus markings, we were struck by the difference between those responses which, however unusual or invented, make the reader's problem with the text clear and those which do not. We found that responses we felt were unclear or even unclassifiable could be put into four general categories.

One form of ambiguity was created when the labels and/or markings failed to indicate just how much text was considered errorful ("revise" written above a line without underlining) or just how many errors were indicated by a particular label. An example of the latter was the use of "punctuation" over the phrase "tone deaf and therefore" in the last sentence of the essay's first paragraph. As we mentioned earlier, such a vague label fails to indicate either the kind of punctuation in question or how many punctuation marks are missing.

A related category of ambiguity concerned responses that, instead of labeling an error, instruct the writer to revise without indicating either how or why this should be done: "change ending," "omit," "delete," or even, in some cases, marks through the text with no label or comment of any kind. Again, the reader of these responses has no way of knowing the nature of the error: Was a rule broken? A phrasing awkward or offensive? A vocabulary choice confusing? Or something else?

A frequent form of response (not surprisingly, considering the problems of clarity this essay poses) was one that simply noted that the choice of word is "wrong": "word choice," "phrasing," "wrong word." Here, we could see that the reader has some quarrel with the text as it stands, but it was often difficult to know why. Consider, for example, some of the responses to the sentence in the essay's last paragraph: "If there is something in this world that you want *they* go out and get it." Twelve teachers wrote *wrong word* over "they." Did they refer to a problem of pronoun agreement (imagined correction: "If there is something in this world that *you* want you go out and get it")? To a problem of misspelling, probably careless ("If there is something in this world that you want *then* go out and get it")? Both reconstructions appeared in many of the other responses to this error, but "wrong word" doesn't help us know which one the reader had in mind.

A fourth category of vague label consisted of teacher jargon words that are too imprecise to be useful to anyone trying to understand the reader's error analysis. Of 17 instances of the label "mechanics," for example, 1 seemed to refer to punctuation, 2 to logic, 1 to style, and 2 to grammar, while 11 more were unclassifiable even with the most generous guessing. We had similar problems with terms like "grammar" and "usage"; they were too vague and appeared in too many different contexts to mean much more than just "error."

In criticizing these imprecise and unhelpful labels, we do not mean to suggest that unanimity among members of the profession about our jargon is desirable or even feasible. But we can't help but think that more could be done in teacher education and staff development to encourage teachers both to use specialized jargon more accurately where it is called for, and to do more to make clear what is to be corrected even where a ready-made label does not spring to mind. As this text makes especially evident, the irony is that should these teachers respond to their own students' writing with such vague, ambiguous, confusing, or otherwise unclear language, they would perpetuate the very problems of logic and clarity they condemn in student writing.

Which Errors Were Considered Most Serious, and Why?

Fifty-four teachers responded to our second major request: to name the three most serious errors in the text and to explain why these were serious. We left it up to them to decide if "most serious errors" meant single errors or types of error. Of those responses that we could classify, 34.3% referred to errors in punctuation, 18.6% to grammar, and 1.4% to spelling, while 25.7% referred to errors in logic/clarity and 20% to style/structure. "Consulting" errors, then, appear to be the most serious problem for these teachers, seeming to confirm the popular impression of teachers as guardians of rules and orthodoxy in language.

When we look at *why* certain errors are considered serious, however, our picture of these teachers' concerns changes radically. Nearly three-quarters of their 140 classifiable responses (104, or 74.3%) said the errors in this text were serious because they got in the way of effective communication of meaning. Of these, 45.2% focused on the text itself; 40 answers indicated that errors were serious because they caused the text to lose meaning and precision: "Without proper punctuation the 'sense' of the sentence can become confusing"; "Author's intention isn't clear." Seven more responses said that error hurt other communicative potential of the text, such as style, credibility, or emphasis: "Destroys cohesion of both a story and an argument"; "If special phrases aren't set aside with quotes they can lose their special importance." A nearly equal number (53.8%) focused on the way that error impairs the reader's process of interpretation: "[The error is serious] because it causes the reader to stumble instead of smoothly following the thought (like hitting a pothole)." The remainder of the 104 answers either combined concerns for textual meaning and reader comprehension or complained of the effect on the reader when meaning wasn't clear: "Irritating to a reader and makes reading extra tedious"; "Makes the reading of the piece very difficult." But whether the responses focused on the text, the reader, or both, the overwhelming majority (86.5%) of these 104 responses regarded error as a serious barrier to meaning.

A second set of responses (16, or 11.4%) said the errors in this text were serious primarily because they represented some problem with the student's education: either she had failed to acquire a basic skill she would need to have, or she would find that this kind of error would pose basic problems for her as a writer: "If you have no sense (or an incomplete sense) of sentence structure, you can do nothing else."

Only a small minority of the teachers (14.3%) seemed to think of the seriousness of error primarily in terms of rules, taste, conventions, or simple frequency. We find that figure impressive — as impressive as the majority's high concern for meaning. It says that for this group of teachers, at least, correctness is not the matter of propriety and rules that it is often made out to be by the pop grammarians; we saw very few expressions of offended taste, condescension, or ridicule. Instead, we find these teachers' responses to be admirably student-centered: wanting to understand what this writer is trying to say and concerned about the course of her development.

Relating these results to the kinds of labels that the teachers used brings out clearly the irony of vague or ambiguous comments. But more important is the fact that even the more precise error labels failed to convey the readers' concerns for effective communication: As we mentioned earlier, our initial impression from simply reading the labels of "most serious" errors was that these teachers were more concerned with rules than with meaning. While we do not assume that error-labeling is the method these teachers would use to respond to texts, we also recognize that error-marking is widely used in our profession as the teacher's main method of teaching editing. Our results lead us to believe that such a practice, if precise and informed, *can* have the positive effect of teaching students a common vocabulary for discussing textual problems with their teachers, peers, and, presumably, other readers in the future. But the labels alone are deeply misleading if the same students were to read them as indications of their teachers' underlying concerns. Labels by themselves do not indicate that teachers' apparent concerns for rules are really problems of trying to understand the meaning of the paper. As such, error labels are ineffective representations of why error is a serious problem for adult readers; if these teachers are at all representative of our profession, error markings do not teach what we most want our students to learn (see also Anson's chapter in this volume).

What Difference Does Level of Teaching Make?

When we examined the responses for our three groups of teachers (elementary, secondary, and post-secondary) we saw some striking differences among them — so much so, in fact, that we feel justified in describing these three groups as different interpretive communities. Global counts of the errors that teachers marked suggest these differences. Although all three groups marked a wide range of errors, stretching from single digits for some teachers into the 50s for others, both mid-range and overall averages increased from elementary to secondary to post-secondary teaching. Fourteen of the 20 elementary teachers marked between 23 and 35 places in the text as errorful, while 17 of 25 secondary teachers marked between 28 and 43 such spots, compared to 5 of 10 post-secondary teachers who marked between 32 and 43 errors. Elementary teachers averaged 28.75 error markings; secondary teachers, 34.56; and post-secondary, 36.1.

The most striking difference we see in these global counts is the jump in average number of errors marked by elementary teachers and secondary teachers — an average difference of nearly six errors. This seems to us a big difference in response to error, and we wonder whether it would not create real problems both for students and teachers from the two levels who try to cooperate in some way. For example, secondary teachers sometimes complain that students are still making errors they should have had under control before leaving elementary school. Perhaps these complaints don't take into account developmental differences and the kinds of errors that can accompany maturing style, but perhaps, too, there is a difference in specialization or practice, or both, that means these two groups of teachers really don't see the same errors when they look at a text.

We also noted differences in the kinds of errors that teachers said were serious. Secondary teachers were only a little more likely to emphasize logic/clarity than elementary teachers, and this held both for their choices of serious errors and their explanations for why errors are serious. However, when secondary teachers chose the three errors they considered to be serious, and when they ranked the most serious of the three, their percentages for style/structure overall were approximately one and one-half times the corresponding percentages for elementary teachers. That is, 25.8% of the three serious errors that secondary teachers named had to do with style/structure, compared to 17.4% for elementary teachers. Secondary teachers considered style/structure as the most serious error 27.3% of the time, compared to 18.8% of the time for elementary teachers.

We see these responses as possible reflections of the particular challenges faced by teachers at different grade levels. Secondary teachers might reasonably expect their students to have mastered the basics for written discourse; their students' problems are more likely to be stylistic, at the level of the sentence, or rhetorical problems of logic, organization, and diction at the paragraph or whole-essay level. In secondary school, too, there is an increasing emphasis upon expository or "transactional" writing (Applebee 1984; Britton et al. 1975; Emig 1971), an emphasis often justified by expectations that this will be the kind of writing demanded later in life, in college and/or on the job. It is a style of writing that, in its forms of organization and impersonal diction, is highly artificial, a kind of translation (as Britton and his colleagues argue) away from the more personal style and associative or narrative organization of expressive discourse. It is not surprising, then, that style would be an important concern for secondary teachers.

Elementary teachers, on the other hand, were more concerned than secondary teachers with what we have called "consulting" errors in grammar and punctuation. Of the errors elementary teachers considered serious, 34.8% were mistakes in grammar, compared to 18.2% for secondary teachers. Another 43.5% of the errors elementary teachers said were serious were punctuation mistakes, compared to 37.9% for secondary teachers. The difference between groups is especially visible for those who chose punctuation as the most serious error: for elementary teachers, 68.8%; for secondary teachers, 40.9%. Even with this student writer's numerous and repeated punctuation difficulties, which would probably lead teachers to consider this category of error serious, the difference between groups is striking.

Again, we would speculate that these responses reflect the special sentence-level problems that elementary-school teachers must face when dealing with the texts of very young and inexperienced writers. As Glenda Bissex (1980) acknowledges in the title of her book, *Gnys at Wrk* ("Genius at Work"), these teachers have to be creative and generous readers if they are to get at the meanings behind their students' invented spellings and irregular or missing punctuation. It is not surprising, then, that elementary teachers do not say this text is particularly puzzling to understand, but focus their concerns instead on basic grammar and on punctuation, one of the major visual features of written discourse that young writers struggle to learn.

The other big difference in the kinds of errors marked occurred between teachers at the elementary and secondary level and post-secondary teachers. In contrast to the other two groups, the professors did not focus concern on violations of written conventions; what bothered them was their own difficulty in making sense of the text. Overwhelmingly, the professors seemed to care about logic/clarity; 81.5% said an error was serious because it caused the text to be unclear or made it confusing to read, compared to 62.5% of the elementary teachers and 58.5% of the secondary teachers. When citing serious errors, professors mentioned cliches that "add nothing that was not said in the previous sentence"; lack of clarity when subjects and verbs don't agree; lack of clarity associated with word choice, with adjectives ranging from "imprecise" and "incorrect" to "incoherent" and "unintelligible."

We do not, of course, expect professors in the content areas to sound like English teachers or to share the same concerns in teaching their own students. College professors typically expect their students to be ready to handle written prose competently, and so this group's focus on content rather than mechanics of diction is, again, what we would expect. But we also feel a certain concern about the very different kinds of response we see when we compare professors as readers to the secondary teachers. We do not want to suggest that high-school teachers are wrong to be concerned with form and style; we do want to raise the question of whether, in the process, they clearly connect style to meaning, to the transaction between reader and writer. This might better prepare college-bound secondary students for the kinds of readers they will encounter in the future.

In summary, our data suggest that the readers that students can expect to have for their writing will differ as they move from grade to grade. Teachers at different levels represent different discourse communities, to some extent. In general, as students move up in grade level, they will get more marks on their papers and the kinds of labels they receive will change, shifting from grammar and orthography to style and then to logic/clarity. This shift may contribute, we suspect, to the sense many students seem to have that there is something mysterious and even arbitrary about being "correct," something arcane that teachers all know about but that students are not a party to. Certainly, if these data are representative, teachers might do more to concern themselves with preparing students for how their writing will be read at the next educational level.

What Difference Does Training in the Composing Process Make?

We asked elementary and secondary teachers if they had had some kind of training in teaching the composing process — in-service, a college course, etc. — and 28 (11 elementary teachers and 17 secondary teachers) reported that they had. Sixteen (8 elementary teachers and 8 secondary teachers) reported that they had not.

Such training doesn't seem to make much difference in the range of errors marked. However, we began to see possible effects of being trained in the composing process when we compared responses on which errors are serious. For both overall averages (8.3 vs. 19.7) and for first choice of a serious error (8.3 vs. 19.2), teachers who had had some training were more than twice as likely to see logic/clarity as the paper's problem. This contrast is especially striking at the secondary level, where four times as many teachers who had been trained in the composing process said logic/clarity was a serious error compared to nontrained teachers (21.3% vs. 5.3%). Of trained secondary teachers, 64.4% said error was serious because the text became unclear or confusing, compared to 50.0% of nontrained teachers. Also, 75.6% of trained secondary teachers said error impeded communication, compared to 55.0% of nontrained secondary teachers. Further, when explaining why communication problems are serious, the trained teachers seem more likely than the untrained ones to speak in terms of problems created for the reader rather than of problems in the text. Again, this gap increases at the secondary level, where 51.1% of trained secondary teachers were concerned with problems created for the reader as opposed to 35.0% of the untrained secondary teachers.

We interpret these figures as suggestions that the composing-process training does convince teachers that there is more to responding to student writing than just marking errors, and that what the student has to say is important. However, we saw some other differences between groups that we have trouble interpreting. Elementary teachers who were not trained in the composing process were more concerned with logic/clarity as a reason for the seriousness of error than were those who had been trained (75.0% vs. 53.6%); they were also more likely overall to say that error is serious because it impairs communication (85.0% vs. 60.7%). This is the reverse of the findings for secondary teachers and perhaps can be read as another indication that elementary and secondary teachers are members of different discourse communities.

What Responses Don't Say

Whenever we ask people to describe how a particular reality appears to them — in this case, what constitutes "errors" in a text — we need to ask ourselves not only what their responses might mean, but also what they are *not* saying, the issues or possibilities that they slight or ignore. In the case of this research, we see these things *not* said in three important ways.

First, hardly anyone raised the issue of the *context* for writing — what the assignment was, how much time the writer had to write, whether this was a first draft, or whether any time elapsed between the composing of the text and its proofreading. We did not mention these issues ourselves, except to say that "the student who wrote the essay had time to proofread it." But none of the teachers mentioned these issues either, although the constraints of both time and task are known to affect writing performance.

Second, as we mentioned earlier, few responses indicated a concern for the student's level of development; most who did comment on what students know or don't know (or typically do) seemed to be referring either to some unspecified "student" or to writers they had seen in their own classes. Yet, we would argue, the issue of whether the errors in this text are serious depends, at least in part, upon the age of the writer. A junior-high student who is not quite sure how to punctuate song titles or introductory clauses might be just average, but for most college-level writers, such problems might instead be viewed as remedial. Similarly, the blurred syntactical pattern, *My parents pleaded with her saying that I would practice all the harder, would she please let have at least a chance at it,* might be a sign of a basic writer attempting to stretch beyond simple sentence patterns toward the complexity of mature prose, as Shaughnessy (1977) and Bartholomae (1980) have argued; but for an average twelfth grader or college freshman, the failure to catch and revise such a sentence might more appropriately be viewed as evidence of proofreading laziness. One professor recognizes this connection between errors and what he can usually expect from college-level students when he writes, "By my standards for undergraduate papers (assuming proofreading): *extremely poor.*" But such comments were rare.

Finally, we were struck by the lack of connection between the *genre* of the text and what was deemed an "error." James Britton and his colleagues (1975) have argued persuasively that the style, organization, and diction of a written text are directly related to the *function* of the writing. They identify three major functions (although in practice these may overlap):

1. *Expressive writing* is personal writing that expresses and explores the writer's own inner feelings, thoughts, values, and memories. In both organization and style, expressive writing is often similar to spoken language.

2. *Transactional writing* is writing that serves the purposes of getting something done — informing, giving instructions, persuading an audience. It is usually public writing directed at others; "expository prose" comes close to meaning the same thing.

3. Finally, *poetic writing* is what we more ordinarily call "literature." Its function is to be a well-made, esthetically pleasing artifact, although its specific conventions may vary from genre to genre.

When we ask ourselves what function of writing this particular text might be said to serve, our answer is that it seems mostly *expressive,* with a very brief attempt at the end to generalize in a way that moves toward the transactional. But what does that interpretation have to do with how we determine the errors in this text? Quite a lot, we'd say. The paper's expressive function does not account for or excuse the writer's failure to observe punctuation conventions or mistakes such as writing "preformed" instead of "performed." But many of the writer's choices that readers objected to on grounds of diction or sense look quite different if we see this piece as a humorous example of first-person storytelling, one close in style to oral discourse: the writer's exaggerated representation of herself as having been drafted into music lessons ("[My parents] enlisted me in a musical program"); her inclusion of expressions that typically link pieces of dialogue, such as "well" and "of course" and "by all means"; the underscoring of certain words to achieve emphasis ("*total* creativity," "*Goal!*"); the breezily informal diction ("take me on," "cleared up my mind"); and even the shifting of verb tenses, the kind one hears from someone recreating a story ("my parents decided that its time . . ." and "now comes the hard part . . .").

Few subjects, however, gave the effects of the text's generic function much mention, and those that did rarely connected it to the problem of determining error. Forty-five of our 55 subjects wrote brief responses to the final request to "please comment on this student's overall strengths and weaknesses as a writer." Taking these comments together with their responses to Part II about serious errors, we see that 17 subjects seemed to have what might be called all-purpose standards for good writing. For these teachers, the strengths of the paper were matters such as "paragraphing," "organization of theme," and "good sentence structure," and, similarly, the major weaknesses were matters such as "punctuation" or "grammar." Nineteen subjects did refer to one or more elements of expressive storytelling, such as narrative structure, vivid description, use of specific details, and the expression of the writer's feelings. But it is not clear that these comments formed any evaluative framework for determining what was or was not an error in the text. Finally, a small group of 8 subjects did make what we would consider connections between function and the writer's achievement: 2 elementary teachers, 3 secondary teachers, and 3 professors. The problems in this essay with logic, sentence-level coherence, cliches, and punctuation are important *because*, these teachers argue, the student is trying to appeal to the reader to share her ideas and feelings about this story, and the errors she makes get in the way. Further, as one response suggests, *writing* a story is not quite the same as *telling* it; what is acceptable in one kind of discourse becomes an error in another:

> The strength of this piece is its conversational tone. I can imagine listening to someone say all of this, and I'd have understood what was to be conveyed. Paradoxically, this student's verbal impact does not transfer well into prose.

We don't suggest that there are no standards common to all good writing; carefulness in proofreading and orthodoxy in spelling (unless one is writing in dialect) are conventions with which we have no argument. But there are so many kinds of writing in the world, for so many purposes, that it seems unworkable to imagine all-purpose rules for word choice or organization. More to the point, as we see in many of these responses, many seemingly universal standards are really specific to transactional prose and would hardly be appropriate in many other kinds of writing. Instead of using many absolute labels like "wrong word" or "not necessary," teachers might try instead to help students differentiate between the kinds of errors that can be found in any kind of writing and "errors" that are really violations of genre conventions. This student, for example, might be asked to "translate" her story into both a poem and a prose argument, in order to be able to consider what in the process has to change and what remains the same.

Conclusions: The Dream of a Common Language[1]

We do not offer here extensive advice about *how* students are to be taught what error is and what to do about it. We assume that part of the work of education is helping students understand that written language is governed by rules and conventions. We also assume that teachers, schools, and districts must decide how much of such instruction should be in the form of explicit teaching and how much implicit in ways that teachers and students talk about student papers.

Our concern is this: Whether conventions and their violations ("error") are addressed out of context (by drill or discussion of workbook examples) or in the context of particular student texts (in conference, class discussion, or by means of written remarks), teachers and students need a shared language. They need a common vocabulary that will inevitably be somewhat specialized and precise, i.e., a jargon. And they need a commonly understood set of procedures that will signal more than the jargon alone can express — understandings about, for instance, the ways that error boundaries can be marked or about how to distinguish those teacher responses that are relatively conventional from those that express more individual readings of style and content. Without such a language and such procedures for using it, we would all be as hapless as those philosophers encountered by Gulliver who pointed to objects they carried about in sacks instead of using words to represent them.

But the research we have reported here and the work of other colleagues in the field suggest that we can no longer take the existence of such a common language for granted. And so our conclusion is both obvious and radical: We think that student teachers and teaching staffs need to put aside their handbooks and lists of error symbols and talk among themselves about what they mean by "error" in student texts. To what extent do they share common assumptions about what is to be labeled an error? What do they call the errors they see and the conventions that these errors imply? Which kinds of errors do they consider serious, and why? When they speak together, are they talking about the same thing? Then, perhaps, teachers might also consider their own classrooms as interpretive communities. When they talk to their students about error and its seriousness, instead of testing students to see if they "got" it, they might ask: How do the students really hear what they say? How do students interpret their teachers' interpretations?

We suggest, in other words, what many others have said before about improving the teaching of writing: that teachers become researchers of their own teaching contexts. They need to be aware of what they do and how this is perceived by their colleagues and students, and they need to do this *before* they address issues of what textbooks say or should say, what they should do in their classrooms, or whether what they have been doing improves student writing. We can only teach what we know, and (as Ann Berthoff likes to say) until we know our knowledge, questions about how and why to teach it are not useful because they are not well founded.

We realize that these suggestions may seem controversial and even threatening. Some participants in our study, for example, expressed concern lest our research be seen as advocating a return to the drill-for-skill approach that the composing-process movement has sought to replace. Their fear is that if we talk about error, we will focus our colleague's attention on rote learning instead of on composing and interpretation. But our analysis of teacher responses suggests that this is far from the case. These responses reveal how much error-identification entails an active interpretation of a writer's ideal, "intended" meaning, a reader's act of composing.

Our data also imply the many ways that students must be active interpreters of their teachers' responses, readers of their readers. Students must, for example, understand that for particular teachers errors may have several different and interchangeable names; that different teachers may name the same kinds of errors differently; that certain jargon terms like "usage" have different meanings depending upon the teacher; that what teachers consider an error in writing may vary considerably; that a teacher's labels may be imprecise or even missing, so that they must be attentive to other cues such as boundary markings or questions to infer the kind of error the teacher perceives; that suggested revisions or comments like "wrong word" imply a version of the text that the teacher is constructing, not exactly the one they wrote or intended; and that even if all errors are identified with labels, some require consulting a rule or convention to be corrected while others involve revisions that are more negotiable. In short, we suspect that students who have the most success with editing are those who learn all these unwritten procedures so they can interpret their teachers' comments the way successful readers read any text: holistically, constructing meaning by perceiving larger patterns.

Re-seeing teaching about error as a form of reading instruction may raise, however, a different set of fears. To admit that error is not the binary matter of interpretation it is often thought to be may seem to threaten a loss of authority in the classroom and in the staff room. To admit that the teaching community is divided in its practices and that texts are not univocal when it comes to error may open the profession to the same "vision of political anarchy" that has bedeviled teachers of literature ever since the advent of reader response and other post-structuralist forms of criticism (Crosman 1980, 157–59). But again, this research leads us to feel that fears of "relativism and solipsism" would be exaggerated. The teachers we surveyed perceived clear patterns of error for the kinds of textual problems that can be corrected by referring to a handbook or dictionary; their sense of what was conventional in matters of grammar and punctuation was widely shared, even when their expression of it could have been more precise. We saw patterns, too, even for those responses that initially seemed to reflect a much lower consensus, comments about style or clarity. Even though responses to perceived problems of style and clarity took numerous forms and varied in how the error was located, we saw that many teachers shared a general sense of the kinds of difficulties this student was having in making herself clear, even if they did not express these perceptions in the same way.

Finally, we want to repeat a conclusion we drew earlier in the chapter because it is so important: focusing instruction on identifying and correcting errors (as is so often done) may disguise the striking kind of agreement expressed by so many of these teachers about the real reason to teach editing — to ensure that what the student has to say is understood by her reader. Despite the apparent evidence of the error labels, these teachers were not bent on socializing the student at the expense of her self-expression. Their values were as generous and as student-centered as any that have been advocated by proponents of teaching invention and revision.

Would that not be heartening for more of us to discover?

Acknowledgments

We wish to thank all those who helped us in the research and preparation of this chapter, especially: JoAnne Eresh and Paul LeMahieu of the Pittsburgh Public Schools; Bill Fitzgibbons, Ellen Hyatt, Anne Picone, Norma Greco, Jane Biggerstaff, and Joyce White for helping us locate volunteers to be our subjects; Carolyn Ball for help in data analysis; Bill Gilquist and Conrad Wall for their assistance with the computer data base and formatting; and most of all, the fifty-five teachers who generously shared their time, energy, and knowledge.

Note

1. We owe this phrase to Adrienne Rich, *The Dream of a Common Language: Poems 1974–1977.*

References

Applebee, A. N. 1981. *Writing in the Secondary School: English and the Content Areas.* NCTE Research Report 21. Urbana, Ill.: National Council of Teachers of English.

Applebee, A. N. 1984. *Contexts for Learning to Write: Studies of Secondary School Instruction.* Norwood, N.J.: Ablex.

Bartholomae, D. 1980. The Study of Error. *College Composition and Communication* 31:253–69.

Bissex, G. L. 1980. *Gnys at Wrk.* Cambridge: Harvard University Press.

Breland, H. M. 1983. *The Direct Assessment of Writing Skill: A Measurement Review.* College Board Report No. 83–6, ETS RR No. 83–32. New York: College Entrance Examination Board.

Britton, J., T. Burgess, N. Martin, A. McLeod, and H. Rosen. 1975. *The Development of Writing Abilities (11–18).* London: Macmillan Education.

Crosman, R. 1980. Do Readers Make Meaning? In *The Reader in the Text: Essays on Audience and Interpretation,* edited by S. R. Suleiman and I. Crosman, 149–64. Princeton: Princeton University Press.

Eagleton, T. 1983. *Literary Theory: An Introduction.* Minneapolis: University of Minnesota Press.

Emig, J. 1971. *The Composing Process of Twelfth Graders.* Research Report 13. Urbana, Ill.: National Council of Teachers of English.

Fish, S. 1980. *Is There a Text in This Class? The Authority of Interpretive Communities.* Cambridge: Harvard University Press.

Greenbaum, S., and J. Taylor. 1981. The Recognition of Usage Errors by Instructors of Freshman Composition. *College Composition and Communication* 32:169–88.

Hairston, M. 1981. Not All Errors Are Created Equal: Nonacademic Readers in the Professions Respond to Lapses in Usage. *College Composition and Communication* 41:794–806.

Hirsch, E. D., Jr., and D. P. Harrington. 1981. Measuring the Communicative Effectiveness of Prose. In *Writing: The Nature, Development, and Teaching of Written Communication,* edited by C. H. Frederiksen and J. F. Dominic, 189–207. Hillsdale, N.J.: Erlbaum.

Hull, G. 1985. Research on Error and Correction. In *Perspectives on Research and Scholarship in Composition,* edited by B. W. McClelland and T. R. Donovan, 162–84. New York: Modern Language Association.

Hull, G. 1987a. Constructing Taxonomies for Error: Or Can Stray Dogs Be Mermaids? In *A Source Book on Basic Writing,* edited by T. Enos, 231–44. New York: Random House.

Hull, G. 1987b. The Editing Process in Writing: A Performance Study of More Skilled and Less Skilled Writers. *Research in the Teaching of English* 21:8–29.

Iser, W. 1972. The Reading Process: A Phenomenological Approach. *New Literary History* 3:279–99.

Lees, E. 1986. Is There an Error in This Text? What Stanley Fish's Theory of Reading Implies about the Teaching of Editing. Paper presented at the Conference on College Composition and Communication, March, New Orleans.

Mellon, J. C., and the Committee to Study the NAEP. 1975. *National Assessment and the Teaching of English.* Urbana, Ill.: National Council of Teachers of English.

Mitchell, R. 1979. *Less than Words Can Say.* Boston: Little, Brown.

Mullis, I. V. S. 1984. Scoring Direct Writing Assessments: What Are the Alternatives? *Educational Measurement: Issues and Practice* 3:16–18.

Rich, A. 1978. *The Dream of a Common Language: Poems 1974–1977.* New York: Norton.

Rosenblatt, L. 1978. *The Reader, the Text, the Poem: The Transactional Theory of the Literary Work.* Carbondale: Southern Illinois University Press.

Shaughnessy, M. 1977. *Errors and Expectations.* New York: Oxford University Press.

Suleiman, S. R. 1980. Introduction: Varieties of Audience-Oriented Criticism. In *The Reader in the Text: Essays on Audience and Interpretation,* edited by S. R. Suleiman and I. Crosman, 3–45. Princeton: Princeton University Press.

Williams, J. M. 1981. The Phenomenology of Error. *College Composition and Communication* 32:152–68.

Appendix A

We are interested in learning how errors in writing are recognized and labeled. By *errors*, we mean mistakes in grammar, syntax, punctuation, spelling, mechanics, and usage.

On the following pages is a short editing exercise and questionnaire. Please take all the time you need to work through it.

Please note: Although we want to study how errors are recognized and labeled, we don't mean to suggest by our interest in this topic that teachers should or should not mark errors in students' papers. We understand that teachers respond to much more than sentence-level error when they read and comment on student papers and that they may sometimes choose not to respond to error at all.

Part I

On the next page is a sample student paper. We'd like you to:

1. Read through the paper one time just to get a sense of what it's about.
2. Then, read the paper again in order to identify its errors. Specifically, we'd like you to:

   - Underline each error that you see in the paper. Make sure that you underline the entire error, so that we can see where you think each error begins and ends.
   - Label each error right above the underlining. By *label* we mean supply the term you think of when you see that kind of error. Please give the label in full; don't use abbreviations.

Note: In this part of the exercise we are asking you to respond to an essay, not as a teacher, but as an error analyst. That is, we're interested here in seeing which errors you identify and how you label them. We're NOT interested here in how you would deal with this piece of writing if the student who wrote it were a student in your class. So, even if you wouldn't mark every error or any error if the student were one of your own, please underline and label the errors for us for the sake of the exercise.

Part II

We're not only interested in what errors people see and how they label them, but in which errors teachers consider the most serious and what they do about them. Look over the student essay again, and from among those errors you have already labeled, choose the three errors that you consider most serious. (Please assume that the student who wrote the essay had time to proofread it; that is, the errors that remain in the paper represent mistakes that the student couldn't correct on her own.)

Then, on the next page, after you have chosen the three errors that you consider the most serious,

1. Describe the error and tell us the line(s) in which it appears.
2. Tell us why you believe the error is serious. (Is it an error that would offend a lot of readers, for example? Is it an error that is difficult for

students to learn to correct? Is it an error that makes the text hard to understand as you read? Or something else?)

3. Tell us how you would address the error with the student. (Some ways of addressing the error might be to mark or write on the student's paper in some way, create a lesson for the whole class, refer the student to a handbook or assign him workbook exercises, or work with the student in a conference in some way.)

A. Most Serious Error

1. Description of the error and the line(s) in which it appears:
2. Why it's serious:
3. Way(s) of addressing the error with the student:

B. Second Choice

1. Description of the error and the line(s) in which it appears:
2. Why it's serious:
3. Way(s) of addressing the error with the student:

C. Third Choice

1. Description of the error and the line(s) in which it appears:
2. Why it's serious:
3. Way(s) of addressing the error with the student:

Part III

Now that you've read the essay, please comment on this student's overall strengths and weaknesses as a writer.

Appendix B

When I was in the fifth grade my parents decided that its time for me to acquire a musical talent. They enlisted me in a musical program known as the once a week piano lesson. At first I was excited about this idea until I met the piano teacher. She had me sit down at the piano beside her while she played notes and asked me to sing that note. The next thing that she told my parents was that I was tone deaf and therefore it was out of the question for me to learn how to play the piano.

My parents pleaded with her saying that I would practice all the harder, would she please let have at least a chance at it. Well with all their pleading the piano teacher gave in and decided to take me on as her student. Next began the difficult task of learning Mary Had a Little Lamb. I seemed to have been progressing quite well, learning all classical music.

Five years later came my experience of *total* creativity at the piano. My piano teacher had asked me to prepare a variation of the song Heart and Soul. She obviously thought that I was capable of doing this. Much to my surprise I was able to sit down at the piano and work on the right hand which is the melody of the song. Of course there was no problem on that hand, since that as the part of the piece well known. But, now comes the hard part putting in the harmony with the left hand. Forget it was all I kept saying. I had been spending hour after after trying to put the two hands together, but nothing worked. Finally, I decided to take a break. This cleared up my mind allowing me to try some new tactics. I decided to play songs I already knew and enjoyed. After doing so, I went back to Heart and Soul. Believe it or not I finally came up with an original addition to it. At my lesson I preformed my version of Heart and Soul. She was astounded. "My I never heard it played so well and I told you you were tone deaf."

From this I have learned a great lesson. If there is something in this world that you want they go out and get it. By all means if you are creative about it you will in the end achieve your *Goal!*.

14 A Theoretical Framework for Studying Peer Tutoring as Response

Ann Matsuhashi, University of Illinois at Chicago

Alice Gillam, University of Wisconsin–Milwaukee

Rance Conley, University of Illinois at Chicago

Beverly Moss, University of Illinois at Chicago

Each quarter at the Writing Center of the University of Illinois at Chicago, peer tutors write case studies detailing their ongoing work with a student. The best of these case studies are reproduced for new tutors, providing them with a profile of the activity of the Writing Center from the tutor's point of view. Most case studies characterize the developing interpersonal relationship between tutor and student and also chart the student's growth; but quite often, as this section from a case study illustrates, a tutor comments on his or her own growth as a writer and a tutor:

> During my first week of tutoring, I met with a young Indian student who had come to the Writing Center. "How can I help you?" I asked. He responded by handing me a composition booklet containing a graded essay. The essay, written in thick blue ink with large, looping, carefully copied penmanship, was awash in red ink. Red sentences were inserted between neatly written blue ones. Red "?'s" and "!'s" punctuated comments written in the margin. On the back page was a twice-underlined, circled red "E."
>
> "What do you want to work on?" I asked.
>
> "Grammar," Satish replied.
>
> When I suggested that there might be a larger, more fundamental problem — "Organization," I said, in a word — he winced. He'd hoped for a quick fix. While I assured him that I could help, I considered my qualifications and responsibility as his tutor and wiped my sweating palms on a sheet of composition looseleaf.

> I had hesitated before becoming a tutor, afraid I'd be embarrassed
> by something that I didn't know. Even though I'd been a successful
> writer, I didn't know any rules or formulas for good writing. I
> only knew when things sounded right in my head. I had no idea
> how to communicate those instincts.
>
> We worked, cautiously at first, rethinking Satish's essays. The
> writing process — adding, deleting, rearranging — was new to
> him. Like many beginning writers, he thought students either
> could write or they couldn't. He put himself in the second category.
> I won't suggest that he ever put himself in the first category, but
> over the quarter in which we worked, he learned to use the
> process of writing and revising, just as every good writer does.
> And in the process, I might add, pushed his grade to a letter not
> nearly as red as the one to which he was accustomed.
>
> Talking about writing — coaching and editing — was new to me.
> Even with experience, writing had been an unconscious, somewhat
> mysterious, process for me. By tutoring, thinking out loud, I was
> forced to draw on my own unconscious process, and learned to
> verbalize some of the instincts which had made me a successful
> writer. I learned some of the why's for the way things sound
> when they work in my head. (Tuzik 1986)

The growth process that this tutor recounts comes as no surprise to those who work regularly with peer writing tutors. Bruffee (1978) was among the first to recognize this growth in a group of tutors with whom he worked: "The tutors' commitment to the value of their own and each other's writing and the quality of their writing improved dramatically" (451). A national survey of college and university writing-program directors indicated that independent writing labs, workshops, and peer tutoring activities are among the most successful aspects of college writing programs (Witte, Meyer, Miller, and Faigley 1981). Yet much of the literature on peer tutoring, of necessity, concerns the pragmatics of establishing, justifying, and maintaining such programs (Harris 1982; Hawkins 1982; Olson 1984; Reigstad, Matsuhashi, and Luban 1978; Reigstad, Williamson, and Matsuhashi 1980). Even so, we are beginning to see studies that explore, in some detail, this rich instructional context; for example, the chapter by Nystrand and Brandt in this volume reports the effect of peer response on the student writer.

Our special interest is in the experience of the peer writing tutor. We see this experience as crucially important in studies of writing, but important, as well, in the broad context of undergraduate education. In the classroom or writing-center setting, we can observe writers of different levels of education, class, language, and social background articulating what they know about writing. The practice they receive as writers, listeners, editors, readers, and problem solvers is integral to the writing process. These settings provide a naturalistic, ongoing laboratory for the study of writing processes and the growth of writing ability. The kind of learning that goes on in these settings is precisely the sort that a recent "blue-ribbon panel" (Lloyd-Jones 1985) recommends as crucial to improving undergraduate education. The report contends that, in spite of increasing enrollments and limited funding for lower-division courses, universities must recognize the importance of active learning: students involved in independent projects with faculty and students involved in interdisciplinary learning and problem-solving experiences (NIE 1984).

In the first section of this chapter, we identify peer tutoring as a response event and, in doing so, broaden traditional views of response. Next, we propose a theoretical framework for studying the nature of peer tutoring, the development of peer tutors, and the training of peer tutors. In the last portion of the chapter, we discuss the evaluative strategies one peer tutor uses in response to a student essay.

Peer Tutoring as a Response Event

Until recently the term *response* has been used, quite narrowly, to refer to teachers' comments on students' texts, and studies of response have focused on what teachers actually do when they write such comments. The prevailing attitude of the teacher, as seen by Sommers (1982) and Brannon and Knoblauch (1982), is one of appropriation and authority, one that ignores what is known about the writing process and focuses on error, and, finally, one that illustrates the discrepancy between the extant student text and some unreachable ideal. These researchers conclude that useful comments should motivate revision. Beyond this, response should allow teachers and students to think about the match or mismatch between the student's intent and the text's effect. Teachers and students could then "negotiate" appropriate options for revision (Brannon and Knoblauch 1982, 166).

In this context, researchers have been most concerned with the effects of the response: Did the response result in an improved text? In more revision? In improved attitude toward writing and writing instruction? Response, in this view, may be characterized as the means to an end or as a "means-end" strategy (Boden 1977) in which the writer or teacher works backward from a goal — that is, a complete, effective, and correct text — to eliminate the differences between the current text and the completed text, usually by a series of revisions. The goal, in this case, is often represented so prominently that attempts to reach it (i.e., attempts at revision) sacrifice the learning process which should accompany the changes. In addition, since challenging writing tasks usually present quite ill-defined problems, it is unlikely that the writer could, at the start, construct a detailed "picture" or representation of the completed text.

It is crucial to think of response in terms of the role or strategies engaged in by the respondent. As Purves (1984) demonstrates in his anatomy of the teacher as reader, the teacher's role can extend beyond that of a judge. A teacher may act as a "common reader," one who reads purely for pleasure; or a teacher may read as a literary critic, psychologist, linguist, or anthropologist, all of whom function as analysts studying interpretations of the text or studying the processes that give rise to the text. Finally, a teacher may read as a diagnostician, locating problems in the text. This anatomy, though limited to teachers' roles, suggests a method for focusing on the function of responses in other contexts and by other agents. As shall be seen in the last portion of this chapter, Purves's anatomy of teachers' roles helped us to think productively about the roles a peer tutor adopts when reading a student draft.

The teacher's role as respondent and the pedagogical effect of response are but two important aspects in the study of response. Response, viewed broadly, can be studied as the feedback processes at work during the language event. Viewed as feedback, response allows writers to test hypotheses about the effectiveness of their communication, written or spoken. Thus, response plays a central role in the development of oral and written skills, as well as in intellectual skill acquisition (Freedman 1985). The notion of response as feedback implies a "to and fro" strategy that emphasizes the intermediate stages of the process. Feedback processes allow the writer, teacher, or peer tutor to respond continually to differences between the current state and a proximate goal state (Matsuhashi 1987; Simon [1969] 1981). With the focus on feedback, it is then possible to study the response as it occurs. For example, rather than focusing exclusively on the end result of the teacher-student writing conference, Freedman focuses on the conversational pattern and on the structure of the conference (Freedman and Sperling 1985; Freedman and Katz 1987). Similarly, close analysis of the talk in peer editing groups can tell us how students perceive their own and others' drafts (Gere and Stevens 1985).

When response is seen as a feedback process, the link between response and revision can be seen as more than a means to an end. Revision is more than changes wrought in the visible text; it can be changes in plans or changes in invention processes, or even changes in understanding (Matsuhashi and Gordon 1985; Matsuhashi 1987; Witte 1985). This view of revision implies a "revision of cognition itself . . . [a] cognitive reorganization that must take place for transferable learning to occur, a reorganization that stems from response" (Freedman 1985, xi). Response, viewed broadly as an event, then, should encompass the developmental learning process, verbal interaction, sequences of writing events, and a variety of contexts.

Our specific interest in response centers on the peer writing tutor and the response event that occurs during the one-to-one writing conference. The nature of this response situation is unique in many ways. The tutor is not a novice or an expert, but somewhere in the middle. At the Writing Center at the University of Illinois at Chicago, the tutor is trained as a reader of student drafts, providing feedback for students on a full range of concerns, from grammar and mechanics to discourse-level issues. Thus, tutors are called upon to evaluate drafts or plans for drafts, question the writer about his or her intent, and suggest priorities for the session's work, all the while taking into account the interpersonal nature of the interaction.

Examining the nature of the tutor's response, his or her growth as a writer and tutor, and the training of tutors becomes a challenging enterprise which can contribute, in general, to our understanding of response. As we noted above, our purpose in this chapter is to mark out a theoretical framework for studying peer tutoring as response and to illustrate how, with a portion of data from an ongoing investigation, this framework can guide research.

The Theoretical Framework

Before planning a particular study or adopting a particular methodology, it seemed essential to think about the key questions that could generate a framework for inquiry. The kinds of questions which may be posed for research and the ways these questions might be classified (Dillon 1984) should contribute to our understanding of peer tutoring as a response event. We have chosen to classify our questions in a matrix format.[1] By asking fundamental questions and then by mapping them against appropriate knowledge domains, we generate a network of relationships that links theory to practice and that promotes interdisciplinary inquiry (Beaugrande 1987). The three fundamental questions that inform the matrix are:

What is the nature of peer tutoring?

How do peer tutors develop?

What occurs during the training of tutors?

Under each of the three questions, we have designated three foci — language, cognition, and context. These foci are not limited to specific disciplines (e.g., linguistics, cognitive psychology, anthropology); rather, they represent a central interest. Within each cell we list the materials, processes, and activities that comprise the peer tutoring experience. Our intention in presenting the matrix is not to offer fixed categories or a comprehensive list, but rather to offer a fluid and dynamic perspective for studying peer tutoring as response. This matrix organization functions as a heuristic, marking the parameters of particular studies while placing them in a broader field of inquiry.

The Nature of Peer Tutoring

One of the earliest classification schemes for inquiry was proposed by Aristotle in Book II of *Posterior Analytics*. Aristotle directs us to pay close attention to the kinds of questions we ask and the relationships among the questions. A central question concerns existence and affirmation on the one hand, and essence and definition on the other, "... when we have ascertained the thing's existence, we inquire as to its nature" (89b Aristotle; quoted from McKeon 1941, 328).

For the study of peer tutoring as a response event, questions about the nature of the event create the "center of gravity" for the matrix. Most of our assumptions about peer tutoring are based on experience, reflection, and speculation — not on formal inquiry (North 1984). In fact, North questions the existence of such a person as a peer tutor: "What do people have to have in common to be peers in a writing tutorial, and how is the relationship different from other tutorial relationships?" (33). We define peer tutoring as two students, one trained as a writing tutor and another seeking feedback or help with writing, who have been brought together in a particular setting by a specific set of circumstances.

Both the character of the interpersonal dialogue and the relationship between the participants — their status as students — differentiate this encounter from other writing tutorials. According to Bruffee (1983), peer talk about writing is more than a helpful pedagogical technique; it is essential to writing because, in Bruffee's view, "writing is internalized conversation re-externalized" (1984, 641). Thus, the tutor-tutee conversation about writing stimulates and productively expands the internal dialogue that occurs when a writer plans, composes, reviews, and revises. During the writing conference, the peer tutor may function as a translator or interpreter, offering his or her own responses as a reader and articulating the expectations of various writing communities

	Nature of Peer Tutoring	Development of Peer Tutors	Training of Peer Tutors
Language Focus	oral interaction nonverbal phenomena such as pauses and gestures perusal of notes, drafts, teachers' comments, resource materials, written plans, completed texts, and readings	increased knowledge (tacit and explicit) of written language and oral interaction	oral or written guidelines for tutoring examples of student writing oral presentations sample dialogues videotapes of sample sessions written information (articles, textbooks, handouts, etc.)
Cognitive Focus	processes involved in reading, writing, and tutoring	acquisition of effective strategies for reading, writing, and tutoring	active learning experiences such as modeling, text analysis, role-playing, and writing activities
Contextual Focus	physical setting language and social background of tutor and tutee attitudes, values, and personality of tutor and tutee exigence	increased awareness of differing language and social backgrounds, attitudes, values, and personalities increased awareness of exigencies in writing situations	discussion of attitudes toward language simulation activities self-awareness profiles self-assessment materials rhetorical analyses of situation, motive, and purpose

Figure 1. A Theoretical Framework for Studying the Responses of Peer Tutors

within the academy. As Fishman (1982) explains, "by extending to their peers a sense of themselves as writers and by inviting their peers to see themselves in the same light, tutors do much to counter what Bruffee calls 'intellectual paralysis' " (88). For many students the peer relationship is, quite simply, less intimidating than the instructor-student one, allowing freer communication and, ideally, a new sense of possibilities on the part of the writer.

The language shared in peer tutoring — verbal and nonverbal communication, written notes and drafts — demonstrates to tutor and student writer the collaborative nature of writing. At our Writing Center, we encourage the writer to read the text aloud to a tutor; through this experience the writer hears her or his language in a new way, and as the tutor responds, the writer's understanding of her or his own language changes. While the writer is reading aloud, we encourage the tutor to read and evaluate the text as well, setting a mental agenda of questions and issues for discussion. This agenda then forms the basis for the tutor's work with the tutee.

From a cognitive perspective, the tutor's evaluation strategies during the response process provide many questions for studies of reading and writing. We need to know, for instance, how these evaluative responses differ when assessing one's own writing as opposed to assessing another's. We need to know how these responses differ when reading and when writing. Also, we need to know how the purpose and context for the language activity influence its outcome. Learning about the evaluation process is central to studies of the development of writing ability (Hilgers 1984, 1986; Scardamalia and Bereiter 1983) and studies of revision and error (Flower et al. 1986; Hull 1984; Matsuhashi and Gordon 1985). What all this research on development and revision has in common is an emphasis on how writers "see" or represent a draft, their own or someone else's, for a particular purpose. In the tutor response we examine in the following section, we are particularly interested in the evaluative strategies a tutor uses while constructing an initial representation of a draft.

The contextual perspective includes the social status of the participants, the physical setting, the socio-cultural background, the personality and attitudes of the participants, and the exigency which prompts the encounter. In the traditional educational model, learning is transmitted from an authority to a student. Collaborative learning, of which peer tutoring is one manifestation, turns this model inside out, creating a context in which learning takes place because of the interaction between peers.

The concrete features of the setting — the size and color of the room, the noise level, the way in which the desks, chairs, or tables are arranged — constitute one aspect of the physical context. In addition, the actions of tutor and tutee create a particular climate that is part of the physical context (Erickson and Shultz 1981). The proximity of tutor to tutee, the eye contact between the two, the tone of voice, and other body movements are all called "contextualization cues" by Gumperz (1976). In the peer tutoring encounter, these contextual cues affect how a tutee receives and interprets a message from the tutor and vice versa.

Other aspects of context include the linguistic, cultural, social, and ethnic backgrounds of the tutor and tutee, as well as their particular personalities, attitudes, experiences, and values. In these respects, each encounter is unique, for as Hymes (1982) reminds us: "Even though one may live nearby, speak the same language, and be of the same ethnic background, a difference in experience may lead to misunderstanding of the meanings, the terms, and the world of another community" (25). Finally, the exigency — the particulars of the writing task, the writer's reason for requesting tutorial help, his or her attitude toward such help — profoundly affects what occurs between tutor and tutee.

The matrix organization is intended to suggest the varied possibilities for research on peer tutoring. Some of the questions the matrix suggests about the nature of peer tutoring are:

> What language do tutors and tutees use to discuss assignments, notes, and drafts?
>
> What features of the written text do tutors devote the most time to?
>
> How does the tutor communicate her reading of the text to the tutee?
>
> How does the tutor make explicit his knowledge of written language?
>
> How do differences in linguistic, social, and cultural background affect the peer tutoring encounter?
>
> How do the tutor's perceptions of good writing affect the response to the tutee's written text?
>
> How are peer tutoring conferences like or unlike teacher-student writing conferences?

The Development of Peer Tutors

We expect that over time, tutoring experience will result in certain kinds of growth for the peer tutor, growth that can be defined in linguistic, cognitive, and contextual terms. More specifically, we expect that the tutors' knowledge of written language and verbal interaction will increase; that they will acquire new strategies for comprehending and evaluating writing tasks and texts and also new methods of intervening productively in the composing processes of their tutees; and that they will increase their awareness of the importance of context and develop an appreciation for social, linguistic, and cultural differences. In addition to developing a facility for tutoring, we speculate that the tutor's growth will transfer to other activities, such as writing, critical reading, interpersonal communication, and, perhaps, general problem-solving skills.

These expectations are untested and come from our own observations and the anecdotal observations of others. Bruffee (1978), for example, claims that his peer tutors' ability to critique the writing of others increased in "perspicacity, balance, depth of understanding, and tact" after tutoring (451). Others, such as Argyle (1976), contend that tutors develop new social understanding and communication skills as a result of tutoring. Furthermore, our expectations are influenced by related developmental research, which suggests that expertise in higher-order problem solving comes with practice and is accompanied by increased metacognitive knowledge and conscious control of various cognitive strategies (Frederiksen 1984; Bracewell 1983).

Questions about tutor development suggested by the matrix are:

> How does a tutor's ability to talk about writing develop over time?
>
> Does tutoring practice influence a tutor's growth as a writer?
>
> How does the tutor's increased awareness of differing language and social backgrounds affect the tutoring situation?
>
> How do a tutor's strategies for writing and for tutoring change over time?
>
> How does a novice tutor develop into an expert tutor?

The Training of Peer Tutors

Until recently, most literature on peer tutoring has dealt with practical matters such as training, and the recommended training procedures often originate in the assumptions about peer tutoring already mentioned — that peer tutoring establishes an important social context for tutor and tutee; that peer tutors acquire new knowledge about language and new rhetorical sophistication in analyzing texts. For example, some training techniques like role-playing and sensitivity exercises are intended to promote awareness of the interpersonal dimension of peer tutoring (Sherwood 1982; Brannon 1982; Garrett 1982). Other techniques, like written responses to a variety of student texts, aim to increase the tutor's ability to analyze and evaluate writing (Garrett 1982; Bruffee 1978). Still other practitioners recommend that tutors read various articles about the writing process and about linguistic matters, such as dialect differences and usage conventions (Bannister-Wills 1984; Reigstad and McAndrew 1984).

Sound as these practices may be, we do not yet know how or if these training procedures translate into effective tutoring practice. As we test various assumptions about the nature of peer tutoring and the development of peer tutors, we expect that the results will confirm the wisdom of many familiar training techniques. But we also expect that research may cause us to reevaluate some practices and develop new ones.

In addition to the need for research into the nature of peer tutoring and the development of peer tutors, we see a need to study training directly, asking such questions as:

> How does training method A (for example, a semester-long writing course that involves peer critiquing) compare to training method B (a sequence of introductory sessions followed by immersion in the tutoring experience)?

> How can we achieve balance in tutor training between learning about writing and language on the one hand, and practical tutoring strategies on the other?

> How should we evaluate the success of tutor training: In terms of the tutor's tutoring ability? The response of the tutees? The tutor's writing growth? The tutor's linguistic and rhetorical awareness?

The questions listed (see Figure 1) under each of the three major strands in the matrix — Nature of Peer Tutoring, Development of Peer Tutors, and Training of Peer Tutors — suggest the range of studies which might be conducted on peer tutoring. Individual studies, carried out within the framework of a comprehensive research program, gain in interpretive power through their connection with other studies. For instance, our own research interests concern the nature of peer tutoring

and the development of peer tutors. Currently, we are conducting a
study of the responses of ten peer tutors and nine entry-level composition students to a draft of their own work and to a student-written
draft (Matsuhashi et al., in preparation). Our central question concerns
the evaluative process a tutor must engage in at the beginning of each
conference. We want to know how the tutor represents a text (written
by him- or herself or by others) before initiating a tutoring or revising
process. Thus, our study incorporates both a linguistic and a cognitive
focus. By comparing the tutor's evaluative responses at the beginning
and end of the academic quarter, we add a developmental dimension
to our study. Further, by comparing the peer tutors' responses to those
of nontutors, we hope to learn if and how peer tutoring promotes
development.

One Tutor's Reading

In this section we focus on how a beginning tutor, Brad, evaluates a
student-written draft. Brad's monologue was chosen from data collected
in the ongoing investigation described above. To generate the language
sample we discuss below, Brad repeated an interview activity in which
potential tutors are asked to respond to a student-written draft. The
purpose of this activity is to assess the potential tutor's ability to
perceive the widest possible range of strengths and weaknesses in the
draft and the ability to articulate those perceptions to a peer. The draft
to which Brad responded, "Let's Ban Handguns," is included in the
appendix, page 315. It was selected as a typical freshman draft which
might be brought to the Writing Center by a student seeking help.
The draft was chosen for its flaws in logic, organization, development,
style, and mechanics.

 After Brad read the draft and summarized it in writing, he responded
orally to two requests from one of the Writing Center staff: "Explain
thoroughly the major problems with this draft," and "Suggest ways
to improve the draft." The staff member listened, offering nonsub-
stantive prompts that might clarify the tutor's references to the draft
and that might encourage the tutor to produce the most complete
response possible. Typical prompts included: "OK," "What else," "Can
you elaborate on that," or "What sentence are you referring to?"

 The response task Brad engaged in was a complex one. He was
asked to read as he would at the beginning of a tutoring session, not
as Purves's "common reader," not as a student reading for a course,
but as writer *qua* editor, reading to discover how to improve another

writer's text. This task and the evaluative strategies it engages are of critical importance during both writing and reading. To analyze Brad's comments, we worked inductively, reading and rereading the transcript until a pattern emerged. At the same time, though, our analysis was influenced by theoretical advances in the understanding of reading and writing processes. Some reading researchers have even suggested that the thoughtful reader is "the reader who reads as if she were a writer composing a text" (Pearson and Tierney 1984, 2). A tutor's reading is certainly informed by his or her purpose: to assess a draft for its strengths and weaknesses and, in a tutoring context, to communicate that assessment to the writer who must revise the draft.

A transcription of Brad's oral monologue was then coded into idea units, according to a procedure which simplified the coding scheme developed by Turner and Greene (1977) and used by Kintsch (1974) in studies of discourse comprehension. Idea units are the basic information units that convey the meaning of the text; in terms of surface syntax, they carry about as much information as clauses. The transcribed oral monologue discussed here contained 159 idea units.

We found that the best way to characterize Brad's representation of the handgun essay was by identifying groups of idea units as particular kinds of evaluative strategies. These strategies are described in detail in Figure 2. We found, too, that it was helpful to think of these strategies as either primarily *comprehension-based, production-based,* or *context-based.* Both the comprehension-based evaluation strategies and the production-based evaluation strategies involve actively constructing meaning. For Brad, comprehension-based evaluative strategies involved constructing the meaning of the existing text, whereas production-based evaluative strategies involved utilizing his representation of the existing text as a basis for planning the construction of new text. Context-based evaluation strategies involve interaction with the interviewer. Our ongoing study, of which this data is a small part, examines that portion of the tutoring process which is not interpersonal; that is, it reflects the period of time when the tutor reads the student-written draft in order to make an assessment of what he or she thinks should be accomplished during that conference. Thus, the strategies engaged by the tutors concern the evaluation task, resulting in only a few context-based strategies.

Brad moved through the essay recursively, constructing an initial representation of the essay and later returning to particular segments of the text to refine his representation. Initially, Brad relied heavily on comprehension-based strategies, but later — having constructed an acceptable representation of the current state of the text — he had

Strategy (Frequency)*	Definition	Example
Comprehension-based		
Diagnose (25)	Label a problem or a strength in the text.	"... it was very vague."
Judge (23)	State values explicitly (good or bad).	"It's a good example of ..."
Survey (11)	Scrutinize, review, or confirm the content of the text.	"[Paragraph 3] tells that parents do store [handguns]."
Read (9)	Read verbatim from the text.	"The handgun is used in fifty percent of all murders. ..."
Comprehend (4)	Assess the meaning of the text or of a portion of the text.	"I don't understand the meaning of 'cost-worthy situations' for Americans."
Audit (2)	Examine a portion of the text for accuracy.	"[Did] somebody pick that [statistic] out of the hat?"
Production-based		
Recommend (31)	Advise a change in the text.	"[The writer] could tell how Robert Kennedy was killed."
Model (22)	Adopt the role of the writer.	"... [Imagine] a criminal who comes up to him [the homeowner] with a gun. .."
Propose (22)	Offer a plan for revising the text.	"[The writer] could go into the cons of having a gun around the house."
Compose (2)	Generate language for use in the text.	"And then say, 'It should be implemented in the U.S.'"
Context-based		
Respond (10)	Respond to verbal prompt.	"Yes, the second paragraph."

* The total number of idea units is 159; the numbers in parentheses indicate the frequency of idea units.

Figure 2. One Tutor's Evaluation Strategies

reduced the cognitive load sufficiently to think productively about how the text might be improved. Thus, in the later portion of his monologue,

Brad relied heavily on production-based strategies. Brad's shift from comprehension-based strategies at the beginning of the monologue to production-based strategies at the end can be illustrated by comparing the first ten strategies with the last eleven:

> *Initial strategies* (in sequence): respond, diagnose, judge, survey, comprehend, respond, diagnose, respond, diagnose, judge.

> *Concluding strategies* (in sequence): judge, read, diagnose, propose, recommend, model, survey, propose, compose, recommend, respond.

Initial Evaluation Strategies

Brad's first ten strategies have a haphazard quality about them: they are unelaborated, too general to be of any use for revision, and follow no apparent plan. Brad's first strategy was to respond to the interviewer's prompt ("Explain thoroughly the major problems in the draft") by asking for some direction, "Starting from the beginning?" After the interviewer's noncommittal response, Brad began to characterize, in a scattershot way, the problems he saw in the text. First, he diagnosed a general problem with the draft:

> "First of all, I noticed/ that it was very vague with all of its parts./ It would present a point/ but it would use mostly generalizations and no real specific examples."

Then, he offered a brief judgment on a segment of the draft ("It was good, the way it . . ."), which he surveyed as follows:

> ". . . it began and ended with the same question of/ you know/ what England does./ It uses comparison all through till the end."

Brad then skipped to a phrase that caught his eye and applied a comprehending strategy:

> "I didn't really understand the meaning of 'costworthy situation for Americans.' "

Brad's query leaves us wondering if he recognized that "costworthy" is not a word. Or if, in his mind's eye, he had replaced the word "costworthy" with "costly" and might be wondering about the author's intent. Costly in human terms? Costly in monetary terms? Brad's early readings of the draft are like a backyard treasure hunt. His first impulse seems to have been to pick up the shovel and dig; only later, after realizing his energy was misplaced, did he organize his search, locating the most productive places to work.

Next Brad located and diagnosed several problems in the text:

> "The thesis thing was kinda . . ./ It doesn't flow very well . . ."/
> "Then sentence five, it asks a question,/ but it doesn't really
> answer it . . . / and it brings up an issue/ that it only touches on
> lightly,/ . . . doesn't use examples."
>
> "There's no real transition between the second paragraph and the
> third . . . / It just stops on one/ and then starts up another one."

Brad's final strategy in this group of ten was to make a judgment
about the example used in sentence ten:

> "It's not really . . . with the example they try to use/ it's a good
> example/ except they don't really use it specifically."

Since Brad's comments jumped around so much, the interviewer needed
to ask about the location of the sentence or paragraph to which Brad
was referring. Brad, therefore, responded three times to these requests.

The ten initial strategies reviewed above seem to provide a trou-
bleshooting guide for Brad's evaluation process. These ten strategies are
always short, composed of just a few idea units; yet they signal
problems to which Brad returns, again and again, throughout the
monologue. For instance, Brad returns again to probe his early diagnosis
for sentence three: "The thesis was kinda . . . / It doesn't flow very
well." Later in the monologue, when prompted by the interviewer to
think of ways to improve the text, Brad returned to the thesis with a
much more elaborated response, engaging production-based strategies
as well as comprehension-based ones. First, he recommended: "I would
suggest a different thesis." After reading aloud the sentence he considered the thesis (sentence three), he diagnosed the problem again:

> "I think/ that's pretty much a run-on/ and — uh — a little too
> much in there."

He has moved from a general diagnosis about "flow" to a more specific,
if inaccurate, diagnosis, naming sentence three as a run-on. We learn
from Brad's next idea unit that he was not using the term run-on as
a textbook would. He defined the term by explaining that there's "a
little too much in there." While his use of the term run-on is not
correct, his understanding of the problem is: the sentence needs
unpacking. With this understanding, Brad made a specific recommendation for the writer to delete a portion of the sentence:

> "They could limit it to just . . . / because they've mentioned before
> to just . . . 'Handguns lead either to a killing accident or a cold-
> blooded murder'/ and drop the rest of that/ or use that separate,
> out of their thesis."

The monologue, on tape, was produced haltingly, with long pauses, as Brad reviewed the draft, attempting to characterize its faults. Most of his early diagnoses were unelaborated, indicating that he sensed a problem but was unsure of its precise nature or of its impact on the text. In the two instances above, we observe Brad's attempts to locate and name problems in the text. In the first instance, he applied a comprehending strategy, questioning, in a general way, the meaning of the term "costworthy." This is, in fact, a strategy that we recommend to a novice tutor who detects a problem in the text but cannot define the nature of the problem. During a tutoring session, the tutor could ask the tutee what he or she meant and based on the new information make a more useful diagnosis. In the second instance, Brad incorrectly diagnosed a sentence as a run-on, but still offered a useful strategy for revision. Even so, had he been working with a tutee who knew what a run-on was, confusion might have resulted.

Concluding Evaluation Strategies

In the concluding eleven strategies, Brad returned, recursively, to two of his initial diagnoses and judgments, demonstrating a more complex understanding of the draft's strengths and weaknesses. In the examples below, we see Brad engaging nearly exclusively in production-based strategies, recommending changes, proposing a plan for revision, modeling how the writer might make these changes, and actually composing some prose for a revision of the draft.

The first time Brad mentioned the draft's conclusion was early in the monologue. He made this rather general recommendation to make the conclusion look more like he thinks a conclusion should:

> "And then the conclusion. It should be more all together here from 14–16./ If they start a paragraph/ and then ask a question at the end,/ and they could've incorporated that all together."

During the final portion of the monologue, Brad returned to these concluding paragraphs with a new recommendation, reflecting a closer reading of the draft and allowing him to become actively engaged in production-based strategies, and thus, actively engaged in the writing process. He then offered a much more complex and elaborate plan for revising the text. He saw each paragraph as fulfilling a different purpose — paragraph five serving as an elaborated concession and rebuttal and paragraph six as a fully developed conclusion.

Brad's discussion of the final two paragraphs began with a general judgment about sentence fourteen:

> "And then ... uh ... this is a good point,/ a good contention here."

He then read that portion of the sentence which functioned as a concession:

> " 'Even if the laws of other countries prohibit handguns/ it doesn't mean/ there won't be any handguns ... ' "

He reaffirmed his judgment by offering a diagnosis, "and that's a strong point." Brad then went on to propose and recommend the following:

> "That can be used to turn it around/ because people are always going to say,/ 'Well, crooks will be able to get handguns anyway.'/ But with this ... they can use this as an example/ of how it's going to limit it/ is going to more or less limit all the accidental deaths."

Although Brad did not use the terms concession and rebuttal, the proposal and recommendation suggest that what he judged as a "good contention" and then read aloud was actually a concession. What he seemed to have in mind was further development of this section. He used the term "turn it around" to suggest that the writer needed to anticipate the possible counterarguments and to back up the rebuttal with an extended example.

Brad went on to model such an example by setting up the following scenario:

> "Chances are/ the average homeowner who has gun/ and there is a criminal/ who comes up to him with a gun,/ the guy's gonna be shot,/ the owner's gonna be shot ... / and that's just making his chances greater/ and the accidents are greater/ and there's ... more likelihood of somebody being murdered/ because there's more guns out there."

Even though Brad did not specifically mention sentence fifteen, it's clear that this sequence of strategies — judge/read/diagnose/propose/recommend/model — was aimed at developing the ideas in this sentence.

The next sequence of strategies — survey/propose/compose/recommend — aims at expanding the final question (sentence sixteen) into a more adequate concluding paragraph. To start this process, Brad surveyed the text, observing that the writer used the comparison between England and the United States as a frame: "And then to conclude it with the point that it made in the beginning." In fact, Brad had made this same observation early in the monologue, but had not elaborated on it. He then proposed that the writer explain how the strict handgun laws in England helped reduce the crime rate and reduce accidental deaths due to handguns:

> "You know/ that when you're comparing us to England/ how it helped England./ Maybe it reduced their crime rate/ or maybe there were less handgun accidents/ and relate it back to that."

Again, Brad identified a problem accurately, even though he did not articulate the problem in the terms of formal argumentation. The problem is that the writer tries to argue by analogy, arguing that these strict handgun laws now in place in England should be adopted in the United States. This argument is flawed on two counts: The writer ignores the burden of proof, failing to produce evidence that the British laws have indeed reduced the crime rate and reduced accidental deaths due to handguns. And, the writer uses the analogy as proof rather than as an illustration, suggesting erroneously that what works in one country will automatically work in another. Indeed, Brad's proposed plan, if completed, would provide the needed explanation of how the British handgun laws have succeeded. What is also needed, and what Brad provides by composing actual text, is a clear-cut statement of the essay's proposition:

> "And then say,/ 'It should be implemented in the U.S.' "

Brad's final comment on this section of the text reiterated his judgment that framing the text with the analogy was a useful strategy:

> "Bring it all . . . to start and end with the same thing./ That would probably make it all right."

Brad's final comment was in response to the interviewer's prompt, "Anything else you'd like to say about it?" He replied,

> "No, I'm just getting a little tired of the topic/ I guess./ Because that's all/ we did in [Composition] 101, this topic over and over."

With Brad's concluding statement, he moved from comments about the text to an acerbic evaluation of the discourse community he shared with the writer — freshman composition.

This analysis of one writer's evaluation strategies illustrates a strongly recursive process as the writer moves from diagnosing and judging strategies to production-related strategies. Throughout the monologue we observed Brad struggling to name and elaborate the key problems in the text, from problems in diction to problems in the argument structure. Our work with this single monologue raises several questions which we hope to address as we continue our work on the evaluative strategies of peer writing tutors and entry-level freshmen. Does the pattern we observed in Brad's monologue — moving from comprehension-based strategies to production-based strategies — apply for other tutors? How do tutors and entry-level composition students learn to name and elaborate textual faults? Does one experience — either tutoring or attending a writing class — have a particularly strong influence on the growth process? The answers to these and other questions about peer tutoring, considered in the context of the theoretical framework we propose, should add to our understanding of writing processes and the growth of writing ability.

Acknowledgments

For help with the manuscript, we thank the staff of the English Department and Helen Karstens. For their contribution in the early stages of the project, we thank Gwen Talley, Jack Ritter, Carol Severino, and Juan Guerra. For a very helpful reading, we thank David Jolliffe.

Note

1. The matrix concept for organizing research questions comes from a team effort during 1985 to develop a proposal for a national center for research on writing. We wish to acknowledge the authorship of that proposal by institution and by individual: University of Illinois at Chicago — Marcia Farr, Ann Matsuhashi, David Jolliffe, Alice Gillam, Sheldon Rosenberg, Michael Kamil, and Timothy Shanahan; New York University — Gordon Pradl, Angela Jaggar, Trika Smith-Burke, Lillian Brannon, John Mayher, Miriam Eisenstein, Mitchell Leaska, and Bee Cullinan; Northwestern University — Elizabeth Sulzby and Robert Gundlach; Illinois Writing Project — Harvey Daniels and Steven Zemelman; University of Pennsylvania — David Smith and Perry Gilmore; American Institutes for Research — Janice Redish; Lehman College/CUNY — Sondra Perl; and Teachers College, Columbia University — Dorothy Strickland.

References

Argyle, M. 1976. Social Skills Theory. In *Children as Teachers: Theory and Research on Tutoring*, edited by V. L. Allen, 57–73. New York: Academic Press.
Bannister-Wills, L. 1984. Developing a Peer Tutor Program. In *Writing Centers: Theory and Administration*, edited by G. Olson, 132–43. Urbana, Ill.: National Council of Teachers of English.

Beaugrande, R., de. 1987. Writing and Meaning: Contexts for Research. In *Writing in Real Time: Modelling Production Processes*, edited by A. Matsuhashi. Norwood, N.J.: Ablex.

Boden, M. 1977. *Artificial Intelligence and Natural Man.* New York: Basic Books.

Bracewell, R. 1983. Investigating Control of Writing Skills. In *Research on Writing: Principles and Methods*, edited by P. Mosenthal, L. Tamor, and S. A. Walmsley, 177–203. New York: Longman.

Brannon, L. 1982. On Becoming a More Effective Tutor. In *Tutoring Writing: A Sourcebook for Writing Labs*, edited by M. Harris, 105–10. Glenview, Ill.: Scott, Foresman.

Brannon, L., and C. H. Knoblauch. 1982. On Students' Rights to Their Own Texts: A Model of Teacher Response. *College Composition and Communication* 33 (2): 157–66.

Bruffee, K. 1978. The Brooklyn Plan: Attaining Intellectual Growth through Peer-Group Tutoring. *Liberal Education* 64:447–67.

Bruffee, K. 1983. Writing and Reading as Collaborative or Social Acts. In *The Writer's Mind: Writing as a Mode of Thinking*, edited by J. Hays, P. Roth, J. Ramsey, and R. Foulke, 159–69. Urbana, Ill.: National Council of Teachers of English.

Bruffee, K. 1984. Collaborative Learning and the "Conversation of Mankind." *College English* 46:635–52.

Dillon, J. 1984. The Classification of Research Questions. *Review of Educational Research* 54:327–61.

Erickson, F., and J. Shultz. 1981. When Is a Context? In *Ethnography and Language in Educational Settings*, edited by J. Green and C. Wallat, 147–60. Norwood, N.J.: Ablex.

Fishman, J. 1982. On Tutors, the Writing Labs, and Writings. In *Tutoring Writing: A Sourcebook for Writing Labs*, edited by M. Harris, 86–93. Glenview, Ill.: Scott, Foresman.

Flower, L., J. R. Hayes, L. Carey, K. Schriver, and J. Stratman. 1986. Detection, Diagnosis, and the Strategies of Revision. *College Composition and Communication* 37 (1): 16–55.

Frederiksen, N. 1984. Implications of Cognitive Theory for Instruction in Problem Solving. *Review of Educational Research* 54 (3): 363–407.

Freedman, S. W. 1985. Introduction. In *The Acquisition of Written Language: Response and Revision*, edited by S. W. Freedman, x–xv. Norwood, N.J.: Ablex.

Freedman, S. W., and A. Katz. 1987. Pedagogical Interaction during the Composing Process: The Writing Conference. In *Writing in Real Time: Modelling Production Processes*, edited by A. Matsuhashi. Norwood, N.J.: Ablex.

Freedman, S. W., and M. Sperling. 1985. Written Language Acquisition: The Role of Response and the Writing Conference. In *The Acquisition of Written Language: Response and Revision*, edited by S. W. Freedman, 106–30. Norwood, N.J.: Ablex.

Garrett, M. 1982. Toward a Delicate Balance: The Importance of Role Playing Peer Criticism in Peer-Tutoring Training. In *Tutoring Writing: A Sourcebook for Writing Labs,* edited by M. Harris, 94–100. Glenview, Ill.: Scott, Foresman.

Gere, A. R., and R. Stevens. 1985. The Language of Writing Groups: How Oral Response Shapes Revision. In *The Acquisition of Written Language: Response and Revision,* edited by S. W. Freedman, 85–105. Norwood, N.J.: Ablex.

Gumperz, J. 1976. Language, Communication, and Public Negotiation. In *Anthropology and the Public Interest,* edited by P. R. Sanday, 273–92. New York: Academic Press.

Harris, M., editor. 1982. *Tutoring Writing: A Sourcebook for Writing Labs.* Glenview, Ill.: Scott, Foresman.

Hawkins, T. 1982. Intimacy and Audience: The Relationship between Revision and the Social Dimension of Peer Tutoring. In *Tutoring Writing: A Sourcebook for Writing Labs,* edited by M. Harris, 27–31. Glenview, Ill.: Scott, Foresman.

Hilgers, T. 1984. Toward a Taxonomy of Beginning Writers' Evaluative Statements on Written Compositions. *Written Communication* 1 (3): 365–84.

Hilgers, T. 1986. How Children Change as Critical Evaluators of Writing: Four Three-Year Case Studies. *Research in the Teaching of English* 20 (1): 36–55.

Hull, G. 1984. The Editing Process in Writing: A Performance Study of Experts and Novices. Paper presented at the American Educational Research Association, New Orleans.

Hymes, D. 1982. What is Ethnography? In *Children in and out of School,* edited by P. Gilmore and A. Glatthorn, xx–xxx. Language and Ethnography Series 2. Washington, D.C.: Center for Applied Linguistics.

Kintsch, W. 1974. *The Representation of Meaning in Memory.* Hillsdale, N.J.: Erlbaum.

Lloyd-Jones, R. 1985. Blue-Ribbon Panels and Singin' the Professional Blues. In *Profession 85,* 23–29. New York: Modern Language Association.

Matsuhashi, A. 1987. Revising the Plan and Altering the Text. In *Writing in Real Time: Modelling Production Processes,* edited by A. Matsuhashi. Norwood, N.J.: Ablex.

Matsuhashi, A., and E. Gordon. 1985. Revision, Addition, and the Power of the Unseen Text. In *The Acquisition of Written Language: Response and Revision,* edited by S. W. Freedman, 226–49. Norwood, N.J.: Ablex.

Matsuhashi, A., A. Gillam, B. Moss, L. Anderson, and B. Stolarek. In preparation. Peer Tutors: Strategies for Evaluating Text.

McKeon, R., editor. 1941. *The Basic Works of Aristotle.* New York: Random House.

National Institute of Education. 1984. *Involvement in Learning: Realizing the Potential of American Higher Education.* Washington, D.C.: U.S. Government Printing Office.

North, S. 1984. Writing Center Research: Testing Our Assumptions. In *Writing Centers: Theory and Administration,* edited by G. Olson, 24–35. Urbana, Ill.: National Council of Teachers of English.

Olson, G., editor. 1984. *Writing Centers: Theory and Administration.* Urbana, Ill.: National Council of Teachers of English.

Pearson, D. P., and R. J. Tierney. 1984. *On Becoming a Thoughtful Reader: Learning to Read like a Writer.* Reading Education Report No. 50. Champaign: University of Illinois at Urbana–Champaign, Center for the Study of Reading.

Purves, A. 1984. The Teacher as Reader: An Anatomy. *College English* 46 (3): 259–65.

Reigstad, T., and P. McAndrew. 1984. *Training Tutors for Writing Conferences.* Urbana, Ill.: National Council of Teachers of English.

Reigstad, T., A. Matsuhashi, and N. Luban. 1978. One-to-One to Write: Establishing an Individual-Conference Writing Place. *English Journal* 67 (2): 30–35.

Reigstad, T., M. Williamson, and A. Matsuhashi. 1980. The Buffalo City Schools "Writing Place" Project: Evaluating the Effectiveness of a Supplemental Tutorial Writing Program. *The English Record* 31 (2): 2–9.

Scardamalia, M., and C. Bereiter. 1983. The Development of Evaluative, Diagnostic, and Remedial Capabilities in Children's Composing. In *The Psychology of Written Language,* edited by M. Martlew. New York: John Wiley.

Sherwood, P. 1982. What Should Tutors Know? In *Tutoring Writing: A Sourcebook for Writing Labs,* edited by M. Harris, 101–104. Glenview, Ill.: Scott, Foresman.

Simon, H. [1969] 1981. *The Sciences of the Artificial.* 2d ed. Cambridge: MIT Press.

Sommers, N. 1982. Responding to Student Writing. *College Composition and Communication* 33 (2): 148–56.

Turner, A., and E. Greene. 1977. *The Construction and Use of a Propositional Text Base.* Technical Report No. 63. Boulder: University of Colorado, Institute for the Study of Intellectual Behavior.

Tuzik, R. 1986. Unpublished case study. The Writing Center, 107 Addams Hall, University of Illinois at Chicago.

Witte, S. 1985. Revising, Composing Theory, and Research Design. In *The Acquisition of Written Language: Response and Revision,* edited by S. W. Freedman, 250–84. Norwood, N.J.: Ablex.

Witte, S., P. R. Meyer, T. P. Miller, and L. Faigley. 1981. *A National Survey of College and University Writing Program Directors.* Report No. 2, Fund for the Improvement of Post-Secondary Education, Grant No. 6008005896. Austin: Writing Program Assessment Project GRG 106-A, University of Texas at Austin.

Appendix

Assignment: Handguns should be banned by federal law. (Agree or Disagree)

Let's Ban Handguns

(1) In other countries, such as England, there are strict laws prohibiting handguns from the general public, while people in the United States can

purchase and receive legal ownership of a handgun because of the right to bear arms. (2) But so many times a handgun falls into the wrong hands, creating a dangerous and costworthy situation for Americans. (3) Handguns lead either to a killing accident or a cold-blooded murder, while handguns also provide the criminal with weapons to commit the crimes, such as murder in our country.

(4) The reasons so many people carry handguns in our country is simple — to protect ourselves. (5) But do handguns really protect ourselves or do they kill? (6) Handguns can give protection to a certain extent, but they also can cause a great deal of danger to the person who uses them or to the people he or she lives with.

(7) Parents usually store or lock up things which could be harmful to their children, such as poisons, knives, and tools, but fail to do so with handguns. (8) Many children are shot accidently with handguns because the parents neglected the thought of locking them up. (9) Throughout the United States, we read in our newspapers about how children are either accidentally wounded or killed by a handgun. (10) In the Chicago Tribune we see stories about a gun being handled by a father accidentally firing, fatally wounding his daughter in the head or about a child finding a hidden handgun and accidentally shooting a brother or a sister.

(11) The handgun is used in more than fifty percent of all murders and a high percentage of all crimes committed in the United States. (12) A handgun makes the perfect weapon to commit a crime; it is small, easy to use, and easy to hide. (13) Handguns were used to kill Robert Kennedy and John Lennon; one was also used in the attempted assassination of Ronald Reagan.

(14) Even if the laws of other countries prohibit the ownership of handguns, it doesn't mean that there won't be any handguns in circulation, but there will be fewer of them. (15) Because of the law, there is less chance of obtaining a handgun and less chance of a handgun causing another death.

If other countries like England can prohibit handguns, why can't the U.S.?

15 The First Five Minutes: Setting the Agenda in a Writing Conference

Thomas Newkirk
University of New Hampshire

Freshmen are usually allowed to hide — at least at large universities. Most of their courses meet in large lecture halls where they are taught by professors who don't, who really can't, learn the names of their students. In class, students listen and take notes, but do not speak. Examinations, by necessity, take the form of multiple-choice or short-answer questions, and the results are posted by Social Security number with an accompanying distribution curve to indicate where the student ranks.

The invariable exception to this pattern is freshman composition where, for better or worse, the student cannot hide. The student is called by name and, on an almost weekly basis, receives a response to his or her writing. Hiding is particularly difficult in the composition course where teacher and student meet for regular conferences in which the student must speak, explain, evaluate; where he or she must make what are often the first awkward steps in the direction of analytic conversation, the staple of the academic world. I will contend in this chapter that these meetings, and in particular the first few minutes of these meetings, constitute some of the most poignant dramas in the university.

I don't mean to overemphasize the confrontational nature of the writing conference by echoing Joe Louis's warning to Billy Conn — "You can run, but you can't hide." Most conferences seem casual, supportive; there is regular laughter and, at the end of the course, appreciation for the personal attention received. But the seemingly effortless, conversational quality of conferences belies their complexity, for both teacher and student are filling paradoxical roles. The teacher must balance two opposing mandates: on the one hand to respond to the student, to evaluate, to suggest possible revisions and writing strategies; and on the other to encourage the student to take the initiative, to self-evaluate, to make decisions, to take control of the paper. There is no neat way to reconcile these mandates, no formula to prevent missteps — just the endless prospect of gambling, of risking silence at some points and assertiveness at others.

The student meets this dilemma from the other end and fills a role at least as paradoxical. When asked the question, "What did you think of your paper?" or one of its many variants, the student knows that the question is really, "How did you (acting as member of a community that you are not yet a member of) react to this paper?" Furthermore, the person asking the question *is* a member of that community and very likely has a better answer — at least in the opinion of the student. Yet, despite the awkwardness of the situation, the student recognizes (usually) that the question is a valid one and works to formulate an answer. So if the teacher is a gambler, the student is often the actor, pretending her or his way into a role.

To complicate matters further, both student and teacher need to come to a meeting of minds fairly early in a writing conference; they need to set an agenda, agree to one or two major concerns that will be the focus of the conference. The agenda often deals with a possible revision of the paper, but there are other possibilities: it could deal with the writing process of the student or with a paper that is yet to be written. Unless a commonly-agreed-upon agenda is established, a conference can run on aimlessly and leave both participants with the justifiable feeling that they have wasted time. The efficient setting of an agenda is particularly important in the conferences that will be analyzed in this chapter. Each lasts about fifteen minutes and, in some, part of this time is used for reading the paper. There is little time to meander.

The conferences were held as part of the freshman English course at the University of New Hampshire and occurred in the third week of the course (in most cases they were the second student-teacher conference). In virtually all sections of freshman English, students are not graded until mid-semester and then only on work that both student and instructor feel is the best produced to that point. For that reason, instructors in these early conferences are not under pressure to give or justify grades. Each conference was taped by the instructor, a first-semester teaching assistant, who transcribed the conference and then annotated it, identifying crucial junctures and critical mistakes. The procedure used by Carnicelli (1980) served as a model.

I will present the opening segments, lasting about five minutes, of three conferences that show different ways in which agendas are negotiated or fail to be negotiated. The papers for these conferences are similar; they are first drafts dealing with personal experiences, and, like many early papers in freshman English, they lack focus. An instructor reading these papers away from the student could conceivably write a similar comment for each. But the student is present, and this presence changes the nature of the teaching act.

"It Might Be Kind of Dumb ..."

The paper for the following conference was entitled "My Favorite Course," five double-spaced pages which began with the student's love for horses as a child (she had a toy palomino). From this beginning she moves on to describe how she was admitted to a horsemanship course, the things she has learned so far in the course, and positive and negative points about her horse. After reading the paper (and before reading the transcript), I expected the conference to deal with the issue of focus. But it didn't, and the reason why should be evident from the opening segment (in this and the following transcriptions, *T*=teacher and *S*=student):

> *T:* All right, now let's talk about your paper. I'm going to spend a few minutes on it now and then we'll talk about it.
>
> *S:* OK.
> [Teacher reads paper]
>
> *T:* OK. Uh, why don't you tell me a little about your paper. What was it like writing it?
>
> *S:* Oh, I liked it. I really like the class, you know, and I liked writing about it.
>
> *T:* So you enjoyed it?
>
> *S:* Yeah. It's a fun class.
>
> *T:* Was it a fun paper?
>
> *S:* Yeah. Well, you know, I wanted to write about it. Maybe it's really boring because I really just wrote it for me, but I guess I just wanted to. It, you know, doesn't say much. Just about my class.
>
> *T:* Well, I enjoyed reading it. It was fun reading it. I could see, I could tell that you liked the class and I liked the way your enthusiasm really shows.
>
> *S:* Yeah.
>
> *T:* Was there a part that you really enjoyed writing?
>
> *S:* Well, I enjoyed writing the whole paper pretty much.
>
> *T:* Uh huh. Is there a part you liked best, you know, a favorite part?
>
> *S:* Oh, yeah. I really liked the part about Trigger [the toy horse]. Remembering him. I still have him somewhere at home. It might be kind of dumb though, a plastic horse.

> T: Oh no. I really liked that. I had a dog, a stuffed shaggy dog that I remembered while reading it. He's somewhere now. I guess everyone grows up with these animals and then keeps them forever. [Laughter.] But I liked that part, I could really relate to it. Was there a part that you thought needed work still? You know, something you were sort of unhappy with?
>
> S: Well, I wondered if it would be boring. You know, too long. It doesn't really say much.
>
> T: Did you, uh, did you want it to say something? What did you want to tell me?
>
> S: Oh, well. I just wanted to tell you about my riding class.
>
> T: Uh huh.
>
> S: That's all.
>
> T: Uh huh. Um. You know you told me about yourself, too.
>
> S: What?
>
> T: Well, that part about Trigger?
>
> S: Oh yeah. [Laughs.]
>
> T: And you know, about being tested. Your dedication. Not only getting up at the crack of dawn and all, but the work. Like it sounds like you're really working your body, so it's a lot of hard work as well as fun.

This conference stumbles at the beginning over the reference to "it." In the first five exchanges, the teacher uses "it" three times, in each case referring to the paper or the writing of the paper. The student uses "it" three times, each time referring to the horsemanship class and ultimately leading her to misunderstand the teacher's question:

> T: So you enjoyed it?
>
> S: Yeah. It's a fun class.
>
> T: Was it a fun paper?

One senses the student's lack of familiarity with the intent of the conference and her lack of awareness that the teacher's primary concern at this point in the conference is with the process of writing. The student doesn't, in fact, quite know what it means to "talk about your paper." This discomfort with the analytic intent of the conference becomes even more evident when the teacher pushes (ever so gently) for a critical evaluation of the paper.

In response to the teacher's request for an analytic judgment, the student consistently gives a global evaluation — of the paper, of the class, and most devastatingly, of herself. When asked to tell about the writing of the paper (an implicit request for analysis), the writer replies with, "Oh, I liked it." When asked, this time more explicitly, if there was a "*part* that you really enjoyed writing," the student replies that she liked "writing the whole paper pretty much." And again later in the segment, when asked about the main point of the paper, she replies globally that she "just wanted to tell you about my riding class." The only tentative move toward an analytic view is the student's admission that she liked the part about the toy horse. For this student, the text seems to exist as a whole that cannot be differentiated into features or parts. And because she brings this frame to her paper, the teacher comes up empty in most of the exchanges.

But not totally empty. For in these replies, the student is making clear her lack of confidence in her own writing ability and her doubts about the validity of her experience as a topic for writing. In these first few minutes the student characterizes her writing as: "boring" (twice), "it doesn't say much," "it might be kind of dumb," and "too long." It is this message that the teacher picks up on and makes the focus of the conference agenda. In her analysis of the conference, the teacher wrote:

> She told me in a previous conference . . . [that] she is the first one of her extended family to go to college. Her self-confidence is very shaky, and she considers her acceptance into UNH to be a fluke. She doesn't think she is "college material." She has a pattern of trashing herself, telling me how "dumb" she is compared to all the "real" students around her. . . . I have an agenda of support for her and, if possible, some sort of positive response against her habit of self-denigration.

So the teacher gambles. She focuses on supporting the student, allaying the student's fears that she is an inadequate writer and that her experiences are "boring." The gamble is that by ignoring, for a time, various technical problems in the writing and by emphasizing the positive, the writer will, in the near future, gain enough confidence to deal with these technical matters. Another gamble is that this support will not be taken by the student as a definitive evaluation — "I enjoyed reading it" may be translated by the student into "This is an *A* paper." The teacher gambles . . . and waits.

"... Like a Mack Truck"

The second conference deals with an untitled paper about the function of pets. It begins in a fairly technical way with the sentence, "I wonder what part domestic animals play in the ecosystem." For most of the paper, however, the writer shifts to a more casual language to describe her own relationship with her dog as they went out in the woods after a snow:

> She would suddenly stop, lie on the ground and chew at the ice.
> Sometimes it was severe enough to cause her paws to bleed
> leaving red splotches on the snow. I knew it was more painful
> for her if I attempted to yank out the ice.

At the end of the paper, the writer returns to the more distant
vocabulary of the beginning, when she concludes that "Pets are
machines for us to lavish affection on or proclaim superiority over."

The paper alone suggests two major issues. The radical shift of tone
after the beginning is jolting, and the conclusion comparing pets to
machines seems at odds with the affectionate description of the writer's
relationship with her own pet. Ironically, both teacher and student in
the following excerpt agree on the central problem in the paper, yet
the conference misfires badly.

T: Now, what did you think your purpose was in writing the paper?

S: Well, I was just kind of dealing with the fact that people have animals.
And are nice to them. And we're not really nice to other organisms
besides ourselves. You know, I wonder why people are so uncommonly
nice to domesticated animals.

T: Yeah? So — umm — did you come to any conclusion about that?

S: No. [Laughs.]

T: But at the end you say: "I have had a pet as a companion. Pets are
machines for us to lavish affection on or to proclaim superiority over."
That sounds like you've come to a conclusion.

S: Well, it's more of an observation.

T: Oh. You see, I think it's a false conclusion. I mean I think you still
don't know.

S: I don't.

T: And I think it's better that you don't know. I mean you're saying there
ought to be some reason for this, but I love my dog.

S: Yeah.

T: And so for me the last paragraph was — I think I said that before —
that you have a tendency to be asking questions and think you have
to find some answer.

S: Umhumm.

T: And I don't think — I mean whatever answer you find, it's probably
going to be a question and it's probably going to be inherent in the
whole piece.

S: So I don't really have to . . .

T: You're saying, "God this is strange, we're funny creatures." And that's
the answer. You don't have to what?

S: I don't have to make it so — like I ought to stick on this conclusion —
which is unnecessary.

T: And also, when you do that you tend to lapse into this scientific language that really — you sound like you've turned into a computer or something. . . . Were there any parts of this that you liked better than other parts, that you enjoyed writing?

S: Yeah, I liked describing — like the skiing and walking through the woods and stuff. I enjoy writing like that. 'Cause I enjoy doing it so . . .

T: And were there any parts that gave you trouble?

S: I don't think so. It's kind of like — I felt that it wasn't — like I — this first part, you know, I was just wondering in general and then I kinda switched into my own experience and that wasn't too smooth, I don't think. Yeah, you know, I just — the part where I was describing what we did.

T: Yeah, well you need the — let's see: "I wonder what part domestic animals play in the ecosystem. . . . Domesticated animals are personalized diversions for humans." See, you've answered it too soon.

S: But . . . that's like an observation.

What stands out in this conference is the domination of the teacher. She speaks more than twice as much as the student (351 to 162 words), but a word count alone does not make clear the nature of that domination. The teacher seems to have in mind what Knoblauch and Brannon (1984) call an "ideal text." She has an image of the true version which this paper should ultimately conform to. In this truer state, the paper would illustrate, through the description of the author and her pet, the reasons why we treat pets in special ways. The language of the paper would be "human" and avoid broad assertions that might *answer* the question raised in the paper; rather, the author should indicate no more certainty than to suggest that, "God this is strange, we're funny creatures." Indeed, just after the excerpt I've quoted here, the teacher offers the student language from this ideal text, urging the student to qualify her assertions with "it seems to me . . ." — whereupon the student reminds the teacher that their textbook tells them to avoid "it seems."

Many changes that the student might make in moving toward this ideal text *would* improve the writing. The conclusion does seem too assured, and it doesn't deal with the complexity of the question raised. The problem is the lack of negotiation in the conference. The teacher identifies a problem and suggests remedies before the student is even convinced that a problem exists. Even at the very end of this first segment, the student repeats her justification of the conclusions as "observations." Paradoxically, when given an opportunity to state her own judgment of the paper, the student identifies the mismatch between the opening and the descriptive parts which, she claimed, she enjoyed writing more than the "scientific" opening. This judgment is not really so far from the agenda the teacher opens with. The conference might have looked a great deal different if the teacher had begun by focusing on the effectiveness of the descriptive passages and then encouraged the student to fit the opening and conclusions to this effective writing.

But because the teacher's agenda is set rather inflexibly early on, she misses this and other opportunities to build on the observations of the student. The student is shut out in two ways: first, she is put on the defensive when the instructor calls her conclusion "false." Then, even when the conclusion/observation issue is momentarily dropped, the teacher doesn't hear the student's contributions. When the student attempts a summary of the teacher's suggestions about the conclusion, the teacher changes the subject:

> S: I don't have to make it so — like I ought to stick on this conclusion — which is unnecessary.
> T: And also, when you do that you tend to lapse into this scientific language.

It is not at all clear that the student understands what is to be done with the ending, but the teacher moves on. Similarly, she fails to follow up on the student's comment about enjoying the writing of the descriptive parts. In her analysis of the transcript, the instructor admits that when the student identifies the problem with the shift from scientific to more casual descriptive language, she "stubbornly cling[s] to my diagnosis about questions and answers."

This conference illustrates what Freedman and Sperling (1985) call "cross-purpose talk":

> With no match in focal concern, T and S will likely be talking at cross purposes and may not even be attending to what the other is saying. . . . This cross-purpose talk manifests itself in a T-S conference when S and T each bring up a topic of concern over and over again, no matter what the other wants to focus on, indicating that T and S often have different agendas for what needs to be covered in the conference. (117)

The teacher reviewing the conference put the problem a bit more bluntly: "Mea culpa. I ran over this kid like a Mack truck."

"It Just Didn't Make Sense"

The final conference excerpt deals with a paper called "Mailaholic," which attempts to explain the writer's addiction to getting letters. It starts out in a lighthearted, almost "cute" way, detailing her love of various kinds of stamps and stationery and the way she and other dorm members place unopened letters on their lunch trays to flaunt the fact that someone has written to them. Then, as in the previous paper, there is a shift in tone, and, in brief paragraphs, the writer explains what letters from mother, boyfriend, and best friend mean. At first reading, this short paper — about 700 words total — seems the least promising of the three (the word superficial comes to mind). But like an expert canoeist, the teacher follows the current of the student's language to a real insight.

T: How do you feel about this paper?

S: I don't like it. I like the topic. I like the title, but I had a hard time . . . I had a lot of ideas I wanted to put in . . . and they didn't seem to flow. Like I read the paper that you gave us Thursday . . . I just liked it. Like everything flowed and went together smoothly. And this, I'm like . . . it just doesn't say anything. I wanted to say something but I didn't say it the right way.

T: OK. Tell me what you were trying to say . . . in a few sentences . . . if you had to tell me what your paper was about.

S: How much getting a letter means to me. But I just . . . I don't know . . . I like a lot of times, you know, it just didn't make sense. It was like I didn't know how to say it.

T: Do you think you addressed that anywhere on the page?

S: Yeah. I think where I'm saying about how I go about reading a letter. You know after I . . . if there's one there . . . after I've gotten a letter and just sit there and let everyone see it. And then when I get in the privacy of my own room . . . then I read it, 'cause then I feel I'm with the person rather than having all this noise around me and I can't concentrate.

T: Yes?

S: And then if I don't get a letter . . . I like sort of envy them and am real jealous. And it's like when they do what I do . . . it's wrong because they're hurting me. I do the same thing. I put it on my lunch tray and let everyone see the letter.

T: Yes?

S: I like that part of it. Maybe I just don't like the beginning or how I get into it. I don't like the transitions. Sometimes I don't see how I get where I'm going.

T: OK. Then you think that perhaps you were trying to find your topic, found it, and then ran out of it?

S: Yeah.

T: Where do you think you really started to get into it?

S: On the second page.

T: All right . . .

S: But I don't really dig into the mess. What I understood about it is . . . think that's where I actually start talking about what I mean to say about it, you know.

T: Yes?

S: So I suppose if I just cut off the first page and start it out with the rest?

T: Yes?

S: What I should try to do . . .

T: What other kind of things are you trying to say?

S: Uh . . .

T: When you think about what getting a letter really means.

S: Well, on the last page . . . about when I get a letter from my boyfriend, or my best friend, or my mom . . . what feelings I get when I get it . . . a letter from them.

By this point the agenda is set. The rest of the conference explores what these feelings are, and as the writer talks, she moves beyond the juvenile tone of the original draft to an insight into her own need for letters:

S: And like I was really close to my mom this summer. So it's like I'm up here and I don't want them to forget me. And so I just want to keep grasping . . . you know . . . to make sure that life is still going on. And when I go home . . . everything isn't going to be the same, but it isn't going to be dramatically different.

While this observation still relies, to a degree, on the commonplace "make sure that *life is still going on,*" the writer seems to have found a reason for her need for letters.

She has been able to make these moves toward understanding because the teacher gave her room. The ratio of teacher talk to student talk differs radically from the second conference quoted earlier. Here the teacher speaks only 97 words to the student's 397, and in many of the exchanges she simply prods the student with a "yes." Such a ratio, of course, may not be an "ideal" to work towards; so much student talk could be digressive. But in this case, the student seems to be working from a global and unformed dissatisfaction with her paper to a more analytic evaluation that will guide her revision. The writer's initial evaluative responses were scattered: it doesn't "flow," it has a lot of ideas, it "doesn't say anything," and "I don't think I did it the right way." The teacher's question about the intent of the paper causes the writer to identify her purposes — to explain what letters meant to her. And again, in response to the teacher's question, the student notes that only on the second page does she really deal with her newly stated purpose. The writer is closing in; she admits that although she begins to deal with her focus on the second page, she doesn't "really dig into the mess." The teacher then pushes her in this direction by asking what things she was trying to say about getting letters; the agenda for the rest of the conference is set.

Or almost set. The student does offer up a concern early in the conference — a concern the teacher wisely ignores. In her first evaluation of the paper, the student says, "I don't think I did it the right way." This comment, common in an early writing conference, suggests that the student has been taught some ironclad rules for writing essays, and she wants to see whether these rules still apply. Toward the end of the conference, this concern once again surfaces as the student asks about her conclusion:

> S: When you write a conclusion, is it supposed to be restating the beginning of the thing? I had a hard time. I didn't know how to end it.

The teacher responds that the writer must decide for herself and that each paper is different.

Finally, this conference illustrates the role of talk in revision. Revision is often used synonymously with rewriting; we change our writing by writing again and making changes. The student in this conference is revising by talking; she is creating an alternative text, an oral text that can be juxtaposed against the one she has written. The next draft she might write is not simply a nebulous possibility; rather, it is a draft that has, to a degree, been spoken. Near the end of the conference the teacher asks what she might do next, and the student answers, "I think I'll probably cut off the first page and a half and work on . . . I don't know . . . giving examples. *Like what I told you a few minutes ago.*"

This emphasis on allowing students to speak these oral texts may seem almost insultingly self-evident. But in reading and annotating these transcripts, teachers were appalled at the opportunities that were missed — when they cut off students, and when they *told* students to expand a section rather than allowing them to expand orally. Students did not get a chance to hear what they know.

Implications

The lessons to be learned from this kind of self-examination are painfully obvious — but worth remembering because, in our eagerness to teach, we often forget the obvious.

1. We all tend to talk too much. The little lecturettes that pop up in writing conferences usually bring things to a grinding halt.
2. The opening minutes of the conference are critically important in giving the conference direction — they act as a kind of *lead*. The student's contributions in these opening minutes need to be

used to give the conference a mutually agreeable and mutually understood direction.

3. These agendas should be limited to one or two major concerns. Conferences seem to break down when a discussion about a "high-level" concern like purpose veers abruptly to a discussion of sentence structure.

4. Potentially, student contributions to the agenda-setting process often are missed if the teacher has *fixed* on a problem early. It is particularly easy for the teacher to fix on the agenda if he or she takes the papers home and marks them up before the conference. Furthermore, a marked-up paper indicates to the student that the agenda has *already* been set.

5. While the teacher must be responsive to the student's contributions in the writing conference, this does not mean that the teacher is nondirective. Students, like the one in the first conference, may at first be unfamiliar with the evaluative-analytic language of the writing conference. These students often need to see how the teacher reads so they might get an operative understanding of what a term like "focus" means. The modeling described by Richard Beach (this volume) is vitally important in this type of conference.

Unfortunately, listing conclusions like this implies that the difficulty of conferences can be smoothed out and problems prevented. This is not my position.

I see the writing conference as a dialectic encounter between teacher and student, in which both assume complex roles. The teacher, in particular, cannot escape the difficult choices between praise and support, suggestion and silence, each choice carrying with it a risk. For that reason, I am uncomfortable with some of the metaphors increasingly used to describe this complex relationship, many of which echo private property and contractual law. The writer, we are told, "owns" the text, which should not be "appropriated" by the teacher (Knoblauch and Brannon 1982). Graves (1983) has similarly urged that the student has "ownership" of the text. Knoblauch and Brannon (1984) describe the ideal reading of a student text as follows:

> It is the rare composition teacher who reads student writing with the assumption that composers legitimately control their own discourses, who accepts the possibility that student intentions matter more than teacher expectations as a starting-point for reading, and who recognizes that the writer's choices are supposed to make sense mainly in terms of those intentions, not in proportion

> as they gratify a reader's point of view of what should have been said. (120)

The polarization of terms in this description is striking: student intentions/teacher expectations, student control/teacher control. And the term "legitimately" introduces, once again, the implication that in defining the role of the teacher we are working within clear, almost legal, boundaries.

But if we push on these metaphors a bit, they wobble. Ownership implies clear property lines guaranteed by legal statutes that are (at least to lawyers) clearly spelled out. For the most part, those who own property can do what they want to with it, so long as the owner is not creating a major inconvenience to others. Those of us who view the property may have opinions about the esthetics of the house built on it, but the owner need not listen, and we need to be very careful about passing on these judgments.

The metaphor of ownership is not slippery enough. To a degree, the student owns his or her paper, but the paper is *intended* for others in the way property isn't; and so, to a degree, the writing is also owned by its readers. No one (I hope) condones the practice condemned by Knoblauch and Brannon in which students must guess at some Platonic text that exists in the teacher's imagination. But by the same token, the expectations of the teacher, the course, and the academy must interact with the intentions of the student. Intention, in other words, cannot be an absolute, a "God-term."

Let's take this paragraph you are now beginning to read. Who owns it — you or I? Does my intention *matter* more than your response? Questions like these divide the writing act in an unhelpful way. The text is neither mine nor yours — no one owns it. Even in writing it, I didn't feel that I was putting *my* meaning into language that would fit *your* needs. Rather, there was a constant interplay between audience and intention so that I can no longer disentangle my meanings from your expectations. I did not feel set against you, my audience; rather, you became part of me in the act of writing. And so it is in a good writing conference, like the third one I quoted, where the teacher becomes an active instrument in the student's search for meaning.

I began this chapter by claiming that few courses at the university push freshmen to assume responsibility for their own learning. I'd like to close with an instance of one that did, a philosophy course, which caused an almost Copernican shift in the writer's view of what it is to be a student. It is, I believe, the same kind of shift that a good writing course can initiate. The paper, written for a freshman English course, is entitled "Philosophy Is Messing Up My Life," and it begins

with the anxiety the student felt about taking an introductory philosophy course. At first the professor appeared intimidating, with a
"strong philosophical nose, and eyes that could eat a question mark
right through you." When the roll was called the writer barely managed
an audible "here." Once the class started, the student opened his
notebook and expected the instructor to begin by writing a definition
of philosophy on the board. But he didn't. He asked questions to
show the students that philosophy is, in this student's words, a "process
of questioning and answering things you don't understand in an
attempt to arrive at the 'right' answer, which usually doesn't exist
anyway."

This process of questioning has taken hold and started to "mess up
his life":

> I start out by asking myself questions about life. I've come up
> with some disturbing answers. . . . The reason I called this paper
> "Philosophy Is Messing Up My Life" is because most of the
> answers make me look bad. I don't like that at all. Realizing that
> I have a philosophy has opened up a whole new world for me
> that I never knew existed. I'm not sure I'm ready for the truth
> yet. But I've made truth my responsibility . . .

When we push students to speak, to evaluate; when we listen and
don't rush in to fill silences, we may be able to transform the rules of
studenthood in the way this philosophy professor did. And when we
pose this challenge, we will be working at the very epicenter of a
liberal education.

Acknowledgments

I would like to acknowledge the help of graduate students who
recorded, transcribed, and annotated the conference excerpts used in
this chapter. Thanks also to Elizabeth Chiseri Strater for her help on
this project.

References

Carnicelli, T. 1980. The Writing Conference: A One-to-One Conversation. In
Eight Approaches to Teaching Composition, edited by T. Donovan and B.
McClelland, 101–32. Urbana, Ill.: National Council of Teachers of English.

Freedman, S., and M. Sperling. 1985. Written Language Acquisition: The Role
of Response in the Writing Conference. In *The Acquisition of Written*

Language: Response and Revision, edited by S. Freedman, 106–30. Norwood, N.J.: Ablex.

Graves, D. 1983. *Writing: Teachers and Children at Work.* Exeter, N.H.: Heinemann.

Knoblauch, C., and L. Brannon. 1982. On Students' Rights to Their Own Texts: A Model of Teacher Response. *College Composition and Communication* 33:157–66.

Knoblauch, C., and L. Brannon. 1984. *Rhetorical Traditions and Modern Writing.* Upper Montclair, N.J.: Boynton/Cook.

16 Response Styles and Ways of Knowing

Chris M. Anson
University of Minnesota

Interviewer: What did your writing teachers tell you about your papers?

Mindy: They went through like what's a verb, what's a prepositional phrase. In Senior [high school] English you had to turn in one essay a week, and he'd go through everyone's paper and mark every grammatical error that was made.

Interviewer: Did he care much about what you said?

Mindy: Oh, no, as long as you had a good conclusion, a good introduction, and you had, like, topic sentences and concluding sentences with all your paragraphs, it was OK. And on grammatical, every place you had a wrong comma or something, they marked off, like a point or something.

Interviewer: What kinds of things did you write about?

Mindy: Um, he just said anything.

Interviewer: What do you think writing teachers value? I mean, what do you think they want to see that would help you get a good grade?

Mindy: Um, all the grammatical stuff right, and if it says what it's supposed to say. (Anson 1984, 246)

As writing teachers who hope to encourage growth in our students' literacy, we often focus on language to the exclusion of many other dimensions of their intellectual development. Thinking becomes style, sentence structure, and the control of surface mechanics. Even when we respond to meaning, our perspective is often narrowed to linguistic and rhetorical concerns — the logical progression of ideas, the appropriate use of evidence, the presence of a thesis, the sophistication of cohesive ties. As Vygotsky puts it in *Mind in Society* ([1930] 1978), our focus on these sorts of particulars recalls the development of a technical skill such as piano playing: "The pupil develops finger dexterity and learns to strike the keys while reading music, but he is in no way involved in the essence of the music itself" (105–106).

As suggested in the common theme of this collection, we must begin to think of response as part of the social and interpersonal dynamics of the classroom community. Our focus must therefore widen to include all that surrounds the texts we read, write, and discuss — not just in the methods we use to create a context for response, but also in how we think about literacy more generally, and what sorts of attitudes toward the world of knowledge we associate with its growth in our students.

Fortunately, there are adequate theoretical resources for making connections between writing and intellectual development, cognitive style, or systems of personal belief (see, for example, Chickering 1981). But many of those connections are still weak. Large gaps exist in our understanding of the relationships between the development of writing abilities and the "ways of knowing" that are part of students' intellectual, cognitive, and social backgrounds.[1] What sorts of worldviews, particularly views of knowledge, do students bring into academia? How are these views related to their abilities as writers? What beliefs about learning do we convey through our responses to students' writing, and in what ways do these encourage (or inhibit) the further development of literacy?

In this chapter, I will describe a study that explored how teachers responded to student essays reflecting different ways of interpreting the world. In many ways, a student's writing and a teacher's response to it represent a transaction through which two separate epistemologies come together, interact, and grow or change in the process. In conducting this study, I was especially interested in the relationship between students' ways of analyzing the world, as expressed in their essays, and the views of knowledge, learning, and writing implied in teachers' responses to these essays. The conclusions, albeit descriptive and based on a small sample, suggest some ways in which teachers' own beliefs about writing inform their responses, which in turn may encourage or inhibit the growth of students' perceptions of writing and, ultimately, their views of knowledge.

Knowledge, Worldview, and Writing

The impetus for this study began several years ago when some of my colleagues and I were exploring ways of applying theories of learning and intellectual development to research on writing ability. As we surveyed the work of Kohlberg, Piaget, Kolb, and other educational psychologists, we were immediately drawn to William Perry's *Forms of Intellectual and Ethical Development in the College Years: A Scheme* (1970). In this book, Perry charts the development of undergraduates' ways of viewing the world, especially the acquisition of knowledge, through nine distinct stages, beginning when they enter college and ending when they have developed commitments to pursuing a particular career or exploring the problems inherent in a chosen discipline.

Perry's work is so widely known now that a brief description of his scheme, in this case glossed with reference to students as writers, will suffice to give the background for this study (for other useful overviews by language educators, see Bizzell 1984; Burnham 1986; Lunsford 1985). However, it should be noted that I see Perry's work as a starting point for further exploration of the relationship between epistemological perspective and response to writing; several theorists have recently called into question the sample from which Perry drew his conclusions (undergraduate males at Harvard) and are also challenging the underlying implications of "intellectual development" charted in his scheme (see, for example, Belenky et al. 1986; but cf. Erwin 1983).

The early stages of Perry's scheme describe an approach to learning that is "dualistic." When students begin college, they often see the world of knowledge in polar terms: right vs. wrong, good vs. bad. Authorities (teachers) possess all the answers, because they strive to accumulate Absolutes in their role as givers of truth. In attitude questionnaires, dualists will answer "true" to such statements as "For most questions there is only one right answer, once a person is able to get all the facts" (see Perry 1968). Learning means collecting these right answers by passively receiving them from Authority. Dualistic students believe that if they adhere to the rules and regulations of Authority, they will succeed — a view built, in part, from the social and behavioral patterns often reinforced in the context of elementary education.

As I have described elsewhere (Anson 1986a, 1986b), typical dualistic writers constantly seek a formula or solution to writing tasks, asking, "What do you want in this essay?" or "Have I done this the right way?" or "But didn't I change everything you told me to?" Because uncertainty is a mark of not knowing the "right way" to compose a text, they feel ashamed of revealing tentativeness in their writing process, assuming instead that a piece of writing is finished as soon as they've reached the end. For this reason, they are not very extensive revisers (Anson 1986a; Beach 1976). When these students talk about their writing, they treat it as an artifact that either conforms or doesn't conform to some preestablished "truth" or norms for correctness (Sirc and Anson 1985).

The content of dualists' essays also reveals a dogmatic view of the world. In argumentative writing, many dualistic students will express attitudes often associated with "cognitive egocentrism" (Kroll 1978) and "writer-based prose" (Flower 1979); they find it difficult to decenter and see their ideas from perspectives other than their own. In a content analysis of 500 basic writers' essays, for example, Andrea Lunsford (1980) found "striking" and "overwhelming" evidence that basic writers have difficulty "decentering or achieving what Piaget refers to as a 'non-egocentric' rhetorical stance" (Lunsford 1980, 26–28).

In addition to showing signs of egocentrism, dualists' writing is often disingenuous or lacks conviction. The student hopes to mimic the established dogmas which, etched in stone by Authority, are incontrovertible truths to be memorized like so many lines of a sacred text. These often take the form of platitudes or blindly citing famous authorities; Slattery (1986), for example, describes a dualistic student who supports the use of painful medical experiments on animals by referring to the Bible, which "tells us that animals were put forth on earth by God in order to serve mankind." Dualists are also prone to making statements that conform to the dominant political or social ideologies of the time, perhaps in an attempt to show the teacher that they, too, know what is right.

For dualists, then, there is a "correctness" both in the proper form and the proper content of a response to a task. The way to succeed is to write a "correct" essay, either through artful guesswork or by persuading the teacher to specify the necessary formal criteria or the ideas to be regurgitated.

As students move through college, they begin to take on a more relativistic view of learning, recognizing that not all areas of knowledge are absolute. There are some questions that don't seem to have ready answers. In the early stages of relativism, many students hold what Perry calls a "pre-multiplistic" view of knowledge: Authority still knows what is right, but withholds it from students so they can find it on their own. Later, students begin to realize that some questions don't yet have answers — but they continue to believe that the answers are still findable by Authority, with enough hard work and fact-gathering.

As writers, students just making the transition into the multiplicity of relativism often believe that the teacher knows the "correct" way to write an essay but is craftily withholding this wisdom for the sake of pedagogy. Fearing that they won't find the answer in this game of rhetorical hide-and-seek, these students may cling desperately to what is tangible in the classroom — the teacher's procedural guidelines.

Such students often refer to or guess at what the teacher "expects" them to do, without knowledge of any underlying reason for doing it: "I figured you'd probably want us to start the paper by telling who we interviewed," or "I did everything we were supposed to do — did my interview, did all that prewriting stuff, and followed the revision guide, so I think my paper's pretty good now" (see Anson 1986a).

As students work their way through relativism, they begin to recognize that knowledge depends on context. They analyze concepts and ideas more fully, often using Authority to support generalizations they eventually reach after systematic exploration. But once it becomes clear that even experts are uncertain in areas where solutions aren't immediately available, relativists often begin to wallow in a kind of abandoned skepticism; since knowledge is no longer absolute, everyone has a right to their own opinion. Floating in a sea of indecision, some relativists can, as Perry points out, become anxious; the student "sees, in wonder and terror, Sisyphus' wry smile bespeaking his awareness that he must again resume the quest for certainty of meaning, a labor that forever ends in the same defeat" (1981, 90).

In the middle stages of relativism, students take an approach to writing in which all decisions are equally tenable and defensible. Since no one can be an authority about what constitutes "good" or "bad" writing, "correct" or "incorrect" decisions, then personal idiosyncracy can prevail, immune to criticism: "But that's just your opinion," or "Why should I worry about my audience, anyway? What difference does it make?" Like dualists, relativists often resist making extensive revisions to their texts because the ends don't justify the means. In conference groups, as Doe (1985) illustrates in a Perry profile of one student, relativists sometimes let other students' comments "run off them" like water, seeing the class community as a place made up of different people trying to understand things in many different ways (27). Opinion for the relativist is, as Perry puts it, "related to nothing whatever — evidence, reason, experience, judgment, context, principle, or purpose — except to the person who holds it" (1981, 85). Any idea or opinion that can't be proved wrong is therefore acceptable. This axiom is even more readily adopted in areas of study where indeterminacy is the norm, such as philosophy and literature. As a result, relativistic students will often become angry or frustrated if the content of their essays is criticized but there are no problems in mechanics, grammar, etc. Since they've done nothing wrong in those areas in which one can define "wrongness," then their ideas are invulnerable to everything but personal disagreement.

More commonly, the content of relativists' essays shows an endless weighing of alternatives, a kind of inconclusiveness born of entertaining diversity. Some students acknowledge all authorities as if they were equally valid, and then avoid making judgments on them. In form, their essays may seesaw from opinion to opinion, perspective to perspective ("on the one hand/on the other hand," "some people feel/others believe"), without ever reaching a solid conclusion. Slattery (1986) gives the example of a student who, in writing about soap operas, lists the opinions of several experts and then concludes, "All in all, whether you should watch soap operas or not seems left up to your own judgment."

In the final generalized stage of Perry's scheme, the student continues to recognize that the world is void of absolutes or "right answers," but now begins to see order and stability within this tentativeness. What is important to the self now becomes reinterpreted in the context of what has been "rendered important by one's family, friends, religious and ethnic traditions, and intellectual interests" (Bizzell 1984, 448). Perry describes this highest stage in terms of evolving commitments about one's life goals, career choices, values, and beliefs. The difference between a commitment and a dualistic belief, however, lies in the intellectual process. Committed relativists weigh alternatives and carefully consider other points of view before making a commitment. (The stereotypical example is the minister who respects the beliefs of other religions but is firmly committed to her own. The religious fundamentalist, in contrast, believes everyone else's religion is "wrong"; he takes a dualistic perspective because he hasn't worked through relativism in forming his beliefs.)

Committed relativists also recognize the fluid and dynamic nature of commitments themselves, and are at first "perilously vulnerable" and "alone" in their convictions (Perry 1981, 97). By becoming members of peer groups who share similar values, some of this peril of relativism is reduced; but most importantly, committed relativists are always open to new ideas, values, and perspectives that might challenge whatever commitments they've already made. Instead of "suffering the ambivalence of finding several consistent and acceptable alternatives," they assert an identity and assume a role in what they must always see as a pluralistic and ambivalent world (Burnham 1986, 154).

In discussing committed relativism, Perry (1981) describes the dominant epistemological view in this stage as *reflective,* perhaps because commitments involve a "dialectical logic," a paradoxical necessity to be both "wholehearted and tentative" (96).[2] Citing the work of

Basseches (1978) and Fowler (1978), Perry describes the central role of dialectical thought in the higher ranges of intellectual development; it simultaneously maintains its coherence and vision of meaning while being conscious that it can be contradicted or modified. An idea or belief is just a resting place in the quest for Truth. It is the importance that the learner gives to the *process* of this quest, and not the Truth itself, that marks him or her as intellectually mature.

As I have described in other studies (Anson 1986b; Sirc and Anson 1985), the most mature student writers are not only unafraid of tentativeness, welcoming it during the writing process, but seem to know that eventually, with enough reflection, they will settle on a particular position or view, find an appropriate rhetorical stance, and reach decisions about their text's structure, style, and so on. When they discuss their writing, they often talk about *possible* areas for further exploration, pinpointing what else they need to think about fully before they can settle on a clear direction for their essay. For this reason, reflective writers are very good at invention and revision, and their composing process reveals the weighing of alternatives, the intellectual byroads that come from exploring one's way to resolution. They are also excellent participants in collaborative activities such as peer-revision conferences where, as Burnham (1986, 157) points out, personal beliefs must be clarified and elaborated and integrated into the emerging values and beliefs of the classroom community (see also Doe 1985).

In contrast to relativists, then, reflective writers eventually find stability and resolution in the chaos of diversity, by analyzing alternatives in the content and structure of their writing. These conclusions must remain to some degree tentative, since the acknowledged relativism of the world allows for their modification. But even in grappling with the most difficult moral and intellectual questions, reflective writers assume that some perspectives are more logical, sensible, and well supported than others. This is writing we are familiar with as professionals — balanced, informed, reasoned. In describing the characteristics of reflective prose, Slattery offers the example of a student writing about terrorism. After considering several remedies to this problem (increased security, increased intelligence, military retaliation, etc.), the student eventually commits himself to a personal but well-reasoned solution (a combination of actions), but quite strongly rules out military retaliation because of its high risks and its way of furthering anti-U.S. sentiment. Unlike the relativist, who might end up saying that the best solution is a matter of personal preference, here the student is willing to take a stand; but unlike the dualist, whose stand is uninformed and dogmatic, here the writer's commitment to an opinion is based on a process of analysis and balanced thought.

Correlation of the Perry scheme with characteristics of student writing must remain tentative and generalized. We know very little, for example, about how the traits of dualistic, relativistic, or reflective writers appear in different sorts of texts (such as exploratory journals or personal narratives) beyond the rather obvious genre of argument. We must also beware not to let the scheme gloss over individual differences in students' development, especially in light of recent work on gender differences (see Gilligan 1982; Belenky et al. 1986). Nevertheless, the Perry scheme is theoretically rich enough to provide a useful lens for analyzing teachers' response styles.

Response Styles and Ways of Knowing: An Exploratory Study

The power of Perry's scheme lies partly in its way of explaining and taxonomizing what teachers see constantly in the work of their students and have known tacitly all along. When most teachers learn of the scheme, they immediately recognize the dualistic, relativistic, or reflective tendencies in their own students' writing and become excited about the scheme's developmental potential (see Bizzell 1984, 450–51). In essence, the scheme charts the intellectual transition away from the accumulation of "right answers" and toward the reflective worldview inculcated by a liberal education, which is an overarching goal of college teaching.

If the scheme is an adequate reflection of the cultural indoctrination into certain "ways of knowing" encouraged by college education, then it would seem to hold much promise for teachers of writing, who hope to move students toward the epistemological values associated with its most mature stages.[3] As Perry puts it, the educated person takes on a worldview that welcomes thinking about one's own thoughts, examining one's own assumptions, and comparing these with the thoughts or assumptions of other people (1968, 39). The academy is so saturated with these epistemological characteristics that only the most dogmatic and educationally sterile teacher would disagree with them in principle.

Accordingly, I set out to study teachers' responses to student essays that clearly reflected, in their content, the different epistemological assumptions categorized in Perry's scheme.[4] In particular, I was interested in discovering what tacit effects (if any) the manifestation of these frameworks in the content of students' writing would have on teachers' styles of assessment and response. Assuming that the scheme is a fairly "coherent framework through which students give meaning to their educational experience" (Perry 1981, 77), we might expect teachers to be at least subconsciously influenced in their judgments of content reflecting one or another generalized epistemological position. Bringing such assumptions to conscious attention could help teachers more systematically to encourage students' intellectual development through appropriate response styles.

Collecting a Writing Sample

For the writers in this study, I chose students enrolled in a special summer program at a large midwestern university. The program was designed to help high-risk, mostly minority students from inner cities to prepare for freshman-level college work. The students' admission to the university was contingent on their successful completion of this intensive, eight-week summer program, in which they took several introductory courses and were involved in career-planning sessions, study workshops, and other extracurricular activities designed to acquaint them with university life.

One of these courses was a precollege introduction to composition, where students learned about the writing process by drafting and revising several freshman-level assignments and by developing an understanding of the basic concepts they would be working with in the fall: sensitivity to audience, methods of organization, modes of argument or development, and so on. Most of these students had performed poorly as writers in high school and had weak control of basic sentence-level skills. As a whole, however, the group represented a range of basic writing abilities, from those who were almost ready to enter a standard freshman composition course in the fall to those who would need further basic writing instruction and additional tutorial help throughout their first year or two of college.

Given the nature of this student population, I imagined that teachers would understand the need to encourage more flexible models of intellectual exploration in the students' analysis of topics for writing. As Bizzell (1986) argues, "basic writers, upon entering the academic community, are being asked to learn a new dialect and new discourse conventions, but the outcome of such learning is the acquisition of a whole new worldview" (297). I hoped that by using a population of basic writers for my corpus, I could see more clearly how teachers encourage the acquisition of this worldview through their responses.

The Writing Task

In searching for an appropriate writing task, I was drawn to the work of several researchers actively extending Perry's ideas into new areas of student learning and career development. The most attractive instrument was an essay task developed by Widick and Knefelkamp (n.d.). I was worried about intruding on the natural classroom context by asking teachers to administer a writing assignment unrelated to the course. For this reason, I slightly modified the original into the following assignment:

> Please write a brief essay on the following topic:
>
> Think of a time when you had to make a decision about something of major importance to you, or the last time you had to choose between some significant alternatives. In your essay, describe the situation and your decision in as much detail as possible. Some things you might want to consider in writing your essay are how you felt about having to make the decision, what factors influenced your decision, and how you felt after you made the decision.
>
> Before writing the essay, think carefully about the topic and try to plan what you are going to say. Then try to write a couple of pages in response to the topic. You may make any changes you wish on your draft.

Eight teachers in the summer program administered this task in their classes of between ten and fifteen students, yielding a sample of ninety-one essays. These were copied and returned so the teachers could use them in their instruction.

Rating the Essays

After asking the volunteer teachers to administer this assignment, I developed *a priori* criteria for classifying the essays, based on Perry's original descriptors (see appendix). In specifying the criteria, I focused mainly on the characteristics that might appear in the essays themselves — perhaps as a reflection of underlying epistemological assumptions, but not necessarily the predictable outcome of a writer who is always seeing the world in exactly the same way.[5]

To rate the essays, I and two other teachers of writing at the same university participated in a norming session. We began the session by discussing Perry's scheme, by examining the writing task and my criteria for classifying the responses into the three categories, and by working through several trial readings until we had normed our judgments. We then independently sorted the essays into the three categories.

Our initial ratings yielded an agreement of 86%; any essays without a unanimous rating were discarded.[6] We then rank-ordered the essays from most to least representative within the three pools, and selected the essays in the top 10% of each of our pools for an additional rank-ordering. From these final pools, I chose the six essays (two in each category) with the highest combined scores. One essay in each category appears verbatim in the appendix (p. 364).

Choosing the Teacher-Responders

Sixteen moderately experienced teachers of writing at the university, all of whom were thoroughly familiar with the college preparatory program and had taught basic writing or freshman composition for three or more years, volunteered for the study.

The participants were told they would be reading papers by basic writers and then responding to or assessing these papers in a way as consistent as possible with their own typical methods and behaviors in a basic writing classroom. Admitting the artificiality of the procedure — divorced as it was from the context of a real classroom with real knowledge of the student, task, and previous instruction — I asked the teachers to imagine that they had given the assignment at the beginning of the term, before getting to know the students well or providing much instruction.

For some participants, I also experimented with a "responding-aloud" method: using the same directions, I asked the teachers to speak into a tape recorder, as discussed in the literature on alternative methods of responding to writing (see Hunt 1975; Klammer 1973; Johnston 1983). I asked the teachers to imagine that each student would be listening to the tape as a way of reviewing his or her paper after it was returned.

To avoid the possibility that some teachers might alter their usual response styles because they knew that their comments would be analyzed, I explained that I was studying the characteristics of basic writers' prose by looking at what teachers said to them about their writing. After the study, I also collected samples of writing (with commentary) from all the teachers' actual classes and analyzed their responses against those they had given in the study. In all cases, the teachers simply did more thoroughly in the study exactly what they did in their classes; there was no change in the nature of their response styles.

Pseudonyms were written at the top of each essay so teachers could refer to the students by their first names if they wished.

Toward a Typology of Response Styles: Some Results

Before conducting this study, I imagined that the volunteer teachers would shift their response styles across the three categories of essays, tacitly "matching" the focus and content of their comments to the different epistemological assumptions reflected in the content of the students' writing — a process described and supported by several educational theorists (e.g., Hunt 1970).

As I read their comments, however, I was surprised to discover that there were very few differences in the style of each teacher's responses across the six essays; the teachers focused on the same concerns, in the same way, regardless of the differences reflected in the essays. These consistent response styles, on the other hand, varied greatly across the group of teachers, with some teachers using radically different styles than others. Lacking any tangible evidence of teachers' adjustments to differences in the essays themselves, I was then compelled to make sense of the varieties of response styles across the entire group of volunteers.

As I analyzed the specific features of the responses, they began falling into patterns. Just as the students' essays seemed to represent different stages of intellectual development, so the teachers appeared to have different visions of classroom writing and of learning to write. The epistemological assumptions in Perry's scheme, which I had used as a framework for analyzing students' responses to the essay-writing task, now returned in force as I began to map consistent characteristics in the teachers' responses. These characteristics, like those of students' writing, would appear to reflect different assumptions about the world of knowledge and about learning to write.

For economy, these general tendencies can be described as categories of response styles. While I remain suspicious of taxonomizing and oversimplifying what is a complicated network of values, beliefs, and processes in teachers' ways of interacting with their students (Anson 1988), such categorical distinctions can be seen as places along a continuum of instructional development. I will gloss these distinctions with reference to the responses of several teachers who participated in the study, showing different patterns in the teachers' assumptions about writing and learning.

Dualistic Responders

The majority of teachers — about three-fourths — used response styles that focused almost entirely on the surface features of the students' texts, and did so consistently, in spite of the differences in the essays' contents. The tone of the responses implied that there were standards for correct and incorrect ways to complete the assignment, and that a teacher's job was to act as a judge by applying these standards to the student's writing. Few alternatives for revision were suggested, and very little was said about the student's rhetorical decisions or composing processes. On the whole, the student's intentions or meaning were ignored.

Mr. Jones, whose responses are typical for this group, wrote these comments on Bobby's essay (Figure 1). At the end of the essay, Mr. Jones then wrote:

> There are some serious problems with this paper. For one thing it is far too short, and the ideas in it, if any, are at the moment barely articulated. All you have done is merely tell us what happened, in the starkest outline. Why? If this event was an important and educative one for you, surely you should have written on it some more? One obvious reason why you did not write more, is that you have very serious deficiencies in your knowledge of the mechanics of writing. I am referring here to *tense, spelling, punctuation,* and *sentence structure.* I strongly recommend that you see me *immediately* about your problems.

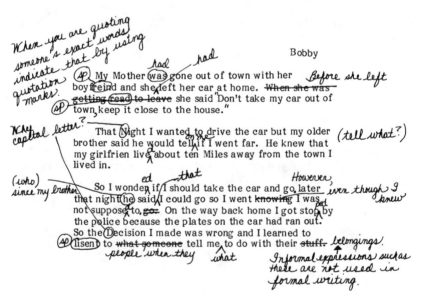

Figure 1. Mr. Jones's Response to Bobby

Interpreted in relation to Bobby's essay and its placement along Perry's scheme, the characteristics of this teacher's response are revealing. Bobby's essay is so classically dualistic in the subjugation of its persona to a recognized authority that even teachers wholly preoccupied with the brevity of the essay would (I thought) encourage Bobby to think more deeply about his experience — for example, the tensions between his own urges, his brother's authority, and the irony of his mother's irresponsibility in not renewing her license plates.[7]

Imagine, then, Bobby's experience in reading Mr. Jones's comments. Mr. Jones tells Bobby, in so many words, that he hasn't done the essay correctly. He admonishes Bobby for not writing more by linking the essay's brevity to Bobby's lack of control over surface mechanics and grammar. Clearly, Mr. Jones is more concerned with the formal features of Bobby's writing than with Bobby's experience, or with ways of responding to Bobby so that he can see more potential in his experience for elaborating his essay. In his predominant focus on Bobby's grammatical problems, Mr. Jones essentially suggests a view of learning, thinking, and writing that is dualistic.

For Bobby, writing more means risking more, since he is unsure about what's right and wrong in the essay. The next time around, if he takes the risk, he may well be penalized for making more errors. Forced to choose between an undesirable brevity or the outright penalty of error, Bobby may opt to continue writing less in the hope that eventually more of what he does write will be written correctly (see Shaughnessy 1977). Most importantly, his dualistic way of seeing the world is being reinforced and encouraged. Since he will continue to believe there is a right and wrong way to produce an essay, and since experiments end in futility and further error, Bobby will increase his fluency slowly and painstakingly, caught endlessly in a cycle of trial and error from which he can't escape.

Karen's essay, on the other hand, reveals a different sort of writer. In discussing a recent conflict of interest, her essay shows a more reflective position: she has made a commitment to her religion and can analyze her transgression (missing an important meeting in the college prep program) in relation to this commitment. Although she's still to some degree uncertain about the outcome, she can reflect on her decision in a world that doesn't often provide ready answers. As a basic writer, Karen may have produced such an essay by chance; nonetheless, as a text, it reveals patterns of thinking that are clearly more intellectually mature than Bobby's.

On Karen's essay, Mr. Jones made the comments seen in Figure 2.

346   Chris M. Anson

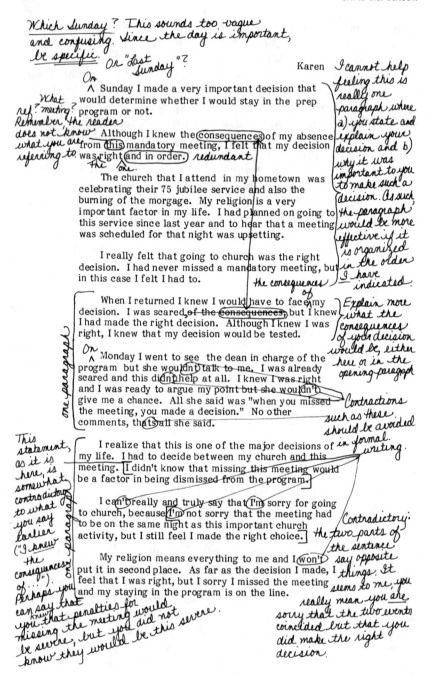

Which Sunday? This sounds too vague and confusing. Since the day is important, be specific. Or "last Sunday"?

Karen   *I cannot help feeling this is really one paragraph where a) you state and explain your decision and b) why it was important to you to make such a decision. As such, the paragraph would be more effective if it is organized in the order I have indicated.*

On
^ Sunday I made a very important decision that would determine whether I would stay in the prep program or not. *What meeting? rel? Remember, the reader does not know what you are referring to.* Although I knew the consequences of my absence from this mandatory meeting, I felt that my decision was right and in order. *redundant — the one.*

The church that I attend in my hometown was celebrating their 75 jubilee service and also the burning of the morgage. My religion is a very important factor in my life. I had planned on going to this service since last year and to hear that a meeting was scheduled for that night was upsetting.

I really felt that going to church was the right decision. I had never missed a mandatory meeting, but in this case I felt I had to. *the consequences of*

When I returned I knew I would have to face my decision. I was scared of the consequences, but I knew I had made the right decision. Although I knew I was right, I knew that my decision would be tested. *Explain more what the consequences of your decision would be, either here or in the opening paragraph*

On
^ Monday I went to see the dean in charge of the program but she wouldn't talk to me. I was already scared and this didn't help at all. I knew I was right and I was ready to argue my point but she wouldn't give me a chance. All she said was "when you missed the meeting, you made a decision." No other comments, that's all she said. *Contractions such as these should be avoided in formal writing.*

one paragraph

I realize that this is one of the major decisions of my life. I had to decide between my church and this meeting. I didn't know that missing this meeting would be a factor in being dismissed from the program.

This statement, as it is here, is somewhat contradictory to what you say earlier ("I knew the consequences of..."). Perhaps you can say that you knew that penalties for missing the meeting would be severe, but you did not know they would be this severe.

I can't really and truly say that I'm sorry for going to church, because I'm not sorry that the meeting had to be on the same night as this important church activity, but I still feel I made the right choice. *Contradictory: the two parts of the sentence say opposite things. It seems to me, you really mean you are sorry that the two events coincided but that you did make the right decision.*

My religion means everything to me and I won't put it in second place. As far as the decision I made, I feel that I was right, but I sorry I missed the meeting and my staying in the program is on the line.

Figure 2. Mr. Jones's Response to Karen

At the bottom of the paper, Mr. Jones then wrote:

> Overall, the paper shows sensitivity and understanding. What the
> paper does not have is a coherent paragraph organization and
> composition. This is unfortunate because it mars the effectiveness
> of what has been for you clearly a painful but educative experience.
> Try to organize your thoughts in terms of paragraphs that explore
> and describe *one* thought at a time. It would also have helped if
> you had established a "theme" (simply an overall controlling
> idea) for the paper in the opening paragraph. The paper also has
> an awkward, contradictory and repetitive sentence. You make a
> free use of contractions that are much too casual and not used in
> formal writing, you have clauses in the same sentences that
> contradict each other, and you make the same statement several
> times without adding anything substantial to what you have
> already said ("I knew I had made the right decision" is an
> example). So, overall I would say, in future exercise more caution
> in planning your paper and more control in writing clearer, more
> precise and effective sentences.

Given Karen's way of seeing the world, as this is reflected in her essay, Mr. Jones's comments don't strike us in quite the same way as do his comments to Bobby. After all, Karen may interpret these comments through a different epistemological lens than Bobby, and the force of Mr. Jones's focus on correctness seems somehow less threatening. What stands out here is Mr. Jones's cursory *response* to Karen's writing as a reflection of a human being coming to terms with her commitments. The *meaning* of Karen's text, within the dualistic response style, suddenly fades from view, and the assignment becomes a kind of rhetorical trick simply to get Karen to reveal her practices in paragraph structuring and adherence to the conventions of "formal" discourse. Whatever beliefs Karen has developed about the world, she may begin to think that the written language, in the rigidity implied by Mr. Jones's constraints on organization and development, is not the medium through which to explore them.

The tendency to fall into a dualistic response style was just as evident in the tape-recorded mode as in the written mode of response, in spite of the more personal and direct features of the spoken voice. Mr. Beyer, for example, provided taped responses very much like those of Mr. Jones's written comments. After making a few remarks about the brevity of Bobby's essay ("The assignment was to go over two pages and what you've written barely fills one page in very large handwriting"), Mr. Beyer then focuses mainly on what he calls the "form" of the essay:

> You write the way you speak, probably, but if you look at the
> last sentence, let me read it to you: "So the decision I made was
> wrong" — that's one sentence — "and I learned to listen to what

someone tell me to do with their stuff." The first part of that
sentence — "so the decision I made was wrong" — is an OK
sentence that can just stay like that. But the second part — "I
learned to listen" — and it should be the infinitive form, so "I
learned to listen" spelled l-i-s-t-e-n, no "t" in the end (this may
just be a typo) — "to what someone tell me to do." Someone is
one person, and this is in the present tense, and therefore, in
written English, this has to read, "what someone *tells* me to do,"
and then it's a little problematic to say "they" if you're talking
about one person, and therefore I suggest you write "what
someone tells me to do with her or his stuff," instead of the
"their." There are some other problems of that kind in your essay;
if you can't pick them out on your own, please come and see me,
because I don't want to go through the whole essay correcting
every little thing, because I do think that some of the things you
can pick out yourself. [Tape recorder is clicked off; then clicked
on again.] And, of course, not everything is wrong in your essay.

In a typically dualistic way, Mr. Beyer chooses to focus on those
concerns that can be objectively assessed as right or wrong; as a result,
the tone of his comments is highly authoritative and "teacherly." He
spends much of his response discussing Bobby's last sentence, explaining the problems in subject-verb agreement and pronoun reference
(leading, ironically, to a rather awkward revision). Then, in an especially
revealing remark tagged on at the end of his commentary, he reminds
Bobby that there is still a glimmer of hope: It's possible, with enough
perseverance, to learn how to produce an essay the *right* way.

It is important to recognize that dualistic teachers are not necessarily
dualists by any moral or intellectual measures, nor are they unconcerned
about their students' development. When they walk into a writing
class or go home to read student papers, however, it is likely that *they
assume a dualistic perspective toward learning to write.* Later, I'll return
to this tendency as part of a developmental pattern in teachers' own
pedagogy, and suggest some ways of helping them to acquire more
intellectually productive models of writing.

Relativistic Responders

A much smaller group of teachers provided a strikingly different kind
of response to the six sample essays. Typically, they wrote little or
nothing in the margins of the student's paper — no correction symbols,
no circled spelling errors, no comments about paragraph structure or
apostrophes. Their responses were written modestly at the end of the
essays, as if textually unattached to them. Addressing the students in
a much more casual and unplanned style than the dualistic responders,
their comments resembled letters or short notes. Once again, these

teachers' response styles did not vary across the three categories of essays, though their language seemed slightly more sophisticated for the more mature writers. In contrast to dualistic responders, these teachers seemed entirely unconcerned with giving the students anything more than a casual reaction, as if this is the only kind of response that can have any validity in a world where judgment is always in the eye of the beholder. In this style, very little is imposed on the student; the text seems "owned" by the writer and the teacher stands outside it, as if on the edges of someone's property, unwilling to trespass but able to enjoy or respectfully question. Even the most minimal *textual* preferences — words, structures, details — seem too appropriative to venture.

Ms. Evans's comments on Bobby's essay are typical of this group:

> Bobby, you certainly had a hard teacher. Did you get a ticket? What happened when Mom came home? Did your brother snitch on you? What happened to you? This kind of thing eventually happens to all of us, but what did you do? How angry was your mother? I'll bet she was hot when she got home, or was she calm and very understanding because she knows how important it is to be with someone you care for. If you had to do it all over again, would you? Tell the truth.

While it's clear what Ms. Evans is up to in this response — encouraging Bobby to be more fluent by asking him heuristic sorts of questions — the existence and purpose of the text itself have almost faded from view. In contrast to Mr. Jones and Mr. Beyer, Ms. Evans focuses her response entirely on what Halliday (1975) calls the "ideational" function of writing, as opposed to the manifestation of this in a specific text. While her response implies a sort of readerly preference for more information, it is rendered in a seemingly relativistic way, as if, finally, such preferences or any other judgments on the text are idiosyncratic and personal. For Bobby's stage of intellectual development, on the other hand, such a response style would seem appropriate, since his lack of fluency may be tied to his fear of error.

Tony's essay (see appendix) portrays a writer who has no lack of fluency, though he makes frequent surface errors. In a typically relativistic way, Tony describes his inability to make up his mind which of two girlfriends he wanted to "keep." Beneath its attempted humor, the essay reveals a young man who, in this instance, floats in a sea of indecision, weighing the "advantages and disadvantages" of each girlfriend without making a commitment, choosing instead to let fate sort out the details of his life. In a characteristically relativistic way, Tony ends his essay without a sense of closure or resolution.

In responding to Tony, Ms. Evans once again avoids focusing on the text, instead providing the idiosyncratic response of a single reader:

> Well, Romeo, you are fortunate things turned out as well as they did! What happened later? I'm sure the women were upset — and did you really stop seeing them? I just imagine you tried to go on with your same old story. How did things finally turn out? Are you still friends?

Seen through the lens of relativism, Ms. Evans's response style now takes on a different quality — a set of opinions or reactions that, to use Perry's words again, are "related to nothing whatever... except to the person who holds [them]" (1981, 85). What distinguishes the relativistic from the dualistic response is not so much the *existence* of preferences for each type of reader but how (or whether) those preferences are revealed to the writer. The relativistic teacher seems to avoid couching her preferences in the language of determinacy. Perhaps for this reason, teachers using this style provided no options for revision, which would imply a readerly preference or some directive for the student to follow. Instead, the writer must *infer* new directions for the essay from the teacher's personal response. In Tony's case, for example, Ms. Evans's response implies the need for closure; but from the perspective of the relativist writer, this may seem like nothing more than a reaction.

Once again, the taped responses in this category showed no differences from those in the written mode. Mr. Young, for example, said this to Karen:

> Hi, Karen. You had a, you had a really tough decision here. I kept thinking, you know, as I read through this, um, what Dean [_____] will do, so it's kind of now switched, with the decision in her hands and not in, and no longer in yours. I know she's not all that tough inside as she seems on the outside; I think she wants people in the program to, you know, to think of this as a kind of bootcamp, but she's really very supportive. I bet if you just talk to her and explain, or, you could just send this paper to her, though that might also seem kind of artificial. Religion versus education, that's a tough issue. [Continues for another minute or two, focusing on the dean of the program.]

In contrast to dualistic responses, such comments privilege the *meaning* the student is conveying — a tendency that, given recent theories of response (e.g., Hunt 1986) would seem preferable to error-hunting, in spite of the absence of any reference to the text as the medium through which this meaning is conveyed. Still, many practitioners would argue that a relativism so extreme that it lets the text fade entirely from view may simply encourage some students to continue wallowing in the slough of indecision, or reinforce a model of writing that doesn't privilege careful planning, attention to rhetorical and linguistic choices, and thorough revision.

Reflective Responders

Finally, another small group of teachers seemed neither dualistic nor relativistic in their responses. Instead, their comments emphasized a range of concerns for each student — ideas, textual decisions, personal reactions — which wove in and out of their commentary. Unlike the relativistic responders, who gave no options for revision, these teachers often ventured into some further possibilities for the papers. Unlike the dualistic responses, however, their comments were never put dictatorially or appropriatively; they frequently used phrases like, "maybe you could think about . . . ," "what if you . . . ," and "how about seeing if there's a way to . . . ." Furthermore, these teachers often did express preferences for certain options, but made it clear that they were doing so as *representative* readers — members of the classroom and the wider social community. Typically, the comments also implied that the papers were in-process drafts or that, even if they were final texts, they could become vehicles for what Beach (this volume) calls "predicted revisions," and thus serve as tools for further learning.

In talking to Bobby on a cassette tape, for example, Mr. Kane gave the following commentary:

> Hi, Bobby. The first thing that strikes me before I even read your story is that it's very short. I don't really like to compare one student's work with other students' work, but it's the shortest one I've seen so far. So right away, I'm wondering if it's short for a good reason, or is it short because you just couldn't think of things to say. It's possible for a piece of writing that's very short to be very good. Poetry is that way, certainly. On the other hand, the more you put in, the more chances are that your reader is going to be able to get into the story. Stories generally — and this essay is a story — are fairly well-detailed, and one of the reasons is that the reader wants to experience the event in some way. If you just keep it short and don't put in many details then we never really get into your story at all.

At this point Mr. Kane reads through Bobby's essay on the tape, adding comments and predictions along the way about what he's experiencing. He then spends another four or five minutes outlining some possibilities for Bobby to consider in expanding the essay and adding details. Note in the following excerpt how certain readerly, personal preferences (for humor, detail, etc.) are woven into the fabric of a reflective response style, which never actually "takes over" Bobby's text and makes decisions for him, but nevertheless provides him with some options. The thinking and revising will then be up to Bobby, as he "learns" his way to an improved text. Note also how the *text* stands at the center of the commentary, as the medium through which Mr. Kane responds to Bobby's *meaning:*

> It has the potential to be a good story. I think this could be kind of a funny story in some ways. I mean, it's obviously not a big tragic sort of event but it was probably pretty exciting when it happened, right? Especially when the police stopped you and your mother got home and found out what happened. I imagine that must have been very exciting too. . . . Maybe you could think more about the events that happened and break them down into more, smaller and smaller events, and describe more, explain more. . . . Maybe just some more details so we understand more about what kind of person your mother is; do you always disobey her without getting punished, or is she the kind that won't let you get away with much? So if we know that, then we would know how big a decision you had to make there. . . . Now, you could also develop that whole [middle] part there, maybe with some dialogue — describe your older brother a bit, describe the circumstances here? Were you watching TV together? Sitting on the front porch? What time of year was it? What exactly did your brother say, as best as you can remember? What did you reply to him? [Continues for 150 words.]

What we see in Mr. Kane's response, then, is a teacher who models a reflective style of thinking — not simply about the events or ideas surrounding Bobby's essay, but the way these are being or might be rendered in the text itself. It is an intellectual, mature, balanced style, one that neither dogmatically insists on one set of concerns nor abandons the need to work on and improve the text; a style that neither ignores meaning in favor of criticizing surface mechanics nor forgets the text in an effort to interact with *Bobby* through his writing.

The tendency of reflective responses to place more responsibility on the writer was clear, not just in the style or form of the response, but in its focus on content. In challenging the writers to rethink their essays, the reflective responders also seemed to challenge the students to rethink their ways of viewing the world, to be both "wholehearted and tentative," to make decisions but to do so undogmatically, through careful exploration. Note how Ms. Song, another participant in the study, encourages Tony to think about the underlying attitudes he reveals in his essay about his relationship with the two women:

> At the very end, I guess some readers might like to know a little bit more, because I find it hard to believe that they forgave you that easily, and that things ended so smoothly. Maybe you could add a little bit there about the long-term outcome — although I suppose it is one logical place to end the paper. I think this was a good choice for you to write about; it's certainly an interesting story, a kind of natural drama that everyone can identify with. One problem you might have here is that you don't really work too hard at getting the reader on your side, and I think that may be a problem here because what you do might be seen as being dishonest; you might be seen as using these two girls. So you might want to guard against people thinking of you as some sort of casual playboy, who just toys around with these girls' feelings. I believe that can't be the case, because they both agree to be your friends; but maybe there's something you could include that showed you had genuine feelings for each of them. But think a bit about that, and then decide if you want to change it or add to it.

While Ms. Song's and Mr. Beyer's comments show how radically teachers' response styles may differ, it is important to point out that there were at least some universally recognized problems in the six essays — for example, the extreme brevity of Bobby's paper. At issue here is not necessarily the *focus* of teachers' responses, but how each teacher's particular model of writing and learning is translated into his or her response style. Unlike dualistic or relativistic responders, those with a reflective style provided comments that were simultaneously tentative and goal-driven; their tentativeness seemed to originate in their attempt to weigh options, toss the responsibility for making decisions back to the writer, and offer possibilities for a potentially better text. At the same time, these responders' sense that reaching the goal of a better text was not only possible, but desirable, did not seem aimed toward writing "the" perfect text (as if one existed); instead, they seemed to imply that the main goal of striving toward improvement was to further the writer's learning process. This simultaneous support and challenge has been at the heart of several scholars' work with the Perry scheme and other theories of intellectual development (see, for example, Sanford 1966; Slattery 1986; Widick and Simpson 1978).

In tone, the few reflective teachers in the study tended to be more casual than formal, as if rhetorically sitting next to the writer, collaborating, suggesting, guiding, modeling. While they did write marginal comments, these were generally sparse and almost always raised questions that seemed geared toward rethinking certain decisions, or praised the writer for an especially effective choice (e.g., "That's a great image!" for Tony's line, "I looked up at her and I almost chocked on my Big Mac"; most of the dualistic responses, in contrast, criticized this line for the misspelling of "choked"). Finally, reflective responses, perhaps because they saw each paper in the context of the writer's individual struggles as these were apparent in the text, more readily adapted their styles to each student's particular problems.

Toward Change: Ideology and Response

Mindy, the young college freshman in the opening transcription of this chapter, was not only describing her own dualistic attitudes toward writing; she was also revealing the source of those attitudes in the instructional approaches of her high-school teachers. Even young children often see their teachers as dictators, controlling the form and content of students' writing instead of acting as facilitators in their development (Black and Martin 1982). When we think of correlating "ways of knowing" with "ways of writing," then, we must not focus on students alone but on the symbiotic relationships they have had with teachers, and how these relationships have contributed to the development of their beliefs.

Like learning to write, responding well to students' texts isn't a matter of gaining simple expertise in the "mechanics" of teaching writing. What a teacher says to a student about writing is saturated with the teacher's values, beliefs, and models of learning. Just as students' awareness of such rhetorical concepts as audience, purpose, and persona lead them to think in more mature ways about their writing, so must teachers' own behaviors in the classroom be affected by their awareness of student development and intellectual style, their knowledge of educational theory and research, or their exposure to a variety of instructional modes and techniques.

Although I began this study by using Perry's work as a template for thinking about response to writing, my conclusions move well beyond the Perry scheme itself and into the wider and more varied terrain of instructional ideology. While not restricted entirely to matters of pedagogy, instructional ideologies generally refer to the integrated patterns of ideas or beliefs that inform teachers' decisions — what sort of syllabus they design or which textbook they choose, what kinds of assignments they require, how they respond to students and their work, even how they physically arrange the tables and chairs in their classrooms, and where they place themselves in relation to their students (see Bernier 1981).

The relationship between teachers' ideologies and their behaviors in the writing class — including, perhaps most importantly, their responses to students' writing — has not been explored very fully in the field. However, several theorists have proposed general models of ideology to explain the varied behaviors of writing teachers (see Berlin 1988; Diamond 1979; Dowst 1980; Fulkerson 1979; Kroll 1980; Mosenthal 1983; Root 1980). Kroll, for example, suggests two such models that correspond quite closely to the dualistic and relativistic response styles; these he calls the "interventionist" and the "maturationist." Interventionists focus on standard usage, sentence and paragraph structure, and other written conventions. Their instruction emphasizes the student's lack of basic skills and is imposed from above, as an "environmental" influence on the student's behavior. Maturationists, on the other hand, believe that students' growth and development is natural. Instruction centers on the experiences and emotions of the student and is aimed at fostering personal growth. The maturationist evaluates writing in terms of its context, the writer's intentions, past performance, and effort. Little is imposed on the writer from above; free expression and the building of confidence are the main goals. For Kroll, a more balanced position — perhaps akin to the reflective style — privileges neither extreme but makes the best use of each approach. The reality of his models has also been supported by empirical research on teachers' attitudes (see Gere, Schuessler, and Abbott 1984).

Although schemes of instructional ideology vary considerably, as do the research methods that inform them, they all strongly suggest that teachers' underlying beliefs about why, what, and how students should write are powerful determinants of their actual behaviors — even in the midst of external pressures such as curricular mandates. But while categories of instructional ideology may be useful as a way to describe general systems of belief that inform practice, they don't say much about how one *moves* from one belief system to another. What causes teachers to modify their belief systems and begin behaving differently in the classroom? How and why do teachers' response styles change over time?

The present study, of course, did not seek to understand the *source* of the teachers' response styles, nor the development of their styles over time, nor even the rich interactions that occur between teachers and students in the fuller context of instruction; the analytical method was entirely static, focusing on textual artifacts (essays and responses) as possible reflections of various attitudes and ways of knowing. It may have been the case, for example, that the teachers imagined the context of this writing task differently, some thinking of it as a rather casual short assignment and others as an essay of considerable importance. Nonetheless, the data at least suggest the power of ideological beliefs by the consistency with which teachers responded to essays representing different ways of viewing the world. As Louise Wetherbee Phelps demonstrates in this volume, teachers appear to follow their own developmental pattern with respect to their classroom practices. Perhaps, then, the three types of response I have identified are really positions along a continuum of development, from the rigidly dualistic style to the balanced, mature, reflective style. And perhaps this continuum of development is related to the depth of a teacher's explorations into the practice and teaching of composition.

The current/traditional paradigm of writing instruction, with its dominant focus on the objective characteristics of written products, clearly manifests itself in a dualistic response style which has historical antecedents — both in the field of writing instruction and in most teachers' prior exposure, as students themselves, to patterns which then become powerful models in the absence of any substantive training or instructional development. Novice teachers of writing, who are unsure of their own expertise and authority, may be especially vulnerable to this dualism. Threatened by the prospect of admitting to students that they can't say with certainty what makes writing "good" — that "good" and "bad" are actually relative and often subjective concepts — these teachers cling desperately to what they do know and can impose objectively as standards for assessment: the rules of punctuation, grammar, spelling, and other rudimentary and skill-centered concerns such as thesis statements and topic sentences.

For the dualistic teacher, response is teacher-based and egocentric, a way of displaying intellectual prowess, a way of asserting authority. As Mina Shaughnessy (1976) so elegantly put it, such teachers at first see their role as the "guardians of the tower," protecting the academy from the intrusion of students who don't seem to belong to the community of learners. Once the teacher accepts, sometimes reluctantly, the bald fact that he must somehow reach his students, he takes on the role of "converting the natives," filling empty vessels with truths — usually the mechanics of the sentence, paragraph, and essay.

It is only when the teacher recognizes that these rules and formulas don't work — that the "flawless schemes for achieving order and grammaticality" are instructionally inadequate — that she is pushed toward what Shaughnessy calls "sounding the depths": carefully observing her students (and herself) to seek a deeper understanding of writing and how it is learned. When teachers question the current/

traditional paradigm, they often reject entirely (and sometimes with feelings of guilt or disgust) the dualistic beliefs they had once accepted through blind indoctrination as practitioners. As their previously held truths crumble around them, they may fall into the critical nihilism reflected in relativistic responses. Suddenly challenged by the assumptions of contemporary writing theory, some new teachers may take on the same sort of abandoned relativism characteristic of students who have come to recognize that most questions don't have ready answers. Like their students, these teachers find themselves floating in a sea of indecision, searching, entertaining multiplicity without a sense of commitment. Not having explored many alternatives in their teaching, they feel tentative about standing behind a single approach. But challenged for the time being by new perspectives, they can no longer hold to the narrow line of dualism.

Rejecting the dualism of the current/traditional paradigm comes to many teachers as a kind of epiphany; I have heard both teacher-educators and teachers themselves speak of this stage as a "revelation," a "rebirth," an "awakening." Such a drastic upheaval of one's beliefs can't occur without considerable anxiety (some teachers even express dismay at thinking about all the past students they have "ruined" through their earlier approach). Too much challenge all at once, however, and some dualists panic: there is no support, no structure within which to make decisions. As Perry's scheme suggests, this overchallenge can lead to retreat (dogged adherence to the old ways) or even escape: many teachers in traditional literature departments become "threatened" by advances in writing theory to which they are nescient and "give up" teaching composition in the face of a newly developing and alien professional community.

Committing oneself to a particular approach, and simultaneously admitting that this approach may be challenged and even later abandoned, takes the kind of courage typical of mature teachers. At once both "wholehearted and tentative," such teachers are often uneasy questioning their own methods and beliefs and revising them accordingly, but eventually (like reflective writers) settle on an approach informed by careful, relativistic thought. The teacher who has come this far, as Shaughnessy (1976) describes in the final developmental position on her scheme for basic writing teachers, "must now make a decision that demands professional courage — the decision to remediate himself, to become a student of new disciplines and of his students themselves in order to perceive both their difficulties and their incipient excellence" (68). At the center of this "remediation," Shaughnessy suggests, is the need to

> pursue more rigorously the design of developmental models, basing our schemes less upon loose comparisons with children and more upon case studies and developmental research of the sort that produced William Perry's impressive study of the intellectual development of Harvard students. (68)

Equally important to the instructional contexts we create, I would suggest, is the need for more developmental research on teachers themselves. While certain methods of instruction appear to be more successful than others (see Hillocks 1986), we need to know much more about how those methods are understood and acted upon by teachers who interpret them through their own beliefs and attitudes. We must, then, ask ourselves not simply what *works* in teaching writing, but how teachers integrate this knowledge into their own ideology. What sort of "intellectual development" should we privilege at a teacherly level, and can we — or should we — be furthering the cause of this development by more fully invading or challenging teachers' personal constructs and systems of belief?

One way of confronting this issue is to place it in the context of the wider professional community that surrounds the teacher — either the immediate community of the teacher's institution, or the more general collective community with which the teacher has professional affinities. Although ideologies are usually seen as individual beliefs, expectations, or attitudes, they are also, at some level, part of a system of shared group values. For this reason, they are passed on from teacher to teacher, generation to generation, often becoming "value-impregnated" systems of thought that may be perceived as sacred (see Bernier and Williams 1973).

In the context of educational communities, there is great potential in more frequent but unthreatening interaction among teachers. The goal of such interaction should be to enhance our present "practitioner lore" of teaching (see North 1987) as part of an ongoing, collective investigation of who we are as teachers, what sort of "academy" we really represent, and how our own attitudes toward students (and their writing) shape their views of knowledge and, indeed, of the world.

Unfortunately, complacency mitigates the cooperation needed even among very experienced teachers, including, ironically, those among us who claim to have been "converted" and who see ourselves as members of the composition research community. Teachers often create idealized images of their own instruction (including their response styles) which suggest to them that they no longer need to participate in ongoing instructional development. These images are often quite at odds with their actual practices. In an informal study, one of my colleagues and I interviewed experienced teachers about their response styles; these teachers said they took a "balanced" view of error, that they praised their students as much as they criticized them, that they provided many options for revision, and that they preferred to respond more often in the role of "real readers" than teachers. When we later examined papers from these teachers' classes, however, we found that grammatical problems dominated their responses, they gave very little praise, they provided few options for revision, and their end comments were dictatorial, appropriative, and teacherly. Surprisingly, these teachers had created constructs of themselves which, unconsciously, they were not acting upon in practice.

For these reasons, even teachers fully exposed to composition theory and research need to come out of their educational closets and begin discussing their actual responses to their own students' writing — not responses to sample essays plucked from real instructional contexts, but responses informed by knowledge of the *students* themselves, including the instruction they are receiving, their past efforts, and other cues (verbal and nonverbal) that profile them as thinkers and learners. There is no domain more private, more unscrutinized among teachers than response to writing, perhaps because we are concerned about "intruding" on the academic privacies and freedoms of our colleagues. Often the only glimpse we get of how other teachers respond to students' writing comes from the occasional lost paper which floats from mailbox to mailbox with the question, "Is this your student?" If and when we read the teacher's response, we are sometimes amused, sometimes dismayed, sometimes relieved to see that someone else's beliefs and attitudes are like our own. But almost never are we disengaged.

In reflecting on how we respond to students' writing, we may find that even conclusions to which we are firmly committed in the field are to some degree still tentative. We may find ourselves shaken from our complacency, awakened to a more reflective intellectual attitude, neither stubbornly clinging to whatever methods or beliefs we hold nor abandoning the quest for truth to a kind of teacherly indifference, shrugging off our responsibilities as educators in the face of indeterminacy. Perhaps, in the process, we will be reminded that it is finally the quest for truth, and not the truth itself, that really matters.

Notes

1. Lunsford (1980), for example, has argued that we need help from psychologists "in designing studies that will probe the relationships among

self-image, cognitive style, perceptual system, and development of writing abilities. We, as teachers of basic as well as more skilled writers, need assistance in determining how best to foster cognitive and moral development, and what specific writing skills might be developed in that effort" (286).

2. Like Slattery, I find the term "reflective" more useful for discussing writing than "committed," which is more descriptive of the epistemological stance from which reflective writing emerges. To capture this feature of mature writing, I shall use the term "reflective" when referring to writing at this stage.

3. Perry is cautious about the educational implications of what he sees as an inherently prescriptive scheme. "Surely," he writes, "educators cannot coerce students into intellectual and ethical development, even if it were ethical to do so." The scheme's potential, he suggests, lies in its contribution "to the ability of planners and teachers to *communicate* with students who make meaning in different ways and to provide differential opportunities for their progress" (1981, 107). Part of that communication — and a crucial part at that — comes in the form of response to writing. The scheme, therefore, may tell us just as much about ourselves as teachers, as it can tell us about various stages of our students' development as learners.

4. The study reported here is entirely descriptive, preliminary, and exploratory, based on a small sample of texts and a few representative teachers of writing at a large midwestern university. Following Applebee's (1987) recent and well-taken complaint that our constant arguments over methodology are often a "distraction" from the real business of our research, I will not provide a "labored explanation that some authors feel it necessary to make in defense of the methods they have chosen" (117).

5. Bizzell (1984) has wisely argued that the gaps in our knowledge of the application of Perry's scheme to student writing mitigate its use as a theoretically sound system for classifying *students* as writers in any detailed way.

6. The high level of agreement in our rankings suggests that certain patterns of thinking reflected in students' writing *can* be perceived, once teachers are given the appropriate theoretical models and practice recognizing them in actual texts. This fact will become especially important in light of the results of this study.

7. The need to consider the relationship between the academic culture of our teacherly responses and the inner-city culture of Bobby's experience is critically important as well, but that's the subject of another essay.

References

Anson, C. M. 1983. Cognitive Style and the Writing Teacher. Paper presented at the annual convention of the National Council of Teachers of English, November, Denver.

Anson, C. M. 1984. *Composition and Communicative Intention: Exploring the Dimensions of Purpose in College Writing*. Doctoral dissertation, Indiana University, Bloomington. University Microfilms No. 85–06, 080.

Anson, C. M. 1986a. Reading, Writing, and Intention. *Reader: Essays in Reader-Oriented Theory, Criticism, and Pedagogy* 16:20–35.

Anson, C. M. 1986b. Talking about Writing: The Discourse of Commentary. Paper presented at the annual convention of the Conference on College Composition and Communication, March, New Orleans, La.

Anson, C. M. 1988. Toward a Multidimensional Model of Writing in the Academic Disciplines. In *Writing in Academic Disciplines*, edited by D. Jolliffe, 1–33. Norwood, N.J.: Ablex.

Applebee, A. N. 1987. Musings. *Research in the Teaching of English* 21:117–19.

Basseches, M. 1978. Beyond Closed-System Problem-Solving: A Study of Meta-Systematic Aspects of Mature Thought. Unpublished doctoral dissertation, Harvard University.

Beach, R. 1976. Self-Evaluation Strategies of Extensive Revisers. *College Composition and Communication* 27:160–64.

Belenky, M. F., B. M. Clinchy, N. R. Goldberger, and J. M. Tarule. 1986. *Women's Ways of Knowing: The Development of Self, Voice, and Mind.* New York: Basic Books.

Berlin, J. 1988. Rhetoric and Ideology in the Writing Class. *College English* 50:477–94.

Bernier, N. R. 1981. Beyond Instructional Context Identification — Some Thoughts for Extending the Analysis of Deliberate Education. In *Ethnography and Language in Educational Settings*, edited by J. L. Green and C. Wallat, 291–302. Norwood, N.J.: Ablex.

Bernier, N. R., and J. E. Williams. 1973. *Beyond Beliefs: Ideological Foundations of American Education.* Englewood Cliffs, N.J.: Prentice-Hall.

Bizzell, P. 1984. William Perry and Liberal Education. *College English* 46:447–54.

Bizzell, P. 1986. What Happens When Basic Writers Come to College? *College Composition and Communication* 37:294–301.

Black, J., and R. Martin. 1982. Children's Concepts about Writing at Home and School. In *New Inquiries in Reading Research and Instruction*, edited by J. A. Niles and L. A. Harris. Rochester, N.Y.: National Reading Conference.

Burnham, C. C. 1986. The Perry Scheme and the Teaching of Writing. *Rhetoric Review* 4:152–59.

Chickering, A. W., editor. 1981. *The Modern American College: Responding to the New Realities of Diverse Students and a Changing Society.* San Francisco: Jossey-Bass.

Diamond, C. T. P. 1979. *The Headwaters: English Teachers' Constructs of Teaching Writing.* ERIC Document Reproduction Service ED 198 519.

Doe, S. R. 1985. William Perry and One Student Profile. *The Leaflet: Journal of the New England Association of Teachers of English* 84 (1): 24–29.

Dowst, K. 1980. The Epistemic Approach: Writing, Knowing, and Learning. In *Eight Approaches to Teaching Composition*, edited by T. R. Donovan and B. W. McClelland, 65–85. Urbana, Ill.: National Council of Teachers of English.

Erwin, T. D. 1983. The Scale of Intellectual Development: Measuring Perry's Scheme. *Journal of College Student Personnel* 24:6–12.

Flower, L. 1979. Writer-Based Prose: A Cognitive Basis for Problems in Writing. *College English* 41:19–37.

Fowler, J. W. 1978. Mapping Faith's Structures: A Developmental Overview. In *Life-Maps: The Human Journey of Faith,* edited by J. W. Fowler, S. Keen, and J. Berryman. Waco, Tex.: Word Books.

Fulkerson, R. P. 1979. Four Philosophies of Composition. *College Composition and Communication* 30:343–48.

Gere, A. R., B. Schuessler, and R. Abbott. 1984. Measuring Teachers' Attitudes toward Instruction in Writing. In *New Directions in Composition Research,* edited by R. Beach and L. S. Bridwell, 348–61. New York: Guilford.

Gilligan, C. 1982. *In a Different Voice: Psychological Theory and Women's Development.* Cambridge: Harvard University Press.

Halliday, M. A. K. 1975. *Learning How to Mean: Explorations in the Development of Language.* New York: Elsevier North-Holland.

Hillocks, G., Jr. 1986. *Research on Written Composition: New Directions for Teaching.* Urbana, Ill.: Educational Resources Information Center/National Conference on Research in English.

Hunt, D. A. 1970. A Conceptual Level Matching Model for Coordinating Learner Characteristics with Educational Approaches. *Interchange* 1 (3): 68–82.

Hunt, R. A. 1975. Technological Gift-Horse: Some Reflections on the Teeth of Cassette-Marking. *College English* 36:581–85.

Hunt, R. A. 1986. "Could You Put in a Lot of Holes?" Modes of Response to Writing. *Language Arts* 64:229–32.

Johnston, B. 1983. *Assessing English: Helping Students to Reflect on Their Own Work.* Sydney: St. Clair Press.

Klammer, E. 1973. Cassettes in the Classroom. *College English* 35:179–80, 189.

Kohlberg, L. 1981. *The Meaning and Measurement of Moral Development.* Worcester, Mass.: Clark University Press.

Kroll, B. M. 1978. Cognitive Egocentrism and the Problem of Audience Awareness in Written Discourse. *Research in the Teaching of English* 12:269–81.

Kroll, B. M. 1980. Developmental Perspectives and the Teaching of Composition. *College English* 41:741–52.

Lunsford, A. A. 1980. The Content of Basic Writers' Essays. *College Composition and Communication* 31:278–90.

Lunsford, A. A. 1985. Cognitive Studies and Teaching Writing. In *Perspectives on Research and Scholarship in Composition,* edited by B. W. McClelland and T. R. Donovan, 145–61. New York: Modern Language Association.

Mosenthal, P. 1983. On Defining Writing and Classroom Writing Competence. In *Research on Writing: Principles and Methods,* edited by P. Mosenthal, L. Tamor, and S. A. Walmsley, 26–71. New York: Longman.

North, S. M. 1987. *The Making of Knowledge in Composition: Portrait of an Emerging Field.* Upper Montclair, N.J.: Boynton/Cook.

Piaget, J. [1926] 1955. *The Language and Thought of the Child.* Translated by M. Gabain. New York: New American Library.

Perry, W. G., Jr. 1968. *Patterns of Development in Thought and Values of Students in a Liberal Arts College: A Validation of a Scheme.* Cambridge: Bureau of

Study Council, Harvard University. ERIC Document Reproduction Service ED 024 315.

Perry, William G., Jr. 1970. *Forms of Intellectual and Ethical Development in the College Years: A Scheme.* New York: Holt, Rinehart, and Winston.

Perry, William G., Jr. 1981. Cognitive and Ethical Growth: The Making of Meaning. In *The Modern American College,* edited by A. W. Chickering, 76–116. San Francisco: Jossey-Bass.

Root, R. L. 1980. Humpty, Alice, and the Composition Prism: A Perspective on the Teaching Process. In *Reinventing the Rhetorical Tradition,* edited by A. Freedman and I. Pringle 105–11. Conway, Ark.: L & S Books.

Sanford, N. 1966. *Self and Society.* New York: Atherton Press.

Shaughnessy, M. P. 1976. Diving In: An Introduction to Basic Writing. *College Composition and Communication* 27:234–39. Reprinted in *The Writing Teacher's Sourcebook,* edited by G. Tate and E. P. J. Corbett. New York: Oxford University Press.

Shaughnessy, M. P. 1977. *Errors and Expectations.* New York: Oxford University Press.

Sirc, G., and C. M. Anson. 1985. What Writers Say: Analyzing the Metacommentaries of Student Writers. *Forum in Reading and Language Education* 1 (2): 59–74.

Slattery, P. 1986. Responding to College-Level Writing in Terms of Intellectual Development. Paper presented at the annual convention of the Midwest Modern Language Association, November, Chicago.

Vygotsky, L. S. [1930] 1978. *Mind in Society: The Development of Higher Psychological Processes.* Edited by M. Cole, V. John-Steiner, S. Scribner, and E. Souberman. Cambridge: Harvard University Press.

Widick, C. C., and L. L. Knefelkamp. n.d. Essay-Writing Instrument for Data on Students' Attitudes. n.p.

Widick, C. C., and S. Simpson. 1978. Developmental Concepts in College Instruction. In *Encouraging Development in College Students,* edited by C. A. Parker, 27–59. Minneapolis: University of Minnesota Press.

Appendix A

Criteria for Rating Student Essays

Dualistic

In the dualistic essay, the writer will typically attribute his or her decision to Authority, who has all the answers and knows what is best. There will be little deliberate, conscious attempt to weigh alternatives and see different implications of one or the other decision. The world is seen in polar terms, and answers to questions can be found by appealing to the proper knowledge source: a parent, a counselor, God, or someone in a respected position. Decisions thus come from without and are "findable," though the writer may not see him- or herself as knowing enough about the obvious rights and wrongs of the world to pursue answers alone. Alternative dualist responses can emerge if the writer makes a decision alone but if the reasons for the decision come from some conventional belief and do not question that belief, assuming instead that it is a given, accepted universally. An appeal to Authority in itself, however, does not necessarily suggest a dualistic response, since the writer may be seeking a range of views and questioning them in the process.

Relativistic

The relativistic essay will tend to examine several consequences or implications of a decision, or pursue the consequences and implications of several alternative decisions. Typically, the writer will list the pros and cons of each choice, perhaps considering other people's views and feelings but without realizing that what is best for one dimension of a situation may not be best for another. The relativistic essay will clearly show the writer's self-interests and a preoccupation with what will most benefit him or her given a world of choice and self-determination. The writer's decision, however, does not typically involve sacrificing something desirable, which rather indicates a commitment to a decision. Instead, the writer will make the decision simply because at some point it must be made, and it will be accepted (however uncertainly) without any implications for commitment. The writer may discuss the decision in terms of its necessity, but this necessity is often imposed from without and does not develop from within. The writer may discuss the decision as the "best of alternatives," but without a sense of commitment (although occasionally there will be an expression of temporal satisfaction).

Reflective

The reflective essay will typically review the decision-making process in relativistic terms, but here the difference involves the writer's feelings about the consequences of the decision. The writer will identify him- or herself with the system of values surrounding a commitment to the decision. The decision will often involve sacrificing something desirable for the sake of this identity, and the person will be aware of these sacrifices before or at the time of making the decision. The writer will often express or imply a sense of being "in" his or her life — a sense that sometimes shows up in an identity with the group that shares the value system surrounding the commitment. There is often an understanding that values change and with new values come new attitudes toward the commitment. These responses sometimes are manifested in temporal satisfaction with future uncertainty, e.g., "I'm happy for now with my decision but I realize that as I grow so my values will mature and change." The decision evolves from the relationship between the self and a system of shared beliefs in the group surrounding one's commitments.

Appendix B

Bobby's Essay

My Mother was gone out of town with her boyfreind and she left her car at home. When she was getting read to leave she said Don't take my car out of town keep it close to the house.

That Night I wanted to drive the car but my older brother said he would tell if I went far. He knew that my girlfrien live about ten Miles way from the town I lived in.

So I wonder if I should take the car and go later that night he said I could go so I went knowing I was not suppose to go. On the way back home I got stop by the police because the plates on the car had ran out. So the Decision I made was wrong and I learned to listent to what someone tell me to do with their stuff.

Tony's Essay

It was in the Spring of 1982. I was a junior at Washington High School, I had too make a very big decision in my life. The decision I had to make was to choose between two girls who I had liked. There names was Valerie and Shelia, both was very attractive and intelligent. Both of them had lived on the same street but different blocks. I met Shelia in the Fall of my Sophomore year and I met Valerie in the Fall of my junior year.

During my junior year I had Shelia in my advisory and Valorie in my typing class. It was during the beginning of my junior, that I begin to notice that I was attracted to Shelia and so I begun to make my move on her. As I started talking to her for a couple of nights on the telephone, I found out that she felt the same way about me.

So this little relationship between me and Shelia was going pretty smooth for a about two months, but we didn't tell anyone that we were seeing each other so everyone assume that I was free to talk to anyone. At about this time, one of Valerie friends stop me in the hall and handed me a letter it was from Valerie saying basicly "that she had like me very much and she wanted to know if I had felt the same about her and if I didn't I was to call her that night telling her that I was interested in going out with her." After reading the letter the first time I was so shock that I read it again and I started thinking to my self.

Many thoughts came into my mine, my first idea was to keep Shelia and ignore Valerie, another idea was to grab Valerie and drop Shelia. Then it another idea hit me and that was to keep Shelia and have Valerie to, I thought said to myself that it my work because don't know one know about Shelia and my relationship so it wouldn't be know problem. So I called Valerie back up that night and we talked for about an hour and half and told I was interested. So for two weeks I was splitting my time between two girls. When I was with one I would tell the other one some excuse like I had housework to do or I'am busy doing homework.

This little two way was going find for about two weeks until one night, Shelia saw me and Valerie at McDonald's eating. She came over to our table and tap me on the shoulder, I looked up at her and I almost chocked on my Big Mac. She then asked "What is this?" I responded by saying "let me explain". then Valerie said "explain what I'am his girl then both started arguing at each other and every one in the restaurant was looking and then I broke in and said hold it let me explain the situation. I explain to the girls what had happened and how all this mess got started. After explaining the situation two both girls, they just stared at each other for about 5 seconds and Valerie asked me "well which is it." and Shelia said yeah, which will it be. I looked at both girls and I thought about the advantages that each had and the disadvantages and I said well let me tell you this, I like both of you very much and both of you various reasons so it would be hard for me to just choose one of you, but since I have both of you I guess I have to choose neither of you. Both girls looked at me and each other and then Shelia said well let just all be friends then Valerie and I said good suggestion and we all had dinner together.

Karen's Essay

Sunday I made a very important decision that would determine whether I would stay in the [prep] program or not.

Although I knew the consequences of my absence from this mandatory meeting, I felt that my decision was right and in order.

The church that I attend in [my hometown] was celebrating their 75 jubilee service and also the burning of the morgage. My religion is a very important factor in my life. I had planned on going to this service since last year and to hear that a meeting was scheduled for that night was upsetting.

I really felt that going to church was the right decision. I had never missed a mandatory meeting, but in this case I felt I had to.

When I returned I knew I would have to face my decision. I was scared of the consequences, but I knew I had made the right decision. Although I knew I was right, I knew that my decision would be tested.

Monday I went to see [the dean in charge of the program] but she wouldnt talk to me. I was already scared and this didnt help at all. I knew I was right and I was ready to argue my point of view but she wouldn't give me a chance. All she said was "when you missed the meeting, you made a decision." No other comments, thats all she said.

I realize that this is one of the major decisions of my life. I had to decide between my church and this meeting. I didn't know that missing this meeting would be a factor in being dismissed from the program.

I can't really and truly say that I'm sorry for going to church, because I'm not sorry that the meeting had to be on the same night as this important church activity, but I still feel I made the right choice.

My religion means everything to me and I won't put it in second place. As far as the decision I made, I feel that I was right, but I sorry I missed the meeting and my staying in the program is on the line.

Contributors

Chris M. Anson is assistant professor of English and director of advanced composition at the University of Minnesota, where he teaches courses in writing theory, English language and linguistics, composition, and literature. He is coauthor of the textbook *Writing in Context* and the sourcebook *Writing across the Curriculum: An Annotated Bibliography.* He has published articles in *Written Communication, College Composition and Communication, Reader, English Journal, Journal of Teaching Writing,* and other periodicals, as well as in several edited collections.

Richard Beach is professor of English education at the University of Minnesota. He is coeditor of *New Directions in Composition Research* and *Becoming Readers and Writers from Adolescence to Adulthood* (forthcoming). He has conducted research on response to literature, revising, and the evaluation of writing. He is currently coauthoring a literature methods textbook, *Teaching Literature in the Secondary School.* He is also treasurer of the National Conference on Research in English.

David Bleich is professor of English and professor of education at the University of Rochester. His books include *Readings and Feelings, Subjective Criticism, Utopia: The Psychology of a Cultural Fantasy,* and *The Double Perspective: Language, Literacy, and Social Relations* (forthcoming). His many articles have appeared in such journals as *College English, New Literary History, ADE Bulletin, Style,* and *The Psychoanalytic Review,* as well as in numerous edited collections, including *Literature and Composition: Bridging the Gap, Gender and Reading,* and *Convergences: Transactions in Reading and Writing.* He is currently a member of the executive board of the Society for Critical Exchange.

Deborah Brandt is assistant professor of English at the University of Wisconsin–Madison. A 1984 recipient of the Promising Research Award from the National Council of Teachers of English, she has published articles in *Written Communication, College English, Reader,* and several other journals, and has contributed chapters to recent collections on writing and writing research. She is presently writing a book on the nature of literacy.

Rance Conley is the assistant chair of English education in the English Department at the University of Illinois at Chicago. A doctoral candidate in composition and rhetoric, he is working on a dissertation that focuses on collaborative learning. He previously taught in secondary schools for eight years, including three years in Switzerland and Scotland.

Donald A. Daiker is professor of English at Miami University, where he teaches courses in writing, the teaching of writing, and American literature. He is coauthor of the textbooks *The Writer's Options* and *Literature: Options for Reading and Writing,* and coeditor of two essay collections — *Sentence Combining and the Teaching of Writing* and *Sentence Combining: A Rhetorical Perspective.* His articles appear in *College Composition and Communication, Research in the Teaching of English, Freshman English News, WPA, Studies in Short Fiction, The McNeese Review, New Methods in College Writing Programs,* and the *Fitzgerald-Hemingway Annual.*

Toby Fulwiler directs the writing program at the University of Vermont. He is the author of *Teaching with Writing* and editor of *The Journal Book.* He has written numerous articles on writing across the curriculum for NCTE publications. He is currently trying to figure out how to write a successful grant proposal.

Alice Gillam is assistant professor of English at the University of Wisconsin–Milwaukee, where she coordinates the peer tutoring program and teaches writing. She has served on the executive committee of the Conference on College Communication and Composition and on NCTE's Commission on the Status of Women. Currently she is conducting research on peer tutorials, collaborative writing in the work place, and the essays of black women writers.

Glynda Ann Hull teaches courses on composition theory and research in the graduate school of education at the University of California, Berkeley. Her publications include articles and chapters on editing, literacy theory, and computer-assisted instruction in writing. She was named an NCTE Promising Researcher and received the Outstanding Dissertation Award for Empirical Research from the American Educational Research Association. Her current research focuses on adult literacy.

Russell A. Hunt is professor of English at St. Thomas University. A specialist in eighteenth-century English literature and literary theory, he currently devotes most of his attention to the study of reading and writing considered as social acts, particularly the social dimensions of the phenomena of literary reading. He has published on these issues in *College English* and (with Douglas Vipond) in *Poetics, TEXT, Reader, Reading Research and Instruction,* and *English Quarterly.*

Ann Matsuhashi is associate professor of English and director of the Writing Center at the University of Illinois at Chicago. She teaches courses in the doctoral specialization of composition and rhetoric and directs a campus-wide peer tutoring Writing Center. Her research has focused on the cognitive processes involved in writing and revising, and, more recently, she has been exploring the strategies writers use to evaluate their own drafts and the drafts of others. Her articles have appeared in *Written Communication* and *Research in the Teaching of English.* She has contributed chapters to the volumes *What Writers Know: The Language, Process, and Structure of*

Written Discourse; The Psychology of Written Language; and *The Acquisition of Written Language: Response and Revision.* She has recently edited a volume of theoretical chapters and research reports, *Writing in Real Time: Modelling Production Processes.*

Beverly J. Moss is a doctoral candidate in English with a specialization in rhetoric and composition at the University of Illinois at Chicago, where she is currently the assistant director of composition. She is completing her dissertation on "The Black Church Sermon as Literacy Event." Her major interests include literacy studies and the relationships between oral and written language.

Thomas Newkirk is associate professor of English at the University of New Hampshire, where he directs the freshman English program and the New Hampshire Writing Program, an annual summer institute for teachers. He is the editor of *Only Connect: Uniting Reading and Writing; To Compose: Teaching Writing in the High School;* coeditor (with Nancie Atwell) of *Understanding Writing: Ways of Observing, Learning and Teaching;* and coeditor (with Jane Hansen and Donald Graves) of *Breaking Ground: Teachers Relate Reading and Writing in the Elementary School.* In addition, he has published essays and research reports in *Written Communication, Research in the Teaching of English, Harvard Educational Review,* and *College English.*

Martin Nystrand is professor of English at the University of Wisconsin–Madison and faculty associate of the Wisconsin Center for Education Research. He is editor of *Language as a Way of Knowing* and *What Writers Know: The Language, Process and Structure of Written Discourse,* and the author of *The Structure of Written Communication: Studies in Reciprocity between Writers and Readers.* The latter volume, which examines the impact of readers on the writing process, outlines a social model of the writing process. Nystrand is currently engaged in a five-year study of the effects of discourse quality on learning in high-school English and social studies.

Cynthia S. Onore is assistant professor of English education at the City College of the City University of New York, where she directs the graduate program in language and literacy. She is currently codirecting two funded projects — a "Stay in School Partnership Program" and a school-centered teacher education project. She has served on the New York State English Council executive committee, and is currently a member of the NCTE Committee on Language across the Curriculum. Her articles have appeared in *Language Arts, English Education, The English Record,* and other National Council of Teachers of English affiliated journals. She is currently writing a book about in-service teacher education with Nancy Lester, entitled *Transformation and Stasis: The Impact of New Ideas on a School System.*

Robert Probst is professor of English education at Georgia State University in Atlanta. Previously he was a high school English teacher in Maryland and supervisor of English for the Norfolk, Virginia, public schools. Interested in the teaching of both writing and literature, he has written *Response and*

Analysis: Teaching Literature in Junior and Senior High School and was part of the team that prepared *New Voices,* a high school English textbook series. His articles have appeared in *English Journal, Educational Leadership, The Clearing House,* and elsewhere. He has served on NCTE's Standing Committee on Research and the Commission on Reading, and is currently on the board of directors of the Adolescent Literature Assembly.

Louise Wetherbee Phelps is professor of English at Syracuse University, where she directs a new university writing program. She has taught at Cleveland State University and the University of Southern California and currently serves on the NCTE Standing Committee on Research. She has published essays in various journals and research volumes, writing on conceptual issues in composition theory, rhetoric, and teaching practice. Topics of her current work include composing over time, literacy development, gender themes in composition, and theory-application in institutional settings. She is coeditor of *Encounters with Student Texts* (on teachers' reading processes) and author of *Composition as a Human Science: Contributions to the Self-Understanding of a Discipline.*

Geoffrey Sirc is an assistant professor of writing at the University of Minnesota's general college. His two chief research interests, on which he writes regularly, are discourse-based studies of the writing process and computer applications in writing. He is currently at work on a three-year grant to study the effects of a local-area-networked writing environment on basic writers.

Jeffrey Sommers, associate professor of English at Miami University–Middletown, serves as executive director of the Miami University Center for the Study of Writing. He has published articles on responding to student writing in a number of journals, including *College Composition and Communication, Freshman English News,* and *Teaching English in the Two-Year College.* He is currently at work on a composition textbook entitled *Model Voices: Finding a Writing Voice.*

Dene Kay Thomas is assistant professor of English at the University of Idaho, where she is also director of writing. She teaches courses in writing, composition theory, English education, and introductory literature, and trains new instructors in composition. Her dissertation, "A Transition from Speaking to Writing: Small-Group Writing Conferences," which is available from ERIC, followed one conference group through a freshman writing course. She is currently at work on a textbook for freshman composition.

Gordon P. Thomas is assistant professor of English at the University of Idaho, where he teaches writing, composition theory, and introductory literature. He has published on the philosophy of language in *College English* and on computers and writing in *Computers and Composition.* He is currently developing a software program called SLICE (System to Link Inventing, Composing, and Editing).

Susan V. Wall is assistant professor of English at Northeastern University and assistant director of the Martha's Vineyard Institute on Writing. Her research interests include case-study theory, teacher training, basic writing, and revision in rhetorical contexts. Her work has appeared in *College English, The Journal of Advanced Composition, The Journal of Basic Writing,* and *English Education.*